CHILD PSYCHOLOGY

RAM NATH SHARMA
RACHANA SHARMA

Published by

ATLANTIC

PUBLISHERS & DISTRIBUTORS (P) LTD

7/22, Ansari Road, Darya Ganj, New Delhi-110002
Phones : +91-11-40775252, 40775214, 23273880, 23275880
Fax: +91-11-23285873
Web: www.atlanticbooks.com
E-mail: orders@atlanticbooks.com

Copyright © Atlantic Publishers & Distributors (P) Ltd., 2002, 2017, 2018, 2020, 2022

All rights reserved. No part of this publication may be reproduced, stored in a retrieval system, transmitted or utilized in any form or by any means, electronic, mechanical, photocopying, recording or otherwise, without the prior permission of the copyright owner. Application for such permission should be addressed to the publisher.

Disclaimer

- The author and the publisher have taken every effort to the maximum of their skill, expertise and knowledge to provide correct material in the book. Even then if some mistakes persist in the content of the book, the publisher does not take responsibility for the same. The publisher shall have no liability to any person or entity with respect to any loss or damage caused, or alleged to have been caused directly or indirectly, by the information contained in this book.
- The author has fully tried to follow the copyright law. However, if any work is found to be similar, it is unintentional and the same should not be used as defamatory or to file legal suit against the author.
- If the readers find any mistakes, we shall be grateful to them for pointing out those to us so that these can be corrected in the next edition.
- All disputes are subject to the jurisdiction of Delhi courts only.

Printed & bound in India by Atlantic Print Services

Preface

The present book, *Child Psychology,* is a textbook dealing with dynamic nature of the field of child psychology. It examines various theoretical view points in highlighting a well balanced view of a child's developmental progress. It covers under-graduate syllabi of almost all the Indian universities. While subject matter has been drawn from standard books published in the West, examples for elaboration have been given from Indian circumstances as far as possible. The presentation of subject matter is analytic, discussing each subject in a separate chapter, each topic classified and further classified into central headings, sub-headings and side headings. This process has been adopted with a view to give easier understanding and quick comprehension of the subject matter to the readers.

Child Psychology is an important subject not only for the university students but also for the laymen, the parents, the teachers, the social workers and in fact every individual in society. It is useful even for one's own understanding of himself. While most of the Western books are overburdened with technical jargon and examples drawn from the West, the present book has been written with an eye on the problems of Indian readers of the subject.

Suggestions, if any, for improvement of the book will be most gratefully acknowledged and incorporated in the next edition.

RAM NATH SHARMA
RACHANA SHARMA

Contents

1

Introductory

Child Psychology, as is evident by the nomenclature, is the psychology of child. A child is a human being of a definite age. Psychologists maintain that childhood continues till the age of twelve. Between the ages of twelve and eighteen children are called adolescents. In order to distinguish the first six years of a child's life from the second stage of development between six and twelve, the term infancy is applied to the former. Development begins when the child is still in his mother's womb, and therefore, the study of the prenatal stage also becomes important. Modern psychologists, therefore, believe that child psychology should comprehend the child's development almost from the moment of conception to its attaining the age of eighteen. Hence, when we say that child psychology is the study of child, we hint at the study of the human being from the moment of the conception to the time when he enters the adolescent period. The one most important fact that emerges from the study of this development is that it is during this period that the foundations of later adult life are laid. It is the age of growth, the period for all kinds of development and growth.

So far we have been concerned with the literal meaning of the term child psychology and have called it the study of the child. Obviously, it is an important branch of psychology, a term which in itself should be understood properly before the meaning of child psychology becomes clear. Modern psychologists define psychology as the positive science of human behaviour which endeavours to understand man in his environment.

WHAT IS CHILD PSYCHOLOGY?

It is essential to define psychology in order to arrive at a precise definition of child psychology because the latter is a branch of the former. Looked at from this standpoint, it too becomes a positive science which studies man in his particular environment with the one limitation that it studies man or human being below the age of eighteen. Child psychology took on its mantle of an individual and distinct branch of psychology in the 19th century when the psychologists gradually realised the importance of the study of child behaviour in isolation from adult behaviour. Consequently, it became important to define it with greater precision. In the words of Crow and Crow, "Child psychology is the scientific study of the individual from his prenatal beginnings through the early stages of his adolescent development."[1] In brief, it can be said that child psychology is a positive science which studies the behaviour of child in the context of his environment treating the child as an individual. In order to eliminate any further ambiguity in the definition the following factors should be stressed here :

(1) **Study in the Context of the Environment.** The behaviour of each individual is influenced by his environment. It is all the more influential in childhood because the child has less developed powers of resistance and of understanding which lead to control of environment. In the study of children, therefore, it becomes very important to study the environment. If one were to trace the cause of one child learning to steal while another does not, it would soon become apparent that this cause lies in the environment.

(2) **Study of the Individual.** Child should be studied as individual. It is necessary for the teacher, while teaching, to be aware of the individual differences of his pupils. If this individual variation is disregarded, children cannot be taught effectively. Child psychology must, therefore study each child as an individual in his own role. Yet, it is only natural that while children exhibit individual differences to a great degree one can discover universal laws and principles that apply to children all over the world.

(3) **Study of the Child.** What is a child? The stage between birth and early adolescence in a man's life is called childhood. It is in this part of his development that man is called a child. Child psychology studies human beings belonging to this category.

(4) **Study of Behaviour.** Reaction to any stimulus is behaviour. Study of a *child's* behaviour requires study of its external reaction and internal experience, and in either case the environmental factors play their part and must be taken into consideration.

(5) **Positive Science.** Child psychology is a positive science. In the words of Watson, "Child psychology came into being from

[1] Crow and Crow, *Child Psychology*, Barnes and Noble (1958).

the scientific study of the child."[1] A positive science is factual while a normative one is idealistic. The one studies that which exists while the other that which ought to be. Examples of the normative sciences are ethics, aesthetics, logic, etc. Examples of positive sciences can be found among all the natural sciences. Child psychology studies the behaviour of the child as a positive science.

VALUE OF CHILD PSYCHOLOGY IN EDUCATION

All modern psychologists stress the need for every educator being acquainted with child psychology. The following benefits can be derived from a knowledge of child psychology:

(1) **Understanding the Student.** John Adams decreed that the teacher must know the student better than he knows the subject he is to teach. He has said, "The master taught John Latin. The teacher must know both Latin and John and since the knowledge of John is psychology, the teacher must study psychology." Pestalozzi is of the opinion that education should be based on a realistic and accurate knowledge of the student's mental processes. A teacher must be equipped with detailed information concerning the student's needs, the bases of his behaviour, mental level, interests, abilities and personality, etc. Any successful education must be based on these fundamental forces that control behaviour. It is common knowledge that these basic motive forces cannot ever be eliminated from the child's behaviour pattern, they can be modified or given a new direction. There is close relation between the child's education and his needs. The needs of most backward and handicapped or problem children cannot be satisfied in school. It is for this reason that they turn to trouble making as a source of relief. A teacher who knows the psychology of children is aware of the fact that the source of a child's defects lies in the incomplete fulfilment of a child's physical, psychological and social needs. Such knowledge also helps the teacher to know the interest, nature, intelligence and individual differences of his students so that he can adjust the curriculum and mode of teaching to their requirements.

(2) **Improvement in Teaching Methods.** Child psychology has brought a revolution in modern educational methods. It has put an end to the role of the rod and the whip. Children are taught

1. Watson, R.I., *Psychology of the child,* John Wiley and Sons, New York (1958), p. 9.

to be disciplined by psychological methods, not by force. Such new innovations as the montessori and the kindergarten methods are based on the child psychology. Teaching has become more scientific, easier and goal-directed. Child psychology gives the teacher information about the processes of learning, methods of teaching, important factors, conditions which help or impede the process of learning, allowing the teacher to make use of this information in his teaching.

(3) **Improvement in Curriculum.** Child psychology has led to important improvements in the curriculum for teaching children. It has laid stress on such activities as games, scouting, picnics, camps, dancing and other extra-curricular activities which supplement rather than supplant class room teaching of academic subjects. Education thus becomes an interesting process and develops various facets of the child's personality which remain untouched under more formal teaching conditions. The curriculum of a school should be based on the individual differences of children, their motives, the values and principles of learning, all of which can be known only through the study of psychology. In deciding the subjects to be taught, such things as the students' ages, their individual and social needs and the responsibility they are expected to shoulder in later life must be taken into consideration. Besides, the methods of presenting teaching material should be based on psychological facts.

(4) **Evaluation and Testing.** In the process of education, both the teacher and the taught are constantly in need of knowledge of how far they have progressed, whether they have failed to progress and if they have, then why? Besides, they are always anxious to know how to improve their performance. It is for this that evaluation and testing are required. But neither can be efficiently performed if the teacher is unaware of the principles of child psychology.

(5) **Diagnosis and Solution of Classroom Problems.** Many problems are created in the classroom by the relations between individual students and the teacher, the mental abilities of the students, the fact of their being backward, etc. These problems can be solved only by psychological methods. Basically, all such problems are behaviour problems of children which require psychological knowledge in order to be solved. Child psychology can assist the teacher in tackling such problems as the backwardness of children, maladjustment, indiscipline, juvenile delinquency, sex crimes, defects in the child's progress, mental defects of problem children etc.

(6) **Discipline and Administration.** If the teacher is unaware of the principles of child psychology he will be unable to solve the problems of his students and will thereby fail to induce order and discipline among them. Generally speaking, order and discipline in an institution depend upon the extent to which the rules and regulations applying in the institution are psychological and the extent to which the teacher makes use of psychological devices. An example will serve to make this point clear. In one particular institution the boys were apt to be very troublesome during the lunch hour. They threw food at each other and wasted it. The warden tried to frighten the children into submission but he could not check this tendency among the boys. He was later replaced by another warden who took stock of the situation and decided to make use of his knowledge of psychology. He announced that the table which appeared to be the cleanest and the smartest looking during the lunch hour would be awarded a flag, and also a double helping of the most delicious food. The effect of this announcement was immediate. At each table the boys tried to appear more clean and smart than their neighbours, and if one boy was inclined to create trouble, he was immediately checked by his neighbours. Application of child psychology solved a problem which had defied all show of power and force.

(7) **Improvement in Teacher-taught Relationship.** Basically, the teacher taught-relationship is psychological. If the teachers and the principal of an institution wish to maintain cordial relations with their students it is essential to be clever and understanding. Child psychology can provide many hints towards such an understanding.

(8) **Experiment and Research.** Knowledge of child psychology encourages the teacher to make experiments in the field of education. By his research he can bring new facts to light and improve education. All experiments should be adapted to psychological methodology.

It should be apparent from the foregoing account that knowledge of child psychology helps in teaching and is of immense value to the teacher.

SUBJECT MATTER OF CHILD PSYCHOLOGY

The subject matter of child psychology is the child itself. The term child' denotes a definite stage in the development of the human being. This stage extends from the time of birth to the adolescent period. Obviously, the subject matter of child psychology is man's development from his birth to the time he reaches adolescence. Clarifying this, Crow and Crow have stated, "The science of child psychology deals with (i) the stages of growth and maturation, (ii) the effect of environmental influences, upon individual patterns of development and (iii) the psychological and social interactions between a child and the other members of the society into which he is born and in which he is reared."[1]

SCOPE OF CHILD PSYCHOLOGY

The following aspects of the scope of child psychology are clear by the foregoing account of its subject matter:

(1) **Stages of Growth and Maturation.** Growth starts, for the child, within the womb, and therefore psychology takes into account the experiences of the prenatal condition also. Development in the prenatal condition passes through three phases—the stage of conception which lasts from the moment of conception till two weeks later, the stage of the immature embryo which covers the period from the third to the eighteenth week and third stage of mature embryo which continues upto the time of birth. Two kinds of growth or development can be seen during the prenatal stage, motor and sensory development. Between the time of birth and the attainment of adolescence the human animal passes through the stages of infancy and childhood. The first six years of the child's life constitute his infancy and the next six his childhood. Between the ages of twelve and eighteen boys and girls are adolescents. In each stage, development can be studied in its five aspects — physical, mental, emotional, — moral and aesthetic. In infancy, childhood and adolescence the first three years are believed to be the time of growth and the later three the period of maturation. Child psychology studies each one of these stages of growth and development.

(2) **Environmental Influences upon Development.** A child lives in a geographical, social and psychological environment which, in its totality, influences his behaviour patterns, the rate of development, the nature and direction of his development. It is the task of child psychology to study all such influences and to find out the different types of environments which encourage various types of development in children. From this information it is possible to deduce causal laws concerning environment and from this one can proceed to change the environment to suit

[1] Crow and Crow, *Child Psychology*, p. 1.

the needs of a particular child. It may also be possible to create an ideal environment ensuring complete development of every faculty of the child.

(3) **Interaction between the Child and the Society.** A child necessarily spends some part of his life in the family, the neighbourhood, the playground and the college. Any development that he undergoes in one or all of these situations is the result of the interaction between the child and the members of his family, the neighbours, other children on the playgrounds or his colleagues or teacher. Such interactions are psychological and social. Social interactions are either conjunctive or disjunctive. Examples of conjunctive social interactions are cooperation, accommodation, and social integration. Conflict, competition and contravention etc., are examples of disjunctive interactions. All social interactions have psychological consequences, and for that reason each one of them is important for the child since it influences some or the other aspect of his personality.

(4) **Mental Processes of the Child.** While child psychology, was itself in its infancy it was discovered that the mental processes of the child varied somewhat from their adult equivalents. Child psychology makes a minute study of the child's perception, memory, thinking, imagination, learning, association, personality and other mental functions, the influence of the environment upon them and the individual differences generated thereby.

(5) **Individual Differences between Children.** Many experiments have indicated that all children are not alike. These differences between the children result in major differences in their development and behaviour and can be seen to occur in respect of family background, economic condition, racial difference, nationality, sex difference, special abilities, mental age, motor ability, personality development, learning and interest. Child psychologists study these individual differences and try to find the universal laws that may be derived from the data collected.

It should be fairly apparent that child psychology is a detailed, composite and comprehensive study of children. Put differently, it studies all aspects of a child's development and behaviour. Its scope comprehends the child's conative, affective and cognitive aspects and behaviour. It analyses the child's efforts at knowing, experiencing and decision making, and the mental processes, concerned in such activity. Another aspect of it is a comparative study of the heredity and environmental influences upon the child, and a study of the changes in development and behaviour brought about by a changed environment. This entire body of knowledge can be put at the disposal of teachers, parents and guardians who can solve their children's problem because of a better understanding of the child behaviour.

AIMS OF CHILD PSYCHOLOGY

The aims of child psychology, as a positive science studying the behaviour and development of the child, are the following :

(1) **Discovering Facts Concerning Child Psychology.** In general, the aim of any particular science is the discovery of facts within a specific area on a definite subject. Child psychology tries to discover causal relations and universal laws concerning the child's development from the time of conception to the beginning of adolescence. Hence, the primary aim of child psychology is the discovery of facts about the psychology of children.

(2) **Solving Problems Concerning Child Psychology.** Most social sciences aim not only at the academic pursuit of collecting facts relevant to their field of study but also at the diagnosis and solution of problems infesting their field. This is only natural since the main concern of social sciences is to improve human life and to increase its element of contentment and organisation. The same is true of the psychologist, although he pursues his study with complete scientific objectivity and fidelity. His aim is not merely to discover psychological facts but to employ them to solve psychological problems. Child psychology is concerned with the problems of children, juvenile delinquents and backward children, the difficulties of creating a suitable environment and allied conditions.

(3) **Making Suggestions for the Improvement and Development of Children.** Normally, of course, the development of children takes place under the care of parents, teachers and guardians, but the child psychologist, by virtue of his special knowledge of children, is better placed for making practicable suggestions in this direction. He can help cure psychological shortcomings in children and to create situations in which they can develop their abilities. This is the practical aspect of child psychology.

It is clear that in its theoretical aspect child psychology is concerned with the discovery of general and universal laws concerning facts about children, and in its functional aspect with the solution of problems concerning the development of children, with making suggestions to parents and teachers towards such solution and creation of proper environment. In the words of Watson, "In child psychology the aim is to develop predictive accuracy about child behaviour and experience, — that is, to establish the lawful relationships among the phenomena which can be observed. To chronicle the facts of child development is not enough, laws or principles must be discovered which will explain and give order to the facts."[1]

CHILD PSYCHOLOGY AND CHILD CARE

Among the more important things that the parent, teacher or the guardian has to consider are: What does a child do, how and why he does it and how can he be of help in this field? What will the child become when he grows up and what can be done to ensure that he will become what he wants to? It is for the child psychologist to provide answers to such questions. Obviously, the child psychologist's function is of value not only to the parent and the guardian but also to the society as a whole. The following facts should be considered:

(1) **Understanding the Child as an Individual.** The main utility of studying child psychology is the help one can derive in understanding the child's behaviour as an individual being. A child psychologist discovers universal or general facts that apply to the behaviour of most children. These laws can then be applied to find out whether a particular child is progressing in a particular direction or not. Is the child normal or not? What new things can he be taught and how? Is his physical, mental, social, moral and aesthetic development proceeding at a normal pace? If he is backward, then what can be done to change this situation? To quote Mussen, Conger and Kagan, "Child psychology includes the study of the child's heredity, physical constitution (biological, chemical and psychological processes within the body), and environmental forces to which he is exposed."[2] Once the subject matter of child psychology is understood it becomes possible to solve one and all problems of children. The child psychologist can be of help to juvenile courts, social welfare clinics and doctors who treat children. Should the parents of a child be dubious about the rate of his development in all spheres, they can take him to a doctor who can examine the child's physique and also his

---

1. Waston, Robert, *Psychology of the Child,* p. 38.
2. Mussen, Conger and Kagan, *Child Development and Personality,* Harper, IInd Edn. p. 2.

psychological condition, apply the child psychologist's knowledge and evaluate the rate of the child's progress. Similarly, if a child is found stealing things in school or breaking the windows of rooms it is better to treat the child than to send him to jail. But such cure cannot be affected if there is no child psychologist, for it is he alone who can tell us the cause and effect of child behaviour and help us to arrive at the cause of delinquent behaviour and to cure such behaviour.

(2) **Rapid Cure of Mental Weakness.** Some very attractive and apparently intelligent children mislead their parents into imagining that they are capable of great things. The truth is discovered only when they are sent to school or taught new things at home, when they are seen to be slower at performing tasks than older children. This difference is due to mental weakness. Many parents cannot digest the information that the children of parents as intelligent as they are, could possibly be mentally weak. But when the child fails to progress even after considerable effort they tend to become fed up with him. It is then time to turn to the child psychologist. He can examine the child's intelligence even in infancy and tell whether the child is below average, average or something akin to a genius. Feeble minded children have to be taught in a special environment for the normal school condition does not suit them. And, in any case, it is better to consult the child psychologist and accept the conclusions of his examination than to remain in the dark and make futile plans for the future.

(3) **Rapid Diagnosing and Curing of Problem of Mentally Diseased Children.** Many a time a problem child or one suffering from mental disease is allowed to go his way for a long time with the result that the defect becomes deep-rooted. This makes cure very difficult. It is part of the child psychologist's job to discover the causes of problematic behaviour or mental disease in children and to suggest ways and means of curing it. With his help the defect can be removed at an early age and the child can be helped to progress normally in later life.

(4) **Knowledge of the Child's Special Abilities.** Another way in which the child psychologist can be of help is to point out the age in which a child may be expected to display unusual proficiency in a particular field. He can also point out the special abilities a child may have. Knowledge of the former kind may eliminate much unnecessary anxiety, for, being possessed of such knowledge we would not expect a child to show proficiency

in a field at a particular age. Besides, if the ability is not shown at the appropriate time we can discover the backwardness and try to cure it. If we are aware of the special talents of a child we can guide his education more effectively. We can help him select subjects for study, and even select a possible profession for him and to provide that particular kind of education which would fit him for that profession.

(5) **Scientific Attitude towards Children.** Before child psychology came into existence as a science in its own right, many unscientific views concerning children were current. Some people believed the child to be a small adult. Yet others believed that the child was an innately sinful and degraded creature, only to be contradicted by others who looked upon the child as a member of the kingdom of God. Plato advised that the child should be treated as the citizen of the state and should be educated as such. Rousseau, the French philosopher, thought that the child was pure at birth and was later contaminated by the social circumstances. Ever since the evolutionary theory of Charles Darwin became prevalent the child has been regarded as a stage in the development of man. Before this time, nobody took much interest in the child's development. Theory of evolution initiated the scientific approach towards children which later developed in the form of child psychology. Child psychology considers the child as a growing and developing being, and childhood as the most important and difficult period of man's development. Freud went so far as to say that the fundamental structure of a man's personality was created in the first four or five years of his life and that all later development was merely the filling in of details. Modern child psychology does not subscribe to this viewpoint, yet it does not deny the fact that childhood is the most important and tender stage of human development. Obviously, it is child psychology which has created this scientific attitude towards the child in parents, teachers, guardians and leaders.

(6) **Programmes of Child Welfare and Improvement.** The children are the future leaders of a country, and the future of the country depends upon the children. Hence, the importance of the proper care of a child's development can hardly be overestimated. All programmes for child welfare should be made in accordance with the laws of child psychology, for otherwise there will be greater possibility of harm than of advantage. To take a simple example, it was used to be taken for granted that the child is slothful and

lazy by nature, that it is his nature to be tricky and naughty. Hence it was felt that he should be kept under a strict discipline and corrective measures should be taken without hesitation. There can be no denying that the parents and guardians who resorted to the use of force did so with no malignity in their hearts, and had the future of their wards in mind, but child psychologists have now come to conclusion that such corrective measures do more harm than good. It is for this reason that the programmes of child welfare and improvement should be conducted under the guidance of a child psychologist.

(7) **Understanding Adult Behaviour.** It has been said that the child is the father of man, meaning that if one wants to understand the adult one must understand the child. Child psychology thus provides the background to an understanding of adult behaviour. Freud and other psychoanalysts have established through their analysis of many mental diseases that the causes of most such diseases develop during the childhood of the patients. Many childhood memories and traumatic experiences are the root causes of many such mental diseases. Apart from the abnormal aspect even most of the fundamental forces of normal behaviour achieve their form and strength during childhood. If this fact is clearly perceived it becomes possible to avoid many difficulties to occur during adult life. One individual may be a criminal, another a mentally diseased individual, a third may indulge in antisocial behaviour while the fourth may be interested purely in domestic work. All these differences occur in individuals because of the social conditions through which they passed during their childhood. A study of the great philosophers, leaders, scientists, pioneers and saints will show that the causes of their greatness had taken root during their childhood. The fearlessness of Shivaji must in part at least be traced to the training given to him by his mother, for she told him tales of bravery in his infancy. Mahatma Gandhi has admitted that his love of religion was engendered in him by his mother. Thus, the personality, behaviour, nature, goal of life, philosophy of life, interest, etc., all have their beginning in the childhood. Jersild has rightly observed, "Why study this little child? The answer is that if one wishes to understand human beings at any stage of their growth, one must study their beginnings."

(8) **Understanding Social Problems.** The great amount of research carried on in the present century has indicated that many of

the social problems seen around us originate in the individual's problems concerning the mind and personality. Social or collective tension, for example, is the result of individual tension present in individuals. This collective tension is at the root of such problems as casteism, linguism, regionalism, communalism and similar problems that infest our society today. If the problems are to be understood in their entirety it becomes necessary to understand the prejudices, dogmas, destructive tendencies, hatred, potential violence, etc., that exist in the different linguistic groups, communities and regional groups. It has already been pointed out that the root of all such adult tendencies and psychological activities are to be found in the social and cultural environment of childhood life. Child psychology, therefore, can also help in the understanding and explanation of social phenomena peculiar to adults. One example will help to make this clear. Before the partition of the Indian Union, Hindu children were inclined to hide with fear in their homes on the occasion or Moharram, a Muslim festival. Their parents advised them to close the doors and to hide. It is this fear of another community experienced in childhood which later develops into communal hatred. And even today we find little intermingling, friendship and comradeship between Hindu and Muslim children in the Indian communal life. How then can we expect that members of this community will grow up to live with each other as friends? In fact, one of the best cures of racial intolerance, communalism, regionalism and all such social malaise is to help the children of different communities to come into contact with each other, live together and to foster a sense of equality. Later on these children will grow up and create a community in which such problems will not occur.

It is evident from the above discussion that child psychology is important not merely for educationists and guardians but also for social reformers, politicians and leaders of the country. In the enlightened world of today each welfare state aims at the complete and all round development of the individual. Among the more important functions of the state are child welfare programmes. But all such programmes should be based on the principles of child psychology. An important part of education is the training imparted during infancy and childhood. This, too, should be based on principles of child psychology. Or put it briefly, knowledge of child psychology can help everybody in almost every situation of life.

NATURE OF CHILD PSYCHOLOGY

Psychology is the positive science of human behaviour. In the role of science its function is to describe, control and predict human behaviour. It aims at discovering universal laws and principles governing the interaction between the living being and his organism. It uses scientific methods and reaches psychological conclusions. In recent years the scope of psychology has been expanding steadily. With every new use of psychology in different fields branches of science have come into being, one such important branch being child psychology. Obviously, the nature of child psychology is scientific but this statement must be analysed to discover the nature of science and its characteristic features.

What is Science?

Science is the systematic study of a limited field. If it is called scientific, the study must necessarily have a limited field and it must be organised or systematic. Yet a study cannot be called a science merely on the basis of its subject matter; what is even more important is the scientific method. It is the method which is science, not the subject matter. It is by virtue of this method that a science differs from an art or philosophy. The characteristic feature of a science is its method either than its field of study.

Scientific Method

A method is scientific if it is applied to a limited field of study the subject matter of which is rendered systematic. The method requires the use of patience, courage, unremitting effort, creative imagination and objectivity. Without these qualities nobody can ask the research worker to study. The greater the details of such analysis, the easier will the work become. The major steps of the scientific method are the following:

(1) **Observation.** The first step in the method is a minute and detailed observation of the subject matter. Most of the fine instruments have to be used for such observation, and if this is so, the accuracy of the instruments must not be taken for granted, but should be ascertained.

(2) **Recording of the Observation.** The second step is the careful recording of all such observations. Complete objectivity is of the essence in this work.

(3) **Clarification.** Once the recording is over, the material collected must be classified. This is an important step. As Carl Pearson has pointed out, it is the function of science to classify facts, to know their order and to realise or to indicate their relative importance.

Classification is done in such a manner that all scattered and disordered facts fall into a pattern and, acquire meaning and mutual relationship. The material collected is organised on logical basis.

(4) **Generalisation.** The next step in the scientific process is the analysis of classified material so that it yields certain general conclusions. This is called generalisation. These generalisations are the scientific laws which are given so much importance.

(5) **Verification.** The scientific method does not stop after discovering universal laws. These laws must also be subjected to verification and the proof of their validity the laws cannot be called scientific.

Essential Elements of Science

The elements that any study requires in order to be called a science are the following:

(1) **Scientific Method.** A science is so called not because of its subject matter but because of its use of the scientific method.

(2) **Factuality.** Science is the study of facts, the search for true facts. Its subject matter is real and not ideal.

(3) **Universality.** Scientific laws are universal and are valid at all times and in all places.

(4) **Validity.** Scientific laws are also valid and are open to examination at all times. They will be found to be invariably true.

(5) **Discovery of Cause-effect Relationship.** Science searches for cause and effect relationships in its material, arid on the basis of such relations it creates universal and valid laws.

(6) **Prediction.** Once the cause and effect relationships are established and universal laws have been formulated it becomes possible for a science to make predictions. Cause and effect relationship is the basic faith of all science. It is believed that one can predict what will happen if one knows what exists, and this is because the laws of cause and effect are universal.

Child Psychology is a Science

If, the above six characteristics are used as criteria one can see for oneself that child psychology is a science, for it possesses each one of these characteristics. The following things should be noted:

(1) **Child Psychology uses the Scientific Method.** Child psychology makes use of such scientific techniques as observation, questionnaire, life history, interview, projection techniques, etc.

In modern times child psychology experiments are conducted in order to verify many facts. In such experiments the child is placed in a psychologically controlled environment and his special form of behaviour studied. It should nevertheless be remembered that it is not simple to compare the method of child psychology with the methodology of the natural sciences. Even the methodology of other branches of psychology cannot be directly compared with methods of child psychology. The main cause of this difficulty is that the child's interests, attitudes, inclinations, etc., cannot be determined very easily. Besides, even when the child knows the object of the experiment he is often unable to provide the answers. Again, it is difficult to except the child to provide an accurate verbal record of his experience and even if such a report is provided it cannot be depended upon. Even then the child psychologists have developed new techniques which can be used on children. For example, in certain conditions a one-way screen is placed between the psychologist and the child through which the psychologist can see the child but the child cannot see the psychologist. Consequently, being unaware of the presence of an observer, the child behaves in his natural manner and thus allows the psychologist to make his observations. Cameras and tape recorders are part of the psychologist's normal equipment. Watson conducted some experiments to note the occurrence of fear in the child. In one experiment, a rabbit was brought to the dinner table while the child was present. A loud noise was made at the same time. The child registered very obvious fear. This was repeated and it was found that the child was frightened every time, and consequently the child came to fear the rabbit although the thing that had scared him was the noise heralding the rabbit's approach. Later on, when the rabbit was brought to the child without the noise his fear slowly vanished. The experiment was designed to show the manner in which fear is conditioned in the child's mind. Now experiments are constantly being devised to discover new material for child psychology. Many of the new experiments are concerned with the educational situation.

(2) **Child Psychology is Factual.** In the words of Ross, "Child psychology is a positive, not a normative science, that is to say, it deals with facts as they are, not as they ought to be." Child psychology, therefore, is factual, and its conclusions are objective and unprejudiced. It describes child behaviour and tries to discover universal laws that apply to it.

(3) **The Principles of Child Psychology are Universal.** Under similar conditions, the laws of child psychology will remain valid at all times and in all places. It is for this reason that the conclusions drawn by American child psychologists from their study of the American children hold good for children in other parts of the world. Naturally, the children of one country differ from other. Yet, general universal principles can be enunciated on the basis of similarities, and these will be seen to hold good in the large majority of cases. For example, the general rule that the development of personality, nature, character, etc., during childhood is influenced by family conditions, the parents' relations with the children, relations between the children, the order of birth, number of children, the financial condition of the family, etc., has been found to have universal validity.

(4) **The Principles of Child Psychology are Valid.** Most of the principles of child psychology have achieved complete validity through continuous verification and re-verification in various parts of the world, under varying conditions. This validity of the principles can be tested anywhere. For example, the general rule that every form of delinquent behaviour and mental disease in children results from some or the other frustration, and that this behavioural defect or disease can be cured if the frustration can be diagnosed, is true any and everywhere in the world.

(5) **Child Psychology defines Cause-effect Relationships.** Child psychology studies the behaviour, mental activity and personality of the normal, the backward and the brilliant child in order to arrive at first causes. It defines cause and effect relationships and on the basis of this knowledge it analyses child behaviour. This makes it possible to know when a child does a particular thing and why he does it. Knowledge of this kind has infinite value for the teacher, the parent and the guardian. Child welfare and child cure programmes are based on the knowledge of such cause-effect relationships. Through these programmes juvenile delinquents, backward children, problem children and the feebleminded have been successfully cured.

(6) **Child Psychology can Predict.** Since certain cause effect relationships concerning the behaviour of children have been established, it becomes possible for the child psychologist to predict the behaviour of other children. He can further predict the development of children in the future. For example, with the increase in population, business and commerce, means of

transportation in large cities, coupled with the shortage of living accommodation, absence of personal contact, the impersonality of relations, tendency of both parents to seek jobs, juvenile delinquency has increased, and will tend to increase under such circumstances. This prediction of the child psychologist can be tested in any large city. This is the basic reason why the incidence of juvenile delinquency is higher in such cities as Bombay, Calcutta, London, New York, Tokyo and other cities of the same size than in smaller cities. In families in which the normal character of the parents is low, or parents who constantly nag each other, or families in which the young men do nothing but wander around the girls or indulge in unnatural acts of sex, it can be predicted that the children cannot possibly develop normal character and personality. Its prediction will be found to hold good for most of the cases. Thus in much the same way an accurate forecast can be made about a child's future in education and in professional life by analysing his intelligence, his talents and his abilities at very young age. Child psychology has found application in vocational guidance and educational guidance only because of its ability to predict.

It is now clear that child psychology is a positive science. A positive science studies facts, that which is rather than that which ought to be, Yet, even though it is, a positive science the degree of actuality that one finds in other branches of psychology can not be expected of child psychology. The very subject matter of this branch, child behaviour, is something extremely subtle, complex and varied. Because the psychologist is himself an adult, he cannot personally feel the experiences of the child and if he tries to rely on his own memory the possibility of error is too great. This difficulty has led some people to conclude that the adult psychologist has no business to dabble in child psychology, and since he cannot make this analysis without being, an adult, it appears that an impossible situation has been reached. But a careful examination will show that this objection is not very fair, because much useful information can be gathered by observing the child, by questioning him and by a comparative study of the reports of different psychologists. It must nevertheless be admitted that the scientific method is faced with grave difficulties in the sphere of child psychology. One major difficulty in this sphere is that, of adequate terms and concepts, and not all child psychologists agree about them. Besides, in experimenting upon a child it becomes difficult to know all the forces that are influencing him. The child's reaction is likely to change if the psychologist is a man or a woman, young or old. A child's behaviour is likely to be influenced by such minor or subtle influences and factors. But the child psychologists have not given up their efforts to make their subject as scientific as they can.

The reality of any science depends upon its subject matter, and it must be admitted that a science studying child behaviour cannot claim the same degree of reality or accuracy that a science studying natural phenomena can. Hence, when we say that child psychology is a positive science we must be aware of its subject matter although even then its limitations cannot be determined accurately. With every new advance in the development of techniques and apparatus the accuracy of child psychology is increasing and there is sufficient reason to believe that this accuracy will continue to increase.

QUESTIONS FOR EXERCISE

1. What is Child Psychology? Discuss the value of Child Psychology for the teachers.
2. What is the Child Psychology? Discuss its significance. How is the study of Child Psychology useful in education?
3. What is Child Psychology? Discuss its nature and scope.
4. Discuss fully the subject matter of child psychology. What is the importance of this study?
5. Discuss the subject matter and aim of child psychology.

2

Relationship with Other Social Sciences

Among the more important social sciences with which child psychology is intimately related are psychoanalysis, clinical psychology, cultural anthropology and education. It is now intended to delineate the relation between child psychology and each of these sciences in some detail.

CHILD PSYCHOLOGY AND PSYCHOANALYSIS

Freud, the originator of the school of psychoanalysis, is one of the important figures in the field of child psychology, for he is responsible for providing it with a lot of data. He showed the way to the use of psychoanalytic concepts in the study of children. In addition to that he provided much psychological data for the training of children. He analysed the relations between children and parents and the development of children. He pointed out the causes that result in criminal behaviour in children. He also demonstrated how childhood experiences later on lead to criminal behaviour and personality deformations in adults. In his method of curing personality disorders he laid special stress on analysing and understanding childhood experiences. He thus returned the attention of the psychologist towards the importance of child life. Later on, many of the theories propounded by him were put to good use in curing mental diseases among children. Alfred Adler analysed the family environment and the child's position in the family, and the influence that this has on determining his future pattern of life. Apart from the work of Freud and Adler, much valuable work in the field of child psychology was done by later generations of psychoanalysis. Anna Freud, the daughter of Freud, did important work in this field. She studied child psychology through the medium of games, pictures, day dreams and dreams. Her study helped psychologists and parents in directing the lives of children.

CHILD PSYCHOLOGY AND CLINICAL PSYCHOLOGY

In America, clinical psychology had its beginnings in 1896 in the establishment of the psychological clinic under the directorship of Witmer at the Pensylvania University. Witmer, the director of the clinic, was particularly interested in the study of backward and crippled children. Modern clinical psychology is now taking interest in the study of children who are suffering from emotional disturbance. As has been pointed out, even the psychological treatment of adults necessitates a detailed study of their childhood experiences. For this reason clinical psychologists have always taken interest in the work done by child psychologists.

CHILD PSYCHOLOGY AND EDUCATION

Education is the process of the child's development. Child psychology is the study of the child's development. Hence the two sciences must be intimately related because without knowing the what, why and how of child development education and training become impossible. Education primarily determines the objective of a child's development For example, modern educationists believe that the aim of education is to achieve an all-round development of the child; but it is not an easy objective to reach. Many or the difficulties that arise are concerned with the child and his environment. If the teacher wishes to solve them and to arrive at an adequate method of teaching be must have a working knowledge of child psychology.

By virtue of this intimate relation between education and child psychology, most of the famous educationists have become interested in child psychology. John Dewey and Edward L. Thorndike, the leading educationists of America, have both been keenly interested in child psychology. Extensive knowledge of child psychology is required in every sphere of education, such as methods of teaching, organisation of the school, formation of the syllabi, programming of extracurricular activities, testing of the students' ability, teaching of backward children etc.

RELATIONSHIP WITH CULTURAL ANTHROPOLOGY

In the modern period the anthropologists have studied old cultures and the behaviour of the men and women, and brought to light knowledge which could not have been imagined by the psychologists of a generation ago. This study has yielded much information concerning child psychology and adolescent behaviour. For example, Margaret Mead studied the people of Samoa, which is an island, and discovered that the mental storm through which the adolescents of advanced societies have to pass never did occur in the life of the Samoan youth. The main reason for this is that in Samoan society there is little social control over and regimentation of the behaviour of young men and women. There is little or no control over their intercourse, so much so that even sexual intercourse between them is not frowned upon. One result of this is that they have no occasion to suffer from any mental conplexes or internal struggle. In modern civilized societies, on the other hand, social life of the adolescent is guided by a very rigid code of morality, and they are not considered adult at any stage, although they wish to be recognised as such. Their, normal curiosity and tendencies, are, frustrated. Adolescence in such civilized societies becomes a period of strong internal struggle through which the adolescent must pass in order to became an adult. In this manner the anthropologists have demonstrated that in modern and ancient cultures the cause behind the difficulties of the adolescent is cultural. In the island of Samoa all such difficulties disappear because the cultural pattern does not create any obstacles in the path of the adolescent. In much the same way other difficulties in the child's life arise because of cultural factors and they can be removed, by, adequate cultural variation. In some societies for example the father gives his love to the child while the mother exercises restraint. In a condition of this kind the Oedipus complex will not develop in the child. Obviously, if child behaviour is to be understood with any degree of exactitude it is essential to take guidance from cultural anthropology because man is a cultural animal, not only a social one.

CHILD PSYCHOLOGY AND GENERAL PSYCHOLOGY

General psychology propounds the general principles underlying the study of man's perception, sensation, thinking, memory, attention, learning and other mental activities, this personality, nervous system, etc. Child psychology studies all these things but its subject, is the child. Obviously, the relation between child psychology and, general psychology must be a close one. Yet, child psychology is an independent field of study, because, as has been proved by modern researches, the child is not a miniature of an adult. Hence it is not possible to say that the principles of general psychology can be applied to the study of a child after making necessary changes. Neither is child psychology a branch of general psychology, because it has been found by continuous research that the child's thinking, understanding, learning, perception, emotion and other activities differ from that of an adult not only in quantity but also in quality. It is for, this reason that child psychology carries on its own research rather than taking over the conclusions of general psychology. In spite of these obvious differences one can develop some interest in the study of children if one is conversant with the principles of general psychology and, their application.

CHILD PSYCHOLOGY AND EXPERIMENTAL PSYCHOLOGY

Experimental psychology studies the entire variety of human behaviour by the experimental method. In a controlled situation the behaviour of an individual is studied. Some aspects of human personality and conduct cannot be studied in an experimental situation because they cannot be subjected to any control. An individual's behaviour in a crowd is a subject worth studying but this cannot be created in a controlled situation.

Experimental method has been used to study many of the aspects of a child's behaviour, and much valuable data has been collected concerning the child's personality, emotions, perception, intelligence, memory and other allied fields. But in certain fields it is impossible to study the child's behaviour by the, experimental method. It then becomes necessary to employ other techniques to make this study Child psychology has thus to rely on a variety of techniques, of which the experimental technique is only one. Obviously, child psychology is not a branch of experimental psychology. But, as has already been pointed out, since many aspects of the child's behaviour are amenable to experimental study, much of the data of this field of psychology is gained from child psychology. Putting it differently, experimental psychology covers the part of child psychology which can be experimented upon. And this is the field in which there is the greatest possibility of making predictions.

It is obvious from the above account that although experimental and child psychology are independent branches of psychology they are intimately related. It can be as the further conjectured that as the uses of experiments in child psychology increase the latter will become progressively, more real.

CHILD PSYCHOLOGY AND EDUCATIONAL PSYCHOLOGY

Literally interpreted educational psychology means the study of human behaviour in educational situations. Skinner puts it in this way: "Educational psychology utilizes those findings that deal specifically with the experience and behaviour of human beings in educational situations." Education is the process of human development. It is for this reason, concerned with the process of human development. As Judd has put it, "Educational psychology may be defined as the science which describes and explains the changes that take place in individuals as they pass through various, stages of development from birth to maturity." Briefly, educational psychology studies human development, maturity and learning, and uses the results of this scientific study in real educational situations in order to achieve the objectives of education.

Defining educational psychology Crow and Crow write, "Educational psychology describes and explains the learning experiences of an individual from birth to old age." These definitions serve to highlight the differences between educational and child psychology. They can be briefly stated as under:

(1) **Difference of Scope.** The scope of educational psychology extends from birth to old age, while child psychology restricts its study of the individual from birth to the reaching of adolescence.

(2) **Difference of Viewpoint.** The viewpoint of educational psychology comprehends nothing more than a study and analysis of the individual's experiences in the process of learning. Child psychology, on the other hand, has a more comprehensive viewpoint. It pays attention to all aspects of the child's development. It studies child behaviour in the educational situation, the family environment and the normal social situation. It aims at the solution of the problems affecting this sphere, for which it traces causal relationships.

Both educational and child psychology are in fact the branches of psychology. Being psychology each one is a positive science of behaviour. Each makes use of the scientific methods in its study. In either case the unit of behaviour is the individual. As has been pointed cut, the subject of study in both cases is the child. The one difference is that in the case of child psychology this study comprehends a greater area. Both are, therefore, mutually complementary. Child psychology helps in the understanding of educational psychology while on the other hand knowledge of educational psychology is of help in the understanding of child psychology. Compared to child psychology educational psychology is more practical but child psychology is more comprehensive.

QUESTIONS FOR EXERCISE

1. Define child psychology and give its nature and scope so as to distinguish it from General Psychology and Experimental Psychology.
2. Give a brief account of the historical development of Child Psychology and bring out the relation between Child Psychology and General Psychology.
3. How is child psychology related to educational psychology? Discuss.

3

Methods of Study

Like all other sciences psychology also aims at the examination of cause and effect relationships and the discovery of principles and laws which can form the basis for predictions concerning human behaviour. Child psychology is the study of the child. Parents, relatives and teachers alike take interest in the child, take pleasure in observing his antics and noting his progress, trying all the while to remove any obstacle that seems to mar his progress. Everyone wishes that he should develop in every possible way. From this standpoint, everyone of them may be said to be studying the child. If one asks parents about the behaviour of their child, they will be able to provide much information based on casual observation. Many such reports and descriptions can be collected to provide much useful information for the child psychologist, yet in must be granted that such reports cannot be said to be scientific. It is commonly believed, for example, that the parents teach their children to walk but recent research has proved beyond a shadow of doubt that when the child reaches a particular stage of maturity he will naturally begin to walk. It is for this reason that reports based on casual and informal observation of this kind cannot be made the basis of any casual deductions and enunciation of laws and principles. Methods made use of in the other branches of psychology must be brought into play in child psychology also. Methods of studying, child psychology should be objective, organised, systematic and real. They should be able to provide an analysis of behaviour based on well defined terms for only then can the conclusions be valid. The reliability of any scientific method bears direct relation to its degree of validity.

No one method can possibly comprehend each, fact of the child's behaviour. This necessitates, the employment of more than one method. One important factor in almost any method of child psychology is that the person conducting the study should be able to establish close and intimate relationship with the child and also adjust his technique in such a manner that he should have minimum difficulty or resistance in obtaining the child's reaction. Obviously, greater presence of mind and agile thinking on the part of the observe will be required in this field than in any other concerned with human behaviour. It normally happens that the child fails to understand the import of many questions or fails to answer questions which he does understand. He cannot analyse his own mental condition, nor can be provide detailed information about his own self. The observer therefore must be possessed of sufficient mental acuity to be able to get this information even without the child's direct assistance.

Among the many methods of child and developmental psychology the more important ones being used are the following:

1. Naturalistic Observation.
2. Child Biographies.
3. Autobiographies.
4. Comparative study.
5. Psycho-physical studies.
6. Statistical methods.
7. Interview.
8. Psychometric methods.
9. Rating Scales.
10. Questionnaires and check lists.
11. Case Study or clinical methods.
12. Projective Techniques.
13. Experimental method.
14. Psychoanalytic technique.
15. Genetic method: longitudinal and cross-sectional.

NATURALISTIC OBSERVATION

The method of naturalistic observation is one of the commonest for studying the child. In this method the parents and other adults observe the child's behaviour over a certain period. Such observation is not systematic or organised, apart from the inherent possibility of the observer's prejudices being reflected in any analysis he may make. Yet, it can and does provide much useful information. In many of the situations encountered in the study of child psychology no kind of control is possible. If one is to study orphans, for example, one must choose children who are orphans, for one cannot make it by separating a child from, his parents and pretending that he is an orphan. Again, experiments for observations which are likely to cause pain to the child cannot be performed in which case observation alone is the source of information.

Since an uncontrolled observation is not very beneficial, psychologists today are keen on using a maximum of control in observing the child. One such device is the use of the one way screen through which one can see in one direction. By using such a screen the observer can see the child at play or at work without the child being conscious of this spying. Movie cameras can be used at places where the child plays and permanent record of the child's behaviour can be obtained. Tape-recorder is another instrument which can be put to extensive use in such a study. All such devices help to render child observation more scientific and accurate.

CHILD BIOGRAPHIES

A method of child study, much in use these days, is that of keeping a day to day record of the child's behaviour. The biographer of the child is one of the two parents or a close relative who is well acquainted with the child. He makes an orderly record of all his observations every day. One such example of child biography is to be found in the studies made by Charles Darwin, which prove that people other than psychologists have done the work of preparing child biographies. And, in actual fact, any individual capable of scientific detachment can prepare a child biography and then proceed to an analysis of it. Although, if he has no knowledge of the laws of psychology his analysis of it will not be adequate or even dependable. Darwin's record, for example, shows that he did not succeed in keeping distinct records and his analysis of them. The following are the main difficulties in this method:

(1) **Protection of Adult Mental Processes.** One major difficulty in amateurs trying their hand at psychological analysis is that they tend to project adult emotions, attitudes and prejudices on the child's mental working.

(2) **Influence of the Observer's Prejudices.** Any Conclusion reached by the observer can be valid and dependable only to the extent to which his analysis has been free of all prejudices and predilections. If his Prejudices have not been held back then they must naturally have influenced his observation and his analysis of the facts, and rendered them unscientific.

(3) **Difficulties in Generalisation.** The behaviour of one child cannot be taken to represent the behaviour of all other children of the same sex and age, and hence the universal laws enunciated on the basis of his behaviour and character cannot be applied to all other children. Similarly, one observer cannot be treated as a

representative observer because the parents of one child might be prepared to go to any length of trouble to provide accurate observation and reports; other parents may be more indifferent.

(4) **Lack of Organised and Systematic Study.** Most child biographies are prepared without any specific objective and hence they fail to report in detail on any particular aspect of the child's behaviour. Consequently, there is considerable difference of how far such biographies can be treated as representative reports of child behaviour.

(5) **Lack of Precaution.** An other difficulty that must be faced is that often the observer fails to take adequate precautions against the child finding out that he is being observed. When the child does find out his behaviour suffers some alteration.

AUTOBIOGRAPHIES

A child's biography can be prepared either by, the psychologist or by the child himself, and hence it can take the form of autobiography. Adolescents in particular can be encouraged to write about their interests, ambitions, their relations with friends and close relatives in the form of autobiographies. If this method is used intelligently, much useful information can be collected and can be used to provide more information by inference. Laird, Hurlock and Klineberg have used this method in their experiments. A modified form was employed by Crow and Crow. This method suffers from the following defects:

1. Most autobiographies are written by children from memory. Many descriptions may be purely imaginary because it is not easy for the average child to remember things of the past in adequate detail.
2. There is a recognised scientific law to the effect that an individual will remember occurrences from his past which have made some powerful impression upon him. In addition to this he tends to remember the pleasant and to forget the unpleasant experiences. An autobiography may, therefore, fail to report on many incidents which the psychologists would consider very significant.

Yet, this method can provide facts and information that no other method can bring forth. A child in recording an incident, will not only dwell on the details but also include his own reactions to it. This will be evident from what be chooses to describe and what he chooses to smooth over. A psychological analysis of such a report can be of immense value.

COMPARATIVE STUDY

Children and animals are fairly alike in that they have affinity for each other. In both animals and children, behaviour is directed by the instincts. Some psychologists have studied children by comparing them to various animals. Some people studied children and chimpanzees of the same age and came upon many interesting facts. Thorridike conducted many such experiments. But a comparative study can provide limited knowledge about the child.

PSYCHO-PHYSICAL STUDY

Crow and Crow have mentioned the importance of psycho-physical studies in child psychology. Such studies concentrate upon the relation between physical development and developments in behaviour depending upon information concerning different kinds of measurements, medical examination, studies of physical, nervous and glandular development, examination of diet and nutrition.

STATISTICAL METHOD

Another method much in use in the study of behaviour in child psychology is the statistical method. This method provides data not only on the subject of individual differences but also makes it possible to establish standards for comparative study. Mean, median and mode can be found out in any data of given information. The mean is calculated by dividing the total points scored by the number of individuals. It is useful because the further the mean is from the given standard the further will the student be from the average in whatever sphere it is under consideration. Median is the figure that is in the centre when all the scores of the individuals are placed in proper ascending or descending order. Mode is the figure that is seen the greatest number of times among the scores obtained by the individuals. These three figures are useful devices for discovering information in any field of research. Mean is considered the most reliable among them.

INTERVIEW METHOD

To begin with, the interview method was employed in the field of child psychology when treatment was required, but now it is used for eliciting specific information. In this method the subject, the child, is present before the psychologist who, if he is skillful, will ask the child a variety of questions. He finds his information not only in the answers of the child but also in the facial expression and general conduct of the child during the interview. The aim and object of the interview is determined before hand and questions are framed to suit the aim, so that only the required information is elicited. That the questions be scientific need not be remarked, because the questions put must be precise enough to draw the information required by the psychologist. Whether they do so or not is the test of their scientific quality. It is better to use a tape recorder because if the child notices that his answers in such an interview are being recorded, his reaction may change and become unnatural. This difficulty can be obviated by the use of a tape recorder The information received during the interview is then processed and evaluated on the basis of a score card or rating scale. Ordinarily, the work of evaluation is carried out by more than one person. If some question is so general that its answer is likely to vary from one person to another then many individuals have to be interviewed before it can go on the rating scale. The chief advantage of this method lies in the psychologist's getting not only the formal information but also his own observations of the subject's behaviour. This is not possible if a questionnaire is used. Yet this method is faced with the following drawbacks:

1. If the subject refuses to cooperate with the psychologist no positive result is possible.
2. Since the method makes it necessary for an experienced and skilled psychologist to interview one subject at a time, it involves the expenditure of much money and time. Some interviews are even spread over an entire week.
3. In an interview the subject is relying solely upon his memory in answering questions. There is grave possibility of mistakes being made.
4. Most people do not like to reveal their innermost secrets to people in an interview, and at least they do not like to say anything which may be derogatory to themselves.

In spite of the difficulties described above, the interview method has been put to very good use in many fields of research in child psychology. But the best results have been obtained by interviewing the child's parents, guardians, teachers and friends, beside the child himself.

PSYCHOMETRIC METHOD

Psychometric methods are used only in spheres in which measurements are required. The first to use one such method was the French psychologist. Alfred Binet who, in 1905, used the method to discover the intelligence quotients of children of different ages. He gave them intelligence tests and gathered much useful information. Nowadays such methods are used to find out facts about intelligence, interest, personality, and a number of other things, Psychologists have constructed many psychological tests to measure various facts concerning children. These tests have a wide application.

RATING SCALES

The rating scale method is very useful for studying the characteristics of a child's attitudes and personality. It is put into use in two ways. In the first place the child is asked specific questions intended to bring out relevant information concerning definite aspects of his personality. The child's personality is revealed either by the answers that he gives or the answers that he picks out of the suggested answers given in the scale. In the second place the child is observed in the situation natural to him, his habits are noted and the main traits of his character are deduced from his behaviour pattern. Most questions put before the child can be answered by a simple 'yes' or 'no', and the scores obtained can be recorded in terms of percentages. The chief drawbacks of the ratting scale method are:

1. If the method is to be used successfully, an extremely skillful and imaginative examiner is required. Most observers are inclined to present their own evaluation of the child's behaviour, instead of allowing the facts to speak for themselves.
2. There is the possibility of partiality in this method because the observer might observe a particular fault in the individual and be inclined to reject him entirely or to project shortcomings on other aspects of his personality too.
3. It is extremely difficult to evaluate any important trait of personality. Besides, the rating scale method makes a quantitative study of items that are fundamentally qualitative. Hence, the quantitative reading can never be dependable.

Despite these drawbacks the rating scale method has been used extensively in child psychology research work and it has done much good.

QUESTIONNAIRES AND CHECK LISTS

Questionnaires are used to a, great extent in the investigations of child psychology. A questionnaires or a check list is a list of selected questions to be answered, questions that are designed to bring out specific information on definite aspects of the personality. The questionnaire can be open or closed. In the open questionnaire the child has to provide his own answer to the questions he has been asked, while in the closed variety he has to select the answer that he fancies and strike out the ones he thinks are wrong. G. Stanley Hall of America was the first to use the questionnaire method on children when he investigated the children of a school in Boston. He made the children answer 123 questions. One important fact discovered in this experiment was that the child's perception of quantity and quality differs considerably from that of the adult.

The questionnaire method is considerably superior to the child biography. In the first place the questionnaire is designed to fulfil a particular purpose and the questions are formed to elicit definite information. It further economises very much on time because the research worker can, within a much shorter time, collect a representative sample. Many research workers for example, have made minor changes in the questionnaire of Stanley Hall and have discovered the relations between chronological age, mental age, intelligence quotient, social status, economic status etc.

Many different forms of questionnaires are used in the study of children, but in the main they can be divided into two classes, the questionnaires to be answered by the child and the ones to be answered by the guardian.

In the first kind the child has to write the answers by himself. This variety has the following drawbacks :

1. A child will not answer or answer incorrectly because he does not understand the question.
2. At times, the information given by the child will, not be what the observer requires.
3. Many adolescent girls and boys fail to answer questions that throw light on their personality or give wrong answers to show themselves in a better light.
4. Many children answer the questions without trying to understand them fully, and this enhances the possibility of mistakes.
5. It is difficult to measure the validity of the answers given by child.

In spite of the above difficulties the questionnaire has been used successfully in studying the child, particularly where information concerning his personality is required. It is also useful for a comparative study.

Questionnaires to be answered by guardians and parents are sent to them by, post, to be answered by them on the basis of their observation and experience. Such questionnaires can be given to teachers also because while teaching in the class they too have the opportunity to observe the child. But this technique suffers from the following defects which detract from its scientificity:

1. Many parents do not take adequate interest in research of this type. Hence they often cannot be persuaded to bother themselves with answering questionnaires. When they can be persuaded to do so, they often provide unintelligible answers.
2. Many parents want to hide such faults in their children as are likely to show them as below average. Hence their observations cannot be relied upon.
3. Another difficulty is that the parent is likely to try to show off his own learning and will then fill the questionnaire with a lot of nonsense, while missing all important points.
4. The parent's attitude towards the questionnaire causes important differences and makes generalisation difficult.

It takes an intelligent and skilled psychologist to derive useful information from such questionnaires. For example, the purpose of a research worker may be simply to find out the attitude of the parents towards different subjects, in which case correct or wrong answers will not influence the research worker's result. Besides, the research worker can forestall lying and falsehood by predetermining the percentage of wrong answers he can get, so that he can evaluate the answers accordingly.

Check lists are used to discover the child's different interests. In such a check list the child is provided with a long list of interests out of which he has to select his own and to list them properly. Such a list is valuable because the child is often unable to put into words the different things that interest him but when he sees them listed before him he can make a selection.

PROJECTIVE TECHNIQUES

One of the most popular method of child study is the projective techniques. In such techniques the child is confronted with situations in which he projects his personality on the situation or the things contained in it. The research worker is primarily concerned with the latent implication of the projection achieved. One major advantage of the method is that the child behaves naturally because he cannot visualise the possibility of anyone finding out anything about his response. In this method, obviously, the main responsibility rests on the observer. In most projection techniques definite research material is employed and principles for analysing the reactions to the material are determined before hand.

The chief advantage in the projection technique is the facility with which it elicits information which cannot be got by direct question and enquiry. Because of the projection the individual's inhibitions are removed and his actual reaction is obtained. Many tests have been devised to make use of the projection method, such tests being concerned with the criterion for analysing the reactions to the projection material. A preconceived stimulus is provided and the individual reacts to it. His reaction is then analysed. Supporters of the technique opine that the individual, in reacting to the stimulus, provides at least a small explanation of his reaction to the stimulus. He forgets the personality he puts on for the benefit of all and can be seen in his true colours. Psychiatrists make much use of the method to diagnose many mental diseases, and they have met with much success. It has been observed that emotionally and mentally diseased individuals do not react to the stimulus in the way a normal person would. Hence it is possible to use the projection technique to find out the causes of emotional imbalance and mental disease. Some of the chief techniques which form part of the projective method will be described here.

RORSCHACH INK BLOT TEST

In 1921 Hermann Rorschach, the Swiss psychiatrist, put forward his ink blot test. He presented the subjects with 200 ink blot tests and evaluated their reactions to them. He finally selected ten and standardised them. In the actual test the subject is given one such card and his reactions are noted. Five of the ten ink blots are black, two are black and red while the rest are multi-coloured. In some of them the perceptible forms are more organised while in most these cannot be perceived distinctly. Rorschach aimed in the main, at the discovery of mental aberration. He found that when the ink blots are given to mentally diseased individuals, the reactions of individuals with particular diseases follow definite patterns which are distinct from the patterns of reaction given by people suffering from some other form of mental disease. After conducting the test with a great many individuals Rorschach defined the laws by which reactions to the ink blots are to be analysed. Many psychologists, Skinner among them, were sceptical of Rorschach's technique. But Rorschach proved the validity of the test by establishing a definite relation between an ink blot reaction and the type of mental disease. This test is useful for discovering internal traits of personality and for measuring them. While some reactions evince a perfect harmony with the social environment other reactions to the ink blots definitely indicate emotional tension, persecution and frustrated needs. The Rorschach ink blot test has been used successfully by many psychologists for studying children, and some of them have gone so for as to define laws for evaluating the reactions of pre-school children. Apparently the ink blots are meaning less, but their utility lies in this apparent lack of meaning. Since the ink blot itself has no manifest meaning it is invested with different meanings by different individuals and even when one individual is seeing it from different angles he may see many things in it. When children are the subjects of this test, more often than not their reactions are almost novel. While one child may see a flower in the ink blot another might see raw flesh and spite blood. One calls the ink blot a puzzle while another discovers a gorrilla in it. One child sees a butterfly in an ink blot but another is frightened by the face of a ghost in the same ink blot. Obviously, the reactions of the second child, in the last example, hint at some abnormality of emotion and personality.

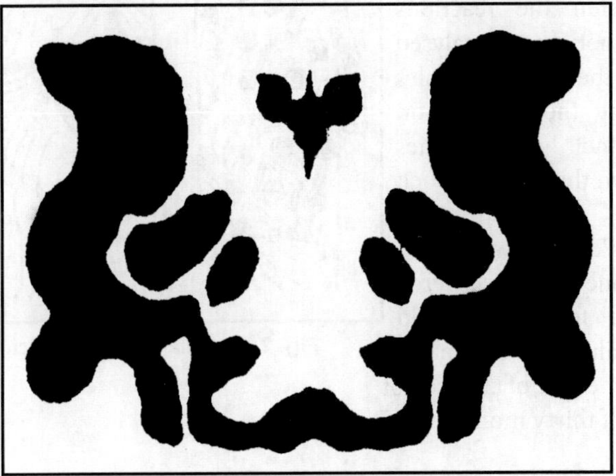

Fig. 1. An Ink Blot of Rorschach.

In actual practice the child is given the ink blot and asked to mention all that he sees in it. If the child wants to know whether he can tilt and turn the card, he is told to do with it everything that he likes. After he has finished with one card he is, given the next, nothing being said about his reaction to the first. Normally, he is allowed to see each of the ten cards, so that his reactions can be formed into a pattern.

After the child has done his work the psychologists analysed his reactions from three viewpoints-what, where and how. The first thing to be noticed is what the child saw. Secondly, one must determine where, on what spot in the ink blot, did he see it. Finally the psychologist is faced with the task of imagining how the child produced that particular reaction. It should be remembered that before the test the child should be told nothing about the what, where and how of his reaction. Some reactions are seen in such a large majority of individuals that they are accepted as normal reactions.

While the ink blot has no meaning of its own, most children see two animals, man's head, two living beings, two lions, the heart etc., in it.

One great difficulty encountered in the beginning was that when the Rorschach test was applied to children the reactions could not be analysed because there were no rules governing them. Later on Ames and his associates laid down the rules for such analysis.

While this work was being done it was discovered that the technique could yield valuable information even in the case of children of the age of thirty months.

Fig. 2. An Indianised T.A.T. Picture.

Murray's Thematic Apperception Test

Another well known projection technique is the thematic apperception test, more popularly known as the T.A.T. In this test the subject is provided with certain pictures depicting human beings in a particular situation. Some of these pictures are useful for children and others for adults, while some can be used for both. The child is given the picture cards one at a time, and within a limited period of time not exceeding a few minutes, the Child is asked to make a story centred around the picture. In composing the story the child has to imagine the circumstances in which the situation in the picture could have been precipitated. He also has to see what is happening in the picture and what could possibly be the sequel to it. If the child asks any questions concerning the picture he is not given any distinct answer for he is left free in making up the Story.

The main point in the test is that in making up the story the child identifies himself with the main figure in the picture. He does this by projection. Hence, the story that he makes up tells the psychologists that in a similiar situation the child would behave in the way he makes the main figures behave, and that his own attitudes and feelings would be the ones he has foisted on to the hero.

Many methods of analysis of the story told by the child are adopted, the simplest one being the reading of the story, examining and digesting it. It is necessary to recognise the person with which the child has identified himself. Then one can analyse the incidents that occur and the events that happen to the hero, his feelings, his mental state of happiness, disgust, pain or rejection. Another thing that must be understood is how he has got into a particular state of mind. What are the needs of the hero? Is he capable of winning a victory at any price or does he want to escape from the environment? What are the different forces which he is facing? Is his family acting as an obstacle in his way, or is there some other entity barring his progress? What is the outcome of his efforts? Does he achieve his goal or does he fail? In all these stories it is necessary to see the blot that has been used more than once. It has been seen that such tendencies as conflict between father and son, consciousness of guilt, hatred, enmity and conflict are the ones that find most common expression in the stories told by children in this test. If the same child repeats this basic kind of plot, then his manner of reacting to the environment can be seen as a definite behaviour pattern. By comparing such tendencies with the normal reactions much valuable information about the child can be arrived at. This will tell the psychologists that the child has suffered from emotional injury or possesses some complex which compels the child to take a warped view of a normal situation. If a child finds suggestions of pain and suffering in stories obviously suggesting optimism and goodwill, then he must have something seriously wrong with him. Obviously, the T.A.T. can be put to good use in the case of children.

Travis Johnston Projection Test

This test was devised by Travis and Johnston. Its main objective is discovering the relationship between the child and his parents. In other words, the condition and general situation of the family is judged from the child's own standpoint. In the process the Child's internal and psychological world comes to light, so that one can see how he adjusts himself within the family environment.

In this test child is given 44 free hand drawings, each picture depicting children and adults in differing situations, some of which are important for the socialization of the child. They may also represent difficult situations. Such fields of family relationships are sibling rivalry and jealousy between the child and the parents, discipline, training in eating and cleanliness, sex, development etc. Different pictures are given to children of different sexes. When the child has been given the drawings he is asked to process his reactions to the individuals in the drawing, the situation and the relations between the individuals. This test, in this way comprehends two major fields the first, sex activity and the other specific traits and presenting the structure of objects; the second, presenting the various spheres of adjustment. Because of these two traits the test is valid for examining the mobility of the child's behaviour, or his flexibility in facing different situations. After the test had been applied to 200 children it was found that it was useful not merely for creating prosperity in the child's life cycle, but also for determining the child's personality, its dynamism and nature as well as the fields of his behaviour which are likely to cause him pain. It can therefore be useful in curing the child of his mental afflictions.

EXPERIMENTAL METHOD

What is Experiment?

According to Garret, experiment is a question asked methodically. In an experiment the researcher is faced with a specific problem to which he has to find a solution through his experimentation The clearer his own conception of the problem or question the better will be the possibility of getting the solution. This question is based on hypothesis which is itself derived from, argument. Then this hypothesis is either proved or disproved by conducting experiments. This can be made clear by a simple example. A person may have been struck by the thought that motives influence an individual's study. This wandering thought is only a conjecture. If it is to be tested then one must ask the question, "Does motivation influence study?" Experiments were then conducted by the individual to find an answer to his question. If the conclusions of the experiment show that the motivation actually does influence study then the hypothesis is proved. Another question which can then be asked is; how far does motivation influence study to advantage? Experiments can then be conducted to find out this. Many related questions can be studied and examined, proved or disproved, through experiments. Other hypotheses such as the influence of smoking on study, the effect of the family environment, the effect of intelligence the effect of repetition, etc. can also form the basis of many experiments. In any experimental method the tests are carried out in a situation which is previously controlled. For this reason any experiment can be described as controlled observation. It is nothing other than the study of the activity of an object or living being within a controlled environment. The chief advantage of the conclusions of such a test is that the test can sometimes be repeated with the same results. So long as the controlled factors remain identical the result will not vary.

In the field of child psychology experiments are made to study the child in a controlled situation with a view to finding out the changes in his development. Before the Second World War a great controversy arose over the influences upon the brain arising out of nursery school experiences. Some people opined that much of what is said on the, subject is not reliable. In order to test this proposition the experiment was started with the hypothesis that the nursery school experience improves the intelligence quotient. In the first place the intelligence quotient of children who had studied in nursery schools for a year was tested. Had the intelligence of the majority of them been generally above the average, it would have been possible to conclude that this development of the mind was a result of nursery school experience. But such a conclusion could not have been scientific because it is perfectly possible that most of the children going to nursery schools may already have possessed intelligence which was above average. Therefore, in order to make this experiment more scientific, a small group of children of the age of five was chosen at random. They were given intelligence tests and were then sent to a nursery school for one year, after which they were again subjected to an intelligence test. If this second test had shown an improvement in their respective levels of intelligence, the claims made on behalf of the nursery schools would have been vindicated. But many other factors could also have been responsible for the improvement in the levels of intelligence. Obviously, any tenable conclusion could not be reached examining only one group of children. Therefore, an experimental group was chosen. This group was kept away from the nursery school. The members of both the groups were chosen from a large group of children without any discrimination, it having already been decided that no emphasis was to be laid on predetermined characteristics. When two kinds of groups bad been created only one variable was left independent, the nursery schools. In this condition it is now possible to find the influence of the dependent variable by comparing the two groups. The experimental group was given nursery school treatment while the controlled group was not given this training. Before the start of the experiment the intelligence quotients of both the groups had been recorded. They were again recorded at the end of the year. Now had the intelligence quotient of the experimental group been perceptibly higher than that of the controlled group the hypothesis would have been proved, but then if the opposite have been the case the hypothesis would have been invalidated.

In the above example, the chief thing in the experimental situation which was emphasized was that while all other variables are fixed only one variable is allowed to function independently or is varied as necessary.

Although the experimental method is the most important method in child psychology, and is the one which can be relied upon to provide the most accurate results, yet, it fails to examine many of the aspects of child development. In studying many important problems the researcher cannot control the independent variables. The parents' love or hate for the child, for example, is an important factor in the development and adjustment of the child's personality, but this factor cannot be controlled by any of the devices of the researcher. In such a case, the only alternative before the researcher is to examine children who have, in the past, been either loved or hated by their parents These two children can then be compared and some conclusions reached as to the influence of the parents feelings to wards the development and adjustment of the child's personality. Yet another difficulty is put in the researcher's path, for it is necessary for all other factors in the children's case to be equal'; otherwise the result will not be valid.

PSYCHOANALYTIC TECHNIQUES

Psychoanalytic techniques are used to a great extent in solving many of the child's behaviour problems and in finding out their root causes. Two chief methods are employed in such activity dream analysis and free association. The child is asked to provide a detailed description of his dreams, which are then analysed by the psychoanalyst in an effort to discover the frustrated' desires of the child. Besides, the child is asked to describe his own life history so that the psychologist can know all the traumatic experiences that the child suffered. The chief exponents of this method were Freud, Adler and Jung. Many were the facts that they discovered. Witmer used a somewhat modified form of the psychoanalytic method.

The following difficulties are experienced in applying the psychoanalytic technique to children:

1. As much time is required in this technique, it proves fairly expensive.
2. In order to be able to apply the technique the psychologist has himself to go through an extended course of training.

In spite of the above difficulties the psychoanalytic technique is used with great success on children in certain circumstances. In fact, the use of this technique becomes absolutely imperative. There is no other method which can be as useful in finding out the root causes of a child's maladjustment and mental diseases.

GENETIC METHOD

Many problems of the child cannot be solved without making genetic study. This research reveals, in the first place, the various characteristics brought forth by the child at the various stages of his development. Besides, it is possible to offer advice and cause improvement after the relation between these characteristics and the factors that cause them has been established in addition to this, all development in the wrong direction can be prevented, while progress in the right direction can be encouraged by the removal of all obstacles. It is for this reason that many modern child psychologists favour the genetic method.

Genetic study normally takes two forms-the longitudinal study and the cross-sectional study. In the longitudinal study the same child is studied over a period of years while in the cross-sectional study different children of same ages are examined at the same time. Another method of study forming part of the genetic method is the convergence approach, a synthesis of the longitudinal and the cross-sectional methods. In this approach children of different age levels are studied, but within the group there may be a number of children of the same age levels. For example, four groups of children belonging to the age levels 6, 8, 10 and 12 are studied at an interval of three years. In this measurement the data available run not into three but into 12 figures. Besides, the development of the different age levels groups can also be compared, because the age measured at three year intervals occurs many times.

In child psychology studies relating to the child's development follow two main lines — the longitudinal and the cross-sectional. The child's development is both vertical as well as cross-sectional and for that reason it is necessary to employ methods which can study both. On the one hand the child is studied as he grows up and goes through a variety of varying situations. On the other, in a single duration of time the child's physical, intellectual, social, emotional, motor and linguistic development is studied. For the first it is necessary to adopt the longitudinal approach and for the second the cross sectional one.

(1) *Longitudinal Method:* As has been pointed out, this method is put into use when the child is to be studied over a long period of time. Its use is like taking photographs of the same object after long intervals. On the basis of this method it is possible to evaluate the development and changes which have taken place in the child with the passage of time. Change of the age is not the only factor, Other things like change of environment can have a vital influence. For that reason it is necessary to be aware of all such factors while

making use of the longitudinal method. It is used chiefly when trying to find out the importance of various methods of child's upbringing. Using this method Shirley examined the motor., intellectual and personality development of twenty-five children from the moment of birth upto the age' of two years. In the first week the children were examined every day in the hospital. During the second week the children were examined on alternate days. After this, for the entire first year, the children were examined at their homes at intervals of a week. In the second year the interval was increased to two weeks. During this entire period the reactions of the children were carefully noted, both by description and by qualitative analysis. Mothers of the various infants also gave their own accounts of the children's behaviour. Conclusions reached on the basis of this data were extremely useful. This is an example of a longitudinal experiment over a short period of time. There are other examples where the study has continued over much longer periods of time. In Minnesotta, U.S.A., for example, the entire 3,200 students of the fourth form of Nobles county were studied from 1950 to 1957. Many important facts were brought to light by this study.

This method proves rather expensive for it involves study over a very long period by a set of skilled enthusiasts and the selection of appropriate subjects from among the children, constant testing and experimentation. Yet, it has proved valuable in many ways, for it has provided much useful information.

(2) *Cross-sectional method* : Many people turn to the cross-sectional approach because the longitudinal approach proves very expensive. In this method children of different ages are studied. Templin, for example, selected young children in 1957 to study linguistic development among children. He chose small children of three years, three and a half, four, four and a half, five, six, seven and eight years of age, with sixty children in each age group. Much research was done on the child's ability to create words, to distinguish between words, to make sentences and the child's vocabulary. Obviously, the cross-sectional method economises time over the longitudinal method and hence finds greater application. By using this method the researcher need not carry on his research for many years. Time which would have been spent in the study of one child is better utilised when he makes a comparative study of a number of children over a very short period of time.

And yet, there are many problems concerning the child's development which cannot be studied by this method. Why does one peculiar form of behaviour appear only at a particular age level or why are individual differences present at every stage are questions which cannot be answered on the basis of data provided by cross-sectional study. The longitudinal method is useful when one studied the deviations of personality. If a particular child is to be studied the cross-sectional approach is inappropriate, because different children show different patterns of behaviour at different age levels.

QUESTIONS FOR EXERCISE

1. Describe and compare the main methods for studying human development.
2. State the importance of the study of child mind and give a short account of some of the methods of studying it.
3. What are the various methods of child psychology? Critically evaluate any two methods.
4. What methods are usually followed in the study of children? Consider the advantages and disadvantages of each of these methods.
5. Outline the principal methods of child study.
6. What are the scientific methods available for the study of the child? Discuss the merits and demerits of any one of them.
7. Describe the principal methods of child study and indicate their comparative merits.
8. Give a brief account of: (a) biographical method and (b) the experimental method of child study.
9. Write short notes on: (i) Comparative study, (ii) Psychological study, (iii) Statistical method, (iv) Interview and (v) Psychometric method of child psychology.
10. Describe and evaluate rating scales and questionnaires as methods used in the study of children. Give suitable examples.
11. Explain fully the projective method adopted in the study of the child mind.
12. Outline the application of Experimental and Psychoanalytical method in collecting data for child psychology.
13. What are the methods of Child Study? Give the advantage of the genetic method.
14. Explain and evaluate longitudinal approach in the study of genetic development.

4

Heredity and Environment

According to John Locke, the British philosopher, at birth the mind of a child is like a slate on which many and varied stimuli make their impression, which take the form of simple and complex thoughts. Modern child psychologists do not subscribe to this view. Many studies have adequately proved and established that when a child is born he is possessed of many hereditary impressions and that education and environmental factors can change these original impressions to a limited extent only. Modern developmental psychologists are of the opinion that human personality and development are the result of interaction between heredity and environment. In this way the value of innate abilities and impressions that a child receives from his heredity cannot be over-estimated in the process of his development. The child is born with physical characteristics, facial features, mental abilities common tendencies, instincts, etc. A study of them will reveal what the child receives from heredity at the time of his birth.

WHAT IS HEREDITY?

Heredity involves all those physiological and psychological traits which a person inherits from his parents. The traits are transmitted to us through the gene. In this way the children of white parents are fair while those of dark parents are generally dark. Negro children exhibit all physiological traits of their Negro parents. If one of the parents is fair while the other is dark, the child may be either fair or dark complexioned. It is heredity which determines the structure and colour of the skin, the colour of the hair, structure, height, facial features, nasal index, cephalic index etc.

How does Heredity Work?

Before the advent of scientific investigation in this field, it was believed that the effect of heredity arises from the mixing of the bloods of parents.

But nearly one hundred years ago, a priest Mendal proved the fallacy of this theory by his experiments on the seeds of peas. Mendal's experiments and the investigations of other scientists proved that the effect of heredity is transferred from one generation to the next through the gene. By the intercourse between male and female, the sperm cell of the male meets the egg cell of the female and the child is conceived. These cells are made of protoplasm, and they have chromosomes in their nucleus. There are genes inside these chromosomes. The heredity of the child from these genes, determines his physiological and some psychological traits. In human beings every physiological trait has a definite gene corresponding to it. This gene is never found in other because both the parents contribute one gene each. Thus the person gets a pair of gene from his parents for every physiological sign. This is heredity. If these two genes are similar, the child inherits that quality, but if the two are dissimilar it is the dominant of the two genes which gives its characteristics to the child. Take an example. If both parents are not fair, and their genes are of a fair colour, the children too will be, in all probability, fair. If the gene of one of the parents is fair while that of the other is dark, the colour that the child will inherit will come from prominent of the two, though it is not inevitable that the child will be fair if the parents are both fair. The real importance is that of the genes. If the child of fair parents is dark, it means that one of the two is carrying a dark gene from his previous generations which became dominant at that time. Sometimes one gene lies dormant for generations but flares up or becomes extremely active in one generation. Sometimes there is a change in the power of transmission of the gene. This mutation causes a sudden change in the gene. No one gene can however, produce some physiological sign by staying away from the other genes. In, reality different genes create a condition in which all the physiological signs are determined for the child.

HEREDITY *VERSUS* ENVIRONMENT

Scholars are not unanimous about the relation between heredity and environment. Some psychologists opine that all physiological and psychological characteristics of the individual find their determinant in heredity. Galton, the eminent author of *Hereditary Genius,* maintained that genius is an innate quality immune to environment. On the other hand, some psychologists think that environment alone is responsible for moulding the character of a person saying that heredity does not in any way affect the individual. Dr. Watson claimed that given any child be can make him anything. Thus the supporters of heredity and those of environment theories have been engaged in an extreme controversy.

Relation between Heredity and Environment

In fact, both heredity and environment are important. MacIver and Page have said very correctly that "Every phenomena of life is the product of both. Each determines the character of the individual. Neither can ever be eliminated nor can ever be isolated."[1] Experiments relating to heredity have proved that it is not the sole factor which determines development of the personality of human beings. And similarly, experiments conducted in the field of environment also indicate that it is not the only factor influencing personality. In Altenberg's words, "Each trait requires both heredity and environment for its development."[2]

Heredity and Environment are Complementary

Actually, heredity and environment are the two aspects of the same element. Davis writes, and very correctly, "Terms like heredity or 'environment' do not refer to anything tangible but to an abstraction." In relation to human development, heredity cannot be imagined apart from environment and neither can environment, be imagined apart from heredity. Lysenco has taken an example from Nature to explain it. Only wheat will sprout from a seed of wheat and the same applies to mustard. But when the farmer decides to sow wheat he has in mind all those things which he needs to make that seed sprout and the extent to which he can lay his hands on them. Obviously the sprouting of the wheat seed and its development depends on both environment and heredity. David Abrahamson wrote, "What the individual can do is decided by heredity and what he does is determined by the environment." The energies of the individual are in the heredity but it is upto the environment to extract these energies. Lumley has beautifully described this relation between heredity and environment. He wrote, "It is not heredity or environment, but heredity and environment."[3]

EFFECT OF HEREDITY

Effect of Heredity on Physiological Appearance

To study the effects of heredity on physical appearances, children of many varied races were compared with their parents. From these experiments it was concluded that it is heredity which determines physical appearance. But other scientists pointed out that the effects of food and environment are by no means negligible.

---

1. MacIver, RM., and Page, C. H., *Society: An Introductory Analysis,* p. 95.
2. Altenberg, E., *Genetics,* p. 22.
3. Lumley, *Principle of Sociology,* p. 50.

Franz Boaz collected examples in which Japanese and Jews residing in U.S.A. had increased in height and the shapes of their heads had also changed.

Effects of Heredity on Intelligence

Having experimented upon Negroes and white soldiers in connection with their intelligence, Yerkes concluded that due to heredity, there is a difference of intelligence between the two. Clark experimented in New York and Los Angeles and contradicted Yerkes in his conclusion that the difference in intelligence between Negroes and the Whites is insubstantial. In an imposing school in New York 10% of the selected 500 students were Negroes, equivalent numerically to the ratio of the Negro population of New York. Besides this, a 9 year old Negro girl registered an intelligence quotient of 200, twice the intelligence of a normal child. Even among the Negroes Klineberg found a disparity between those of the North and those of the' South, the former being the more intelligent because of better developed education and environment. Then, again, scientists have pointed out that the Negroes are always at a disadvantage in these tests designed specifically for the Whites. Intelligence tests developed for one group do not suit other groups.

J. Mackeen Cattell, in his book *American men of Science*' wrote that if the generations of 885 American scientists are studied it is seen that l/5th of them come from the tradespeople, another l/5th from the agriculturists, notwithstanding the fact that the agriculturists comprise 40% of the population while the handful of tradespeople represent only 3% of the population. From this study, attempts have been made to prove that due to effects of heredity, some specific groups or classes show a greater propensity or ability for trade than those belonging to other groups. But Cooley, in his assay *Genius, Fame and Domparision of Races* disproved this opinion by recounting the examples of 71 scientists of Europe.

Importance of Heredity for Personality

It is indisputable that heredity determines the difference of sex and on this basis some scientists contend that heredity determines personality because it is the difference of sex which determines the personality of men and women. People, in general, believe in a fundamental difference in the personality of men and women due to the difference in sex. Thus the qualities of patience and emotion are attributed to woman and she is called the very picture of love and affection. It is generally believed that their main function is to give birth, to look after their offspring and to work in the house. Every literature holds such typical thoughts that woman is like a creeper which lives entwined about man. Her personality is considerably influenced by man's personality. On the other hand, man by nature is hard, persistent, intelligent, independent and self-supporter. While women take an interest in art and literature, men take an interest in science, mathematics and war and other difficult works.

Effect of Sex Difference

The popular thought which attributes difference in the personalities of male and female to the difference in sex is not borne out by facts. One can find among women those who are dangerous criminals, fighters, scientists, mathematicians, politicians. History contains evidence to show that when occasion arose the women did not lag behind the man in any field. Some famous examples such as Joan of Arc, Madame Curie, Rani Lakshmi Bai etc., support this view. To some extent it is possible to assert that the fundamental difference in the personality of man and woman is not due to the difference in sex. This can be proved by conducting experiments in controlled environments. But most of the information collected on this subject comes from the researches of 'the anthropologists and it has been proved that in varied cultures men and women develop varying personalities and the difference in sex plays very insignificant role. The famous anthropologist, Margaret Mead studied the cultures of Arapesh, Mundugumor and Tshambuli, three native tribes of New Guinea. In the Arapesh tribe no difference in the personality of males and females was discernible, both being equally co-operative and efficient. Men and women in the Mudugumor tribe were equally ruthless and aggressive. In the Tshambuli tribe there was an unmistakable difference between the two. Margaret Mead concluded from this that the development in personality depends upon the culture, not excluding the effect which sex has on the personality of an individual. It is universally accepted that the physiological structure, too, has a significant effect upon personality. The physical energies of man and woman are not the same. When compared to man the average weight and height of a woman is less. Her body is naturally adapted to reproduction and the care of her offspring. Her body is more delicate than that of man and due to the physiological difference caused by the difference in sex, they occupy different places in society and consequently the difference in their personality is quite natural. The extent of difference in the personality of individuals however, varies with the variation in culture. Thus the extent to which difference in sex affects personality is governed both by heredity and environment. Landis and

Landis correctly said, "Heredity explains man the animal, environment man the human being."

Effect of Temperament

Besides difference in sex, difference in temperament is also an important part of personality. The nature of an individual depends very much on the environment. Temperaments develop according to the environment in which the child grows. Thus the difference in environment affects temperament. Family relations, social circle of friendship and working conditions all have an effect upon the temperament of an individual. In poverty, temperament becomes hard, irritable, over bearing etc. Even though it may not be accepted as a law, no man of experience will deny that the financial status, occupation, nature of life partner and living conditions all have a profound effect on temperament and all these collectively constitute the environment. But the effect of heredity on temperament is more profound than the effect of environment. Temperament depends, to a large extent, upon internal drives which are deeply effected by endocrine glands. In modern times extensive research has been carried out to find out the effect of endocrine glands on temperament and some scientists have gone to the extent of saying that glands determine personality. People have been classified on the basis of the effects of glands. Scientific discoveries have proved beyond dispute that the effects on temperament once attributed to the environment are actually the effects of glands. The change which occurs in the temperament of boys and, girls caused by the increased activity of the sex glands with the coming of youth is inevitable. Besides as the secretion of the Thyroid increases, an individual becomes restless and active and if it decreases he becomes slow and lazy. If the parathyroid secrets more a person remains calm but he becomes excited with every fall in the secretion. Research on the effects of the glands located in various parts of the body is in progress. Attempts are being made to bring about artificial increase or decrease in the glandular secretions. Undoubtedly, many ways of improving human personality will be evolved but to conclude from this, that temperament is determined by glandular secretions or that heredity determines everything in the subject, would be completely one sided. These secretions have tremendous but unperceived effect. A big change in these secretions is effected by cultural and social environments. For example, the mental disturbance through which adolescents in our societies pass when they attain youth is absent in many tribes because in those tribes there are no restrictions upon sex relations. Obviously, the change is not exclusively due to the activity of sex glands, but it is also due to social customs. Heredity then does not mould the personality. The above description of the effects of heredity' on personality can be beautifully summed up in the words of Biesanz and Biesanz, "Personality is the organisation of a person's habits, attitudes and traits and arises from the interplay of biological, social and cultural factors."

The above exposition of the effects of heredity upon physical appearance, intelligence and personality, makes it quite obvious that its effects are not similar and equal in all cases. We know from experience that heredity has its most pronounced effect upon physical appearance, somewhat less on intelligence and least of all upon personality. This conclusion is supported by scientific researches.

EFFECT OF ENVIRONMENT

Environment has a very significant effect on man. Its effect starts from his birth and continues almost till his very death. The status of the child, youth and old man in the family and society is not the same and as a result of this difference a man's personality, roles, temperaments, ways of thinking, tendencies, inclinations, and character is affected. In the same way, the status of the person in places like school, office, occupation, etc., affects his role to a great extent.

Environment can be roughly divided into two parts-controlled and uncontrolled environment and social and geographical environment. In both the social and geographical environment of man, a part of them is controlled and the other part is not controlled. Both these types of social and geographical environments, have a profound effect upon the individual.

Effect of Social Environment

The various parts of society like the family, school, occupation, social customs and primitive concepts all effect the individual. In this, context one example from family life will suffice. In the opinion of the famous psychoanalyst Sigmund Freud the personality of a person is fashioned in the first seven years, the rest of the life being an expression of those tendencies. Whether all thinkers agree with Freud's opinion or not, all have agreed with regard to the effect of the environment on the family, upon the character, nature, mental tendencies, habits and behaviour of the individual, and there are enough existing causes which justify family's influence upon the individual. This special knowledge can be gained by comparing children brought up in families and those bred in government institutions. Havelock Ellis in his essay *The Problem of Race Regeneration,* says, "The advantages of a mother suckling her baby are more than merely physical, it is a stimulus to her affection for her child and a guarantee that the child will receive in other respects the loving care it needs." In childhood parental love affects stability of the emotions for the child. It is inevitable that excessive love and care spoil the children and lack of affection leaves their feelings undeveloped, which are then unnaturally expressed. The famous psychologist Alfred Adler said that even the birth order of the child in the family affects personality. This may be expressed or clarified better thus — in the family mother, father, husband, wife, elder brother, younger brother, elder sister, younger sister, beloved child, unwanted offspring all have their respective, dissimilar status which affect their personality.

What is heredity? It is, in a mixture seed form all that a child receives from his parents. The child is born by the combining of two genes of the mother and father. But this seed does not sprout similarly under all conditions. The farmer ploughs the field and sows the seed in it. The seed which lands on the stone does not sprout while the one which lands on the hard land does so with difficulty. The seed away from water sprouts but does not grow because it dries up due to lack of water. If the farmer fails to look after the crops, wild-animals and birds would destroy it. The absence of fertilizers would restrict the proper growth of plants. Thus, the mere planting of wheat will not allow one to reap it. It is essential that the crop be given manure, water, etc., at the proper time and it be protected from animals.

The same principle holds true with human beings. Admitted that the child is born with many physiological and mental qualities in a seed form but do these qualities develop similarly under any and all conditions? Two twin children have identical heredity, but W.E. Blatz in his book, *Collected Studies on the Dionne Quintuplets* proved very clearly that even identical twins develop differences. Newman, Freeman and Holzinger bred 19 identical twins in dissimilar environments and the studies revealed very slight physiological dissimilarities but very marked differences in the peculiarities of personality. Obviously, change in environment changes the effects of heredity. Thus, even if the most intelligent child is placed in a bad environment, the growth and development of his genius will become limited and on the other hand, the qualities of an average child can be developed to their maximum by placing him in good and helpful environment.

But does this mean that the seed has no importance? Can the mere change in environment make anybody just anything? If a seed of cactus is sown, mangoes cannot be had. Environment develops the traits received from heredity but only to some extent.

In brief, it can be said that heredity is the seed, the environments are conditions for its development. The development of inherited qualities will be according to the environment.

Thus both heredity and environment are important for the education of the child. Both must be improved to realise all round development of personality, while the family provides the heredity, the school may provide such environment and may help in maximum utilization of the hereditary traits.

QUESTIONS FOR EXERCISE

1. Bring out the relative importance of heredity and environment in the development of child.
2. What is heredity? How does it influence the formation of the personality of a child? Give instances in support of your answer.
3. Define Heredity. Evaluate the relative role of Heredity and Environment in the mental development of a child.
4. What do you mean by heredity? State the nature of carriers of heredity.

5

Response Mechanism

Response mechanism is that system which helps the organism to adjust itself with the environment and controls its activities. Thus it is due to response mechanism that one finds selection, adjustment, synthesis etc.; in human behaviour. The response mechanism in animals is divided into the following parts:

(1) **Receptors.** Eye, nose, ear, tongue and skin etc., are receptors. They receive the sensation. Human behaviour begins through the receptors. It is only after the receptors have received the sensation that the response in the organism begins.

(2) **Effectors.** Effectors include muscles and glands. They make the actual response possible.

(3) **Nervous System.** Nervous system controls the response. It connects the receptors and organs.

Human organism is effected by the environment. The sun, heat, cold etc., affect our body. The body responds to external stimuli. This response changes the external environment. When something pinches, the pinched one feels a sensation. The sensation is received by the nervous system through which the receptors and motor organs are connected and the muscles of the hand react immediately so that the pinching object is removed. Thus the receptors receive stimuli from the environment and the motor organs change the environment by response. The human organism has innumerable receptors cells. In the eye alone there are millions of cells. Similarly, the receptor organs, *e.g.,* muscles etc., have innumerable muscle fibres. The nerves connect the receptors and the muscles and thus make response possible. These nerves carry the message from the receptors to the muscles. This communication has a speed of 75 yards, a second. Thus, response takes a very small fraction of a second. In times of emergency, it becomes even more rapid.

NERVOUS SYSTEM

Nerve is the most important part of response mechanism. It joins the receptors and the effectors. The nervous system is divided into two parts: (1) Central nervous system and (2) Autonomic nervous system. In the human organism there is a whole net work of nervous system. The central nervous system, too has two parts (1) Spinal Cord (2) Brain, which has three parts (i) Cerebrum, (ii) Medulla oblongata, (iii) Cerebellum. The autonomic system has two parts: (a) Sympathetic, (b) Parasympathetic. The following chart shows this structure:

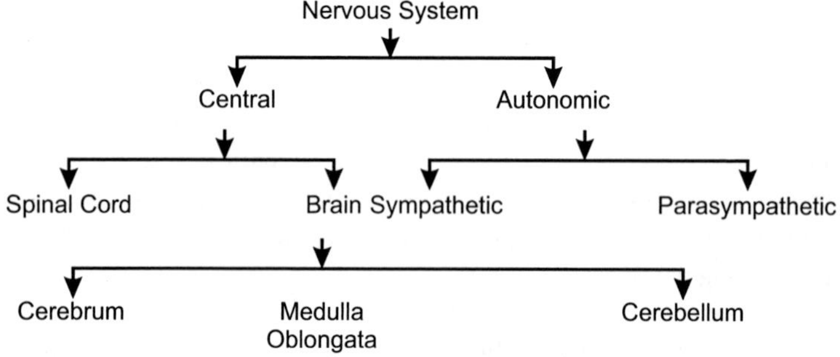

A nerve net work spreads throughout the body, similar to the telephone cable net work spread over the city. These nerves reach every receptor and muscle just like the cables which reach every business centre, office, hospital, college etc. All the nerves of the body are connected to the spinal cord and this central body resembles a telephone exchange where all the wires from the different telephones meet. Information is sent from any telephone in the system to the telephone exchange and the desired telephone connection is got. Thus the exchange of information between two centres is always through the medium of the telephone exchange. A similar state of affair's exists in the nervous system. Sensory nerves bring information to the centre from the receptors and the motor nerves carry directions to the muscles. But there is a big difference between the telephone system and bodily nervous system. The telephone exchange is merely a medium which has no say in anything which goes on. On the other hand, the nervous centre is not, merely a medium because it decides upon the response to the stimuli and the part of the, body to obey it. So, in reality it is this centre which controls the whole response mechanism.

The nerves of the central nervous system reach every sense organ and muscle. These nerves are connected with the central gang of the spinal cord. All the nerves meet at this centre. The nerves carrying the message from the receptors to the centre are known as sensory nerves.

The nerves carrying the message from the centre to muscles are known as motor nerves. The response mechanism works by systematic working of the sensory and the motor nerves. Besides these two types of nerves there are nerves connecting them.

Thus, various responses of the human body function through nerve centres. These nerve centres are very complex. When seen with the help of a microscope, many subtle fibres are seen in other nerves. Some of these are even some yards in length. The complexity of the nerve centre can, be imagined from the fact that the optic nerve alone has about 4,000,000 fibres. A nerve is made, up of a bundle of fibres. Fibres are connected outside the nerve centre, but again meet in the nerve centre. It is not necessary that one fibre should carry one message. Sometimes an outgoing fibre takes several messages. When the nerves are broken and the muscles are unconnected with the centres, these fibres become useless.

The nervous system is made up of nerves. The nervous system and the nerve, cells are connected through the blood vessels. These nerves also include their branches. These branches are of two types-Axons and Dendrites. Axon is one and alone while dendrites are many. Axons are several feel long. The dendrites extend like the small branches of a tree. The axon is covered by an insulating substance. The axons of the sensory nerves are sensory while axons of the motor nerves are motor. A motor axon extends from the brain or spinal cord to the muscle or gland. The sensory axon extends from the nerve cells to the brain. Thus these axons connect the receptors and the nerve centres.

The connection between the two cells is known as synapse. In this synapse an axon of a nerve finishes in fine branches and these fine branches get connected with the dendrites of some other nerves and a sensation is carried from one to another. The axon carries the sensation and the dendrites receive it. Thus the message is communicated from the axon of the nerve to the dendrite of another nerve. This message is in the form of nerve impulse which is like an electrochemical current found in the nerve. The force of the reaction of any muscle depends on the total number of these electro-chemical currents per second, as it increases and decreases simultaneously.

The Spinal Cord

There are two parts of the central nervous system: (A) Spinal cord and (B) Brain.

The spinal cord is situated in the back bone of the human structure. It is a white soft substance like a rope. Its upper surface is made up of white matter and is thick. There are two types of nerves in the spinal cord: (1) sensory or afferent nerves and (2) motor or efferent nerves. These nerves connect the receptors and the nerves centres. The sensory nerves carry the sensation from the receptor to the nerves centre. The motor nerves carry the message from the nerve centre to the muscle. This coming and going of the sensation and messages is through the grey substance of the spinal cord. 50% of the spinal cord is made of grey substance and the rest of the white substance. The pathways of the spinal cord are situated just below the skin. In their centres are the cell bodies and the pathways are in the peripheral portion. In the white matter there are tracts coming up and down. In the grey matter there are associative nerves.

The spinal cord directs the reflex action. In the reflex action the sensory nerve carries the sensation to the brain and the message from the brain to the motor or efferent nerves. This action is so rapid that it takes almost no time. Besides the control of the reflex activity, the spinal cord links the brain with the external parts of the body. In it are connected 31 pair's of the nerves coming from outside. Every pair has one sensory and one motor nerve. These nerves connect the spinal cord with external parts of the body. Thus the various functions of the external parts of the body, *e.g.*, the movement of the hands, feet, etc. are directed through the spinal cord. It has free control over all the learned activities including writing, reading, cycling, typing, walking, running etc. The brain has not to interfere with these habitual actions.

Cerebrum

Besides the spinal cord, another important part of the central nervous system is the brain. The brain is divided into three following parts: (1) Cerebrum, (2) Cerebellum and (3) Mid Brain or Medulla oblongata or, brain stem.

The cerebrum is bigger than the cerebellum or the mid brain. Hence it is known as cerebrum or the bigger brain. Beginning with the eye brows, it extends to the middle of the skull. Thus, it is the frontal part of the skull. It is the highest part of the brain. In it the arrangement of the white and the grey matter is exactly opposed to that of the spinal cord. Its upper surface is made up of grey matter while internal part is made up of white matter. As has already been pointed out, in the spinal cord the upper surface is made of white matter while the internal part is made of grey matter. The upper grey part of the cerebrum is known as cortex. In it there are clusters of nerve cells which make the sensory area and the motor area of the brain. The white matter forms the nerve fibres. The grey matter forms the nerve cells.

In the cerebrum there are two hemispheres separated from the fissure and are known as the right and the left hemispheres. Most of the part of the right hemisphere is linked with the left part of the body. The left hemispheres is linked with the right part of the body. Thus between the hemispheres of the cerebrum and the body there is a crossed relation. On the surface of the cerebrum there are small convolutions or gyri. These convolutions are separated from each other through the fissures. These fissures go deep into the matter of the cerebrum. But the brain is not actually divided, into these fissures because under the surface of the brain there is a fissure in the centre which is known as central sulcus. It is also known as fissure of Rolando. Besides this, there is also a fissure situated horizontally. This fissure is known as fissure, of silvious or lateral sulcus.

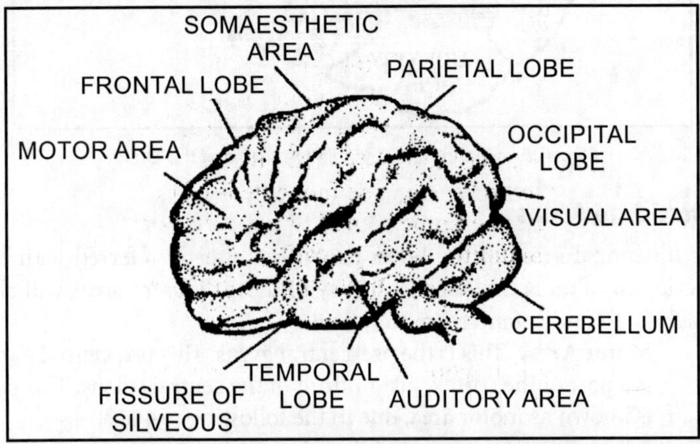

Fig. 3. Lobes, Fissures and Areas of Cerebrum.

The big portions of the, cerebrum are known as lobes. These lobes are connected with each other. Thus, the cerebrum is divided into four parts: (1) Frontal lobe, (2) Parietal lobe, (3) Occipital lobe and (4) Temporal lobe.

All these four parts of the brain are connected by sensory projection fibres. These fibres enter one lobe from another.

These different parts of the cerebrum are connected with different types of sensation. For example, the frontal lobe is connected with thinking. In complex thinking, it is this frontal lobe of cerebrum which works. In the central part on the one side of the central sulcus there is a motor area. This is situated in the frontal lobe. In the parietal lobe there is a somaesthetic area where the sensations from the skin and muscles are received. In the upper part of the temporal lobe there is auditory area where the sensations of hearing are received. In the back part of the brain in the parietal lobe, there is the visual area where the sensations of seeing are received. Near the lateral sulcus there are areas of taste and smell.

Several experiments have been conducted regarding the value of these different lobes in the behaviour of man.

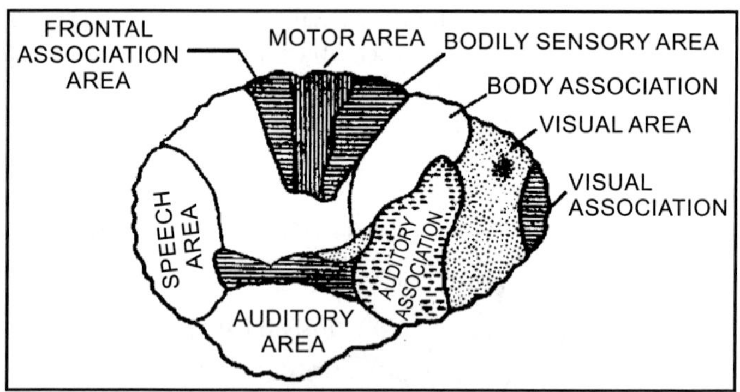

Fig. 4. Functional and Associative Areas of the Brain.

Functional Areas

The functional areas of the brain have been already referred with the description of different lobes. A survey of these different areas will also be helpful to understand them fully well.

(1) Motor Area. This is the pre-central gyrus. This pre-central gyrus is a part of the cortex, just in front of the central sulcus. This part is known as motor area, due to the following reasons:

- (a) A shock to any part of this area results into paralysis of some part of the body.
- (b) Application of electric current to any part of this area results in the movement in different organs of the body.

Hence, this part can be rightly called motor area. But this part does not govern the motor activities of the body. Cortex which is in front of this area also takes part in the movements of the different parts of the body. This part is known as pre-motor area. The motor area governs the single movement while the pre-motor area governs the complex movements.

(2) Sensory Areas of the Cortex. This is concerned with the lower parts of those sensory organs which are situated near one another at the upper end of the cerebellum. The nerve fibres from the eyes, ears and other sense organs meet at this place. The relay fibres also go to meet sense organs from here. It is through this area that the sense organs are related with the cortex.

(3) **Somaesthetic Area.** This is also called central gyrus. It is just behind the motor area. It is here that there is the main cortical centre for sensation from the skin and muscles. A shock in this region destroys sensitiveness of the skin of muscles.

(4) **Auditory Area.** The auditory area in the brain is situated in a small part of the temporal lobe. It is here that the sensations from the ears are received. The relay fibres reach the cars from here. A shock in this region results in the destruction of the capacity of hearing.

(5) **Visual Area.** The visual area is situated in a part of occipital lobe. It is here that the sensory fibres from retina are received. The relay fibres to the eyes also go from here.

Associative Areas

The associative areas are those parts of the cortex which would be included in the motor area. The associative area appears to be divided into two big parts. One associative area is situated in occipital, temporal and parietal lobe between several motor areas. Another associative area is situated in the motor area and cerebrum in the front part. The associative areas are separated by the association fibres. If these fibres are damaged some sensitive part of the brain is also damaged, *e.g.*, with the destruction of the association fibres of the cortex, everything learned is forgotten. With the destruction of the area near the motor cortex, the capacity of speaking and writing is destroyed. With the destruction of the visual area, it becomes impossible to understand language and the, man cannot understand words even while seeing them. Some severe damage to the areas of the front part of the brain results in forgetting of something immediately learned, though one can remember something of childhood.

Mid Brain

The second part of the brain is the brain-stem or medulla oblongata. It is through this part that sensations sent to the spinal cord reach the brain and the responses from the brain reach the lower part of the spinal cord. The work of the spinal cord has already been described earlier.

Cerebellum

The cerebellum is the third part of the brain. It is situated in the portion behind cerebrum. It is divided into two lobes. Inside these lobes there are white nerve fibres which are covered by a thin layer of the grey cells. There are some fibres in this part which are deeper than those of the cerebrum.

The cerebrum controls the kinaesthetic movements and coordinates the muscular activities.

AUTONOMIC NERVOUS SYSTEM

Autonomic nervous system is an important part of the nervous system in the human organism. It is known as autonomic nervous system because it is independent of the central nervous system in its action. There is no interference in its activities from the central nervous system. For example, in the emotional state there are many changes in the body which are governed by autonomic nervous system and in which central nervous system takes no part. But this does not mean that the autonomic nervous system has no relation with the central nervous system. As a matter of fact the spinal cord which is the important part of the central nervous system has also an important role in the autonomous system. Hence, it can be said to be autonomic only in the sense that it controls and governs all those activities in which the brain has, nothing to do. The activities of this system cannot be checked even with the efforts. It goes on acting independently.

The main function of the autonomic nervous system is the adjustment between the activities of the different parts of the body, Many of its nerves beginning from the brain and the spinal cord reach the stomach and nerves carrying blood. These nerves control the activities of the internal and external muscles. It is the autonomic nervous system which controls the activity of the glands, the stomach and the blood vessels. It is this system which controls the activities of the different parts of the body, *e.g.*, lungs, heart, liver, spleen, rectum, sweat glands etc. Thus, as a matter of fact this is a motor nervous system. Many of the ganglia of its nerves, cells and also the synapses are situated outside, the central nervous system and the central nervous system takes part in, their activities.

The left part of the autonomic nervous system is divided into three parts as follows: (1) Cranial, (2) Thoraco Lumber and (3) Sacrel. The thoraco lumber is the part from the brain stem to sacrel. The reason to call it thoraco lumber is that the nerves of this part reach the thorax beginning lowest from the spinal cord. Below thoraco lumber and in the part of the spinal cord is the sacrel.

The autonomic nerves and the different parts of the body are connected with the spinal cord. Thus, the autonomic nerves are extended up to eyes, salivary glands, mucous membrane, blood vessels, heart, liver, stomach, pancreas, intestines, adrenals, kidneys, bladder, colon, rectum and genital areas. Besides these they are also extended up to sweat glands and cutaneous vessels. The ganglia and spinal cord are linked by those nerve fibres which reach the ganglia from the spinal cord. In a ganglia there are 22 sympathetic ganglions. The sympathetic ganglions are on the upper surface of the white matter, known as myline. The axon fibres beginning from ganglia return again to the nerves of the spinal Cord.

The autonomic nervous system is divided into two parts: (1) Sympathetic nervous system and (2) Para-sympathetic nervous system. The activities of both these parts are opposite to each other.

(1) **Sympathetic Nervous System.** The sympathetic nervous system prepares the body for emergency. It saves the body in the time of emergency. It also works in emotional states. Due to its activity the retina of the eye acts at the time of emergency and the blood vessels of the stomach send more, blood to the muscles and brain instead of sending blood to the stomach. As a result of this the digestion stops and so also hunger. The muscles and the brain begin to work rapidly as the intestines stop working and the gastric glands stop giving secretions. The heart beats with a speed as it has to pump blood rapidly. The adrenal glands execrete adrenaline. As a result of adrenaline the blood sugar is increased in the blood resulting into increase of strength in man. Excitement results in the destruction of many cells and the rate of respiration is increased. The water metabolism drops down resulting in dryness in throat and mouth. All these activities can be seen at the time of quarrel or fighting, anger or fear. In the emotional state, the galvanic response capacity also becomes less.

(2) **Para-sympathetic nervous system.** Another part of the autonomic nerves is para-sympathetic nervous system. It is the link with cranial and sacrel The main work of Parasympathetic nervous system is anabolism. It includes the concentration of the energy of the body and strengthening of the different parts of the body by this concentration. As the activity of the sympathetic nervous system decreases, the speed of the heart beat is lessened and the blood pressure also becomes less. The activity of the salivary glands increases which helps in digestion, resulting in the increase in the weight of the body. The pupils of the eyes contract resulting in the relaxation of the eyes. The para-sympathetic nervous system controls the activity of the sacrel division. It keeps the bladder, the colon and the rectum healthy and helps in execrating the different kinds of useless and poisonous matter from the body.

The sympathetic and the para-sympathetic nervous systems differ from each other as explained below:

(1) In the sympathetic nervous system the ganglions are in the spinal cord near those internal organs of the body which they excite. But in the para-sympathetic nervous system the ganglions are not in the spinal cord but near bodily organs.

(2) In the sympathetic nervous system the whole system works together, but in the para-sympathetic nervous system the different parts are independent.

But this does mean that the sympathetic and the para-sympathetic nervous systems are absolutely opposite to each other and they are not related. As a matter of fact they cooperate in spite of these distinctions. These systems do not work independent of each other but cooperate in different proportions according to different situations, *e.g.,* if the organism has to struggle with the environment, the sympathetic system works more and the para-sympathetic system is less active. In the adjustment with environment the para-sympathetic system has to work more while the sympathetic system works less. Thus due to the cooperation of the sympathetic and para-sympathetic systems, there is a balance. In the body in both the states of work and rest.

Glands. These are a special type of structure with secret different types of chemical substances in the body. Generally they are divided into two classes: (1) Duct glands *e.g.,* Salivary, Tears, Gastric and Sweat glands etc., (2) Ductless glands *e.g.,* Pituitary Pineal, Thyroid, Parathyroid, Thymus, Adrenal, Gonads, etc. These glands provide different types of harmones to the body which have important influence on the physical activities as well as on behaviour.

Nervous system. Nervous system is made of, nerve cells which are linked through tissue and blood vessels. There are two types of branches in nerves — Axons and Dendrites. The connecting link between two nerves is known as synapse. Nervous system can be divided into central nervous system and autonomic nervous system. Central nervous system is further divided into Spinal cord and Brain. Spinal cord is situated in the back bone. It has two types of nerves :

(1) Sensory or afferent (2) Motor or Efferent.

QUESTION FOR EXERCISE

1. Explain human response mechanism.

6

Nature and Principles of Human Growth and Development

Developmental psychology studies human development, the study starting not with the infant's birth but before it, while it is in embryonic form within its mother's womb. The child's development within the womb is a very important phase of his entire development. Hence, there have been detailed studies of the human embryonic state. The human being originates in the form of a fertilised ovum. Gradually and continually, this fertilised ovum shows signs of structural and functional development. In the structural development, the ovum cells multiply in number and increase in size. These cells are of two kinds, the germ cells and the somatic cells. The germ cells help the germ plasma to develop from one stage to the next higher level. The somatic cells are concerned with the development of various physiological parts such as bones, muscles, nerves, etc. Besides changes in structure, the functions of the embryo also take on variety and complexity. Functional development occurs with the addition of new activities. While the human being is in the embryo, the structural and functional developments take place in the nature of two mutually supplementary aspects of total development.

EMBRYONIC DEVELOPMENT

Psychologists have divided the embryonic development of the being into several states. These states and a brief mention of them are given below:

(1) **Germinal period.** The period beginning with conception of the child and lasting for a period of two weeks is called the germinal period of the being's development. During this period the being exists in the form of a fertilised ovum, not being given any external nutrition and continuing in an independent and unmixed state,

Lacking nutrition it does not develop. The form of the fertilised ovum is that of an egg, and its cells are equally divided.

(2) **Embryonic Period.** The period from the third to the eighteenth week of pregnancy is called the embryonic period, during which the embryo gets nutrition from its parent. As a result, its form undergoes rapid change. In this change there is a hive related to the ovum and it is situated between the cells that lie in between the Omniotic sac and the Yolk sac. In this hive, the cells lying next to the yolk sac are called the endoderm cells while those lying next to the omniotic sac are called the ectoderm cells. The cells of the first kind prove, of help in the development of the digestive and the respiratory systems, while the latter or second kind of cells lead to the development of the nervous system and the skin or epidermis. The mixing of the two kinds of cells leads to the development of a new layer called the mesoderm. Development of the two kinds of cells leads to the creation of muscles and bones. Cellular structure which is originally flat and convex, gradually spreads out. Every cell has its own peculiar position, and if it is changed, its characteristic features will also undergo some change. For example, if it would originally have developed into skin, it will develop into the muscles of the eye on changing the cells. Certain chemical substances are also of importance in the separate and individual development of the cells. These chemicals are called organisers. Besides these, the development of the embryo is influenced by the use of light, electrical field, X-rays, and other chemical rays.

(3) **Fetal Period.** In the development of the being this state begins with the eighth week, and In it a number of cells increase, following which their size improves. Change in this stage is very rapid.

As has been pointed out above, the child's development during pregnancy is characterised by two types of development, the structural and the functional. The following two laws are accepted in respect of structural development:

(a) **Law of Cephalocaudal Development.** According to this law, in the development of the embryo, the development starts with the cephalic portion or the head and gradually proceeds to the tail portion. In this way, this law or development shows the direction of the bodily development. This law applies to growth as well as differentiation.

(b) **Law of Proximo Development.** According to this law, the progress in development is more rapid in peripheral parts than in the parts situated in the centre.

In structural development, the structure of the nervous system is a very important one. In this development, the first layer of the ectoderm cells turns inwards to form the neural tube, the major portion of which, the spinal cord and the upper part develop into the brain. In the fifth week of development, the medulla, cerebellum and the mid-brain become distinctly visible. The nervous system develops very rapidly during the fetal period. Muscles begin to be formed even before the nerves and sensory organs. Almost all the sensory parts develop in the being before delivery or actual birth. The development of vision starts with the second week, and continues even after pregnancy. Receptors concerned with olfactory sensation reach maturity in pregnancy in the case of some children. Taste cells develop in the third month, that is during the fetal period. Besides this, during pregnancy, the being attains the power of feeling sensations of pressure on the skin.

EMBRYONIC FUNCTIONAL DEVELOPMENT

Functional development during pregnancy is divided into two parts, those of motor development and sensory development. Their description follows:

(1) **Motor Development.** During pregnancy, the embryo shows constant activity that can be discovered with the help of the stethoscope 14 to 16 weeks before birth. During this period, this movement is also felt by the pregnant woman carrying the child. At the age of three weeks, the heart starts beating, and after 18 weeks this heart beating becomes audible. In this period, some motion is also evident in the chest. In the seventh week, the organs of digestion evince some movement while there is sometimes some tension of the urinary bladder. Children born in the sixth month of pregnancy produce certain sounds. Research experts have made study of the embryonic movement in rats, cats and pigs, etc., and compared it with the movement in human animals. This research has shown that till a certain stage of development is achieved, the embryo does not show any reaction to any stimuli. In the beginning the tail section does not show any reaction, but it is evident when maturity of this part sets in. The movement starts with the leg, continues to the knee and can then be seen successively in the foot and the ankle. Menkowski and Hooker have conducted important research in connection with motor

development. The two laws concerning structural development are also applicable to motor development. According to Toghill's principle, in functional development there is a movement from the general to the particular. Putting it more explicitly can be said that first general activities appear, and then through gradual development these general activities are divided into particular activities that become distinct.

(2) **Sensory Development.** The second important aspect of motor development is that of sensory development. In the eighth week, the embryo becomes susceptible to epidermic sensations. Later on, it reacts to pressure and temperature sensations. According to the law of cephalocaudal development, in sensory development, epidermic reaction is the first to appear, while sensibility of the rest of the body are also in evidence, but the sensation of pain does not develop during pregnancy, while the ability to recognise and react to direct smell and taste is engendered during pregnancy. Some experiments have shown that the child can react to strong sensations one month before it is born.

The diagram given below represents the various states of motor development-personal, social behaviour, language, adaptive behaviour, at varying levels of maturity in the child from the time based upon the book *Developmental Diagnosis, Normal and Abnormal Child Development* by Gesell and Amatruda.

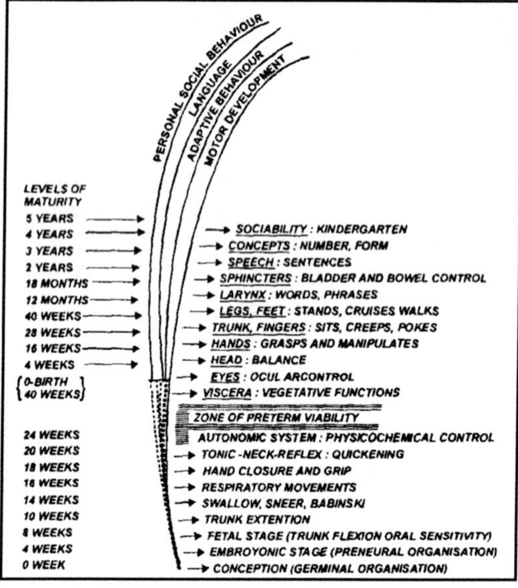

Fig. 5. Maturation of Human Behaviour.

As has been shown in the figure, mentioned below, the bodily parts develop gradually in the child during pregnancy. After birth during the 4th, 16th, 28th and 40th weeks., the eyes, hands, back and fingers attain expertise respectively. In the ninth month movements of the legs and feet are evident. At the age of one year and half, babbling sounds are produced, which are the rudiments of speech. At two the intestines and the bladder are brought under control. At the age of three years, he develops the capacity for thought and reasoning. And when attains five, he shows the tendency to socialization.

MAJOR STEPS IN DEVELOPMENT

Man is a being who is constantly developing in its life time. This development of his passes through various stages. Having passed through these steps, an immature and erring child develops into the properly developed and matured adult. Although there is some difference of opinion among thinkers regarding the various steps in development, yet generally human development has been divided into the following four stages:

(1) Infancy
(2) Childhood
(3) Adolescence
(4) Adulthood

These above mentioned four stages in the development of the human child were determined by Rousseau, the French philosopher. Establishing the age levels that correspond to this division, the educational psychologists have pointed out that infancy lasts from birth till six years, childhood, from six to twelve, adolescence from twelve to eighteen while adulthood should be accepted to extend from eighteen till the individual ceases to develop. It is the common belief among modern educational psychologists that by the age of twenty the individual usually completes all kinds of development. According to Dr. Jones, before adolescence or by age of twelve the child attains to a kind of pseudo-maturity. Following this infancy and childhood are reflected in adolescence and adulthood. According to modern psychologists, the most rapid development in the child, takes place in two stages, the first time when the infant is about two, and the second time when he is between ten and twelve years of age. It will be necessary to reflect upon these above steps in development from the standpoint of physiological development. It should be remembered that though all children pass through these various stages of development, yet all do not o through them at the same age go. The female child, for example, generally reaches each one of these stages some two years ahead of the male sex. Nevertheless, generally speaking, the physiological development that takes in the different stages can be seen in all children.

Major Aspects of Development

As, a general rule, the development of the individual in each step can be divided into the following aspects:

(1) Physical development
(2) Mental development
(3) Emotional development
(4) Ethical and Aesthetic development
(5) Social development

The physical development of the individual includes the development of his various physical parts, his height, weight, nervous system, internal organs, lungs, heart, sex organs, etc. His mental development includes the progress of his intelligence, special abilities, capabilities, tendencies, imagination, reasoning, and other mental elements. In emotional development, the evolution of different instincts and emotions leads to the formation of sentiments and the progress of sentiments to character. Moral development includes the evolution of the moral character, and aesthetic sense and artistic tendencies. In his social development, the individual learns to move and live according to the rules of his family, group and society, and to adjust to it. Educational psychology studies all these aspects of the development of infancy, childhood, adolescence and adulthood. The development of these aspects will be the subject of reflection in the succeeding chapters.

Fig. 6. Spiral Development of the child.

A discussion of the various stages and aspects of development makes it evident that human development is not linear, but spiral. In other words, in progressing further it turns back and then moves forward again. This development moves both horizontally as well as vertically. This nature of development can be understood from the figure given above.

Educational Aspect of Development

Knowledge of the various stages and aspects of the educand's development is of much value for the teacher. The object of education is the complete development of the educand. Hence, it is evident that the teacher should be possessed of the knowledge of aspects of development so that he may be able to discern whether the student is lagging behind in any aspect. The curriculum and other programmes in school should be designed to expedite the overall progress of the educand. Where the curriculum does not seem likely to succeed, recourse should be had to extra-curricular programmes in order to ensure progress. In examining the student, it should be kept in mind that all his various aspects are being evaluated.

Modern education is based on the psychology of the educand. And the educand's psychology conforms to the stage of his development. Hence, by knowing the stage of development through which an individual student is passing the teacher can know his psychology, can base hopes of his development and progress in various departments accordingly, and can mould his method of teaching accordingly. Having a knowledge of the various aspects and steps of development, the teacher can form a dynamic attitude towards education and the educand.

QUESTIONS FOR EXERCISE

1. Write note on Periods in Prenatal Development.
2. Sketch the growth of behaviour during prenatal development.
3. State the different periods in prenatal development. What are the factors influencing prenatal development?
4. Discuss the factors that influence prenatal development.
5. Explain the meaning of development and growth.

7

Physical Development

Four Stages of Physical Development

Although there is some slight difference of opinion regarding the various stages of physical development, the majority of thinkers are in favour of dividing it into the following four stages:

(1) Infancy
(2) Childhood
(3) Adolescence
(4) Adulthood

INFANCY

Infancy is divided into two stages of development, the first lasting from birth to three years, thereafter the second stage lasts till the child is six years of age.

The child develops very rapidly in the infant stage. At birth, the child is bodily unattractive because the skin is lined, the face puffed up and red, the size of the head approximately one-fourth of the body and the rest of the body unbalanced. When born the child is about twenty inches in height, but grows another 10 inches before its first year is completed. Generally, the child is between seven and seven and a half pounds in weight, the male child being taller and heavier than the female. In the first year, both weight and size increase at a very rapid pace. Height increases about 50 per cent in this period while the weight doubles in six months and trebles in another six. The proportion of the head to the body also changes, being one-fourth at the time of birth, the head becomes one-eighth of it as it develops. In the process of development, the head becomes one-eighth of the body, the length of arms and legs also increases as the child comes to require them more and more in his adaptation to life outside the womb.

Weight of the brain increases rapidly during pregnancy and immediately after birth. By the time the child reaches the age of four his brain gains 80 per cent of its final weight, another 10 per cent being added by the time he is eight. The final 10 per cent is acquired by his twentieth year. It is between the ages of 4 and 6 that the main part of the brain develops in weight. Sex organs develop in the opposite manner, as during the first 14 years of development they develop only to 20 per cent while the remaining 80 per cent is completed in the next six years.

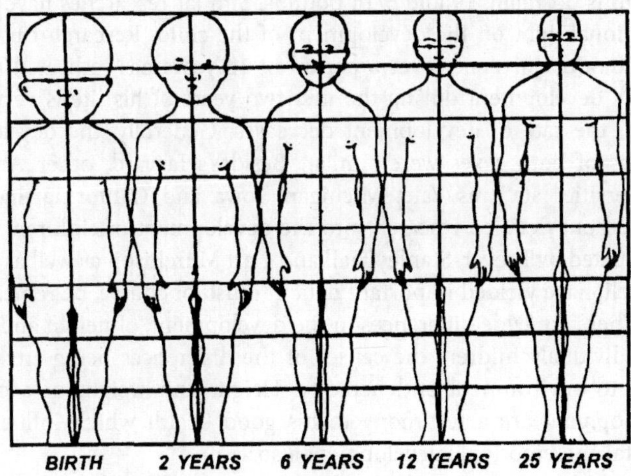

Fig. 7. Proportion of Physical Parts since Birth upto Twenty Five Year's of Age.

Normally, the height of the child at birth indicates the height he will attain in adulthood, but there are about 20 per cent exceptions to this rule. Although there is never any very rapid physical development yet one can see individual differences in the speed and time of it. Normally, one sees an inclination towards the average in the increase in height. Those who grow fast, slow up as they reach the average, but those who increase in height relatively slowly, develop rapidly as they attain to the average.

Describing infancy in respect of height and weight, Thorpe has written[1] that according to a recent survey the average weight of a child at birth is 7.13 pounds, irrespective of sex and race. In this connection, the weight of boys was, on the average, 0.2 pounds more than the weight of newborn infant girls. The weight of white newborn babies was 0.25 pounds more than the offspring of negroes, but the weight of the child at birth is not influenced by social and economic status. Another survey, older than the one mentioned above, indicated that the weight of 85 per

1. Thorpe, L.P. *Child Psychology and Development.* The Lowell Press Co., (1955), p. 102.

cent children at birth is between 6 and 9 pounds, and the height between 17 and 22 inches. The rapidity of the development of infants can be gauged from the fact that on an average, male children increase upto 7 and 1/8 inches in 9 months, while female children increase 6 and 3/4 inches during the same period. Increase in the weight of children is even more significant and well marked, as the average child doubles its weight in six months. The weight of a, male baby whose height is 24 and 1/8 inches is 19 and 11/16 lbs, while the weight of a female child of the same height is normally 19 and 5/16 pounds. Similar researches have thrown additional light on the development of the child. Research carried out at Harvard University over a period of 12 years has indicated that the child's development during the first two years of his life is very rapid. Then, the rate of development decreases. Generally, the development curves of both sexes were similar. Besides Harvard, other American Universities such as Yale, Michigan, Iowa and California, have also carried out detailed research into the development of children. Studies conducted by Preyer, Stanley Hall and Carl Murchison as well as Arnold Gessell, have yielded important data. It must, of course, be remembered that there are wide differences in the development, of height and weight in individual children, the causes of the differences being attributable both to environment and heredity. Height and weight of a child in development are a testimony to his good health which influence his mental and emotional development also.

Another area in which change continually takes place is the proportion between the various parts of the developing child's body. The head becomes smaller and reduces in proportion to the body, while the hands and feet gain in size proportion.

Development of Internal Organs

Teeth are absent at birth, but within a year the child begins cutting teeth that are called milk teeth. In his infancy, the internal organs of the child's body undergo constant development. The most prominent ones to develop are the digestive organs, lungs, muscles, nervous system, nerves, sex organs and glands. This development achieves balance between the various internal organs.

When the child is born, he has a nervous system adequately developed to deal with his environment, to react to its external stimuli and to adapt and adjust to it. Muscles normally do not develop during the child's infancy. There is no evidence to indicate that the child breathes inside the womb, but as soon as he is born he begins breathing and blood circulation continues. While inside the womb, the heart beat is very low, but immediately following birth, the heart beat gains considerably and becomes rapid. As the size of the heart increases, it becomes stronger; the heart beat and the speed of blood circulation in the arterial system both slow down to become steady. According to physiologists, during the first month of infancy, the child's heart beats upto 140 times a minute, but in the first six months it slows down to about 100 times a minute. While the child is still in his infancy, he develops the means of excreting all water waste from the body and combating all attacks of virus and other disease germs. On the contrary, the development of sex organs in infancy is exceedingly slow.

Important Facts about the Infant's Development

The child's weight decreases in his first two weeks of his life because much of the water in him evaporates. But this decrease is soon made up. Some precautions are required on the part of the parents if the child's physical development during infancy is to be maintained. The following are these important facts:

(1) **Food.** Food is one of the most important considerations in child care. The speed of growth being very rapid, it is essential that the child's diet be both balanced and administered at the proper time. In this connection, Laird and his associates conducted an experiment in which some children were kept on an exclusively milk diet, others on a diet of milk and other nutritive foods, and still other children on normal food. After some weeks it was noticed that the children on a milk diet had progressed some 8 per cent more than the children on a normal diet. Similarly, children kept on milk and other nutritive foods had progressed some 16 per cent more than those on the normal diet. Generally speaking, all doctors and scientists believe that milk is the best food during the period of infancy, as in this period the bones develop and strengthen at a rapid pace, and milk is essential for this development. As long as the child retains his so called milk teeth, his best and most nutritive diet is milk, and among the varieties of milk the very best is the variety that is the easiest, to digest. Mahatma Gandhi believed that goat's milk was the most digestible but scientific opinion dares to contradict this view in favour of cow's milk. The latter is beneficial for mental development besides, its more obvious advantages for bodily development and improvement Tinned milk if it be not too old, can also be administered without any ill-effects. In some cases, tinned milk does not prove efficacious and leads to serious

ailments of the stomach which can become complicated and even fatal. Concerning baby food, Spiller has opined that the child should not be given any solid food, but should be given only milk and fruit. The child's milk teeth cannot bite and masticate hard food, nor can his intestines digest it.

(2) **Clothes and Cleanliness.** In infancy, the child's bones are very weak and tender. Consequently, it is necessary that much care must be exercised in cleaning and washing him. The use of good oils for delicate massage is good for the child, but the massage must be very tenderly conducted. Lack of attention to the child's cleanliness can result in his contracting many diseases. In the Indian type of climate the child should be bathed at least once daily, and his bed cleaned with the same periodicity. It can be kept free of urine and other waste matter excreted by the child, by the use of bed sheets made of rubber. More generally speaking, it is desirable that the child's bed and clothes should never exude any bad smell. Bad smell creates bad effects on the child's health. Of course, the best thing that can be done is that the children should be trained to excrete by the clock, that is, at set times. Tight flitting clothes interfere with the free circulation of blood with bad effect on his delicate health. Clothes should thus be reasonably loose, but not necessarily of the toga variety. Of course, it is reasonable that the child should be protected from the cold by warm clothing, but it is better if he is not suffocated in them. He should not be smothered in his clothes the pores of his skin should be given as much change to breathe as his lungs. It is best that the child should be loaded with the least clothes to protect him, since the habit of counteracting the heat and cold that be acquires at this stage usually lasts him his whole life: The sun's rays, so long as they are not strong enough to burn the skin, are always beneficial to the skin, but if one would be convinced of their real utility, one should enquire of the infant, for it is the infant who derives the greatest benefit from them. How surprising it is, that while people in the Western hemisphere, where the climate is much colder, try to keep their children in as few clothes as possible, in a hot country like India people literally load them with clothes. In winter, it does the child's tender bones much good to be massaged with, oil and then laid out in the sun to be strengthened. The body gains by massage and sun bathing because the child gets vitamin D from the sun's rays, which helps in his cutting teeth at the right time.

(3) **Sleep and Up-bringing.** It is in his infancy that the child requires much sleep and can normally get it. He should be allowed to sleep like a sapling, not a log, as long as he feels like it, since the proper amount of sleep helps in adequate and proper development of the body. Normally, at this age, the child awakens only when he feels hungry and goes to sleep immediately his stomach is filled. He spends the larger span of his time in sleeping. In the first month the child wakens only when he is hungry, but sometimes it is also because he has tasted milk, so that it is not a good practice to feed him milk whenever he cries such intemperate feeding spoils his digestive system and has the worst effect on his health, besides leaving him susceptible to many dangerous diseases. It is scientifically more desirable to feed the child by the clock, and to allay his crying by presenting him with toys or by any other means available, such as crooning to him, if that can possibly put a stop to his crooning. Children are normally very much attracted by brightly coloured objects and if they manage to get their hands on them they begin to suck them. On the bed the child flings his arms and legs about, much to his own good as it exercises his limbs though in a some what unconventional manner.

Havelock Ellis, the famous thinker, emphasised that the importance of mother's milk for the child exceeds its purely nutritive value. Besides nourishing the baby, the act of feeding symbolises, the mother's love for the child. From this point of view, it is desirable that the child's care and nourishment should be in the hands of his mother. It is never good to leave this function to a servant or a nurse. It has particular ill effects on the child's emotional development as the love that he bears his mother he cannot give to any other person, and in the absence of adequate reciprocation from the mother, his emotional development is adversely effected. An individual concerned with the child's nourishment and general care has to keep in mind all the needs of the ward as at this stage the child is himself unable to communicate his needs, being unskilled in the use of his tongue. Hence, many of the diseases that the child contracts at an early age are the effect of his parents' or guardian's carelessness. If the child cries, it is best to make some effort to divine, the cause of his discomfort. It may be that his ear or may be stomach paining, and for this it is better to us the medicine a doctor prescribes than to give him more milk and try to put him to sleep.

Love and affection are always very potent influence in the child's life but these should not outstrip the limits of propriety and spoil the child. From the physiological point of view, it is not desirable to carry the child in one's lap for long periods. As far as possible, the child should be allowed to rest in a recumbent position and he should be diverted by the use of toys if he cries. Some people make it a practice to put a rubber nipple in the child's mouth whenever he cries. This too, is not a very commendable habit as it is possible for the child to contract many diseases if the nipple is unclean or unhygienic. What is even more important is that once a child becomes habituated to its use, it is difficult to wean him of it. But even then if it must be used, then all care must be taken to keep it clean. In this stage of his life, the child is a delicate sapling, and he must be handled with the greatest care, the least strain proving harmful. One should never be rough with the child's body. Even over-exhaustion is harmful for the developing child. The child is fully capable of keeping his body requisitely exercised as he is guided by an inner instinct to run and move about as much as his frail body requires. Hence, it is never a very good idea to try to keep the child exercised. Just as a young plant fares well if it is well tended and provided with requisite amounts of sun, water and manure, the child develops well and without difficulty if it is properly looked after giving the correct food and the necessary sleep and the exercise that he requires. Some parents betray unnecessary anxiety regarding the physical development and growth of their children. Although, normally, every child should attain a certain level of height and weight by the time he reaches a particular age, yet there are always exceptions. Some children have a tendency to learn bodily structure while others are more liberally supplied with fat at their birth and they tend to collect it more and more. Hence, it is not sensible to feed the child excessively in trying to make him fat or strong, but is in fact a kind of torture for the child. In this connection, and in connection with all physical development, it is always preferable to adopt the golden mean, since almost all kinds of excess is harmful for the body. And in the child's infancy, his physical development depends upon the intelligence and rationality of his guardians.

INFANCY PRIOR TO CHILDHOOD

Following the first three years of his life, the second stage in the child's development is the time between three and six years of age. This period is considered by some' to be the precursor of childhood, or the last stages of infancy, as it falls after infancy but before actual childhood. It comprehends the development that takes place between the ages of three and six. While the first three years of the infant's life can be called the period of agglomeration, the period under consideration can be called the stage of maturity. In other words, all that the child acquires in the first three years is strengthened and made stable in the next three.

Evidently, no fresh bodily development takes place in this period, only the old development is capitalised upon and made permanent. Children appear to be very naughty and irrepressible in the first three years, but they acquire a modicum of reserve in the next three, and appear comparatively serious. In the first stage, it is easy and desirable to guide him in as many ways as possible, but in this latter period it is best not to interfere in his development and maturity. This stage, too, requires that all possible attention be bestowed on him in respect of his physical as well as his mental comfort.

CHILDHOOD

Physical and other development in the child that takes place between the ages of six and twelve is in the childhood period. In other words, the period from seven to nine years of age is the period of acquisition or agglomeration in which development takes place, while the time between the ages of ten and twelve is the period when maturity of this growth takes place.

(a) **Period of Growth.** The child is as restless in the growth period of childhood as he was in the same period of his infancy. At this stage, his interest in the objects of his environment is continually on the increase. This time is the best to, start his education. His education at this stage should be so designed as to make the most profitable use of his instincts. From the bodily point of view, development is not very rapid, as such rapid development is visible either at the age of two or of twelve. Games are particularly important for the physical development of the child. Every effort should be made to interest the child in games by which be can profit both in respect of body as well as of mind. This age is particularly important in respect of possibilities of ingraining good, habits and high ideals in his mind. He should be taught to lead a disciplined and regular life, and his various physical and mental needs should be quickly attended to. His physical comfort must not be neglected. In fact, bodily development does not imply the child's becoming large and, broad, but rather the possession of such qualities as energy, ethusiasm, freshness, the capacity to labour, etc. It is only when the child possesses these qualities in abundance that he can properly be called healthy. Elementary physical training and light drill at school at this stage is desirable.

(b) **Period of Maturity.** In the maturity period, the child specially develops a social consciousness. He should be encouraged to meet others and cooperate with them, but at the same time a sense of proportion is always to be admired. The child should never be allowed to become a vagabond or truant. Such healthy habits as collecting stamps, postcards, etc., can be inculcated.

ADOLESCENCE

The second stage when the child develops very rapidly is the period of adolescence, after the first stage in his infancy. The same pattern of three years of growth and three following years of maturation can be assumed to exist in this period of the individual's life also. Maximum physical development takes place in the first three years. Normally, adolescence appears at the age of 11 and 12 in girls and at 12 and 13 in boys. Commonly, boys are taller and heavier than girls, but in adolescence between 12 and 14 it is the female who is both taller and heavier as she develops earlier than the male child. It is for the same reason that in these years girls consider boys of same age as younger and prefer to be with boys a couple of years older than themselves. Another characteristic is the desire for mixing between boys and girls. In adolescence, boys and girls attain 90 per cent of the height that they are going to have in later years. In other words, by the time a young boy is 14 he has developed to 90 per cent of his ultimate or final stature. But it takes him another six years to cover the remaining 10 per cent. On the other hand, the weight of the adolescent is only two-thirds of what is going to be. Even after the adolescent has stopped growing upwards his weight continues to increase at a rapid pace. Compared to boys, girls gain in both height and weight faster but the development in these directions also stops earlier. Consequently, the adolescent girl looks more developed than her male counterpart of equal age. Muscles, in particular, develop mainly only after adolescence is over. In this age, physical education is most important and very meaningful. Sex education is equally important as it is in this age that boys and girls develop the characteristic features of their respective sexes. Girls develop lady-like features. Of the many changes in the girl, the most perceptible is the roundness of the breasts and hips while among the boys their faces become adorned with beard and moustaches. While the girl's voice becomes sweet, the boy's sound takes on a deeper and more thrilling note. Within a year or two of adolescence, both male and female attain the capability of procreation.

Notable Facts Concerning Adolescence

Physical exercise and games are important for physical development in adolescence. The well balanced body shows apt proportion between length and weight. Much of this proportionate development depends upon the exercise taken. But neither height nor weight are in fact indicative of the healthy taste of an individual's body. Physical health finds adequate expression and recognition in the enthusiasm, energy, swiftness and interest with which he performs his functions. Although it is always desirable for youth to be active and vibrant in adolescence, yet one should guard against excessive exercise that completely tires the body, as such exhaustion has adverse effects on the body's development. Nutritive food is as important for getting rid of exhaustion as rest is. Exercise, too, should be balanced. It should be remembered that the physical development of a player's body is sometimes impaired by his playing a particular game in which only some of the bodily organs are exercised and strained. Excessive indulgence in such a game can have only the least desirable effect. But even if regular practice of the game benefits these parts, the other organs of the body are not, benefited. Hence, generally speaking, it would be more efficacious to induce adolescents to take interest in physical education rather than spending long and weary hours in the pursuit of perfection in the various competitive games. Schools should divert their expenditure on coaching schemes to the physical education of their students. This measure will help to improve the level of health among adolescents. Proper exercise steps up blood circulation with the result that many waste materials are thrown out of the body, while other parts of the body such as lungs also develop better and faster. Physical capacities are also developed beside the progress of the body itself. Ignoring the exceptions, one could draw up a chart of the various physical capacities as correlated to the various stages in physical development. From adolescence to adulthood, the grip of the hand, the length and strength of the feet, neck and the middle portion of the body, all develop equally. The golden formula for proper physical development at this period of life is proper food and adequate exercise, without excess in either of the two. Of course, there can be no common level of food and exercise for every one. The amount of food, rest, sleep and exercise that an individual requires can be found out from experience or from his friends or teachers. Provision of sex education can help the young boys and girls to form the proper attitude towards bodily development concerning sex. Suppression of feeling on account of fear will only, have adverse effects on them. Their clothing should be such as not to restrict the growth of their bodies. Just as at any other stage in life, it is not advisable to wear very tight clothes, as they will harm the body even if they do appear temporarily attractive and smart. And, particularly among the young girls, it is essential for the development of the breasts and the hips that they wear slightly loose and comfortable clothes. Any female child who aspires after beauty can begin practicing her wiles from this age. Hence, in this respect some intelligence is the adolescent's best companion.

ADULTHOOD

This period of life begins where adolescence ends. By this time the individual usually attains the age of 20 and completes his development in respect of, height, weight, nervous system, bone structure, etc. It is equally important at this stage also that adequate attention be paid to food, sleep, rest, regular pattern of life exercise, etc. Similar principles also hold true, that is, there should be no excess in any one direction. It is perfectly correct to indulge in slightly more exercise than previously since it helps in the development of muscles, and the attainment of due proportion between the various parts of the body.

QUESTION FOR EXERCISE

1. Describe physical development during infancy and childhood. Point out important things to remember in this connection.

8

Motor Development

Stages of Motor Development

Development of the motor ability is an important part of a child's physical development. In motor development, change in activity can be observed through the physical progress For example, before acquiring the ability of walking, the child passes through a number of stages. Although individual differences are visible in motor activity, even to the extent of individual styles of walking being very distinctive, the approximate time of the development and appearance of certain motor activities in physical development can be established. In motor activities, the motor control starts with the head, in other words, the child first starts by holding his head erect and focussing on various objects with his eyes. Following this, the child learns to grip objects and then to crawl and walk on his knees. This is represented in the figure given on next page. In the child's motor development over the first two periods the following stages are evident:

Age in months	*Motor Activity*
1.	chin high
2.	raising the chest
3.	gripping and releasing, object
4.	sitting with some assistance
5.	lap-sitting and holding objects
6.	sitting on high chair
7.	playing with object
8.	standing with some help
9.	standing while holding on to furniture
10.	moving oft knees
11.	raising oneself while holding on to furniture
12.	walking while holding someone

13. climbing stairs
14. standing without assistance
15. walking alone

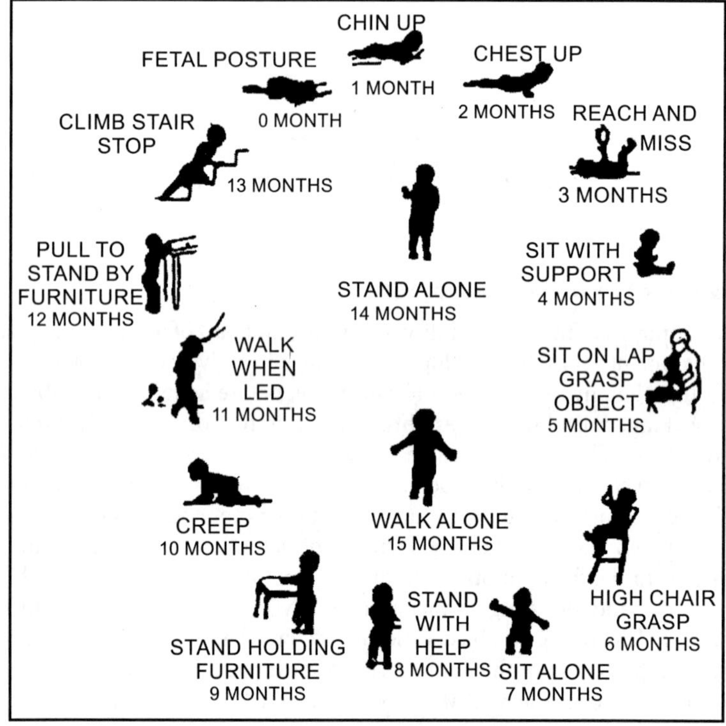

Fig. 8. Motor Development at Different Age in the Child.

For motor development it is essential that the child be given adequate freedom. If the child is always carried and is not allowed to move around, its motor development is likely to be retarded. The child should have adequate space to play in. If it is left to its own devices on the floor, it will be seen moving its legs and feet.

Patterns of Crawling and Creeping

The beginning of a child's motor development is with the activities of creeping and crawling. Different children exhibit different patterns of these activities. In the following figure are illustrated the various physical positions that are adopted by the child in developing from the crawling and creeping to the walking stage. These physical positions have been illustrated in the following order: (1) motion of new born's crawling. (2) less motion in the hind part while it tries to raise the head. (3) Control on the movements of head and shoulders improves. (4) There is considerable development in the upper part, while remains on the floor. (5) Contraction between the motion of the head and shoulder, and the hips, with the result that raising of hips leads to lowering of head and shoulder. (6) Motions of rocking in which the hip bone is kept above the ground. (7) Complementary movements of creeping. In starting movement some children creep on the stomach, others move on all fours while still others propel themselves by swinging their hips along the surface. Different children start creeping and crawling in different ages. Generally, the child who begins his crawling early also walks erect in shorter time. Although motor activity develops along with general progress of the child, but in encouraging the child to walk wooden or other scooters or rollers can be used. This can induce him to learning walking earlier.

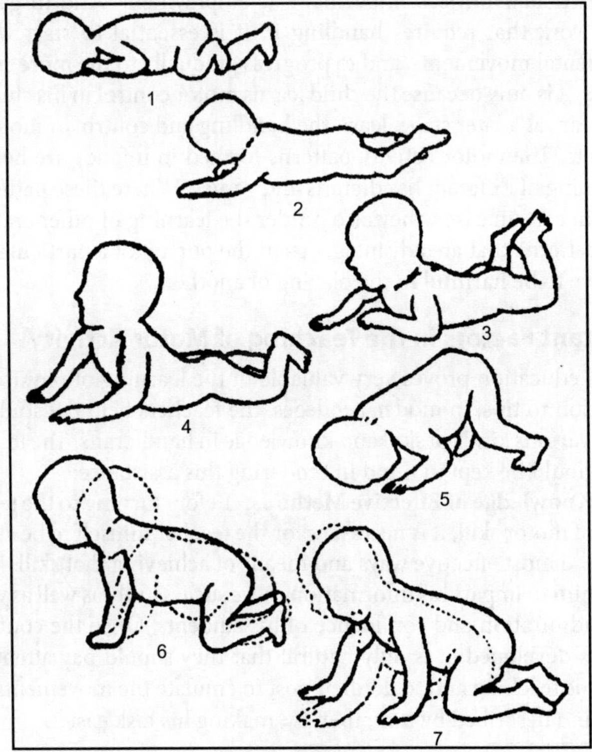

Fig. 9. Patterns of Crawling and Creeping.

MOTOR DEVELOPMENT AND EDUCATION

Motor development is an important prerequisite for man's motor learning. Along with other development, motor development continues during childhood and adolescence. And in this, much importance is, attached to various physical movements and exercises. It is for this reason that in modern colleges, academic teaching and training is accompanied by various physical exercises, game and many activities that require motor activity. It helps to develop in child many handicrafts that assist him in his adopting some particular career. Some such handicrafts are stitching and sewing, wood work, typewriting, cooking, etc. Motor control is essential in all handicrafts. Motor development is an important part of over all comprehensive development.

Important Factors in Motor Development

Many factors cast a very profound influence upon the child's motor development. The object of motor learning is the acquisition of skill in some particular physical movement or employment. And to gain skill in any work that requires handling it, it is essential to start with the fundamental movements, and to progress gradually to the more complex motions. It is only because the child learns motor control in his childhood that he can, at a later stage, learn the handling and control of motor cars, cycles, etc. The motor activity patterns formed in infancy are helpful in the learning of different handicrafts and games. Where these patterns are of help in certain cases, they also hinder the learning of other crafts. The motor patterns that are advantageous to the pursuit of a particular game can prove to be harmful in the playing of another.

Important Factors in the Teaching of Motor Activity[1]

Physical education proves very valuable in the learning of physical skill. In addition to this, in modern colleges, the teachers help the students to acquire various kinds of skill and knowledge in handicrafts. The following points should be kept in mind in rendering this assistance:

1. **Knowledge of Effective Methods.** Before turning to the teaching of motor skill, it is necessary for the teacher himself to be aware of the most effective ways and means of achieving that skill. It helps him to impart his information more successfully as well as win the admiration and confidence of his students. Once the confidence is developed, it is only natural that they should pay attention to his teaching and to do their best to emulate the movements made and described by him, thereby, making his task easier.

---

1. Crow and Crow. *Educational Psychology*, p. 286.

2. **Encouraging the Students in the Use of Effective Techniques.** Having gained confidence in the teacher the student acquires the right mental set for acquiring motor skill. Now the teacher has to encourage him in the use of methods that have proved successful in the attainment of that motor skill. In the beginning he is not able to perform these actions perfectly because the skilled and refined actions can be done there are the unrefined and unskilled actions to be mastered. The student fails repeatedly in acquiring the skill he requires by the use of these unskilled and unrefined movements, with the result that he becomes discouraged, and may even become so despondent as to throw up the training. It is for the teacher to foresee this contingency and to prevent it, by, tendering encouragement and sympathy. Certain people entertain a groundless fear of water and hence of swimming with the result that when they try to learn it, they are, apt to give it up after the first or second ducking. In a situation of this kind, it is for instructor to encourage constantly so that enthusiasm may not flag. As in the case of all other learning, the motor learning is, also susceptible to the inevitable plateau of learning in its curve. The intelligent instructor can discover the reasons whereby this plateau is arrived at, and contrive to remove it. As a result, the student progresses further, and continues to do so. Hence, in, order to develop motor skill, the developed and progressive methods of learning should be employed so that hindrances and obstacles in learning, be reduced to a minimum and progress be the most satisfactory and regular. The method of teaching should conform to the needs of education, and should change as the subject to be taught changes.
3. **Minimum Possible Destructive Criticism.** Just as the student is susceptible to constant encouragement and good words from the teacher, he is influenced by strong critical comment from the same source. He is so affected that he may become despondent and discouraged. Hence, even if he makes mistakes, the student should be corrected and advised sympathetically, and criticism reduced and kept to the minimum. It should be indulged in only if it becomes inevitable, and even then it should be only as much as is absolutely necessary.
4. **Stress on the Right Activities.** The main cause of failure in motor skill is the following of wrong activities or actions by student. On the other hand, it is essential to make a habit of the right actions. It is desirable for the teacher to take each action

involved in any motor activity separately and demonstrate it to the students following it up with continuous practice of it in his own presence.

5. **Stress on Speed and Exactness for Skillful Working.** Generally, some people hold the view that any work done rapidly is not successful. This is quite true of any work at its outset, when one is learning it. In the beginning it is desirable to make a habit of working slowly but avoiding all mistakes and faults. In, learning motor skill it is particularly important to note that no wrong habits are formed, even if progress is thereby quite slow and retarded. The speed of work should be improved gradually. Sometimes accuracy and skill improves by working rapidly at the outset. In learning cycling, one learns the proper balancing and control only if one immediately takes to riding fast, without any fear of the falls one is going to suffer. On the other if he begins by cycling slowly and pays attention to his faults, he is sure to sustain many falls and learn only with great difficulty. But this fact is not true of many motor skills and activities.

   Once a very strong habit of some motor action has been formed, it becomes quite automatic and does not require constant attention to be performed. If a person has learnt his cycling well, he can travel through a crowded market without any apparent attention to his movement. He can in fact allow his thoughts and attention to wander, to some extent, to other things while he continues forward without endangering his own safety or that of others. Having attained motor skill in some department, in addition to the automatic control on the physical movements involved in it, the individual is also in a position to control the mental state involved in that motor skill. An expert cyclist need not ponder over every individual situation to decide when he is to use brake to a hault or when to pick up speed. His unconscious does this for him.

6. **Proper and Adequate Practice.** Constant repetition of some movements is not sufficient in order to generate motor skill in them. It is essential that adequate and proper practice of the activity should be indulged in, in a state, of complete mental consciousness of it. The practice must be mentally attended to. Many such factors as the nature of skill, the age and interests of the educand, the conditions of learning, the time taken in learning and practicing period of rest, the desired, level of skill etc., influence the result of practice, and changes in these factors

are reflected in variations in the final achievement. In practicing it should be remembered that the practice should conform to the method required in actual practice. For example, if a child is required to write with a fountain pen at a later stage, he should be made to practice with a fountain pen and not a quill pen. Similarly, the proper tools of expert use should be employed in training individuals in wood work, carpentry, leather working, etc., and as far as possible the things made during practice should be the same as are required to be made once the training is completed.

7. **Practice with an Aim.** While practicing for the gaining of motor skill, the educand should be aware of the objective, and should be constantly mindful of it. The teacher should measure his progress by examining him in terms of this objective. If the student is aware of his aim, he progresses fester and more satisfactorily, and his interest also is maintained knowing his aim, he is aware of the skill, that he must attain. In this, the teacher can also put some example before him. In the absence of such an example, the student may stop working after he has learnt only a very little, in the impression that he has in fact become skilled in his pursuit.

By keeping in mind these factors that influence the teaching of motor skills, the teacher in college can make very skilled workers of the students. In this, he will have to pay individual attention to each student, because the problems, capabilities and abilities of individual students differ. Some of them can learn one piece of work in very short time, while others may take much longer to master the same. As it is bad to hinder and obstruct the fast workers by holding them up in their progress, it is also wrong and impolitic to force the slower workers to go faster. Similarly, it is not very fruitful to hope for all students that they will attain the same level of competence and skill in any motor activities for which they are being trained. All people cannot be equally successful in one particular skill, irrespective of the quality of implements and equipment used as well as the time taken in training them. Practice should be made to conform to age and capability. Small children should be forced to practice for shorter periods of time, while older people can benefit by longer sessions of work. And the period of rest between the periods of practice should be longer in the case of young children with less skill than in the, case of older people with greater skill in the work. Practice should avoid fatiguing the individual as much as possible, but the time of practice should also not be so short that the workers may not even warm up. In this connection it is best to maintain a balanced and cautious outlook.

QUESTIONS FOR EXERCISE

1. Describe the major steps of motor development.
2. Give an account of the sequences of motor development of the child.
3. Outline the development of locomotion during infancy.
4. Describe the stages of motor development. Discuss the factors that influence motor development.
5. Describe the various stages of motor development during infancy.

9

Development of Speech and Language

If a child's birth has been normal, then he gradually gains command over language after passing through the different stages of linguistic development. This development is a process and its different stages cannot be distinguished from each other. Neither is it necessary that each one of these stages should be distinctly, apparent in the linguistic development of every child. Language ability does not develop and improve at the same rate in all children, and neither does it take the same time.

According to psychologists, a child speaks his first word when he is 13 or 14 months old. Language development therefore should be considered, from this point. The period preceding this can be said to be a kind of preparation for the evolution of linguistic ability because during this period the child indicates his requirements to other by making various audible sounds. These sounds and signs that he makes play an important part in the development of his language ability.

PRE-LINGUAL COMMUNICATION

A child needs some, means of communication by which he can communicate with, the, other people around him. Even during his infancy the child develops some signs and indications which help to transmit his needs to other people. Psychologists differ in their opinion about the first crying sound of the child at the moment of birth. Some consider it a desire to communicate while other think it is a reflex action. Nevertheless, all psychologists agree that the child develops some kind of sign language to communicate his needs. Even when the child is three weeks old he uses different sounds and physical movements to indicate such physical conditions as hunger, cold, pain, wetness etc. In this manner, one observes the following three kinds of signs in a child while it is preparing for language Development:

1. **Crying.** This is the child's first sound and it does not have to be learnt for it is automatically produced by the vocal organs. Crying, is uncontrolled and irregular. According to Leibnitz and Stuart, the child cries during the first two weeks without any particular cause. Crying does not bring forth any tears but the breathing becomes irregular, pulse rate increases, the fist are clenched and the body becomes red. Despite the fact that this crying is not motivated the child normally quietens down if it is picked up by the mother. After the third week this variety of crying grows less. Normally, crying in the first seven weeks indicates an excess of hunger, noise and light. According to Watson the child cries because of hunger, exhaustion and fear. Buhler has indicated numerous causes of a child's crying-birth, light, high pitched sound, physical discomfort, interruption of sleep, exhaustion, hunger, difficulty in movement caused by tight clothes, the taking away of toys, fear, etc. Many children are found to cry immediately before they are fed and before they go to sleep. When a child is of three months he cries when he wants to attract the attention of grown up people. A four month child cries when he is not allowed to play. A nine month child cries when he observes his mother going towards another child. Studies of the crying sound of children have indicated that they utter the first sounds of vowels. If the parents pay too much attention if the child cries, then the child develops a habit of crying whenever he needs any thing. It is better to attend to the child immediately he cries so that he should not have to cry for a long time in order to be attended to. Crying for long periods has a bad effect on the child's digestion, besides which it also causes nervous tension and loss of sleep. This creates a feeling of insecurity in the child, for he feels that he is being ignored by his parents. All these things have the effect of making future social adjustment difficult. Physical development also suffers.
2. **Babbling.** The stage of babbling begins in the third month and continues upto the eighth month. During this period the child's vocal organs develop. A child makes those sounds which give him pleasure, and he repeats them because they add to his pleasure. If his parents indicate their delight at the sounds he is making then the child feels encouraged to go on repeating them. Most of these sounds are meaningless and should be treated as such. Older

people, on the other hand, try to read some meaning into them and they say that the child is trying to say something. The child has to make an effort to produce such sounds. According to Jersild, these sounds later on die out and the child does not make them. In the beginning these sounds have some vocal quality, although the child learns to pronounce consonants only when he sports his front teeth. Some sounds become more definite than others because of repetition. Hurlock believes that the child continues to babble upto the age of twelve months. But it would be more accurate to say that the period of babbling depends upon the development of the child's speech organ's and the encouragement he receives to speak. Babbling gives pleasure to the child and he is often seen babbling to himself. He grins and laughs when he hears the sounds proceeding from his own mouth. Compared to the normal child a deaf one does not babble so much because, he cannot hear the sound that he is himself making. It is in the process of babbling that the child learns gradually to control his vocal chords.

3. **Gestures.** The child uses different types of gestures and signs to express his meaning to others. He uses several parts of the body to make gestures. If he does not succeed in conveying his meaning through gestures he begins to weep. In infancy several types of gestures are spontaneously visible, as for example, moving the head from side to side, smiling, stretching arms, weeping, throwing legs etc. The parents follow the meanings conveyed by the child through these gestures. As the child leams to speak, the use of gestures becomes less and less, because they are not needed any more. But gestures are used even now due to imitation and sometime to emphasize certain words.

After passing through different stages of language development the child gradually begins to understand different words and their uses. At the age of 18 months he can use ten to twelve simple words on an average. Some children can use as many as one hundred words at this age. In next three or four months, the child's vocabulary increases very fast. At the age of 3 years his vocabulary may include words in four figures and this goes on increasing till the age of 12 years when it reaches the limit of 10,000 words or more.

LANGUAGE DEVELOPMENT IN DIFFERENT AGES

Some psychologists have described language development in different ages. This can be divided into the following three periods:

1. **From 2 to 3 Years of Age.** During this period the child begins to use words to form sentences. He uses pronouns though he cannot use 'I' and 'me' properly. At the end or this period he begins to use plural and past tense. A child of three years can make complex and compound sentences.
2. **Four to Five Years of Age.** At the age of four the child's ability to form a sentence is considerably improved and he begins to make use of the rules of grammar. He is very talkative at this age. He is interested in almost everything and asks questions without waiting for the answers. It appears that curiosity is not the only cause behind these questions, a reason is the exercise of the growing vocabulary. At the kindergarten age the child achieves sufficient control over words, though he cannot understand their subtle meanings.
3. **After Five Years.** At this age most of the children go to school. They use language intelligently in talking to other persons. The school and the home play a very important role in language development at this stage. The child also learns to pronounce correctly.

STAGES IN LANGUAGE DEVELOPMENT

The following are the four important stages in a child's language development from the point of various elements of language:

1. **Comprehension.** Comprehension means the ability to understand the meanings of the words uttered by others. According to the psychologists the child's power of comprehension develops even before, he begins to use words. The child can comprehend more words than he can speak. The ability of comprehension plays a more important role in learning any language than the ability to speak. Though it is not definite as, to what part gestures and words play in comprehension, it can be said that they play a very important part in it. If gestures are used along with words in teaching the child, his learning is facilitated. According to Hurlock when gestures are used with a child of 18 months, he understands the meaning more properly as compared with mere use of words. The psychologists Gassel, Termann, Merrill, Cattel, Garrison and Mcarthy have investigated into the child's ability of comprehension during different periods of age. It has been found that an infant of four months moves his head while hearing human sounds, and smiles at her mother. At the age of 6 to 8 months he hears the words attentively and also tries to pronounce them. At

the age of 12 months the child can understand simple commands and instructions and also follow them. At the age of 5 to 6 years the vocabulary of the child is so much developed that he can understand the talks of unknown persons. He can comprehend the meaning of stories told to him. He can understand similarity and distinction between words. It has been found by experiments that the child's power of comprehension can be immensely increased by means of radio and television.

2. **Building a Vocabulary.** The vocabulary of a child increases by hearing of other's using different words. One can find general and particular words in a child's vocabulary. The general words are those which can be used in many situations, *e.g.*, sleeping, walking, good, bad, man, woman, etc. The particular words are those which are used in different situations at different ages. As a general rule the former type of vocabulary is more developed than the latter kind.

   In the development of general vocabulary the child first learns nouns and uses them in language. In these, also he first learns words which are useful for him and which are easy to understand. On the other hand, he seldom uses words which are difficult to pronounce and finds it difficult to learn them. Thus, the child learns pronouns in due course. He learns nouns at the stage of babbling, *e.g.*, daddy, grand-father, uncle, etc. The verbs are used after learning nouns. In the beginning simple verbs such as come, go, get-up, sit down, etc. are used. At the age of 18 months, the child begins to use adjectives, such as cold, warm, good, bad, etc., and adverbs such as here, there, where, etc. According to Jersild in learning pronouns several types of 'I' are used and 'you' is used less often because the child is generally self centred. According to the experiments of Young, Mcarthy and Garrison, the uses of pronouns and adverbs are very much found after the first two years of age. At the nursery school, the child is found to use more pronouns, verbs and adjectives than nouns.

   The growth of vocabulary is intimately connected with intelligence and motivation. These factors are not only conductive to the learning of the new words but also in finding new meanings of words already learnt. In the first two years the child's vocabulary grows slowly. It increases very fast after he enters the school, because there teachers teach new words and their uses. Vocabulary increases by contact with new things, persons and places, hearing a radio, watching television, and reading story books. The psychologists have found out that the range of words in the, vocabulary of the school going children is from 20 to 24 thousand in the first class, 50,000 in the VI standard and 88,000 in the High School. Some psychologists including Smith, Mcarthy and Jersild have supported the conclusion of Crow and Crow that at the age of 12, the average vocabulary of a child is 10,000 words, while in exceptional cases it may go upto 30,000 words or more. The increase of vocabulary helps the child's talking as well as his writing. The progress of a child in education can, be estimated by the range of his vocabulary because he knows the world around him through words. In modern times the wide use or radio, television and films in the school for the purposes of education has very much helped the increase of vocabulary. In the words of Garrison, "In an age of radio, television, films, rapid transportations and world relationship, the child needs to know many words and to be able to use them. Failure tends to result in impaired social adjustment."

The above discussion concerns with the development of general vocabulary. At the age of 3 the child begins to develop particular vocabulary. This includes words of different types, such as, words showing respect, etiquette etc. As the child learns to behave with the elders, he learns such words. Secondly, as the child sees things of different colours, he knows the names of different colours. Again, at the age of 2 years the child learns numbers. At the age of 5 and 6 years, the child learns to distinguish between different seasons, days, months, etc. At the age of 4 or 5 years he can distinguish between different coins. Just before adolescence, the children are seen talking in secret language, which is formed by different techniques.

3. **Formation of Sentences.** Upto the age of one year, the infant generally uses only one word. He begins to construct incomplete sentences involving two or more words at the age of 2 years. At the age of 4 and 5 years he uses compound sentences. This ability of the sentence construction increases upto the age of 9 to 10 years, when the child can construct several types of sentences. The ability of constructing sentences increases with the cultural level of the child. According to Gessel, Garrison, Mcarthy and Jersild, a child of two and a half years uses complete sentences. The girls are generally more advanced than boys in sentence construction, because the speed of their intellectual development is more than that of boys.

4. **Correct Pronunciation.** According to Hurlock the child learns, to pronounce by imitation of others. If the others are pronouncing wrongly the child also learns to pronounce wrongly hence pronunciation can be improved by demonstrating correct pronunciation to the child. In adolescence the pronunciations are more or less established and cannot be easily changed. The child's pronunciation improves after the age of 18 months and it is sufficiently improved at the age of 3. Besides age, one finds individual differences in pronunciation. While some children pronounce very correctly at an early age, others fail to do so, even at the advanced age. The main cause behind this distinction is the differences in the development of vocal organs, occasions of training and the amount of motivation. In the beginning the child's pitch of speaking is high, but upto the age of 3 years he learns to adjust it. The child should not be bluntly snubbed for speaking in the high pitch because this adversely affects the development of his vocal organs.

FACTORS IN LANGUAGE DEVELOPMENT

1. **Physical health.** If the child remains very ill during the first two years of life, it very adversely affects the language development in him, because firstly he does not get contact of other children, secondly he has no motivation to speak because, his needs are fulfilled even without asking and thirdly he is often asked to keep silent. According to Gassel and Garrison, the deaf children learn to speak very late and their pronunciation is mostly incorrect. In comparison with other children their vocabulary is very much limited, because they cannot learn by imitation.
2. **Intelligence.** Almost all the psychologists admit that the level of intelligence is closely related with the ability of speech. The language development goes along with the increase in the level of intelligence. The children who are mentally undeveloped seldom develop average vocabulary. A mentally deficient child of five years of age has generally a vocabulary of an infant of $1^1/_2$ years. On the other hand, the superior child has a vocabulary more than the average. He begins to speak at least four months earlier than the average child. The mentally deficient child, on the other hand, sometimes lags behind the average child for three years. But all the children are not same in this respect. About one third of the mentally deficient children begins to speak at the proper age.

   The superior children not only learn to speak early but adopt the developed pattern of speech at an early age. They can not, however, think with the elders. Sometimes some children who are very much advanced in language development in the beginning gradually lag behind even the average. Similarly, some children who appear to be very intelligent in the primary classes lag behind others in higher classes.

3. **Socio-economic Status.** The psychologists generally believe that in comparison with the children coming from lower socio-economic status, the children from higher socio-economic status have a wider vocabulary and more linguistic ability. Some psychologists have admitted a distinction of eight months period in the language development according to socio-economic status. Among the newcomer children in the schools the children coming from families of higher socio-economic status generally depict a developed vocabulary as compared with that of the children coming from poor families. This, however, does not mean that socio-economic status is the sole determinant of linguistic ability. In fact, the influence of socio-economic status makes distinction in the circumstances of children. Generally, the parents occupying a higher socio-economic status are more intelligent and more educated as compared with others. Thus, it is natural that their children should be more intelligent than those who belong to a lower socio-economic status. Secondly, better means of learning such as radio, television, magazines etc., are available in the family of higher socio-economic status and these in their turn favourably influence the intellectual development of the children. Thirdly, the children learn words by imitation of their parents. It is therefore natural that the modes of speech and the vocabulary of the children coming from families of higher socio-economic status should be more refined than of those children who come from poor families. Again, in the families of higher socio-economic status, the parents pay more attention to the intellectual development of their children. All these factors at the higher socio-economic status favourably influence the linguistic development of the child.

4. **Sex Differences.** A comparative study of the linguistic development of boys and girls has revealed that in comparison with the boys the girls begin to speak earlier and they can use longer sentences at an early age. The language development, length of sentence purity of construction, uses of words, power of comprehension and ability of pronunciation of the girls is much more than that of boys. On an average their vocabulary is bigger

than that of the boy of the same age and they develop a wider vocabulary at an early age. This superiority of the fair sex over the male is maintained upto a considerably higher age, so much so that at the stage of complete language development the girls are generally much more advanced than the boys. This distinction in linguistic abilities according to sex differences has been explained in terms of differences in family situations according to Mcarthy. In infancy the girls generally identify with the mother and the boys with the father. But while the girls get sufficient company of the mother. The boys do not get as much company of the father because he is generally absent from the house. It is due to this lack of contact with the parent that the linguistic development of the boy suffers. The explanation given by Mcarthy has not been admitted by other psychologists. In fact, the superiority of the girls in linguistic ability can be accounted by the fact that their general development is two years earlier as compared with the boys and they reach adulthood two years earlier. It is hence that their linguistic ability is much more as compared with boys of the same age.

5. **Family Relationships.** The studies conducted by Mcarthy, Thomson and others among the children brought up in orphanages have shown that the language development of orphans lags behind the children brought up in average families. The orphan infants weep more and babble less. They begin to speak at a late age and use few sounds. An important cause of this deficiency is the absence of opportunities of the imitation of the parents. The psychologists have also found difference in language development according to birth order in the family. The real reason behind the distinctions, however, is not birth order itself but the difference which it makes in the child's contact with the parents. According to Davis and Mcarthy die language of the elder child is much more improved than that of the younger children because he gets more contact of the adults in the family. But if the youngest child also gets sufficient contact of the parents, his linguistic development will not lag behind because of his birth order. Other studies have revealed that the linguistic development of the twins lags behind the development of children born alone because the twins are generally weaker.

6. **Bilingualism.** An important factor in the language development of the child is the fact whether he has to learn one or two languages in the house in his early age. In some modern Indian families,

the child is so much confused by hearing a mixed language that he cannot pronounce correctly either his mothertongue or English and cannot improve vocabulary in any. From this point of view it is better if the child is encouraged to speak his mother tongue and the same is spoken to him. If the child is taught two languages right from the beginning the burden is likely to hamper his language development and more particularly his thinking because he often fails to decide as to which word should be used at a particular occasion. In order to learn two languages he has to memorise double words everywhere, with the result that his vocabulary in any one language does not improve appreciably. It is more so because often the grammar of two languages is also different. Thus the Indian parents who try to speak in English with their children right from the beginning and encourage them to do so, stunt the mental development of their children and unnecessarily load their mind with a foreign language. The psychologists have unanimously agreed that the child should be taught through his mothertongue and the same should be spoken to him. A foreign language can be taught to him only after he masters his own mother tongue.

7. **General Growth.** The general growth of the child very much influences his language development. If the general growth is better the language development will also be better. The child in this case will begin to speak earlier and his vocabulary may be wider. On the other hand, if the general growth is deficient, the child will be lagging behind others in language development as well.

SPEECH DEFECTS

Sometimes some speech defects are observed among children in small classes and these must be cured before any appreciable development in education takes place. While on the one hand these defects create difficulty for the child while speaking, on the other hand, the social adjustment is also affected, because other children laugh at his defect. If the defect is not removed at an early date, the child develops inferiority complex. He either keeps silent before others or tries to escape from society. He cannot achieve high mark in the class nor can he lead his fellows. He develops a sense of insecurity. Thus, it is necessary to make all efforts to remove speech defects in the children. The main speech defects are as follows:

1. **Lisping.** This speech defect involves change of sound of letters and words. Its main cause is the continuity of the infantile mode

of speech. The infant cannot pronounce words correctly. He changes their sound but gradually this defect is automatically eliminated. If the child continues to speak like an infant till late age, the defect requires to be cured.

2. **Slurring.** An important speech defect is slurring by which the child is unable to pronounce correctly. Sometimes this is due to too much haste on the part of the child, because he wants to express everything in no time. This defect is sometimes found among children who are used to be among strangers, so that when such a situation arises they become tongue tied or whatever they speak cannot be understood. Sometimes slurring is due to emotional tension because of excessive fear or some other emotion. These defects causing slurring can be removed easily, but if slurring is due to some inherent defect in the vocal organs, it cannot be completely removed unless these organic defects are removed.

3. **Stuttering and Stammering.** Stuttering and stammering, though closely related, are separate activities. In stuttering the child pronounces the same letter repeatedly before pronouncing it word. In stammering, on the other hand, he fails to produce any sound for some time, which results in embarrassing types of gestures and facial expressions. These again create emotional tension and difficulty in social adjustment. The tendency of stuttering is generally observed among children of 2 to 3 years of age, but it is gradually removed with the advance of age. Some exceptional children, however, stutter even at a late age. The defect of stammering, on the other hand, is continued till late age. Studies conducted regarding the causes of stuttering and stammering have revealed several important facts. According to Russell and Dunlop stuttering and stammering is due to learning faulty ways, of speech by imitation of others. Other studies have revealed stammering to be hereditary. According to some psychologists stammering is the result of change of handedness which creates emotional tension. According to Johnson, Soloman and others stammering is mainly due to emotional tension as observed in excessive fear. It is, however, observed even in the absence of emotional tension, the causes in such a situation being sense of insecurity and maladjustment. According to some psychologists, stammering is because of lack of balance among the two hemispheres of the brain. According to others, a main cause of stammering is auditory amnesia. Sometimes stammering

is because of physical deficiency or certain inorganic phosphates, proteins and potassium.

From the perusal of the above mentioned causes of stammering and stuttering, it can be easily understood that while some of these can be removed, others cannot be removed. The presence of speech defects in childhood is sometimes due to lack of sufficient training and maturity. As these factors are provided, the speech defects disappear. The guardians and teachers should therefore encourage children to pronounce correctly. If they make haste in speaking, they should be taught to speak slowly. But it speech defects are continued till late age, efficient physicians must be consulted for their cure. Some defects can be removed by means of surgery. It requires much patience on the part of the guardian, teacher and the physician, as well as the defective child to remove various defects of speech.

QUESTIONS FOR EXERCISE

1. Trace the stages in the development of language in children. What are the major environmental factors that contribute to this development?
2. What are the main stages of speech development in children? Give a short account of each.
3. Describe the sequence of speech development in children.
4. Describe the different stages of language development during childhood. Indicate some of the handicaps which interfere with language development.
5. Give an account of the beginning and development of language in children during the first three years of life.
6. Discuss the different stages of speech development in children. State the functions of language usage in the life of a child.
7. Describe the pre-speech forms of communication and give a brief account of the significant influences of language development.
8. Discuss the salient features of a child's language development.
9. What are the factors involved in the acquisition and development of language in children?
10. Describe the types of speech defects in children. Discuss the causes of delayed speech with special reference to the role of parents.
11. Give an account of various speech defects and disorders.
12. Distinguish between speech errors and speech defects. How are the former developed?

10

Intellectual and Mental Development

The mental development comprehends the development of intellect, mental capabilities, imagination, thinking, emotion, volition and other mental processes. The teacher's duty is to assist in the development of his abilities. This development is education. Education that does not result in development is not worth the name. Functions of the human brain are three *viz.*, to know, experience and to reach decisions. It is, the teacher's function to see to it that each of these three activities of the child are developed as completely as possible. Mental education is concerned with knowing, experiencing and reaching a decision. The process of knowing comprehends perception and cognitive knowledge. The individual makes use of an object in its absence through employing his imagination and memory. Knowledge also includes reasoning and deciding. It is for the teacher to help the young child in perceiving, imagining, reasoning and reaching decisions. It is equally the duty of the teacher to understand the child's problems and look at them from the child's viewpoint.

INFLUENCE OF ENVIRONMENT

The social environment is pregnant with influences that affect the mental development of a child. Having grasped this simple fact, the sensible teacher searches the environment for an explanation of the difficulties that arise in the mental development of children. It is of course, not implied that heredity is any the less influential in the mental development of children. Generally speaking, it is from heredity that the child acquires a particular mental level and specific mental abilities. These abilities can be developed further to the best advantage under certain propitious social circumstances. But the objective of improving the environment in order to study the influence that environment has on the child's mental development, that education professes, is very important. Environmental influences can be divided into the following classes:

(1) **Influence of the Family.** The child's education begins in the home. It is within the family that the development of his mental abilities starts. Hence, if the family possesses a favourable intellectual atmosphere, the mental development of the child is speeded. Possession of radio and television help in increasing the child's fund of general knowledge, and he tends to be better informed. In rich families, the child has available many other resources besides these that help to add to his knowledge. Imitating his parents and brothers and sisters, the little infant learns a lot. If their mental development is good, the child is more apt to progress fast than if such is not the case. An atmosphere of autonomy in the family makes a child self-sufficient and self-reliant, and his mental faculties develop properly. Parents should make their best effort to satisfy each inquisitive query proceeding from the child, and to persuade the young child to think for himself. Maternal influence, in particular, is well known on the mental development of the world's greatest saints, scientists, leaders and thinkers. The child's mental development is susceptible to such diverse influences as the relations between his parents, the number of brothers and sisters, presence of other relatives in the family, the relations existing between the child himself and his parents, the social, economic and cultural level of his family, general administration or discipline within the family, peace and comfort, etc,

(2) **Neighbourhood Influences.** Once the child becomes mobile by learning to move about, he moves outside the sphere of household and becomes intimate with other elements in the neighbourhood. As he grows, he even becomes member of the group of children who are knitted into a team because of their contiguity. These friends and colleagues exert an important influence on his mental development. Guardians should pay attention to the activities of this group and to their best do guard against the children acquiring bad habits.

(3) **Influence of Social Environment.** After the house and the neighbourhood, the next potent influence to which the child is exposed is the school. Normally, a child enters school at the age of three or four, and is thence fourth, susceptible to such influence as the conduct of his teachers, the curriculum, methods of teaching, environment of the school, the character and behaviour of his colleagues. In this connection the following facts are worth noting:

(a) *Teacher's Behaviour:* Parents in the family and the teacher in the school take the place of the child's ideals. If the teacher himself has a wide mental horizon and treats his young students with love and affection, the children will be able to develop their minds, in a free atmosphere. On the other hand, a staunch disciplinarian for the teacher may harm the students by deforming their mental development.

(b) *Method of Teaching:* Modern educational psychology places much stress on research in the field of teaching methods. Research already conducted in this sphere indicates that different teaching methods influence the developing mind in different manners. A proper method of teaching will help to develop a healthy and comprehensive outlook, whereas other methods may make the child narrow minded and hinder his mental development. Whatever the teaching method, the teacher should aim at making, the student think and understand for himself rather than force him to learn by rote. And the children should make the best effort to prepare their own notes from books, instead of having them dictated to them by the teacher. Private tuition also helps to make the student narrow minded and dependent upon the work of others. His mental powers are not developed Secondly, students should be dissuaded from the use of brief and inferior help books made with a view merely to pass the examination. Many students prefer to learn answer to questions by rote and thus get through the examinations. But this method is not conductive to proper mental development. The truth of the matter is that there is no shortcut to mental development, it being the outcome of considerable labour, persistence and consistent effort. Children should be encouraged by their teachers to study as much as they possibly can. The extent to which a child car, study continuously depends upon his age and individual ability and this factor should be kept in view when advising a student to study.

(c) *Curriculum:* Mental development in children is also influenced by the curriculum adopted in the various schools in which they study. A study of mental development in children has revealed roughly the various subjects that a child should be required to study at various age levels. Putting too great a strain on him in the form of exercise books can only hinder and obstruct his mental development. Secondly, if the curriculum is such that the subjects taught are dry, arid and mechanical the whole process becomes a burden. Fear of failure in the examination compels him to learn enough material to ensure his success, but his mind does not approach even the least towards the goal of complete development.

(d) *Extra-curricular Activities:* According to modern educational psychologists, complete mental development of the child cannot be achieved only through study, since formal education alone does not provide occasions for the practice of all mental skills and abilities Thus, most modern schools provide opportunities as debates, picnics, travels, tour of historic and important places, gardening, scouting, N.C.C., dancing, music, painting, acting and formal student unions. Such programmes help in the improvement of both mental abilities as well as the various aspects of child's personality.

(e) *Administration and Discipline:* For the proper mental development of children, it is essential that the schools in which they study should be properly administered, but teachers should be advised to maintain discipline, through love, affection and sympathy rather than through physical punishment. In modern educational institutions the discipline of the school is entrusted to a few chosen students themselves. Similarly, the organisation of the various programmes organised within the school such as picnics, games competitions, etc., is also put in the hands of students. This method has the effect of removing any consciousness of a burden, as they learn to discipline themselves. Being self imposed, discipline losses the element of burden. A hostel warden had recourse to a brilliant psychological device for putting an end to organised indiscipline among his students. He announced that the dining table which showed the least disturbance during dinner would be awarded with a flag, which would entitle occupants of that table to twice the normal rations of the choice morsels of food. This system worked wonder with the discipline of the children, and the students strove to maintain discipline among themselves. Even if one of them felt inclined to be naughty, he was speedily dissuaded by his table in mates. In this manner, the use of psychological ingenuity solved the warden's problems without any undesirable strife. Generally speaking, it is likely to prove profitable if the care of furniture and other class room equipment is made over to the students themselves. If this is done, the students themselves will deter those among them who are of a more ambitious but perverted turn of mind. Nevertheless, there, is no way of completely avoiding some system of awards and punishment in schools. There is little to worry about awards, as there is little chance of their being injudicious in nature or in time of presentation, but care must be taken to convince the punished child that he is being punished for his own good. Normally, one should avoid severe physical punishment of children because this adversely affects their personality.

(4) **Influence of Cultural Environment.** The child is open to the cultural environment whether he be in school, in his neighbourhood or at home. The cultural environment is made up of ideals, objectives and values. Mental development is healthy and comprehensive if these elements are themselves valuable. But if these factors lack real value, mental development is likely to be hindered or it may take turns that are not desirable.

Mental development implies living being's adjustment of his conduct with the conditions and circumstances of his environment, with the object to attain certain ends. The correlation between physical and mental development can be seen right from infancy. Consequently, while the two year old is apparently more developed physically than a one year old child, it is equally perceptible that he is mentally developed and superior to his juniors in all. But there is inevitability in that a child of five must also be mentally superior to a child who is of four because individuals differ in respect of the speed with which they develop mentally. Nevertheless, mental development in most children progresses at approximately the same rate which is consequently the average. Educational psychology tries to locate this average. The cells of a child's mind develop continuously, and in this manner the various parts of his brain gain in complexity. Hence, his mental development takes the form of vertical development.

MENTAL DEVELOPMENT DURING INFANCY

The infant shows very few signs of rational behaviour. His main functions are eating, sleeping and fulfilling various other physical needs. In this manner, he is primarily concerned with his own comfort but experiments have proved that the child can react to visual and tactual stimuli although these stimuli and the consequent reactions show lack of order and system. In the first three years the infant begins to give evidence of mental qualities that are to be his capital for the years of life to come. Roughly speaking, in the first six years of life, till he attains the age of seven the following characteristics are to be seen in his mental development:

(1) **Choice of Alternative Methods in the Satisfaction of Needs.** The infant is fully conscious of such physical conditions and needs as hunger, thirst, sleep, regulation of temperature, etc. As he progresses, these needs settle into a definite pattern, and the methods of satisfying them also become definite. In this process, the infant is often seen displaying his selective capacity. In general, the infant makes efforts to avoid all unpleasant and painful circumstances. At the same time, much of his behaviour is motivated by the desire to distinguish between one person from another. He has desire of attracting attention and winning praise from others. In the first year, he learns to walk and to talk. In the next two years there is rapid progress in his ability of walking, talking and detecting various objects within his environment through the use of his sense organs. At this age, the infant slowly but inevitably becomes aquainted with the objects and living beings that form part of his environment. He comes to know them by their names, and also to reckon their spatial distinctions and relations.

(2) **Lack of Temporal Knowledge.** For the infant, the conventional divisions of time such as today, tomorrow, the day after or the

Fig. 10. The Child likes to hear Fairy Tales and Tends to Live in the World of make belief.

week and year are meaningless as he cannot distinguish between them.

(3) **Questioning in such Terms as Why, What and Who.** As has been pointed out, and can be observed without much difficulty, a growing infant evinces a continuous and unflagging curiosity and interest in the objects and living beings in his environment. Hence, he constantly asks questions from his parents and teachers. Questions such as why is this? Why does that not happen? what is this? who is this? are characteristics of the child. His queries are virtually ceaseless, and the questions come so rapidly that the infant does not even bother to wait for an answer to one before going on to another. When he is very much surprised, he often even forgets the very question he has just asked. These questions are not motivated so much by his quest for knowledge and information as they are an expression of his developing mental capacities.

(4) **The World of Make Belief.** In this age, the infant tends to live in a world of make belief, of which he himself is the creator. By donning his father's clothes he impersonates his papa to his own delight, and the acquisition of a stick effects an immediate transition to the schoolmaster. He makes a horse out of a long stick while some fruits suggest dolls to him. On seeing different animals, he assimilates them into his world of imagination. It is equally easy for him to roar like a lion, to bark like a dog to make the sounds of a goat or to impersonate a cock in sound. His imagination also transforms him into objects and machines. One often comes across children playing as trains and aeroplanes. Young boys and girls live the life of their parents in an imaginary world in which they marry off their dolls and make brides and bride grooms, and houses of sand which are as unstable as their imaginings. Such behaviour is as indicative of imitation as it is of a colourful and active imagination.

(5) **Variety of Imagination.** Often enough, the infant himself is the hero of his imaginary world, and away from the real world, he lives delightedly in his own sphere. Evidently, imaginings of a child display astonishing variety.

(6) **Tendency towards Self-assertion.** According to Alfred Adler, the famous psychologist, the most prominent and strong tendency in the infant is the tendency towards self-assertion. He normally yearns to exhibit his physical and mental abilities and win acclaim, of the elders.

(7) **Distinction between Self and Others.** The infant is normally very conscious of his self, being primarily an individualist. He sometimes gives the impression of being selfish, and he does not show to advantage at such moment. He often sticks to his demand and obstinately tries to have his way. And if one infant succeeds in getting something, another who has seen him at it is even more obstinate in his demand for it, even though he may have nothing to gain from it. But if he chooses to decline something, it needs much patience to make him yield the point. In fact, the ego develops gradually in this age.

(8) **Surrender and Enthusiasm.** Even though his ego develops continuously in this period of his life, the infant also exhibits, in certain special circumstances, qualities of surrender and enthusiasm. They are not normally evident.

(9) **Intellectual Development.** The infant's intellect starts developing in infancy, differences between intellect of various children being readily evident. As the infant develops intellectually, his understanding and his knowledge of the various objects around him increases.

(10) **Solution of Simple Problems.** As the infant gains in intellectual maturity, he learns to solve simple problems. At the very beginning, these problems normally relate to the activities and actions of the hand and feet. Having studied infants between the age of 19 and 44 months, Alpert came to the conclusion that infants in this age also manifest evidence of existing insight. Intellectual development is evident from the ability by which the infant solves various problems as they arise. According to Herter an infant of five is able enough to solve problems through the use of concrete material as well as linguistic symbols.

(11) **Development of Memory.** The infant has great ability in learning by rote, as is evident from the success with which they have heard many times. Despite the fact that they hear the same songs and folklore many times, they evince the same rapt interest every time. And as far as stories or poems are concerned, they remember them so well that they can correct the person reciting to them, if he should happen to make a mistake,

(12) **Development of Mental Abilities.** Infants manifest the development of such mental qualities as observation, comparison, decision, etc. As the body develops, their sense organs become more and more sensitive and acute with the result that they can perceive objects better. Simultaneously, linguistic ability also shows signs of improving. Gradually, the infant learns to

distinguish linguistic symbols. Starting with small individual words, he progresses to the understanding to the simple sentences, and in a short time learns to speak with considerable fluency and authority. These mental capacities of children can be seen in their play. He also develops constructive and aesthetic imagination. Coloured pictures are also intriguing for infant. He takes great interest in collecting things and in the construction of things with whatever material that comes to his hand.

(13) **Desire to Assist his Parents.** Infants are usually very much interested in assisting their parents, and when given the opportunity, they become very enthusiastic and delighted. They show preference for cooking with the mother and helping the father to carry small weights about the house. In this the infant not only wins praise from his parents, but also gets an opportunity to give expression to his individuality.

(14) **Development of Mental Abilities.** The infant's mental abilities reach the stage of complete development by the time he is six. These are the one that can help him to conduct himself like an individual in any group of human beings. On the one hand, the infant manifests the desire to co-operate with others, while on the other hand, he expresses differences from others in respect of attitudes and behaviour.

(15) **Development of Sex Tendencies.** Generally, the development of sex organs during infancy and childhood is rather slow, but psychologists as Freud have irrefutably proved that the child has present in him the sex tendency and that it constantly develops. According to Freud, infancy is the state of self love, as the child finds pleasure in exploring the various parts of his own body. On this theory, sucking of the thumb is expressive of the sexual tendency. In this stage, the infant loves himself, but, very soon the infants develop love for their parents. In this love, Freud has also detected the presence of heterosexual love. According to him, one can see the Oedipus complex present in male children and Electra complex among the females. While the male infant loves the mother the female love the father.

(16) **Instinctive Behaviour.** Much of the infant's behaviour in the infant and pre-school period is generated by instincts. Although the infant also develops intellectually, yet he prefers to have his instincts satisfied without delay. He starts crying at the delay in preparation of his food. At the smallest and most trifle things he throws himself upon the ground and becomes adamant. He does whatever pleases him, but avoids anything that promises him

pain. It is evident that in this period of his life, he is not aware of moral and ethical considerations and compunctions in his behaviour.

(17) **Dependence upon Others.** As in the first three years of infancy, in the next three years also is the infant dependent upon other persons such as parents, brothers and sisters, relatives and servants. He needs the assistance of others even in the fulfilment of such elementary needs as taking food, bathing and putting on clothes. As yet he does not process self-confidence and self-reliance. He even fears going out of the house alone, and prefers to take some-one with him for protection and companionship. He depends upon others to such an extent that even the activities that he is capable of performing by himself he requires of others to perform it. If he falls, he tries to attract attention but does not get off the ground without the help of others, preferably the parents.

(18) **Imitation.** Much of what an infant learns of behaviour is acquired through the imitation of other individuals in the family. He is continually influenced by the behaviour of the parents among themselves and other infants in the family. Hence, a majority of the habits that an infant has can be traced to some one or the other individual member of his family because he imitates them without going into propriety of the habit he is thus forming. He shouts if he sees others making a noise, but if he finds them quiet and peaceful, he does not disturb them but chooses to be equally quiet. Such habits as lying or stealing things are formed in like manner.

(19) **Curiosity.** An infant's curiosity is almost always at a fever pitch, and there is no end to the questions he can devise concerning the most mundane and uninteresting object that comes in his way. Answers do not interest him as much as asking questions. He revels in roaming around outside as he comes to see many novel things. This innate curiosity of the infant can be skillfully exploited to the child's advantage by his parents and teachers who can tell him many things and turn his thoughts into desirable and profitable channels.

(20) **Influence of Love and Affection.** An infant is apt to react very violently to the least criticism and disrespect or disgrace. The arrival of a new baby in the family interests the infant but if he comes to be disregarded by his parents his attraction turns into hatred, jealousy and distaste, which can sometimes take a very serious turn. He requires loving and sympathetic treatment

from his parents which, if it is not forthcoming, can hinder his mental development. He hates any correction or reproof. Strong discipline does not win his sympathy and he tries to rebel against it. In this age, the father should pay more attention to the male infant since its absence can lead to the development of hatred in the children. This consideration finds its theoretical support in the Freudian theory of Oedipus and Electra Complexes.

(21) **Creative Impulse.** In this age, of the most manifest tendencies in the infant is the creative impulse. He busies himself in making or collecting things, as the activity gives him the satisfaction is motivated by the desire to do all that he sees his elders doing, and it affords him much pleasure if he is given the opportunity of doing it. According to Western educational psychologists, in this period of the infant's life, it is desirable that the parents should spend some time with the children as it affords them the best education that there can possibly be. The same function can be performed if the infant is sent either to the kindergarten or the montessary school but only in case these schools are really excellent, as otherwise it would be futile to entrust the children's education to them. It is in childhood that the foundation of good and bad habits as well as character are laid so that it is essential that the child be properly looked after.

THE INFANT'S EDUCATION

It is evident from the foregoing consideration of infant's mental characteristics that the teacher must pay the utmost attention to his development in the process of education. It is for the teacher to arouse the curiosity of the infant in any subject that he wishes to teach. Once this is achieved the teacher can confidently leave it to the infant's enthusiasm to understand the lesson properly. Whatever the nature and irrelevance of the questions that an infant asks, he should never be irritably reproved. A teacher must do all in his power to answer each and every question that an infant puts.

(1) **Use of Instincts in Teaching.** The infant's education should be based on his instincts. If the infant's self respect is injured, his tendency to self-assertion is seriously impaired. Sympathetic and loving behaviour can induce the infant to surrender to the teacher and honour his discipline. An infant's enthusiasm should never be suppressed as it may lead to the formation of mental complexes.

(2) **Teaching through Actual Objects.** As the infant normally tends towards imaginative wanderings the teacher should employ concrete objects in training and teaching him. Although it is essential that the infant's imagination and particularly aesthetic imagination be activated through dance, music, painting, etc., his formal education should be conducted through the use of concrete things, such as wooden blocks etc.

(3) **Importance of Sympathetic and Loving Behaviour towards the child.** Modern psychologists unanimously opine that the behaviour of a teacher towards the infant should be one of sympathetic understanding and love. If the infant works to his satisfaction, it should be encouraged further by kindly words of praise.

(4) **Need for Making the Child Self-reliant.** Understanding of infant's mental development makes it evident that the teacher should do his best to provoke self-reliance among his students. In fact, in modern democratic societies, the very aim or education is to make the child self-reliant and independent individual. For this it is essential that he be given small minor tasks to perform on his own initiative. He can be assisted in the process of learning but this assistance should take the form of guidance and should never be so excessive as to render the infant utterly dependent upon the advisor. Actually, the duty of the teacher lies in looking after him as he develops himself, not to develop the infant, whose intelligence mental abilities, and memory and other capacities develop of their own accord as he grows older. It is upto the teacher to satisfy the needs of the infant that arise during this process of development. And for this it is essential to develop the right kind of atmosphere in the school, since once this main task is achieved successfully, the teacher's function is reduced to one of intelligent participation and supervision. The atmosphere depends upon the presence of games and toys, attractive and interesting curriculum, healthy schoolrooms and the right adjustment in the mutual relations between the teachers and students, and the students themselves.

Keeping in view all that has been said above, modern schools are seen employing the latest methods of education and experimenting with them. Western countries are making increasing use of radio and television in the education of infants. The programme is varied when infants are taken to view educationally important films. The infant's stock of knowledge is increased by taking him to new gardens, exhibitions, historic and other interesting places. Communal qualities are generated in the child by encouraging participation in collective programmes that are organised in the school. In this manner, the modern teacher who is at all knowledgeable, keeps in mind the mental development of the infant and tries to set the educative process to conform to the infant's mental mould.

MENTAL DEVELOPMENT DURING CHILDHOOD

The period of childhood extends from a person's sixth to eleventh or twelfth year. The following are the major characteristics of his mental development in this period of child's life:

(1) **Stability.** The most characteristic mental feature of childhood is stability. In other words, this age has been called the state of pseudo maturity because in this period the child gives false impressions of maturation. In his childhood, the little chap becomes fairly well acquainted with his environment, and loses the wide-eyed innocence that marks his infancy.

(2) **Maturation of Gregarious Instinct.** The gregariousness that the child evinces in his infancy reaches its maturity in childhood. Now he prefers more to, be with children of his own age and shows no interest in staying alone. Coming of new people in the family gives him pleasure. He develops interest in fairs or games and becomes a regular member of the group of neighbourhood children.

(3) **Curiosity.** The curiosity of which the infant gives evidence in the infancy increases when he reaches childhood. No longer content with the more passive method of asking questions and waiting for an answer, he longs to make actual and personal acquaintances with his surrounding environment. But he continues to ask his questions. His curiosity can be put to good use by exciting it in respect of many desirable habits.

(4) **Moral Norms.** As a member of a group, the child learns to obey certain moral norms. He is so much led away with the idea of group membership that he does not shrink from telling untruth to his parents and teachers if it is required of him by his group. From this age, the child can be made to think in terms of good and bad, and foundations for his moral character are laid.

(5) **Extroversion.** In this period of his life, the child appears to be pre-eminently an extrovert. He takes less interest in his own self than he does in his surroundings, being more attracted towards concrete objects than the flickering of an imagination. He, has

developed practical interests and yearns to achieve something of real worth.

(6) **Play.** While in his infancy, the child invents imaginatively the modes of play to entertain himself, but in his childhood he turns to the forms of play prevalent in the concrete world. Even his imaginings now take a more mundane turn, as they are closely connected with the real world. He is motivated by the desire to achieve something useful. Hence he can be taught, many things even as he plays.

(7) **Acquisitive Tendencies.** Having reached childhood, the infant is often observed manifesting sense of possession and right. He likes to collect various kinds of things and by encouraging him to collect useful things like stamps, old coins, toys, etc., a very good habit can be inculcated.

(8) **Latent, Sexual Tendencies.** According to Dr. Jones, the child in this age does not manifest any self-love, Oedipus or Electra complexes because in childhood his sexual tendencies are latent.

(9) **Imitation.** In childhood, too, as in his infancy, the child possesses a strong tendency towards imitations of others. Observing others in doing various functions and making things, he is inspired to do something of the same kind. Sometimes he imitates others in private, in order to obviate the chance of other people laughing at him.

(10) **Creative Tendencies.** The child manifests an instinctive creative tendency. He is positively inclined towards making new friends and making objects out of mud and sand. He can be encouraged to play with wooden blocks in this age.

(11) **Influence of Praise and Blame.** In this period, as in most other periods of life the child is happy when praised but pained when reproved. He is encouraged when praise falls to his lot, while he feels discouraged when he is criticised. Consequently, it is his constant endeavour to do only those acts that bring him the praise and acclaim of everyone involved, it being a different matter if be falls foul of his parents or teachers and wins the reproof in trying to do something that his friend's circle thinks praise worthy.

(12) **Extension in the Field of Interest and Thinking.** In childhood, the child's field of interest and thinking widens considerably. He finds much, delight in seeing pictures of and reading about human beings and animals to be found in the various parts of the world. He cannot restrain his curiosity if something mysterious falls in his ear.

(13) **Revolting Against Strict Discipline.** In this age the child resents any strict discipline, be it in the home or in the school, and fosters feelings of revolt against it. If strong discipline is exercised upon the child, outwardly he seems to succumb to it, but inwardly he seeths with revolt and pent up anger which sometimes leads him to run away not only from school but even from the home.

(14) **Solving problems.** In this age, the child takes special delight, in solving puzzles and various kinds of problems, so that the power of abstract thought also develops in him.

EDUCATION IN CHILDHOOD

Knowing the various mental characteristics of childhood, a teacher can do much in the way of making education natural and easy. The following points are important in this respect:

(1) The child can be taught such things in communal situation as telling the truth, honesty, obedience, discipline etc. The teacher can induce many desirable traits in the children by setting a good example and ideal.

(2) Making good use of the gregarious instinct, the child can be indulged to take part in scouting and other team games. These activities can help in the development of qualities like co-operation, humility, leadership, organisation, justice, patriotism, social service etc., in the children so that they may be ideal citizens when they attained their adulthood.

(3) His extrovert nature can be put to good use in sending him on extensive tours of the country so that his knowledge increases. The child's personality develops through participation in extra curricular activities.

(4) Collection of useful things is a good habit and it can be ingrained in the child by teaching him to collect such things as stamps, photographs, rare coins, books etc.

(5) His curiosity can be aroused regarding novel things and he can then he left to learn many new things.

(6) His imitative methods can be put to the most advantageous use by performing useful activities in his presence so that he may learn to emulate them.

(7) The foundations of a good moral character can be laid by praising good things in his presence and condemning all bad things, also in his presence.

(8) New subjects can be introduced in the form of puzzles and problems to the child so that he may be attracted to solve them. Education is simplified in this way.

(9) Creation of an atmosphere of love and affection both at home and in the school, besides creating opportunities for the teachers and students and parents and children to work and play together, can help in his mental development and, in the development of his personality.

It is evident from the above description that a knowledge of the progress of mental development in childhood makes possible better education of children.

MENTAL DEVELOPMENT IN ADOLESCENCE

The English word adolescence is a derivative of the latin 'adolescere' which means to grow to maturity. This age begins from twelve and continues till the age of twenty. In the words of Jersild, "Adolescence is the period through which a growing person makes transition from childhood to maturity." Adolescence, in the opinion of most educational psychologists, begins between the age of 12 to 24 years. Compared to boys, girls enter the period of adolescence a couple of years earlier. According to Dr. Jones, adolescence is the recollection of infancy. It parallels the states of infancy and childhood in being patterned into the conditions, the first of growth and the second of maturation.

(A) *State of Growth:* In this state, the adolescent is seen to be very active and unstable as well as disturbed. He gives the impression of being somewhat lost, and is subject, to rapidly varying moods of dejections and elation, enthusiasm and deep lethargy, etc. The main thing concerning this period in life is that the adolescent is no longer a child but an adult, though the society in which he lives continues to treat him as a child. Secondly, he climbs down from the dizzy heights of imagination that be reached in his infancy and childhood and steps firmly into the real world. Both these factors engender in him a constant fear of reproof and criticism at the hands of others. He often becomes helpless and pitiable, shy and repressed. This does not indicate that be runs away from the real world, but that he tries to modify it according to his own notions. In efforts of this kind, elation and dejection is often seen wearing a look of anxiety.

(B) *State of Maturation:* By the time he enters this stage, he has calmed down a bit and shown signs of stability. He carves a, niche for himself in his society, and gradually, his tendencies, habits and activities become stable and regular.

In adolescence the individual is so transformed that he wears a new and unrecognised look. Mental changes in this period of life find their best expression in the work of poets as they depict the mental states of young men and women. Adolescence exhibits the following mental characteristics generally :

(1) **Development of Mental Abilities.** In adolescence the individual's nervous system becomes more strong with the result that his mental activities show greater tenacity and system. Ability to think, to solve problems, to differentiate and evaluate are some of the more prominent characteristics and abilities that he exhibits.

(2) **Sexual Development.** From the psychological viewpoint the most significant characteristic of the period of adolescence is sexual development. According to Dr. Jones, the repressed sexual force of infancy, that continued latent through the period of childhood, once again awakens as the individual passes through various stages of sexual development. The truth of the matter is, that even if it is not the only tendency, sexual tendency is undoubtedly the most prominent and stable tendency to be found in adolescence. Hence, to disregard it is to make a fatal mistake as it is the most harmful form of negligence conceivable. The development in this sphere is so rapid that his entire personality appears to be coloured by it. Sexual development in adolescence finds its expression in attraction towards strangers, rather than towards parents as in the case of infancy. It announces its presence even in such small activities as the young boy's anxiety and nervousness, biting of fingernails, putting a pencil in one's mouth, tying knots in handkerchiefs, etc. Both physical and mental teaching in this age can use the sexual tendency as an important force. Normally, the development of the sexual tendency passes through the following three stages:

(a) *Auto-eroticism:* In the beginning of adolescence, sexual tendency manifests itself in self-love, but this self-love differs from the infant's, self-love. In infancy, the child finds physical pleasure in exploring and touching various parts of his own body. But in the adolescent self-love, the individual dresses himself well and meticulously, observes his face continuously in the mirror, and does his very best to make himself as presentable as possible. Many young men and women passing through this stage can be seen humming as they look at themselves in the mirror. They are content to be with themselves and love only themselves. As yet they have no time to observe and appreciate others. Freud calls this the state of narcicism. The term has a long story behind it, from which the term originated Narcissus was a Greek prince of almost unparalleled beauty, who could not find anyone more handsome than himself he loved himself probably justifiably. A flower is called narcissus, and it grows by the side of lake in such a manner that its image is visible in the water. Young men and women in their teens behave in a similar manner as they love to look upon themselves and beautify themselves. One of the most prominent and common malpractices in which the adolescents indulge is masturbation. The American psychologist Kinsey, in his famous report, has mentioned the various ways in which young men and women derive pleasure from their sexual experiences. Sometimes the feelings of guilt that arise as a result of indulgence in these activities lead to the formation of complexes that are very harmful to the mental development of individuals. The one and only means of escaping such consequences is proper sex education. In order to impart the right attitude towards the sexual tendency to young people, it is essential that teachers and parents tell them everything frankly so that they may adopt this healthy attitude.

(b) *Homosexuality:* Progressing from the stage of self-love, young boys and girls are attracted to members of their own sex, either older, or younger than themselves. Homosexual love of this age is accompanied by great anxiety and deep affection but latter on it turns into heterosexual love. Persons of this age can often be seen caressing each other, roaming together, preferring only each other's company, sleeping together, praising each other and finding other modes of expressing their mutual attraction. Some girls also develop the habit of exciting each other's sexual organs. Similar aberration is present in boys in the form of sodomy, which leads to feelings of guilt and crime if the person is reproved for these activities. Such bad habits can be got rid of only through the medium of sensible guidance and sex education of the children by the parents and teachers. It is always desirable that adolescence passing through this phase should be controlled sensibly but it is equally essential that all control exercised over them should be in the form of loving advice rather that, punishment.

(c) *Heterosexuality*: The state of homosexuality in adolescents is succeeded by sexual maturity, a state of moral heterosexual relations between men and women. Young men and women who have attained this age can often be seen being attracted to members of the other sex, meeting each other, talking inessentialy for hours on end, putting their best feet forward to attract the other and hold such attention adopting the latest fashions to appear the more attractive, going for walks together, visiting picture houses together, caressing each other and sometimes even going to the extent of actual sexual intercourse, though this often has disastrous results as the girls become mothers even before they are married. The strength of this sexual tendency can neither be curbed nor can an strict control upon it prove efficacious even if it is considered desirable. Excessive restrictions on meetings between boys and girls in colleges and universities only leads to greater indiscipline and misconduct. Hence, many educational psychologists have advised that instead of restricting communication between them, relations should be encouraged. On the other hand, the traditions that have continued our culture stress the complete segregation of the sexes during this period. In the modern context any effort at emulating these traditions can only prove foolhardy in the future, and in any case such efforts are not likely to prove efficacious. Uncontrolled and impassioned contacts can only lead to such ostensible and detestable consequences as suicides, unmarried mothers, social corruption etc. Hence, it is essential that the youth of today be provided with proper sex education and encouraged to develop a healthy attitude towards sex. This will have the desirable effect preparing them for responsible parenthood when they ultimately get married.

Fig. 11

Another method of solving problems of the sexual impulse, besides sex education, is inspiring young men and women to develop interest in various kinds of games and sports, dances, singing, art, painting, etc. It is a matter of universal regret, particularly among the enlightened population of the nation, that nearly 99% of teachers and guardians find it embarrassing to discuss any sexual matter with their young charges. The consequences are undesirable as the young inexperienced adolescent learns the same things from bad and uncouth companions who convey to him all the aberrant forms of sexual information. Such a situation is true of many civilized societies, and all the more of India. When the adolescent observes that his teachers and guardians prefer to keep all sex information secret and concealed from him, he forms a guilt complex regarding sex. Due to the normal stage of development, he can do nothing to abate the force or strength of the urge, and he is helpless as no assistance from his teacher is forth-coming. Thus, he either indulges all his energies in trying to control the instinct, losing all interest in studies in which he cannot concentrate, or forms obnoxious and deforming habits, or as an alternative contracts serious mental diseases through excessive repression. Hence teachers and parents should assist adolescent males and, females to organise, control and sublimate the sexual impulse through adequate sex education.

(3) **Hero Worship.** Generally speaking, adolescents evince a strong tendency towards hero worship, though the criterion of heroism is not the same in all children. Possession of any quality that attracts an individual child the most is sufficient qualification for a man or woman to become his ideals. While one child may, regard a wrestler as a hero, another may profess allegiance to a scientist, yet another may be devoted to a film personality or a political leader. In schools some teachers impress their students considerably with the result that they come to be tenderly and affectionately regarded by them, also being imitated by the tender children. Sometimes this hero worship turns in love. It is not till considerably later that the young man turns his thoughts to his own heroic qualities, when he begins praising them. The tendency to hero worship can be turned to good account by inculcating a proper character and personality in the child's mind. For this it is essential that the teacher himself should represent the highest ideals, as he is the best example that the child can facilely imitate.

(4) **Religious Feeling.** Many adolescents become positively and deeply religious in this period of their lives. One can often observe them loving God in some one image, talking to Him, sacrificing themselves to Him and praying to Him. India is particularly productive of such specimens since, for one, the religious tendency is deeply ingrained in the people's mind, and for another, in Indian society young boys and girls meet great leaders and famous personalities on very rare occasions. While religious tendency protects the young inexperienced child from many bad habits, it sometimes helps in making him somewhat impractical. Teachers can help to create a healthy attitude towards religion.

(5) **Gregariousness.** Adolescents are always acutely desirous of being among their friends, of praising them and of improving their relations with them. Often, they form definite groups in which each adolescent has his specific status and a role to suit him. This status and role plays an important part in determining his status and role in adult life.

(6) **Extroversion.** In this period, the child once again regains his extrovert flamboyancy, taking deep interest in his surroundings and other individuals, their activities and conflicts. In school, too, he likes to take part in all kinds of activities. And it is a matter of joy with him if he can spend the larger part of his time in the company of his friends. Various individuals become engaged in programmes of social service and welfare. In this manner does the adolescent announce the interest that he takes in the real world. This interest can be usefully exploited to ingrain in him such useful qualities as self dependence, self determination, cooperation, discipline, honesty and the quality of maintaining good relations with others or develop the social instinct. This is the age in which the foundations of good citizenship can he deeply laid,

(7) **Lack of Stability and Adjustment.** It has been pointed out earlier, too, that in his adolescence the growing individual is at the threshold of his life although he is rarely if ever considered an adult by his seniors. From the psychological point of view, he takes himself seriously enough not to consider himself a child, and likes to be treated as an adult. Evidently, he shows considerable instability and lack of adjustment. His adaptation to his environment is upset by such small considerations as the growth of pimples on his face or the presence of other small physical deformities. In fact, it is a stage in which he learns to lead adult life in every sphere and direction. Hence, the presence and continual development of problems is only natural. And these problems are susceptible to ready solutions if the seniors are prepared to extend their sympathetic cooperation and guidance.

(8) **Excessive Sentimentality.** The adolescent is very sentimental and emotionally unstable, although at this age his mind is fairly well developed. Of the many feelings that drive him, the strongest are the desire to win praise and self respect, any injury to or repression of them leading to serious malformations and even open rebellion. Sentimentality can be turned to good use in developing cultural traits in the adolescent. Participation in

programmes of dancing, acting, music, painting etc., makes the emotional life more stable.

(9) **Excessive Imagination.** Although the adolescent is as much in this world as any other living, yet he is prone to much imaginary flights into the world of fancy. The smallest thing can persuade him to temporarily abandon the world of reality and turn to the imaginary world. Such excessive imagination manifests itself in the strong tendency towards daydreaming, but some gifted children express their creative and aesthetic imagination through literature, music and painting, besides other arts.

(10) **Particular Interests.** In adolescence, as the individual develops both in mind and body, his interests vary. Progressively the boys and girls develop the interests of their adult counterparts. Girls show this development in such interests as the use of various cosmetics, efforts at appearing beautiful, reading or taking interest in romantic novels, love stories, dramas or poems, participating in music, art and acting programmes etc. Boys manifest their approaching adulthood in the form of various active games, running around, doing acts of valour, developing a vocation that they are to pursue in their adult life. Both boys and girls take constant interest in developing friendship with members of the other sex and maturing it to fruition through conversation, intimacy, letters and romance.

(11) **Development of the Mind.** In adolescence, the mind develops rapidly. The cells of the nervous system increase rapidly, and the chemical composition of the, nerves also undergoes a change. In this way, the mind and the nervous system rapidly matures. In this period along with physical and mental development, practice helps to, develop mental abilities. Linguistic ability also registers improvement during this period. In his adolescence the child develops the vocabulary that he possesses. His vocabulary reveals general intelligence. Mental development, too, reaches its apex in adolescence. Despite the inevitable individual differences that are invariably present, mental maturity achieves its completion normally by the age of twenty. Practice or experience contributes considerably to this maturation. Normally, the individual's intelligence continues on the same level, or, in other words, even in different ages the intelligence, quotient of an individual remains more or less the same. Many detailed studies have revealed that during the first five years of life, the mental development is greater than that achieved during the following five. In this manner, the

mental development during the ages of 10 and 15 is greater than that during 15 and 20, in respect of rapidity. At the age of ten, the mental development of a child is at its fastest. Following this, as the child approaches the stage of adolescence, the speed of mental development slows down. In his infancy, the child only acknowledges and indicates the feeling of sensations, while at the age of three he is in a position to distinguish between objects, animals and human beings. At six, he is capable of describing a picture that he has seen, but in his adolescence he rises above description to the level of interpretation of the pictures that he sees. In this manner, one can see constant development and improvement in the mind's reactions to stimuli. Generally, an individual's memory is tested by the number of digits he can remember after they have once been announced to him. In adolescence, the ability to remember digits improves with age and reaches its highest peak at the age of twenty.

Education of Adolescents

The sensible teacher can make his teaching psychological if he has knowledge of an adolescent's mental development. The intensity and proper use of imagination can help to make an individual a poet, painter, sculptor or a psychologist. Intelligence, observation, reasoning and thiriking having reached the required state of development in adolescence, the school and college curriculum can be fairly diversified and made comprehensive. The truth of the matter is that actual education begins only in adolescence since at this stage the young boys and girls treat themselves as adults and they come to entertain a serious and responsible attitude to their education. What is needed is that the teacher should inspire them to work hard in their studies through self inspiration.

(1) Physical development is rapid during adolescence. The bodily structure develops at a rapid pace. This age is the time of revolutionary physical development as in this age young boys and girls attain to their maximum heights and specific bodily developments, conforming to their respective sexes, take place. Hence, they should be trained in games and beneficial exercises. In educational institutions, they should be specially trained in health and bodily development since, if they do not pay attention at this stage they are not likely to appear handsome later on in life.

(2) The extreme sentimentality of adolescence can be used to induce the girls and boys to learn literature, music, art and science. This age is propitious for the teaching of all subjects. Transfer of learning during this period is considerable.

(3) Good conduct, proper interests and good habits of living can be developed in boys and girls by making adequate use of the strong sexual tendency that is a strong motivating force. In adolescence, the sexual organs of the boys and girls undergo rapid development. In girls, the menstrual cycle starts while the boys are subject to nightly emissions. The sexual organs are covered by hair. Persistent development in the girl's breasts sometimes leads to pain. Lacking knowledge of the basis and cause of all these physiological changes, boys and girls are often subjected to much perplexity. Many of the girls are not even aware that the blood emitted during the menstrual cycle does not happen to them alone but to every other girls passing the same stage of development. This leads to much anxiety and sometimes even results in the creation of guilty, feelings. Not knowing the manner in which they should dress hygienically during the menstrual cycle they are sometimes put in very embarrassing situations that are very painful to them. They are even rendered ridiculous. It is a matter of no little sorrow and pain that much changes are inevitable in the lives of every young men and woman, but almost all of them have to get over them through trial and error. The parents, who have themselves been through these conditions, are content to leave the helpless children on their own resources and wit. This is not a desirable practice. In this connection it is for the parents to inform the children of all necessary details and methods, without making secret of anything. It is never a good practice to hate or scold or deliver moral lectures if one sees an adolescent developing bad habits. It is a matter of physiology and psychology, and it should be treated accordingly. It is for the teacher to inform the growing boy and girl of the complete facts about the male and female body, and to train them adequately in all forms of hygiene.

(4) Hero worship and idealisation are two very useful tendencies with which the adolescent is endowed. This stage in his development is particularly efficacious for laying the foundations for a good character. He should be given the lives of great men to read and to draw what lesson he can from them. High ideals stand revealed to him, and he can think in terms of greater characters as opposed to the imaginative pictures of heroes that he has been sketching to himself. The, adolescent should be persuaded to read extensively, It is never desirable to prevent him from reading stories and novels. All that is needed is that he should be intelligently guided in forming his taste by being taught to read interesting works of great

novelists and psychologist so that his knowledge of human nature increases and his sexual tendency reduces its hold upon him.

(5) The adolescent is by nature a rebel against the traditions and customs prevailing in his society. His rebellious instinct can be chanelled to good use by the teacher who can help to develop a generation which hates all the bad traditions and rids society of them. Adolescents can easily be induced to think of social development and improvement. They can be taught to rise above their narrow interests and comprehend the spirit of nationality, internationality and universal love.

(6) It is no less important to impart ethical, moral and religious education to the child. Although all educational psychologists fail to see eye to eye on this subject, moral and religious education can benefit the recipient only if it is psychological and simple.

(7) In adolescence the individual should be given vocational guidance after his mental capacities, inclinations and interests have been examined. His education should conform to the vocation that he is going to pursue in the future so that he may not be a misfit in any occupation but should rather be able to earn a comfortable, living, establish a household and contribute actively to national development.

MENTAL DEVELOPMENT IN ADULT AGE

The individual steps into his adulthood at the age of 18, having passed through his adolescence. Consequently, in most countries the individual is considered an adult when he attains 18 years of age, and is vested with the rights of responsibility for his own actions, independent judgment, marriage, pursuit of a vocation, establishing a household, and inheriting property, besides other sundry rights. Before this, all these rights are denied to him, transferred mostly to his parents and guardians. It is evident that it is justifiable to treat a person of 18 as fully responsible. His interests are now concerned with the objects and individuals that form part of his environment. Reality replaces the world of imagination. An adult is faced with the necessity of finding solutions of the practical problems with which he is confronted in his day to day life. Among the various functions that he chooses to perform are the necessities of finding a vocation, earning wealth, marrying and finding his place and status in society. Similarly, the erstwhile girl passes through the roles of young women, wife and mother while the boy passes through the stages of young man, husband and father. Both the man and the woman accept the burden of citizenship of the nation.

From the physiological point of view, the individual is completely developed in this period of his life. By the time an individual attains his twentieth year, all his mental faculties are fully developed and he is fully equipped to use them in practical life for performing the greatest of works. In the opinion of some people, an individual's mental capacities start receding or deteriorating after he passes the age of 20, or atleast that there is no further development of them. But many researches only serve to disprove this contention. On the basis of researches and study it can be said that man's mental power and capabilities reach their ultimate peak at the age of 35 and 40. This peak is followed by a general decline in mental powers through the deterioration of the physiological machine or the reduction of energy characteristic of old age. Similarly, in attaining to the ages of 35 or 40, the individual reaches the very peak of his learning. At this stage it is also relevant to keep in mind the importance of practice. Although it can be confidently asserted that after the age of forty the nervous system and sense organs of man are susceptible to such changes as reduce his mental power, but it is evident in the case of many scientists and scholars that they have produced their real masterpieces only after they have passed 40. It is said of Sheikh Sadi, the famous Persian poet, that he began the study of Persian after he had crossed 40. Yet, it can generally be said that man's mental powers are at their peak between the ages of 20 and 40, and it is in this period that he is likely to achieve the greatest mental feats. If practice, experience and maturity continues, mental powers are found virtually intact even when the individual descends to old age.

At this stage, the individual is possessed of the quality of self direction since his knowledge and power of reasoning are acute and developed. An adult should do his best to maintain his good habits. Constantly awake and alert individual always learns something even from the most mundane and apparently insipid situations in life. Ambition is another important factor in this stage of life. It is the motive force that constantly propels the individual towards further progress but one should not be blinded by it to the realities of life. Much research and study has succeeded in establishing the fact that the guidance and advice of old people is always desirable in marriage, vocation, etc. and no adult should ignore it. Moral and religious education assumes special significance in this state. As a matter of fact, it is only now that the individual is fully aware of good and bad, and is in a position to mould his future as he desires. This does not mean that the influence of family and society is in any way lessened, but rather that the individual can create his own environment. Sentiments of self respect and benevolence are the basis of an adult's moral education. Briefly, adults can make a success of their lives by taking advantage of their education, the experience of their parents and other older people and by self education.

QUESTIONS FOR EXERCISE

1. What do you mean by intelligence?
2. Trace the intellectual development of children indicating the role of maturation.
3. What do you mean by adolescence? Describe the principal mental characteristics of adolescence.
4. Adolescence is a period of storm and stress. Discuss.

11

Emotional Development

The word 'Emotion' is a derivative of the Latin word 'emovere' which means 'to shudder'. Thus emotion is that state of the individual which deprives him of his equilibrium. In fear his teeth are clenched together, his body shudders and signs of perspiration can be seen upon his forehead. Emotions shake a man violently. Even when the object of his anger is no longer present, the person's arms twitch uncontrollably. Emotions stimulate the energies of the creature and assist him in dealing with emergencies. In emotional condition he performs action which he is incapable of performing in a normal state. But sometimes, though comparatively infrequently, a person is absolutely stupefied and fails to perform even the ordinary activities. These mutually contradictory results bear testimony to the fact that it is difficult to define emotion. Though psychologists have not differentiated between motive and emotion, everyday experience shows that there is some difference. Similarly, some psychologists do not find any difference in physical activities and emotions. But experiments reveal this difference which is by no means negligible.

P.T. Young has defined emotion thus: "Emotion is acute disturbance of the individual as a whole, psychological in origin, involving behaviour, conscious experience and visceral functioning." In Woodworth's opinion "An emotion is a disturbed state of the body. It is a disturbed glandular and muscular activity. Woodworth rightly says that each emotion is a feeling, and each is at the same time a motor set" In this way emotion is that state of the individual in which the body is externally as well as internally upset. This can be clarified by an example of anger.

The emotion of anger is the painful aspect of the pugnacious instinct. Anger in the creature is aroused by any interference in the execution of an instinct generated activity, or by the failure of such activity. Therefore anger is directed upon the interfering object or creature, though not always because sometimes anger is directed to oneself. For example, when angry, clenching of the eye brows, vociferating, kicking, attacking, trembling-these and many other physical activities, or rather disturbances are apparent. The activities in an emotional condition of anger are the opposite of the activities of a person who is struck with fear. In anger a person becomes aggressive.

A child is born possessing some innate emotions, though there is no unanimity of expert opinion concerning the number of such emotions. According to William McDougall there are 14 emotions attached with 14 instincts. The sentiment of self regard is the basis of an individual's character. Besides, the character is also comprised of such desirable emotions as pity, wonder etc. Their development leads two elevation of character. Other emotions that are part and parcel of character but, are not desirable, are fear, anger, hatred etc. The development of such emotions only deprives the individual of his energy as it is consumed in destructive effort resulting in inadequate adaptation to society. Emotions influence an individual's adjustment with other individuals in society and determine his conduct towards them. Although man is a rational animal, much of his conduct is determined by emotions and instincts. Hence, human development is considerably influenced by the emotions. Various emotions arise due to different stimuli conditions. Besides the presence of stimuli, another factor that sometimes hampers the adjustment of an individual is the excess of some one emotion. This is evident in both mental as well as physical adjustment. Emotions change in form as the child grows into the, adult individual. Many detailed studies have revealed that emotions constantly develop and undergo considerable transformation. Emotional development, too, is studied in relation to the individual's situations and conditions. The normal states of the development of a human being are infancy, childhood, adolescence and adulthood. The present study proposes to adopt this division and study emotional development in this context.

EMOTIONAL DEVELOPMENT IN INFANTS

The emotional element is present in the child from his birth, as is evident from his crying and vigorous movement of body parts. These movements bear adequate evidence to the presence of emotion at birth in the child but it is difficult to determines emotion that is related to a particular form or pattern of the child's conduct. Generally, before any emotional activity can be indulged in, the child should be able to interpret the stimulus. Hindrance in the fulfilment of some desire in a child leads to emotional excitation. In infancy, the child is unable to transfer his emotional reactions from one situation to another. The studies that bridges conducted concerning infant emotional states revealed that the child's emotions increase with experience, but they are very changeable and unstable. Anger and fear in infancy are indicative of general obstruction or pain. As the child develops and passes to a higher stage of life, his emotional pattern can be determined with increasing precision and accuracy. In order to study the child's emotions during this age some scientists took photographs of many children depicting such emotions as pain, anger and fear, under normal conditions. In one cinematic study, in which a movie camera was employed, it was revealed that the individual child's conduct during the first few days after his birth does not show any determinate emotions, but within a year, emotions of his nature become more specific and definite. Most observers of a photograph of a ten month old child could determine the emotions with such accuracy and similitude that the concurrence could not be attributed to coincidence.

By the time a child reaches his first six months, his facial expressions and other bodily positions are specific enough to make it possible to distinguish between such emotions as anger and fear. There is continuous variation in the manifestation of emotions during infancy. For some time after birth, the infant smiles when it, sees a human face and later on it also laughs audibly. In studying children of four weeks. Gesell distinguished between expressions of hunger, anger and pain. Even though it differs from child to child yet the expression of these emotions is so specific that the mother can always determine the cause of her child's crying while another child's crying may not convey any meaning to her. Similar expressions of fear, pleasure and affection can be seen in the child's first year of life.

In the process of this emotional development, the child gradually evolves definite pattern of reaction to stimuli that cause emotional reaction. In the beginning, the child's activity, on becoming angry, is not definite and neither is there any solution of the situation that gives rise to anger. As the child grows older, he exhibits a more patterned effort in solving the problem that arouses anger in him. Nevertheless, some inconsistent activities are always to be seen in an individual's emotional behaviour. Besides emotional expression, the intensity of emotion can also be used as a criterion of distinguishing between emotional states. Emotional expression is intense at times, while at others it is comparatively calm and weak. The child who literally becomes mad when deprived of his feeding bottle, at the age of seven months, shows much more composure and less violence when he has occasion to be angry at seven years. In this manner, the gradual development of emotional states is accompanied by variations in emotional intensity as well, although even in adult life some people behave with almost lunatic violence when emotionally disturbed, As the infant approaches childhood, his crying and yelling becomes considerably less than during earlier infancy. This condition is more particularly noticeable in the child's behaviour outside the house. This change is the result of many factors. By the time he enters childhood, the infant is in a position to express the feelings through language. He can substitute abusive language for crying when incensed at something. He also realizes that it may not be desirable or proper for him to show his anger at all times. Even if he has cause to be angry with someone older than himself, he can indiscreetly express his displeasure as he is likely to be beaten for his trouble. Another reason is that his friends tease him if he cries, and this injures his self respect, with the result that he chooses other alternatives for expressing his feelings of resentment. In the later stages of infancy, the child moreover reacts less violently to emotionally disturbing situations. Nevertheless, novel situations that he comes across provide him with emotional experiences, but the result that any situation will have upon him depends on his learning and maturity. In the first six or seven months, a child runs shy of a strange face and runs from it, because by then it then it achieves enough maturity to distinguish between familiar and strange faces. It is very essential that in one's dealings with children one should understand their emotions. In this connection parents and teachers must exercise proper restraint and caution, since this is the age in which the child can be moulded as desired, and emotional development is an important aspect of his development. The child's emotionality is completely bound up to his hopes, desires and ambitions. An important element in the child's emotional development is the affection that others give him as well as the affection that he himself harbours for others. Any loss of his affection can lead to very strong feelings of jealousy, resulting in serious adjustment problems in the family. As the child starts taking interest in new things that come within his sphere, the occasions that bring him pleasure and satisfaction also change. He finds much pleasure in learning and finds occasion for exercising the knowledge of climbing stairs, riding cycles, etc. The scope of a child's activities widens alongwith the increase and development in his abilities, a corollary of which is an increase in opportunities for greater and more diversified emotional experience. In this manner, a child's emotional development moves parallel to his physical and mental development. One also sees emotional reactions in children to some imaginary situations because in his infancy the child is very sensitively imaginative. Experience of emotions and feeling from novel things increase as his objectives, purposes, desires and plans increase. Watson believed that a new born infant has three, fundamental emotions-fear, anger and love. Sherman and Bridges have criticised Watson's contention on the basis of considerable experimentation. Nevertheless, most other psychologists also accept Watson's enumeration of three emotions in the infant, and that he develops his other emotions by the mixture of these basic emotions. Hatred, for example, is the result of a mixture of anger, fear and indifference. As the age of the infant increases, the, feelings and expressions of these emotions also change. Experiments have indicated that while a two year old child is not afraid of a snake, one of four year is. One important element in these changes is the imitation of the elder's behaviour.

EMOTIONAL EDUCATION IN INFANCY

The parents and teachers should be careful that no particular emotion in the child reaches a stage of excessive or extreme intensity as this sometimes leads to serious physical damage or impoverishment. Extreme fear can even lead to death. Most of the things of which a child is afraid create fear in him only because he has learned to fear them. Parents and other near relatives are capable, of making a child a hero, a coward, an angry or placid individual, irritable or forbearing. Concrete behavioural examples are more effective and influential than lectures. If the parents set the child good example, he is more likely to learn to control his emotional expression. Along similar lines various circumstances can be stimulated in the family whereby the development of undesirable emotions in the child is obviated, while the expression of desirable ones is encouraged. For example, if the parents meet out fair and equal love to all the children there is no jealousy among them on this account. Secondly, if the parents are intimate with the children, many emotional tensions are avoided. Emotional development of a child is further open to such influences as the behaviour of other children in the neighbourhood because when the child is two or three he goes out to play with children of his own age, and takes part in all kinds of activities. The parents should also try to keep an eye on the child's companions and game programmes as bad company is almost certain to have undesirable effect on his emotional development. It is said that many of the world's bravest people become brave because they heard their parents talking of the bravery of bygone heroes. Hence, emotional development depends in the main upon the education given by parents and teachers.

EMOTIONAL DEVELOPMENT DURING CHILDHOOD

Emotional development during childhood is more susceptible to the influence of friend circle than of the family. The friends can either belong to the neighbourhood or to the school. It is this age that the child first goes to school. Hence, his emotional development is now also open to such influences as the teacher's behaviour and the atmosphere within the school and classroom. The proper emotions can be willfully created in the child by the teachers setting the appropriate examples, the same measure also being effective negatively in blocking and preventing the development of undesirable emotions. Creating a proper atmosphere for the child is equally important. He must be encouraged to take interest while at the same time the child should have a sense of belonging and should not feel a stranger in school. These are the methods by means of which ideal character can be developed in the child. In childhood, the manifestation of emotions becomes more specific and precise but the child is devoid of the impetuosity of infancy. At the same time, the child shows no reaction to many things that in infancy led him to react violently. He does not show anger at being bathed or dressed, neither does he show any fear of strangers. In this age, the child is almost invariably the member of some one or the other group, in the activities of which he participates actively. Sometimes, undesirable and harmful tensions and hatred develop among different groups, in which case it is necessary for the teachers and well wishers to intervene and remove the tension generated, as such tensions can lead to the development of undesirable emotions and complexes. Fear is engendered in the child if physical punishment is used to teach him, the outcome being his desire to escape from study. Gentle behaviour on the part of the teacher pays dividends in the form of proper emotional development and adjustment. It is for this reason that more women than men are employed to teach small children. The atmosphere in both school and home should be as free as possible since only then the child can freely manifest emotions. If free expression of emotions is hindered because of the presence of excessive control and strict discipline, the child develops all kinds of mental complexes which are very harmful as regards his mental health and development. Presence of good ideals in healthy school and domestic atmosphere is itself a sufficient condition for the natural development of audible emotions. Similarly, if the ideals present in the school and at home are low and detestable, then even the greatest amount of precaution and care cannot avoid the development of improper emotions. Repression only leads to the suppression or control of the expression of emotions, but not their destruction, and this repression is often more dangerous than if the emotions were expressed.

EMOTIONAL DEVELOPMENT IN ADOLESCENCE

Adolescence is the period of life when the individual shows signs of development in every respect. Hence, it is only natural that the expression of emotion should undergo similar modification. For example, the adolescent is very sensitive to any injury to his prestige. A physical deformity is so magnified in its evil effects that it even enters his dreaming state and modifies it. Many of his emotions he suppresses externally but they find expression in the form of day dreams. The high intensity of the sexual instinct is one reason why the adolescent is more prone to react to love than to any other emotion. This emotion finds expression in the form of excessive and almost obsessional attraction to the individuals of the other sex. As the adolescent's field of knowledge widens, the situations that give rise to emotions in him also change. He becomes angry if his country is attacked by another nation, he can even show displeasure at any instance of injustice that comes to his notice, and he can even rebel against society. He develops hatred for authority if administration is strict.

EDUCATIONAL MATURITY IN ADULTHOOD

Emotional development reaches its maturity in adulthood. In these stages, the various emotions such as fear, anger, hatred, discrimination, pleasure, etc., can be distinctly seen in an individual, and generally their patterns of expression can also be recognised. Emotional reactions in this age are influenced by such complex factors as values, desires, ideals, viewpoints and common ethos of the society. Manifestation of emotions also is relatively refined, the adult being normally possessing the discretion to hide his emotions when the occasion so requires. Even when angry, he does not immediately give it expression but stores it in his mind to manifest it sometime days later when the opportunity presents itself. In this age, the various problems that face the individual concern vocation, marriage, family and new responsibilities, being problems that exert considerable influence on his emotional development. If these problems are properly solved, then his emotional development proceeds along desirable paths. On the other hand, such problems as failure to secure the desired profession, continued unemployment, undesirable marriage, increase in the number of children, unsound economic position, absence of domestic calm and bliss can only help to create such emotions as anger, fear, hatred, jealousy, insecurity, etc.

EMOTION, SENTIMENT AND CHARACTER

Emotion is the intense disturbance of an individual. It is a mental activity which comprehends feeling and motor set, an experience and activity that is directed by the individual's internal structure. It is temporary, though it disturbs the individual while it lasts. On the other hand, sentiment is a permanent structure. It is a mental creation that exists even when the occasion for its manifestation has passed. This difference lies in the mental facts and mental activities, of the structure of nervous combinations or the one extension of mental combinations on the one hand, and the experiences and activities organised by that structure on the other. In the words of William McDougall, "The emotion is a mode of experience a way of functioning and a way of activity. The sentiment is a fact of structure, an organised system of disposition which endures, in a more or less quiescent condition, between the occasions upon which it is brought into activity."

Sentiment determines the form of emotions. In this manner sentiment is the cause of emotions, and emotions are the result of sentiment. But, on the other hand, emotions are also the causes of sentiments and sentiments their results, as sentiments are formed out of emotions. The kind or nature of emotions that we have regarding a person or an object will determine the sentiment that will be formed regarding it.

Development of Sentiment

Some emotions are present innately in the human being. These are called simple emotions, examples of which are fear, surprise, anger, sorrow, etc. Besides these, some other emotions are also developed such as jealousy, love, hate, etc. As the social circumstances of an individual undergo change, these emotions are inspired by various objects. For example, one person may give him cause to fear while another may encourage him to love and affection. When many emotions concerning the same object or individual combine to form a permanent structure, then a sentiment regarding that individual or object is formed that conforms to the original emotions which it had aroused. A child loves the mother and her presence gives him pleasure, as she satisfies his emotions of possession, sexuality, pleasure, love, etc. Hence, the child develops a sentiment regarding the mother. That is a composite of these emotions.

Sentiment and Character

Character is the system or organisation of sentiments. And in this system one master sentiment rules over all the other sentiments. As long as the individual's sentiments are scattered and lack system, he has no character. Thus any individual who exhibits signs of being led by one sentiment at one time and by another at another time is called characterless if the term is interpreted in the psychological sense. It is in this sense that it has been remarked that women have no character. In the character formation, the individual's sentiment of self regard directs his emotions of love, friendship, hatred etc. From the moral viewpoint, a character is high if the master sentiment is high and valuable, but if it is not so, the character is said to be low. In this way, it is one thing for a character to be organised and stable, and another to be high or low. One is a psychological concept while the other is a moral concept.

Moral Character and Character

Here, it is essential to keep it in mind that fundamentally, character does not imply moral character. It was the German philosopher Immanual Kant who chose to interpret the term character in the sense of moral character. In ancient Greece, the term character referred to the moulds used for making coins. In order to prevent the minting of false coins, each mould was so formed as to be difficult of imitation. The same sense continued even into modern English. It is for this reason! that some people qualify the term, and use the expression ethical character if they want to distinguish between good and bad character. In the words of Skinner, "One's character, defined by the history of the word is all that makes him or her unique, different from everyone else." In this manner, character includes all those special features of an individual's personality that serve to make him a distinctive individual. Yet character is more commonly interpreted to be a system or organisation of sentiments.

Sentiment and Culture

The intimate relation between character and sentiment is further evinced by the evolution or different kinds of character in different cultures. Sentiment is closely related to culture, since in every culture attempts are made to develop certain definite sentiments in an individual so that his social adaptation is facilitated. Concerning the importance of sentiment in society, William McDougall has written, "The growth or sentiments is of utmost importance for the character and conduct of individuals and of societies it is the organisation of the affective and conative life. In the absence of sentiments our emotional life would be a mere chaos without order, consistency or continuity of any kind and all our social relations and conduct, being based on the emotions and their impulses, would be correspondingly chaotic, unpredictable and unstable." An individual's social conduct is guided by some values, values that are related to his sentiments Hence, sentiments have a special significance for the individual's character. For example, individuals who attach much value to sacrifice, service or benevolence usually possess sentiments of patriotism, linguistic attachment or philanthropy. It need hardly be pointed out that in the absence of these sentiments no such values could possibly survive.

PROCESS OF CHARACTER FORMATION

The process of Character formation originates in childhood, to which the child's life in the home and school, and social and cultural life in his surroundings contribute. Character is formed of the organization of sentiments. Sentiments are formed of the organisation of emotions. Some emotions are innate while others are acquired. Both the acquired as well as the innate emotions contribute to the formation of sentiments. In social situations different emotions become bound up with different objects due to the simple and natural process of mental association. For example, the child delights in his mothers approach and he manifests the emotion of love towards her. If he comes to harm through the agency of some animal or situation, he learns to fear it. When fear is strengthened by indifference and anger, hatred is generated. Gradually, these various sentiments combine into a complex that is called character. An individual's character is known through the ruling or prominent sentiment which directs all the other sentiments. In the character of a patriot, for example, the sentiment of love of country becomes the sentiment of self regard, and all other sentiments are directed by it.

1. **Character and Culture** Character formation is also influenced to a considerable extent by culture, since different values and different sentiments develop in different cultures. In the words of Kimball Young, "Sentiments are products of cultural conditioning, they may be closely allied to our fundamental values, or they may be relatively fleeting in their strength and importance." In this way, individuals develop differing sentiments in dissimilar cultural situations. For example, on the one hand, at one place the sentiment of world brotherhood is developed, while on the other the sentiment of racism leads the white to hate the black. The sentiments that people of a nation have for their national flag, national anthem, etc., are not to be seen among the nomadic tribes. The presence of the sentiment regarding an object completely changes its value from its material worth. Love letters and engagement rings carry far more value than their material

worth for the possessor. But their value depends upon the worth of engagement of marriage that a particular culture allows or considers feasible. If marriage is considered less valuable, all things attached to it will naturally have less value. Consequently, the sentiments concerning all these objects will be less strong. In this way, the individual's moral, aesthetic, social and religious sentiments are determined by his cultural environment. They change if the environment changes. Sentiments help the individual in his adjustment to culture, so that any change in culture is reflected in changes in this adaptation. Yet, some sentiments may also be caused by the individual's peculiar and unique nature. If they are not consistent with the cultural environment, these sentiments are given the stigma of abnormality and efforts are made to cure the individual. Conforming to the cultural environment they come to be treated as desirable, even though in a different culture they may be regarded with aversion.

2. **Character and Habit.** Habits are important elements in the individual's behaviour. Much of his day to day conduct is determined by his habits. Thus, character is expressed in habits, though it cannot be said that character is the sum total of habits.
3. **Character and Volition.** Volition is a very important element in character. It is will power that develops the character. People of strong wills stick to their principles without flinching, while the weak willed people show a lack of this spirit and are easily diverted from their paths by the least obstruction. Hence, the intelligent teacher tries to develop volition in his students. For this it is essential that every student should be given the maximum possible opportunity for performing some task on his own initiative. This helps to maintain their active tendency, and their volition also improves. The child should be encouraged to complete the day to day tasks that are set to him, and when he successfully, completes his work, he should be praised. Failure to do this discourages the child, and he develops the sense of lack of confidence. It should also be kept in mind that the student should not be loaded with so many tasks that it becomes impossible for him to perform any, since this too reduces his ability to determine the course for himself.
4. **Character and Imitation.** Imitation is an important element in the psychological development of character. It is a matter of common sense that children imitate the conduct of teachers and all family members who are senior to them in respect of age. Teachers and parents represent ideals to the child, whom

he imitates both consciously and unconsciously. Hence, it is desirable that the examples set to the child by the teachers and parents should be of brave and high characters. Before the teachers and parents can hope to improve children, they will to improve themselves.

5. **Character and Suggestion.** Formation and development of character is also duly influenced by suggestion. These suggestions to the child can be conveyed through good stories, tales and high ideals. From the psychological viewpoint, it is the positive rather than the negative mandate that gives the more adequate and effective suggestion to the child. If the children are to be prevented from plucking flowers, it is much better to direct them to protect flowers than directing them not to pluck flowers. Similar sensible and psychological methods should be applied in guiding the child in other matters.

6. **Effect of Reward and Punishment on Character.** Punishment and reward also occupy an important place in the development of character. In the ancient system of education, punishment was an important element. One English proverb prevalent at the time was 'Spare the rod and spoil the child.' But the application of psychology to the field of education has led to continuous decline in the importance of punishment in education. According to Mumford, if punishment can at all be effective, the most it can do is to prevent doing of some wrong. In this way, the main function of punishment is negative, as it can only prevent the performing of some apparently harmful activity by the child. But it cannot help the development of the child's character as such development requires, the presence of high and valuable sentiments in him. But this need not be interpreted to mean that punishment should never be applied. Even modern psychologists are not averse to the occasional and judicious use of the rod; but they sanction it only if all other practices fail to yield any positive results. According to Dumville, we cannot completely deprive the educational system of punishment. Sometimes punishment appears to be the only tool that can prevent some want on misconduct. But punishment is a measure that is to be brought into force when all other tools have failed, In fact, as Pestalozzi has pointed out, punishment can be meted out even when the school is instituted as the house of love, since it helps in the development of character. But it is best to avoid its use as far as possible. What is most essential in this respect is that the individual being punished should harbour no doubts in his mind as to the purpose of punishment. He should be

completely aware of the fact that the punishment is intended for his own improvement and not inspired by a feeling of retribution, because the child's loss of faith in his teachers and parents can have only the worst effect upon him. It is equally incorrect to give extreme punishment since it either causes a loss of confidence in the child or strengthens hatred and disgust. This can only hinder the progress and development of his character.

7. **Character and Emotion.** A child's character development is improved by developing high sentiments in the child. Sentiments are created by emotions, The development of proper and high sentiments in a child demands psychologically effective behaviour on the part or his parents and teachers. From the psychological viewpoint, the conduct of parents and teachers regarding children should be loving and sympathetic, but of course, this, hardly means that the child, be spoiled with excessive affection and tolerance, even in the matter of bad habits If a proper character is to be evolved in a child, it is essential that he be prevented from, acquiring bad habits and this is a task which needs the co-operation of both parents. What more often happens is that while one parent is scolding the child, the other takes his side in the argument, which can only have a bad effect upon the child. Nevertheless, as long as possible the only weapon to be used with a child is the rod of love, wielded with understanding and insight, since the absence of love, and affection leaves the child's emotional aspect undeveloped and he does not attain to the full maturity which is desired.

8. **Character and Knowledge.** Finally, increase in knowledge is also important for the development of character. Herbart has stressed the importance of knowledge in character development. A person who is, not knowledgeable is not in a position to make the distinction between good and bad, with the result the complete development of character does not occur. It is for this reason that education is an important, tool of character development, although this is no reason to suppose that the uneducated or illiterate person is devoid of character. In fact, education brings within reach all the means of developing character. And, as long as the individual himself does not use these means to the best advantage, his character is not likely to develop to any extent. In the process, the teachers and parents can only help.

CONTROL OF EMOTIONS

A child's behaviour is more guided by his emotions than by his intellect or reason. His behaviour distinctly manifests the influence of emotions such as fear, love anger hatred, etc. Some emotions guide him to extremely desirable and likeable forms of conduct but when in the grip of other emotions, be descends to the level of beasts and behaves in the most detestable manner that can only lead to sensure from his elders. Thus, the necessity of controlling emotions becomes evident. Experience and behaviour show the extent to which emotional imbalance is harmful both to the body and the mind, as it results in all kinds of nervous and mental diseases. But the control of emotions through their repression is no less harmful. Psychoanalysts have made a detailed analysis of the various neuroses that result from such repressions. The best methods of controlling emotions, in fact, is to prevent the occasions and opportunities that excite emotions. Auto-suggestion is another means of controlling emotions. If one makes it a practice to avoid using emotions they will weaken through disuse and atrophy. When the stimulus of one particular emotion is willfully conjoined to another emotion, the undesirable emotion will disappear. If the emotions can also be expressed through some harmless and innocent channel, then the excitation that accompanies emotions is destroyed thus facilitating the control of that emotion.

CONTROL OF EMOTIONS THROUGH SUBLIMATION

The best method of controlling emotions is their sublimation. It changes the very form of the emotion. A child's conduct can be improved by instilling in him love towards good habits, hatred for bad ones, anger for injustice, curiosity towards nature, etc. Once these emotions are conjoined to the right object, his behaviour takes a good turn. Sublimation does not destroy the emotion; it only changes the mode of its expression. It achieves the necessary control while avoiding all the damage that is the inevitable corollary of repression. It also avoids the formation of emotional complexes. As psychoanalytic study has revealed, all the greatest poets, authors, scientists, leaders, saints and great persons could contribute to human well being only through the sublimation of their emotions. The compositions and creations of both Tulsidas and Kalidas clearly show the result of sublimation of their love for the opposite sex, as a result of which their sexual instinct was sublimated into love of God. Character development cannot be left to fate. It needs the hardest and unbending effort. And the sublimation of emotions is a very important aspect of it.

ANGER

When a child is in the grip of anger one sees various kinds of agitated facial expressions to destructive behaviour. A child discovers early in life that by feigning anger he can attract the attention of others and can often obtain anything he desires. Hence, as he grows older he learns to adopt varying forms of anger to suit varying situations. But, obviously, the adult has greater occasions to display anger than the child.

Children become angry normally when something obstructs the fulfilment of their natural needs or the performance of some activity, or even if their self-respect is injured. When the child, for example, is playing, he does not like to be interrupted, but if he is then he becomes angry. Even when the child wants grown up people to pay attention to him and they do not, he becomes angry.

Causes and Results of Anger

In an angry mood the child is capable of behaving in many ways. Although his behaviour is determined by the situation, variations can be seen to be caused by virtue of age and sex. Besides, individual differences also account for the variations in the expression of emotion. When the child is angry he can be seen howling, screaming, stamping his feet, scratching and biting, hitting out and throwing things about or breaking them. A child's expression of anger is more vehement than that of the adult, for the child almost goes mad with anger. He throws himself on the ground, without caring whether he will hurt himself and flings his arms and legs all over the place. This anger may come about because of common place things, such as somebody's taking away his marble or toy or not giving him something he wants very much. As the child grows older his anger becomes concentrated upon some object or individual. The patterns of his expression of anger also undergo change. A grown up child will either criticise or resort to abuse, but he will not throw himself upon the ground or start crying immediately. In adolescence the expression of anger takes on an even more explicit form. Although the strength of the emotion does not diminish it normally takes oral expression. In almost all cases the anger is directed to attracting attention or obtaining some desired thing.

The reaction of anger can be seen even in a child of 15 months although it becomes more explicit only when the age of two or three has been attained. Upto the age of nine the child is seen to resort to anger on fewer occasions. Beyond this age anger again takes on strength. It will be seen that college-going children show greater control on their emotion than children who do not attend school because the former realise that expression of anger may bring about undesirable results. Yet some children are seen indulging in antisocial activity in schools because of anger. This activity takes the form of constant wrangling, pushing and shoving, fighting, etc. But in this stage anger is mostly expressed through words.

Means of Removing Anger

In a social situation the child cannot be allowed to express this anger in any way he chooses, although it is true that at times anger helps in adjusting oneself to a particular situation. If the child's anger is to be eliminated it is necessary to draw his attention away from the object agitating him and to turn it towards some other stimulus. This will split his attention and change his mood. If the child is to learn to control his anger it is necessary that the behaviour of the adults around should be determined and explicit, not vacillating. It should be made obvious to the child that his anger will not reap a rich harvest. Yet, when anything is done, it is necessary to think of the child and his situation, for, many times the causes of anger may be biological. Children suffering from ill health and weakness are inclined to the irritable. Another cause of anger is immaturity. In such a condition it is more important to pay attention to his health. He should be given a nourishing and regulated diet, and be allowed to sleep many times. There should be balance between his periods of activity and of rest. He should be encouraged to be happy and this can happen only when he is surrounded by people who know how to be happy. If the child's anger is to be controlled, his expressions of anger must be criticised but not to be such an extent as to further aggravate it. In any case, constructive suggestions are always better than criticism. The child should be helped to understand that anger will only harm him and that controlling anger will give him pleasure. But if the child's anger is justified it should not be repressed. In such cases both the child and the adult must have a clear understanding of the situation. Calming an angry child can be done by praising him and winning his approval. Criticism never reduces the child's anger, it only fans the flames.

As has been pointed out in certain circumstances, he expression of anger is justified. It is only natural for the child to be angry if injustice has been done to him. This helps him to overcome fear and to learn to face situations, yet extremely destructive anger injures the child's mind and body. In this way, anger can help the child to get out of a tight situation when such anger is justified but when his anger is frittered away on useless things he does injury to himself. Adults should teach children to control anger only when they have understood the utility of it. Frustration or repression of anger is not desirable in any situation.

JEALOUSY

Causes of Jealousy

Children can be jealous of other children over almost anything. Normally this jealousy arises when the child observes another child's superiority in some respect. Superiority may be the result of something that he possesses or some power that he may be capable of exerting or his success in some field. This causes the jealous child to feel afraid and inferior. It angers the jealous child although he cannot express anger. Obviously, jealousy is a mental state in which the emotions of inferiority, dependence, fear and anger are mixed up. A major cause of jealousy in children is the loss of the parents' love or the fear of such loss. Whenever a new child enters the family the existing child fears that now the parents will forget him, and if this fear turns into reality the child becomes jealous of the intruder. Apart from the loss of love that he suffers, the child feels that his self-respect has been injured, and this adds to the jealousy. Jealousy, therefore, is normally connected with other individuals. Whenever the child finds that his respect, love or some physical possession has been taken by another child he becomes jealous of him. At times this jealousy is expressed in violent actions but more often its expression is indirect. Anger often accompanies jealousy, along with the desire to attack or to avenge oneself. Fear and inferiority also go to make up jealousy. Jealousy has serious repercussions on the child's personality only when it is permanent, although it can be both permanent or short-lived. Temporary moments of jealousy occur to every individual at some or the other stage of his life, and hence it is normal behaviour which causes no particular harm.

It is obvious from the preamble that the causes of jealousy should be looked for in social situations. At home the parents and the teacher in school are the unwitting agents of jealousy. When a new child is born to them the parents lavish on him so much love and affection that the old child is forgotten and has ample cause to be jealous. This happens particularly when the time gap between the two children is very small. If the difference is more than 18 months then the older child is not likely to become jealous of the fresh arrival. In fact, he will himself shower affection upon it.

Results of Jealousy

There can be many consequences of jealousy in the child. On the one hand he may refuse to eat, or feign illness, or develop a habit of thumb sucking or bedwetting. On the other hand he may try to cause injury to the object of his jealousy. Older children express their jealousy by fighting, quarrelling, boasting, laughing at or spreading rumours about the individual of which they are jealous. Individual differences result in varying, expressions of jealousy. One, major cause of jealousy within the family is the different treatment meted out to different children by the parents. This makes the child feel that he is being ignored or that he is being considered inferior to others. This feeling of inferiority is then compensated by shouting or indulging in destructive activity. Mothers who give very obvious expression to their extraordinary love cause jealousy among their children.

Means of Removing Jealousy

If jealousy is to be done away with, it is necessary for the parents to treat their children equally and to love them equally. If jealousy against the, newly arrived child is to be avoided, it is best to let other children play with his toys. This makes no difference to the little one but it makes the older child feel happy because he thinks that the young one's arrival has been the cause of his getting more toys. Another thing which plays an important part in jealousy is the sense of authority. For this reason it is necessary that all the children in the family be given different things in uniform quantity. In some cases jealousy acquired in childhood is retained for a very long period and the adult then becomes jealous by nature. But in all cases of jealousy the blame does not automatically rest at the parent's door because individual differences also account for it to some extent. When a child learns early in life that he is inferior to his brothers and sisters for some reason, he becomes jealous of them because he is afraid that he will not keen pace with them and will have to suffer loss of respect on that account. For this reasons it is not always possible for the parents to control jealousy within the family. Despite this if one behaves in an intelligent and responsible manner jealousy can be reduced. In any case its more violent manifestations can be regulated and finally controlled. Jealousy can be of advantage when, like anger, it inspires the child to make greater effort to make up for the deficiency. Jealousy, like anger, therefore, need not always be discouraged. It is desirable for the teacher and the parents to behave in such a manner towards their wards that the latter should have no occasion to become jealous.

FRIENDSHIP

Friendship is normally taken to mean the mutual intimacy and ties of affection between two individuals. It may be short enough to last no more than two days or permanent enough to last the lifetime of the two parties. Children normally tend to form friendships from their third or forth year. Often one of the two children tends to overshadow the other, but at times the relationship is reversed and the master takes on the mantle of the slave. Excessive friendship between two children often hinders their forming contacts with others and for this reason such strong relationship should be discouraged in the earlier stages. It is desirable for the child to live in a situation where he comes into contact with a number of children.

Children form friends for the same reason that adults form friendships. Children of the same age easily become friends, although the mental ability and physical stature of the two parties also play important parts. Some children become friends because they are of the same age while more often friendships are formed by virtue of having similar sociability or intelligence or of belonging to the same class. Similarity of interests forms another bond. To begin with, some children may experience difficulty in forming friendships. This happens particularly when a child changes his group, because the children in this group do not immediately take notice of the newcomer. If he is not discouraged by this indifference some one child will gradually befriend him and then his acquaintance will grow. At times the child who has extended the hand of friendship leaves the group to befriend the outsider, but then he is faced with a choice between, his group and the intruder. He may either choose between the two or he may succeed in persuading his group to adopt the newcomer.

In the social situation an individual must be possessed of certain qualities if he is to make friends. Many psychologists have written thought-provoking books on the subject. If the child possesses such qualities he will make friends but at times the child has to be helped by adults in this. If such a child is left to fend for himself he will more possibly make enemies of the other children. This often happens when the child has been allowed to adopt an attitude of superiority in the family.

Children make friends in the family, in school, on the playground and around the neighbourhood. It is believed that friendships formed on the playground are the most lasting. Children do not take notice of sex in making friends, particularly in the smaller classes the child makes friends with both girls and boys. Again, the child's friends in school may not be his friends outside the school because this depends upon the occasions they have of meeting outside the school. Many children from some friendships in college or school, while they have other friends made in a neighbourhood. Children should always be encouraged to behave in a friendly manner towards the other children. They should be encouraged to realise the importance of living peacefully with others. But in the majority of cases the child should be allowed to make his own friends so that he can form normal relationships and understand social qualities.

ROLE OF MOTHER

The mother occupies a very important place in the child's life. In the first few months of his life he is entirely dependent upon his mother for the satisfaction of his physical and mental needs. For many more years it is the mother who satisfies his psychological requirements. Her influence begins to diminish only when he begins to play with other children before he goes to school his mother is the single major influence. When he goes to school the teacher becomes an important influence in his life, yet at no stage during childhood does the importance of the mother ever decrease. It has been seen that male children have greater emotional attachment with the mother than female children.

If a mother so desires she can teach the child anything she wants, because she is loved most by the child. It is necessary for her to attend to the child's physical, mental, emotional, moral, aesthetic and social development. A child's education in these spheres can be achieved through telling him different kind of stories and giving him, examples. Both excessive love and excessive criticisms are undesirable. A child should be confident that his parents will always behave with fairness and justice, for only then will he obey them. A mother can teach the child about good conduct and character by herself putting the right ideals before him. This radical influence of the mother can be seen in the lives of all the great leaders of the world.

PRE-MATURE CHILDREN

One does come across children who behave and talk either like children older than themselves or like adults. Such children are called premature, for they are children who have achieved maturity in advance of their age. In fact, this premature development proves an obstacle in the normal development and health of the child. Such a child does not behave like other children but in a very young age appears thoughtful, serious and anxious like adults. Prematurity of this kind is caused by the family environment. Cases of premature development are common in families in which the child has to shoulder the family burden at an early age, or the child is not allowed sufficient time in which to play and enjoy himself, or the child has to devote much of his time to doing the work in the home. An obvious cause of prematurity, therefore, is that the child, much before his time, has to acquire the traits and behaviour patterns of the adult because his family circumstances have forced him to. They become conscious of the difficulties of life at such an early age that they behave like adults. In poor families, poverty and the lack of the good thing of life themselves cause prematurity. But when children in prosperous families give evidence of the premature development the causes have to be traced to mental and the social sphere. Such children should be encouraged to play with other children of their own age. In doing so they can behave like other children, yet it is not desirable to insist upon this because normal development is then even more hindered.

INFERIORITY COMPLEX

Generally speaking, it can be said that almost every child has to go through a situation in life which he feels backward, inferior and weak. Poverty may cause feelings of inferiority, or the realisation that one suffers from some physiological defect. Under normal circumstances the child can make some adjustment with a situation of this kind by consoling himself. He will then avoid developing any mental complex. If this happens the sense of inferiority may actually prove beneficial because it may spur the child on to greater effort to remove the cause of this inferiority. Demosthenes, the famous Greek orator, used to stutter in his speech as a child. He rid himself of this defect and avoided an inferiority complex by going to the beach and trying to speak with pebbles in his mouth. He gained such mastery over his speech that he became one of the greatest orators of the Greek world. In a similar incident of man's perpetual fight against weakness Theordore Roosevelt turned to horse riding to overcome physical feebleness.

Cures of this kind do take place, but they are not overcome. Some children cannot overcome the cause of their inferiority in such a direct manner and hence the inferiority becomes a complex in their minds. This complex then develops many other mental characteristics. Mental disease is a common result of the inferiority complex. Social adjustment deteriorates instead of improving. In order to compensate for their feelings of inferiority they indulge in anti-social activity. This happens particularly when the child is constantly scolded by the teacher in school and ignored by the parents at home. He turns to crime. When he finds that he cannot restrain his self-respect by any of the specially recognised means he feels compelled to try anti-social means.

If people suffering from an inferiority complex are to be cured, it is necessary that the cause of their inferiority should be removed.

EMOTIONAL PROBLEMS

Individual differences play a minor role in determining the nature of the emotional problems of children, for, in most cases, these problems are common to many children. One major problem, concerns the love of the parents for their child. If the child gets less affection than he needs then his feeling of insecurity and dependence take a deep root, while excessive love serves to disturb the child's balance. The solution of the problem lies in the parent's exercising proper care in lavishing affection on their offspring. Harm is done either when the love bestowed is not sufficient or is in excess. Another emotional problem common in children is created by the behaviour of other members of the family towards the child. A child develops feelings of jealousy, anger, etc., if his social adjustment with his brothers and sisters is not adequate. If the parents pay greater attention to the child his adjustment within the family can change for the better and his problems can be solved. The third major emotional problem of the child relates to his sexual satisfaction. The child seeks pleasure in certain forms of activity, and if he is prevented from indulging them he may develop some harmful complex. It is necessary for the parents to act with restraint and intelligence in this matter. A child, can develop an inferiority complex if he is weaker than other children. On the other, hand some children develop a superiority complex. A child can be rendered normal if the parents are willing to help and if the child can be given adequate training. One comes across many kinds of fears, anxieties, jealousies in children, although none of them have any apparent cause. Parents can, by their advice and conduct, solve these emotional problems of the child.

RESISTANT BEHAVIOUR

Resistant behaviour is not uncommon among children. If they decide upon one thing they make sure that it is accepted by every one else. At the smallest provocation they will fling themselves on the ground, shout, scream, throw things about and in general raise the roof. They do not tolerate the slightest interference in the fulfilment of their wishes. Basically, such behaviour stems from the conviction of the child that he can get what he wants if he sticks to his point long enough and makes a nuisance of himself. But if the parents make the child feel that resistant behaviour will get him nowhere, the child will soon give it up. At the same time it should be realised that often the child's resistant behaviour has its source in many emotional conflicts and physical weaknesses. These defects make him irritable, and if he is threatened and shouted at, his growth is likely to, become stunted. He then suffers mental and physical injury. Another way, therefore, of curing resistant behaviour in a child is to look after his mental and physical well being. In any case it is essential to remember that no attempt should be made to cure the child of it by frontal attack. If a child is physically deterred from doing something he feels insulted. It would be better if he can be, made to see the folly of his action. A simpler way of overcoming resistant behaviour is to distract the attention of the child when he is in the grip of it. A child should not have many occasions of resorting to this kind of behaviour. For this the family environment should be made suitable. And finally, there is never any reason to grow panicky if the child persists in resistant behaviour, because the child's behaviour pattern changes as he grows older.

PREJUDICE

Prejudice, literally translated, means the formation of opinion about something which has yet to be experienced. Prejudices are formed because of psychological conditions. Among the commonest examples of prejudices is the prejudice people have against foreigners whom they have never seen. In India we see prejudices in Hindus and Muslims about each other. Children normally do not form prejudices on their own because their experience is limited. Their prejudices are formed by the information conveyed to them by the adults in the family. In America, for example, many parents tell their children that in playing with black children they can contract a variety of diseases. This information leads to the formation of a prejudice in the white child against all black children. While this may be unconscious, prejudices are consciously created by parents in the child's mind against things, objects and individuals in order to suit their convenience. This does not mean that the child does not form prejudices from his own experience. If a child does not know an individual particularly well, his expectation of the individual's future behaviour will be based on what he has seen of him in the past. This is a prejudice once a child has been frightened by one bearded man, he will tend to avoid all men with beards.

Prejudices are harmful for they create obstacle in the child's adjustment. A child can not develop properly if he has prejudices. For this reason the parents and the teachers should actively try to remove any prejudices he may have formed.

QUESTIONS FOR EXERCISE

1. "Emotion is a reaction of total organism." Discuss.
2. Describe in brief the emotional development in children.

3. Discuss the role of maturation and learning in the emotional development of children.
4. Write short note on characteristics of childhood emotionality.
5. Discuss the emotional behaviour of the infant with special reference to fear or anger.
6. Explain briefly the causes of the major emotions of fear, anger and jealousy in children. What measures can be adopted to allay or lessen them?
7. Describe the causes of children's anger. How do they express their anger?
8. Write a note on Jealousy in children.
9. Write a short note on Premature children.
10. What are the characteristics of Premature children? Discuss in particular, the intellectual development and emotional behaviour of premature children.
11. What are the characteristics of Premature children? Discuss, the intellectual and emotional behaviour of Premature children.
12. Write a short note on Inferiority Complex.
13. Why do children develop inferiority feeling? How does the feeling manifest in their behaviour? How can they be guarded against such a feeling?
14. What are the common emotional problems of young children? How do they arise? Can you suggest some measures to the parents to prevent these problems?

12

Sexual Development

Being related to the sex glands, sex is organic need. It is a means of giving birth and sustaining the species. It is known by the seasonal menstrual changes in the female mammal. Its Manifestation has become very complex, in view of the restrictions placed by the society, though its importance cannot be denied. Sigmund Freud, the founder of the school of psychoanalysis, believed the sex motive to be the most important and comprehensive of all.

The inception of the sex motive is due to the excretion of a gland. In the male it is caused by the excretion of the sex glands, while in the female due to the ovaries. The circulation of the blood carries it to the brain, the resulting behaviour being of a type not normally observed. The normal activity due to this motive is an interest in the members of the opposite sex, and a particular type of behaviour towards them, the goal being the mating of the male and the female. In the lower species, the sex activity is related to the seasons, being the highest in spring when the day light is of a longer duration. The light has an effect on the brain via the eyes, and it excites the sex instinct.

A distinction between sex drive and lust, similar to the one made in the case of hunger and appetite, must be made. While the drive for sex is based upon the sex organs; lust is kindled by either the beauty or femininity of the female or the masculinity and strength of the male which act as stimuli besides the organs. The proximity of a member of the other sex may also create lust. In human society cinema, colourful, clothes, make-up, etc. are elements which excite lust.

Sex activity in human beings is very complex. Hence in order to ascertain its natural or real form, it has been studied among animals. Rats were experimented upon in this connection. A rotating drum was attached to the rat trap. There is a board in the drum which records its rotation in any direction. The rotation of the drum is a measure of the distance travelled by the mice.

Experiments with this instrument proved that male rats show less activity without any particular pattern of change. The female rat runs a mile in the first three or four days, but on the fourth and fifth day her activity is very much increased. When extremely active she covers a distance of 15 miles in a day. The effect of the ovaries should be investigated because the absence of the sex organs does not alter this behaviour. It seems that this behaviour is due to the excretion of the ovaries. The level of sex activity is reduced by castration but not completely stopped. An injection of testosteron steps up this activity. Thus, the effect of the glandular excretion is unmistakable. Besides the sex glands, other glands such as the pituitary and the adrenal, also affect the sex activity. Though the individual analysis of the effect of the three glands has not been made, it is definitely established that they do play a part in sex behaviour.

Seasons do not affect the sex activity in humans as much as they do in animals. The excretions of the sex glands have a specific effect. With the extraction of the ovaries a development of the signs of femininity in a girl is stunted. But the removal of the sex glands does not substantially affect the sex activity in developed people. Quite possibly, this is the result of the habits formed in the presence of the glands. The sex activity can be restored by an injection of glandular extracts, at a late age, if it is impaired in any way.

The sex motive is not equally intense in every man and woman. The intensity of the motive and the means of its fulfilment vary from individual to individual. Quite a few people are abnormally sexual either due to excessive glandular excretion or social stimulation. The famous Kinsey report has thrown adequate light on the vast differences in human sexual behaviour. Excessive repression leads to the reduction of lust in a normal person. Abnormal sexual practices start in childhood because the child tries to satisfy his sexual motive in some way. These result in many perversions concerning sexual behaviour in adults. These perversions are far more numerous in human beings than in animals due to the social restrictions imposed on the sex motive in human society.

But is there some mating instinct, in humans and animals? As has been mentioned earlier, there is undoubtedly a mating instinct in animal like rats belonging to the lower species. The experiments on rats have shown that a two months old rat reared separatly from the female shows an abundance of activity indicative of the sex instinct, and if released with a female ready to mate, he very soon mates like a normal rat. Even in the absence of previous experience, the rats exhibit a definite pattern of sex behaviour and mating activity when they attain adulthood. Apparently, mating is instinctive in rats because they do not have to learn it. In the higher species the pattern is not so well established. Experiments on chimpanzees, carried out at the Yale University, show that these animals learnt sexual behaviour by trial and error over a long period of time and that the pattern is different in each. Though experiments have not been carried out on human beings, it is obvious that he patterns of sexual behaviour are mostly acquired and learnt by seeing, trial and error or other methods. Therefore, it is difficult to say that there is a mating instinct in men similar to the sex instinct.

Cycles of Sexual Motivation

Sexual behaviour, runs in cycle; *i.e.*, it becomes intense and it disappears. These cycles are of three main types:

(1) **Life Cycle.** In this cycle sexual behaviour is seen more clearly in a major period in the fife of the organism. For, example, youth is such a period.

(2) **Seasonal Cycle.** In this cycle intensity of sexual behaviour in males and females is high in some specific seasons.

(3) **Estrous Cycle.** This cycle depends upon the secretion of endocrine glands. For example in mammalian females changes in intensity of sexual behaviour is seen in different phases of menstrual cycles. There is a low beginning period, a peak period and again a low end period of sexual activity in the cycle. In the human beings and other mammals extensive studies have been made on the above three phases of sexual behaviour. It has been found that many endocrine secretions affect the sexual behaviour of the organism. These are Estrogens, Prolactin and hormones from the anterior pituitary. Useful information about sexual behaviour has also been gathered by many studies of pregnancy. For example, it has been seen from the studies on rats that once pregnancy occurs, there is no sexual drive in the female rat till she gives birth to the babies. But a few hours after the birth of the babies sexual drive again becomes intense in the female.

Influence of Environmental Factors

Besides the endocrine secretions, influence of environmental stimulation on sexual behaviour can be seen in almost all animals. Learning and experience of the organism has also a great influence on it. No generalization can be made about the influence of environment for all the species. But the influence of light is seen in almost all animals. Greater length of the day in winter and spring is an important cause of greater intensity of sexual behaviour in fish, birds and mammals. Light also affects Estrous cycles. This is supported by the experiments on rats. Besides light, the effect of temperature on sexual behaviour has also been established. Influence of olfactory stimulation is also well-known.

Influence of Physiological Factors

Influence of various hormones like androgens and estrogens on sexual behaviour has been established. Giving these hormones to many animals makes them sexually active before the age of maturity. Similarly sexual behaviour can be induced off season by injecting these hormones. It has been observed that sexual potency declines in old age in man and other animals. In lower animals like rats, injection of hormones in old age brings back sexual potency. This has not been successful in the case of man. Physiological factors, besides old age are more important in human beings than in lower animals.

It is clear from the above discussion that sexual behaviour of the organism is affected by sex harmones on the one hand and experience and learning on the other hand. These two influences work through the nervous system. As is clear from the factors given below, beside the harmonal factor sexual behaviour of the organism is also controlled by the neural factors like spinal cord and other brain structures. Sensory stimulation has a special importance in arousing sexual behaviour. Androgens influence the sexual behaviour of male whereas Estrogens influence female behaviour. Spinal cord integrates genital reflexes of males and females Hypothalamus as an integrative centre and organizes the patterns of sexual activity.

Influence of Sensory Factors

As has been said earlier, sensory factors have important role in arousing sexual behaviour. One or more senses may contribute in sexual arousal. Substances having characteristic smells secrete from the genital tract of the female rat or dog; specific type of sounds are given by the cat; skin of the sex organs of monkeys becomes red; and many signs are seen in the birds. Besides these, tactual and kinaesthetic cues have important contribution in the total sexual behaviour. In the absence of these stimulations, change in sexual behaviour may occur. Even if the sensory contributions of other organs are not essential, smell, hearing or vision have important influence in sexual behaviour. But it cannot be said that sexual behaviour of the organism depends totally on the sex organs. Female rats showed normal mating behaviour after removal, of the uterus and, vagina. This finding was also-confirmed by the studies on cats. Thus, taken together, it can be said that sexual behaviour is not aroused by any particular kind of stimulation but on the total amount of relevant sensory stimulation. In some instances it has been seen that hormones have a special contribution in sexual arousal. Besides this, the influence of various structures of the brain is also important. The most important neural structure is cerebral cortext. Hypothalamus is another important structure which acts as an integrative centre. Spinal cord mediates in the control of genital reflexes. These findings have been confirmed by the experiments on rats and cats.

It is clear from the above discussion of physiological aspects of sexual behaviour that stimulation from various senses, harmones and neural structures like hypothalamus and cerebral cortex have important influences in the sexual behaviour of the organisme.

THEORY OF PSYCHO-SEXUAL GENESIS

In the opinion of Freud the sexual instinct in man has biological as well as psychological influence, and he believes that most tendencies that result in mental illness have a psycho-sexual aggressivity genesis. According to Freud, the sexual instinct becomes evident in man in infancy and for this reason frustrations of human life have their origin in infant life. Freud also put forward the contention that from the psychological viewpoint there is no distinction between normal and abnormal individuals and that their behaviour should be elaborated on similar principles and theories. The development of mentally ill people does not differ from those of normal people in kind, and this contention of Freud has been borne out by the, observation of normal and ill children. Just as sex problems are evident in adults along with other frustrations or abnormalities, the children also evince them. A fact that is generally recognised by abnormal psychology today is that every mental disease has its psychological as well as physiological aspect.

Sexual Tendency in Children

Freudian theory of the presence of sexual instinct in children was intensely objectionable, and was severely chastised, but modern sexologists and psychologists as well as physicians recognise this fact. For attaining adulthood in sex it is essential that, infantile sexuality be repressed. The sexual instinct passes through a latent period from about 7 to 14 years of age, after the infantile stage has been passed and before adolescence is attained. During this period the sexual instinct is latent, but later on in youth it is again revived. Freud has always seen the human personality as a being that is involved in interaction with the environmental forces. Through the process of this interaction the individual has to suffer many frustrations and repressions that reap a considerable change in the personality.

Stages in Development of Sex Instinct

Freud has described the following stages in the development of the sex instinct:

1. **Oral Stage.** In this much of the actual activity is confined to oral biting and oral sucking.
2. **Anal Stage.** In this two tendencies are prominent the anal expulsive tendency and the anal retentive tendency. In this stage the child is imparted toilet training and this has considerable influence upon his personality. If too much frustration is effected his personality develops all kinds of abnormalities.
3. **Phallic Stage.** In this condition most of the frustrations are concerned with infantile masturbation.
4. **Period of Latency.** In this the experiences of sexuality are latent, not apparent.
5. **Genital Stage.** In this sexuality is again apparent and following this stage sexuality is manifested in normal adult relationships.

Importance of Sex Development

A normal development of human personality requires essentially that the person's sexual development also be quite normal, since its abnormal development can be the cause of many mental diseases and illnesses. Sexual adjustment in adolescence is a very important factor, and, for this, sex education is desirable. In the five stages of sexual development mentioned in the last section there are present four kinds of frustration, such as oral, anal, phallic and genital frustrations. The form of these frustrations changes nominally in differing cultures. And the extent to which a normal personality can develop in some particular culture depends upon the extent to which normal expression to human tendencies is permitted in its environment.

QUESTION FOR EXERCISE

1. Critically examine the various levels of psycho-sexual development of the child.

13

Moral and Aesthetic Development

MORAL DEVELOPMENT

Moral Development within the Family

A child's moral development, no less than his mental, emotional and social development, passes through, various succeeding stages, being a gradual process. The child's first initiation into the mysteries of good and bad is through his parent's acceptance and rejection of his various actions. Any action that meets with his parent's disapproval and invites their criticism is categorised by the child as bad or wrong. On the other hand, all actions sanctioned and welcomed by the parents are accepted as good and correct. A contributory factor to this opinion is the presence of punishment or reward. Here, the child's moral development is dependent upon his emotional development. An action that automatically results in reward brings him pleasure so he considers it good and right. Where punishment is the result of an action, the child's reaction is the feeling that it is bad, conjoined to the realization that it is wrong. In this way, the child forms his concepts of good and bad, although, evidently, many of such conceptions may be incorrect. For example, in families in which the parents think it incorrect for children of different sexes to play together, the children also consider it undesirable. On the contrary, families that impose no similar restriction help their children to think well of the practice. These notions of good and bad that the child adopts in his infancy continue into a fairly large part of his childhood also. The truth of the matter is that the foundations of a child's moral development are laid in his infancy.

Moral development in School and Neighbourhood

While the child quits the boundaries of the house and wanders out into the neighbourhood in search of suitable companions for his play, he becomes influenced by the notions of the good and bad that prevail among his chosen companions. He adopts the ethos of the group of which he, has become a member. He learns to think in concurrence with the group and think well of things that, have its sanction while he castigates anything that his group chooses to look down upon. It sometimes occurs that he is so profoundly influenced by this new ethos, that he rejects all that he has learned at his mother's knee. It is natural that the child's moral conduct in this age and in childhood should exhibit signs of inconsistency. For example, he thinks ill of lying, stealing, deception under certain circumstances but is prepared to condone such conduct when the circumstances are different. The propriety of his moral behaviour depends to a great extent on his learning. It is further influenced by his reactions, daily life, desires and prejudices. Children accept many things as acceptable and beyond censure when they see their seniors doing them in the school and at home, and having done so they adopt it as a part of their own pattern of conduct. It becomes assimilated in their natural behavioural pattern. Hence, the responsibility of parents and teachers in the child's moral development is very great.

Generally speaking, an individual's moral notions and concepts are determined by laws, traditions, religious ideals, customs, etc. in an individual's development, but there are many instances of exceptions to it. Neither does an individual invariably accept the general concept of propriety in a particular case, nor does he invariably proceed upon the actions he himself thinks correct and proper. Hence, moral development is a complex process in which the action and interaction of an individual and other people surrounding him is of great importance. Even in his infancy, the child does not exclusively depend upon another notions of propriety, but chooses to form his own criterion, however rudimentary it may be. Many studies have shown that sometimes these conceptions are so strongly entrenched in the child's mind that it becomes difficult to change or modify them.

Moral Development during Adolescence

An adolescent's moral development, during the most crucial stage in an individual's development, is peculiarly susceptible to the effects of his mental and social development. Detailed study and analysis has revealed that in this age, the sexual urge of both male and female adolescents is particularly intense. Hence, it is only natural for the notions of good and bad to become associated with sexual behaviour. Since the laws pertaining to sexual behaviour differ considerably in various cultures, the moral concepts and conduct or adolescents do not exhibit any universal conformity but differ according to their culture. Sex education has the best and most profitable influence upon the adolescent's moral development at this stage. Actually, in this age, it is best to utilize the technique of sublimation and modification of manifestation rather than that of suppression. Many educational psychologists also advocate moral and ethical teaching in schools. But it is commonly and generally accepted that moral education is best imparted through practical representation of best ideals and values rather than through academic teaching and preaching of them. It is equally important for both teachers and parents to do their best to set the best example to their wards. Another factor that is equally important in respect of its influence upon the moral development of the child is the atmosphere prevailing in the school.

Influence of Society and Culture

Besides the school and family, the general social atmosphere also affects the moral development of individuals. It is for this reason that moral behaviour and conduct of individuals belonging to cultured and uncivilised societies show such marked differences that they appear almost incompatible. It is in society that an individual's axiological concepts are formed. Although the contemplative among society's members do not blindly conform to the social morality, the greater majority of them do follow, more or less unthinkingly, the general morality prevailing in society. Hence all individuals who set examples to the multitude, individuals such as leaders, great personalities, saints, scientists, literature's, actors, etc., influence the moral development of the individual. In addition to this, more indirect matters such as employment or unemployment, inability to secure the desired profession, economic status of the family, practical adjustment, peace in the family, intellectual and educational status, moral level of friends and intimates, presence of immoral institutions such as prostitution etc., in society, also cast a serious influence upon the moral development of the individual.

Moral development normally exhibits individual variations within very wide limits. There can be no saying what the actual moral implications of a particular instance will be for an individual, though generally speaking, good situations normally have a desirable influence.

AESTHETIC DEVELOPMENT

Development of the Aesthetic Sense in Family

The tendency of creativity and aesthetic appreciation is evident in the child from the very beginning. It is this tendency that is the basis of his aesthetic sense. Emotions also help in this. Young children find much pleasure in drawing all kinds of figures with colours and pencils. The artistic compositions and productions of children are their natural self expression, although elders may find it difficult to find anything artistic in them. This self expression can be further refined through guidance and direction from teachers. If children are encouraged to examine artistic creations, their ability to appreciate and to create art increases gradually. But it should be remembered that it is not possible to develop this aesthetic ability in all children. Similarly, the aesthetic sense, too can also be developed only to a definite extent in children. This development includes many hereditary qualities and environmental factors. Fundamentally, family tendencies are very important. Children of parents who themselves possess aesthetic sense and a creative approach can be expected to progress fairly rapidly in this direction. It is only natural to expect a child to praise his parents if, he observes them drawing pictures, and to try to imitate them. He is also encouraged by the criticisms and comments that are forthcoming from admiring parents. Sometimes, such behaviour is found to be so effective that all the children in a, family do their very best to win the admiration and praise of the parents. Evidence of the effect of family atmosphere upon aesthetic-sense and artistic tendency is implicit in the number of artists and aesthetes that are present within succeeding generations of a family when once a great artists is born in it. Here, both heredity and environment are effective.

Development of the Aesthetic Sense in School

The aesthetic sense of the child next develops in the school. Schools that encourage artistic expression, painting and acting normally develop the child's artistic sense better than other schools that, take such subjects as a matter of course. In the beginning, the child does not care to attend to other's remarks on his artistic expression, and neither is be bothered how closely his painting approximates to the model. In the first and second classes a child does his drawing without any model. But by the time be reaches the third class he makes all possible efforts to draw a model. And in this stage, he is more amenable to comments from his teachers. Extreme criticism has adverse effect because it discourages the child, hence even his blunders should be pointed out with the greatest of tact and discretion. If so handled, the child will normally make his own effort to improve his work.

Method of Expression

Expression of the aesthetic sense takes place through the medium of making clay toys, decorating flower vases, stitching, knitting, music, dance and other arts. Individuals differ in the manner in which they give expression to their artistic cravings. Some children prefer clay modelling to other forms of art while other children find it more diverting to draw pictures with pencil or paint. Aesthetic sense finds better expression if the children are provided with the objects that they desire to have. In schools the decoration of school rooms and verandahs can profitably be left to the children. Development of the aesthetic sense is more influenced by informal educational methods than by formal ones.

Aesthetic Development in Adolescence

Informal education is more influential and consequential in the adolescent stage since in this age, young boys and girls go to colleges to learn various forms of art. Artistic expressions and manifestation of the aesthetic sense in this period of life is influenced by the individual's family background, interest, abilities, means of artistic expression, attitude of the parents and teachers, etc. Besides teaching children the intellectual appreciation of beauty, efforts should be made to inculcate in them a sense of beauty. Such training can be made facile by seeing good films, natural scenic beauty, art galleries, beautiful buildings etc. This has the effect of encouraging the students to appreciate beauty.

Many factors cast important influence upon the child's aesthetic development, the more prominent ones among them being the following:

(1) **Age.** As the child grows older, his aesthetic sense in respect of his clothing, mode of life, interests and tendencies, etc. also gradually develops. Although it is not possible to distinctly define the various stages of aesthetic development according to the child's age, in the same child one can observe progress in the aesthetic sense as he grows older. It is also true that the aesthetic sense that some children possess is so acute as to be unusual even in adults. In his infancy, the child's artistic tendencies find their natural and unmodified expression. Gradually, the artistic sense comes under the influence of his experience as well as his mental physiological capabilities. Important results and conclusions were obtained from experiments concerning the development, with age, of the child's aesthetic sense. In this experiment, the ability of children to keep time to music was put to the test. The maximum possible score being 400, children of two scored 84, of three scored 109, of four scored 153 while those of five obtained 192 points. Evidently, then development of aesthetic sense improves with age.

(2) **Intellectual Development.** The main reason why increase in age influences the development of aesthetic sense is that intellect

increases with age. Generally speaking, each art requires many kinds of abilities, such as sensory acuity, motor activity, perceptual acuity, power of imagination, aesthetic determination, etc. It need hardly be pointed out that as these capacities gradually develop, the child's aesthetic sense will also develop. It is another matter if a child develops so rapidly as to equal or improve upon the general level evident in adults.

(3) **Physical Development.** Certain art forms such as dancing require balance, rhythm and unity. And for this, it is essential that the child attain to a certain minimum level of physical development. If the children who are taught dancing are too small, they will not benefit by the training as much as they would if they had attained to a higher level of physical development.

(4) **Experience.** Experience is an important component of aesthetic sense. As the experience of a child in some particular art form increases one comes to expect better performances from him. Even otherwise, adult artists place much emphasis upon experience and practice.

(5) **Means.** Means are an important factor in experience. Different art forms need different means and tools as painting requires colours, brushes, plates and paper, etc. If these means are not available, a child is not in a position to point even if he feels so inclined.

(6) **Training.** Many detailed studies and examinations have indicated that it is in the organised training and atmosphere in school that the child develops and improves his aesthetic sense. Not only are the various art forms taught in the classroom, even such activities as stitching, knitting, decoration etc. need training four proficiency to be achieved. This training in so many spheres, benefits not only the children but also the elders. Nevertheless, in training them, the teacher has perforce to take note of his students' maturity, age, experience, etc.

As long as the child does not manage to attain a certain specific level of mental maturity, it is not desirable to instill art into him through the apparently mechanical tool of training. The knowledgeable teacher collects all proper means for a child's artistic expression only after, he has taken due note of his maturity. Using these available means, the children themselves develop their aesthetic sense. For instance, a child of three or less is, not, in possession of enough maturity to be able to use colours, pencils and other apparatus for drawing. Children, do of course draw things but even they themselves would be hard put to it to explain their creations if they were asked. They give their creations the most bizarre titles, which they also promptly forget.

(7) **Atmosphere.** Atmosphere is another element that exerts considerable influence upon the development of aesthetic sense. As has been pointed out earlier, atmosphere both in the house as, well as in the school is important in this respect. Design of the school room, furniture, the children's dresses, decoration and window glasses can be so arranged as to help in the child's aesthetic development. Further aesthetic development of the child can be effected in the work room where he can be induced to make dining tables and other such items besides taking part in decorating the school, decorously darning clothes and doing numerous other small things. The child's aesthetic sense is further stimulated by the criticisms leveled at him by his friends and colleagues. Importance of social influences on an individual's aesthetic choice is evident. In fact, the, school and home influence the child in their role of parts of a wide and comprehensive social organism. In society, one often sees very wide and overwhelming changes in songs, musical instruments, furniture, general architecture, poetic forms, literature, hair styles, and different fashions, etc., as time moves on, the change helping in the aesthetic development of the individual. It can be made more effective through the use of radio and cinema as media of mass communication.

(8) **Individual differences.** But ultimately, any aesthetic experience is an individual and personal experience. It can originate in many individual factors. For example, an individual can find an ideal adjustment through the constant study of literature or music. But as he gradually attains to perfection in these arts, he again comes to accept praise and admiration. In trying to develop and improve the aesthetic sense of the children, the teacher should keep in mind their intelligence, abilities, physical and mental development, attitudes, domestic atmosphere, quality and defects of personality, social and emotional development, etc., as individual differences, in these respects have the greatest consequences. Generally speaking, the tools used in different arts should differ with the age of the child playing them. The differences in the aesthetic ability of a child of 4, a child of 12, and an adolescent are evident, and their training should confirm to their age level, for which, it must be suitably modified. On the other hand, the, artistic activities of different children within

the same age level will show startling differences. At one end are the really proficient while at the other are children almost completely devoid of all artistic sense, but the majority of them are somewhere between these two extremes. It is only natural for children to have differing aesthetic development. The child's internal emotional life is another normally incalculable factor that seriously influences his or her artistic expressions.

Briefly, then, the following are the important points in a child's aesthetic development:

1. Aesthetic development is a part of the complete development and develops corresponding to it.
2. The associations in which an individual develops create an atmosphere important in determining the nature and direction of his aesthetic development.
3. The individual's aesthetic values evolve from his surrounding and his reactions. In this development the fundamental causes of the development of his internal life can be found.

   It is evident from the above delineation that an individual's aesthetic development is a complex process and despite the influence of many important factors, the most essential elements are the individual's personal abilities and personality traits.

QUESTIONS FOR EXERCISE

1. Trace the development of moral concepts in children. Give illustrative examples.
2. Give a brief account of the development of moral values in children.
3. Explain the effect of family on the moral development of the child.
4. Write short note on Moral Sentiment.
5. Describe the various stages of moral development in children.
6. Write short note on development of morality.

14

Social Development

A big controversy has developed among thinkers on the question of the mutual relation between individual and society, but all are agreed that this relation is an intimate and close one. Actually, the society precedes the individual because society is not an exclusive characteristic of human beings but is also found in animals. Its life is longer than that of the individual and while the latter may come and go, it goes on continually. But, on the other hand, society has no existence in the absence of individuals, of which it is formed. Individuals constitute society. Individuals influence the society. It is society that makes individuals cultured. The child's personality depends to a large extent upon his, social environment. Almost everything that he learns is acquired from society. Only the capacity of learning is his own. It is in society that his self or ego develops whereby he is called a human being. Every society has its individual organisation. Each exercises control over the individual and group which appear to be two independent units. But nevertheless, the existence and development of both depends on each other.

SOCIALIZATION: ITS AGENCIES

Socialization is the process whereby an individual learns to behave in accordance with social traditions and mores. The human child possesses a tendency towards imitation. The child develops according to the environment in which he lives. The individual tries to win the praise of the group in which he lives. Man is a social being. He, of his own' nature tries to adopt the culture of society. Man becomes what he is by socialization and it is by virtue of this that he is believed to be superior to animals. Socialization brings balance to his personality because the social aspect of personality also is very important. Through socialisation the, individual learns to control himself in the interest of society and realizes his responsibility towards others. Socialisation develops in him the community feelings and he learn to cooperate with others.

Individuals influence each other by means of imitation, suggestion and sympathy. In addition to these, social institutions and associations also carry out the individual's socialization. The individual is influenced by many processes in society, praise and blame, cooperation and conflict, submission and ascendancy. These help to form his personality and individuality. Education is the most prominent means to socialization.

Socialization in the family

The family plays perhaps the most dominant role in the individual's socialization. The child finds much to learn in the behaviour of his family members parents, relatives and friends. He imitates them in their mannerisms, behaviour, cliches, etc. He tries to avoid such activities which result in punishment or which considered bad in the family. It is the family environment which forms his good habits and it is in the family that he acquires criminal tendencies. In the book *New light on Delinquency and its treatment* Healy and Bronner have written that juvenile delinquents mostly hail from families which at one time or another, have suffered some hindrance in the fulfilment of social relations. Psychoanalysts, prominent among them are Freud and Adler, have proved that a man behaves in society according to whatever he has become in the family. Termann, the author of *Psychological factors in marital happiness,* has said that only those individuals can make marriage a success whose parents were contented. The preface writer of *Women of the street,* a searching book on London prostitutes, has stated that the problem of prostitution is the problem of the parent-child relationships. Boys and girls are spoiled when family contentment and peace are lacking. Many similar circumstances give birth to many thieves, murderers and prostitutes.

Other Influences in Socialization

But it is incorrect to believe socialization to be dependent, exclusively on the family. Other institutions and associations outside the family also wield influence on the development of man. When the child has grown a bit, he leaves the sanctity and protection of his home to go out and plan, at such a time he is very susceptible to the influence of his playmates. The child in the school, is in addition to the effect of education, vulnerable to the influences exerted by the personalities of his teachers of his friends. In much the same way, young men and women learn to conduct themselves and to give expression to their views, such a process being an out come of education and constant association with teachers, the unique environment, fellow collegiate, etc. Following college education, the individual's occupations and marriage are important factors of socialization. Both men and women are strongly influenced by the personality of their life partner, and their future depends upon this to a large extent. In this way, the child in the family becomes successively the protector, husband and father. These new responsibilities and rights teach him very much. In brief, socialisation is a process which begins at birth and continues unceasingly until the death of the individual. Like education it too is an incessant process.

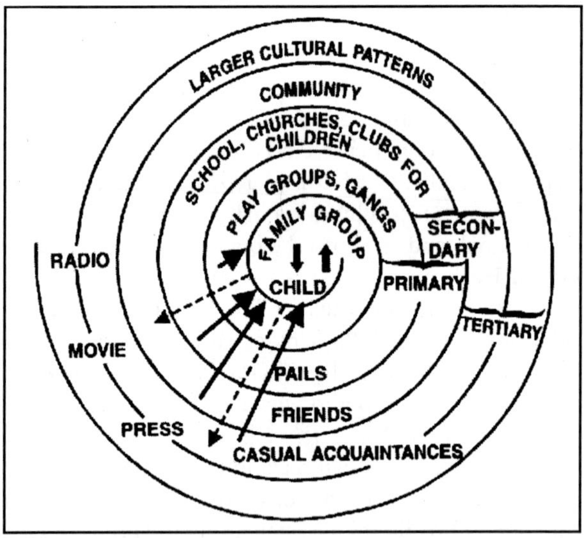

Fig. 12. The Expansion of the Horizon of Child's Experience and the Resulting Interaction.

From P.J. Brown, *The Sociology of Childhood,* p. 45.

In the figure given above the proportionate breadth of arrows shows the comparative influence and interaction of different individuals and groups on the child. Thus family exerts maximum influence then come the play groups, school, religious group, children club, community and larger cultural patterns. Interaction is maximum with pals, then with friends and casual acquaintances.

NEED FOR SOCIALIZATION

The question why is socialization, necessary for the development of the individual is best answered by the examples of human beings who were for some reason, nurtured outside society. Human beings of this kind are described by Gesell in his work *Wolf children and Human child* and by Davis in his essays. In 1920, in India, two children were found in a wolf's den, of which one was eight years old and the other couple of years younger. The second died the lapse of only a few months while the first continued to live for six years. She was named Kamla. The girl was completely innocent of the modes and ways of human behaviour. She walked' on all fours, growled like a wolf and could not speak. She became nervous at the sight of human beings as undomesticated' animals he tend to do. In this way, due to the absence of socialisation possessed none of the characteristics of human being save for her bodily structure. She was taught to speak, wear clothes and eat. In this way, she could learn some human behaviour due to the influence of socialization after a period of some years.

Socialization is not the exclusive but a prominent source of individual's development, because heredity also has its importance. The development of the individual, with the spread of culture through socialization, is impossible. The 'self' of the individual develops only due to socialization. Every social relationship of the individual contributes to this process of socialization. The problem of man's socialization is very complex and it has not yet been completely solved in any human society. In the words of Davis, "The improvement of socialization offers one of the greatest possibilities for the future alteration of human nature and human society."

WHAT IS SOCIAL DEVELOPMENT?

In defining social development, Sorenson has written, "By social growth and development we mean the increasing ability to get along well with oneself and others."[1] Thus, social development is the ability or skill by means of which an individual maintains order and system in his relation with other beings in his, neighbourhood, besides adapting his behaviour to them. Man is a social being influencing the conduct of others and being influenced by their behaviour, in his turn. Social relationships depend upon the mutual adjustment between such behaviour. Interests, attitudes, habits, etc. bear much importance for this mutual behaviour. Development of all these elements is part and parcel of social development in general. During the different stages that an individual passes, social circumstances in his immediate neighbourhood, his relations with others and their expectations of him undergo constant change. Social-development accords an individual the ability to adjust to his present social circumstances and to behave in accordance with the wishes and desires of other people. If adult men or women were to

1. Sorenson, H., *Psychology in Education*, McGraw Hill Book Co., New York, 1954, p. 209.

be seen playing with dolls, it would be considered socially undersirble and improper whereas it is perfectly reasonable for a child to indulge in this sort of entertainment. Due to social development the individual's conduct conforms to the requirements of his age, his Social status and social functions. In the words of Powers, "Social development can be defined as the progressive improvement, through directed activity, of the individual in the comprehension of the heritage and the formation of flexible conduct patterns of reasonable conformity with this heritage."[1] In this manner, stress is laid upon unceasing progress and development. The individual's social circumstances are constantly undergoing change, and the individual must perforce change with these circumstances. This is the process of his actual social development.

Characteristics of Socially Matured Individual

Having understood the behavioural patterns of a person mature from the social standpoint, it will become easier to comprehend the implications of social development. An individual, mature from the social standpoint, is one who cooperates with all those with whom he comes into contact, and contradicts them only when such a course of action becomes inevitable. He is never ill-mannered, choosing instead to appear very well mannered, considerate, and friendly to all and sundry. Consequently he has a large circle of friends. An adult, who has attained that stage, as required by the social standpoint, evinces great interest in art, study, games, etc. He studies the works of the greatest authors, and takes interest in games and forms of recreation suitable to his station in life. His activities and conduct are scrupulously in conformity with his age and sex. He mixes with people easily, yet occasionally prefers some solitude. He has the power of independent decision and judgement. He gives every evidence of being well balanced and adjusted within himself and in his behaviour towards other individuals.

Socially Undeveloped Individual

On the contrary, an individual who is undeveloped or immature as looked at from the social standpoint, is one who hesitates in society and shows signs of being' embarrassed. He experiences nervousness when in the presence of others. He depends to a, large extent upon the decisions of his mother and is attached to her, having a very small circle of friends and acquaintances. He find it difficult to carry on with others.

It is evident from the above description that social development comprehends physiological and mental status, qualities personality and emotional development.

---

1. Power, F.F., *Educational Psychology*, Prentice Hall Inc. (1945), pp. 102-3.

Having understood the meaning of the phrase social development, one is now in a position to study and understand the child's social development in infancy.

SOCIAL DEVELOPMENT IN INFANCY

The child's social development takes place gradually as he advances in age. The newborn baby performs very few social functions, being both consciously and unconsciously concerned. With the fulfilment of his physical needs. But before long, he exhibits signs of reacting to individuals who help him fulfill these needs. The only thing that his early activities shows that he has started understanding the objects and individuals in his environment. By the time he completes his first year he forms specific patterns of behaviour regarding the adults with whom he comes into contact. He is also influenced by their interests and things.

Similarly, as the child grows older, the patterns of his play also evince many significant changes. When he is two months old, the only thing, he is capable of is holding the wooden block preferred to him. But when he is two years old, he plays with his toys without the need of any external intervention, besides which he tries to dispossess other children of their toys and to take all toys for himself. Gradually, the feelings of 'I' and 'mine' develop and strengthen, but at the same time he also learns what 'you' and 'yours' means. In the third year, he also recognises the right of other individuals over his toys, thereby learning to share his possessions with others. It is only after this period that the child shows any desire to co-operate in group games.

Moving from the ego-centric behaviour of the first three years to the pre-school period, the child's conduct begins to appear socialized. In infancy, the child is almost completely ego centric and selfish, not being inclined to give any of his possessions to any one else. As his social development progresses towards ultimate maturity, he learns to divide and share his own with others and to co-operate with them. Even then, the intelligent children maintain some independence and individuality. Most of the child's games in the pre-school period are ego-centric. On entering school, he enters the first stage of his socialization and immediately becomes a member of the group of his own sex. Boys group with boys, and girls with girls. In school, the child is particularly sensitive and susceptible to other's behaviour towards him, particularly the conduct of his seniors. Till four or five years of age boys and girls play together. As the child gets greater opportunity, boys of his own age, his socialization accelerates. In the words of L.B. Murphy, "He becomes a member of a small world of children, all near his own age, although, differences in age may vary with the arrangement in different groups. This world of children furnishes, from this time on, a major part of his social diet. He is constantly assimilating this, by direct imitation of patterns of other children, by spontaneous reaction to things which they do or to situations which they create, by resistance to this pressure, by repeated experience of tensions aroused by their mere presence."[1] In the kindergarten and montessori education systems, the child's social development is further facilitated by the opportunity that, children get to play together. It has been pointed out before, too, that in this age group one can find groups of children formed on the basis of sex differences. But it is equally usual for two children, of opposite sexes to become quite friendly and intimate due to reasons of proximity or convenience or the absence of other children. The truth of the matter is that the presence of sex distinction. Among children's play is the result of criticism or interference from seniors. In

Responses of infants to adults, observed in 60% or more of the cases[2]

	Age in months		
Returns glances of adults with smiling	1	to	2
Is quieted by touching	2	to	3
Cries when adult who is attending him leaves	2	to	3
Smiles back-at adult	2	to	3
Disturbed when approached	2	to	3
Returns approaching glance with 'lalling'	3	to	4
Displeasure when loses glance of adult	3	to	4
Quieted by caressing	4	to	5
Disturbed by the sight of people	4	to	5
Striving for attention by 'lalling'	7	to	8
Stretches out hands towards adults	7	to	8
Cries when adult stops talking	7	to	8
Strives for attention by movements	8	to	9
Pulls on the clothes of adults	9	to	10
Offers adult and object	9	to	10
Imitates movements of adults with a plaything	9	to	10
Organises play activity	10	to	11

1. Murphy, L.B., *Social Behaviour in Child Personality*, Columbia University Press (1927), p. 49.
2. Buhler, C., *The First Year of Life*, John Dev, Co. (1930), pp. 56-57.

this age, friendship normally lasts for no more than a couple of days. Some children of course and it easier than others to make friends.

Living in the group, the child gradually evolves the communal sentiment. As he grows, he also acquires notions of propriety and impropriety, although children are seen differing in their individual opinions on this point. These concepts are primarily influenced by the attitudes of parents and teachers. The child himself, in his play, shows little or no consciousness of sex difference, a state of mind that is normally found to exist in the childhood that immediately precedes the period of adolescence.

Although development of social behaviour in the child exhibits considerable individual differences, yet Buhler saw, from his investigations that more than 60% children show similar patterns in social development. This can be seen from the table given on page 169 constructed by Buhler.

In studying the ages in, which specific forms of social behaviour in children were first manifested, Gassel and Thomson found that although some specific activity could be expected of a child at some specific time period, yet a considerable differences is also in evidence regarding the behaviour of individual children. While Buhler has studied the social development of the child's behaviour towards adults, he has also studied its development in respect of other children. This is to be seen from the following table:

SOCIAL DEVELOPMENT IN CHILDHOOD

Responses of infants to other infants, observed in 60% or more of the cases

	Age in month		
Observes other child	4	to	5
Smiles at other child	4	to	5
Cries if other child receives attention	8	to	9
Offers toy to other child	8	to	9
"Lalls" to other child	8	to	9
Imitates movements of another child	9	to	10
Opposes toy being taken away	9	to	10
Organises play activity	10	to	11
Strives for attention by means of "lalling"	10	to	11
Ill-humour if another child moves away	10	to	11
Setting aside toy and turning towards another child	11	to	12

Most children go to school when they attain to childhood. Hence, the social development of this period, is particularly influenced by the atmosphere in school and play ground. It is a part of the teacher's job to provide by creating such an atmosphere in the classroom, school and play ground in which healthy social development of the child may take place. Games have a special significance for the child's social development during this period of his life. Teachers should organise such games that provide satisfaction of the child's social needs, and the needs of his social development. And, in this, it is desirable if individual differences between children are also kept in mind. As a general rule, the child's social behaviour is not fixed or properly patterned by the age of six, it

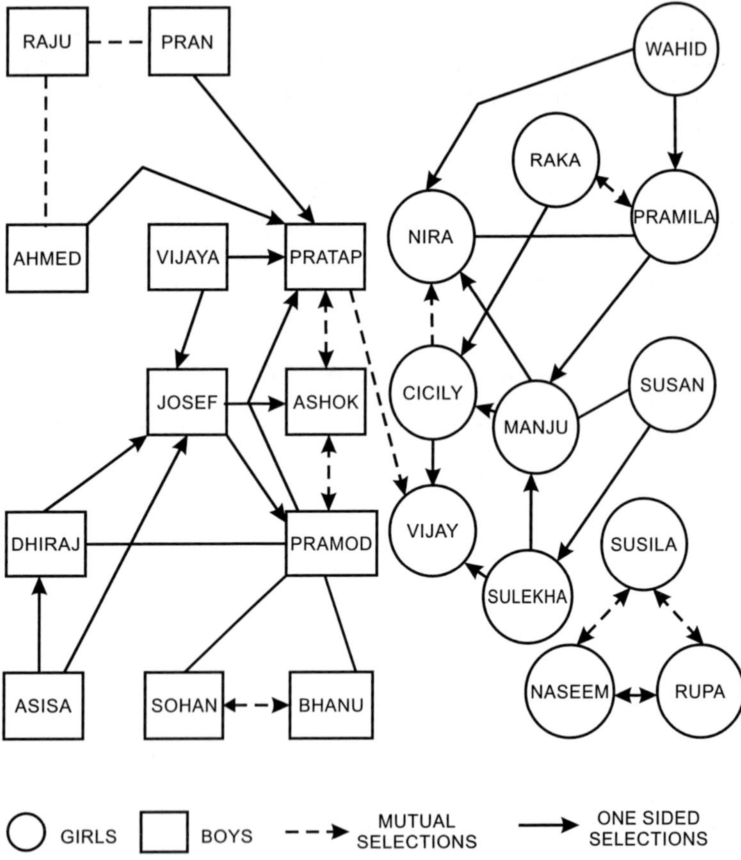

Fig. 13. Based on Ruth Cunningham's *How to construct a Sociogram.*

being influenced by such factors as his social consciousness, the ability to mould himself according to the rules in force in school, physical experience and mental development, etc. The moment a child enters the portals of his school, he is faced with new problems of social adjustment.

Between the age of 6 and 12, the child begins adjusting rapidly to his changing and varying social world. Now he is usually a member of one or the other group, which exhibits a code language, places of meeting a leader, special purpose of various activities, etc. The members of the group evince a definite loyalty to the group, do not hesitate to obey the orders of the leader and to emulate him and experience considerable freedom and independence. These same groups later on, in adult life, manifest themselves in the form of committees and societies. In this age, boys and girls form their groups among members of their own sexes, because of a definite and clear differentiation between their habits, interests, desires, etc. This fact is further clarified by the sociogram drawn on page 171 which is based on a testing of the mutual selection of boys and girls, and of the one-sided selection. In this, only two children have made a mutual selection, Pratap and Vijaya, while all other boys have chosen boy friends, and girls have selected girl friends, Sushila, Nasima, Rupa are girl friends by mutual selection. Manju is liked by four girls, Susan, Pramila Sulekha and Vijaya. Waheeda and Susan are not selected by any one though each of them has selected two friends. Similarly, proceeding on the same lines, find out who is the most popular boy in his group.

In this period of his life, the child is away from home for a considerable part of the day, yet the affection of parents and teachers is in no way reduced. While he aspires to the social values of his own group on the one hand, he is equally anxious to win the love and esteem of his parents as well as of his teachers, although it can sometimes happen that out of loyalty to the group he may feel compelled to neglect his parents and teachers and their entreaties. For, he is particularly anxious to win esteem in the group. Sometimes, in the group he indulges in activities that are considered specifically anti-social. In the case of children who indulge in such activities, fundamentally a great responsibility lies in the environment within the home and family. In families where the parents have no hesitation in giving praise and affection to their children, it will be seen that the young individuals indulge in proper and desirable activity. On the other hand, neglected and consequently rebellious children are apt to indulge in detestable actions, and later on turn into juvenile-delinquents It is necessary that the teachers keep an eye on the development and active manifestation of such tendencies within the child groups within his domain. Groups provide opportunities for the development of the qualities of leadership, so that in their adult and more responsible years, the boys and girls can turn to leading the nation. It should be kept in mind that all children do not evince the same liking for the group. Some children tend to avoid groups and prefer to stay with one or two children of their choice. There may be occasions of conflict between these individualistic boys and the bigger groups. And, there is no essential rule that members of the group are intelligent while these boys and girls who tend to shun the group are slow-witted. It is perfectly possible for the opposite to be true. Secondly, there may be some personal reasons, which may actuate the individual to stay away from the group, but generally it is best to live in the group as it benefits the individual's social development.

The child's social development is influenced in an important manner, by the mutual interaction between childhood groups, competition, conflict, and co-operation.

According to Bridges, the following table can help to reveal the extent to which a child's social development has taken place if at all. Positive answers indicate development, while negative ones indicate the opposite[1] :

1. Played with another child.
2. Spoken to another child.
3. Occasionally made social contact by touching or pushing a child.
4. Imitated other children's, actions.
5. Imitated children's words.
6. Imitated children's laughter.
7. Often spoke to other children.
8. Originated new play activity with other child.
9. Joined group of children in, play.
10. Sought another child's approval.
11. Asked another child for help.
12. Always given up toys at fair request.
13. Usually waited turn.
14. Tried to defend own right to materials or place.
15. Pointed to others' errors.
16. Tried to help others.
17. Stopped work to aid another child.
18. Comforted another child.

Further indication of desirable adjustment can be measured in terms of the extent to which a child *has not* rather has:

1. Bridge, K.M.B., *Social and Emotional Development of the Preschool Child*, Kegan Paul, 1931.

19. Turned away to avoid another child's friendly advances.
20. Usually stayed out of group marching or games.
21. Claimed others' toys.
22. Interfered with others' work.
23. Destroyed others' work.
24. Created disorder in group or led others into mischief.
25. Frequently pulled or pushed others.
26. Frequently complained of other adult for own gain.
27. Harassed new child by scoffing or shunning.
28. Hit or pinched, others for fun several times.
29. Bitten or spit at other for fun several times.
30. Teased in other ways, causing irritation or discomfort.

SOCIAL DEVELOPMENT IN ADOLESCENCE

When the child attains the age of 13-14, he undergoes radical and startling changes of a mental as well as physical nature. It is natural that his social development should also undergo some change, the phenomenon under consideration being influenced by many various factors. It is effected by interests, needs, feelings of insecurity, values, attitudes, responsibility, viewpoint, etc.

In adolescence, the child becomes exquisitely conscious of his sex. Because young girls grow up two years earlier than their male counterparts they prefer to associate with boys a couple of years their seniors. But on the other hand, the social distance between boys and girls also widens, with the result that boys associate with girls or criticise them, but in either condition they are fully conscious of the other sex. Similarly, the girls who are seen continuously blaming and criticising boys pay considerable attention to the boy's criticism and behaviour, besides which they attend to the activities of the male sex in one or the other respect. But immediately the child enters the adolescent stage, he rarely professes extreme heterosexual tendency of a very intense nature. Generally, in this age, the boys and girls are more keen on seeing each other and being seen by the others. They try to attract and hold the attention of each other through such tactics as wearing extraordinary clothes, dressing their hair in the latest fashions, peculiar conduct, etc. They want to make their presence felt and known, so that they are even conspicuous by their absence, if such an occurrence becomes unavoidable. In this manner, relations between heterosexual individuals are not very well defined during the early stages of adolescence. One of the main reasons why they are so disturbed and ill at ease in the presence of each other is that they are conscious of a strange attraction that is new to them and they cannot divine the reasons for it. Consequently, while they like to be with each other, they feel embarrassed and reticent of each other. In social conditions created within the school, girls and boys can adopt the proper patterns of behaviour between the sexes under sympathetic guidance of the teachers. It is essential that teachers as well as parents should be very careful when acting in this connection. In order that they may be able to adjust properly in their roles of husband and wife, it is essential that during adolescence each develops the right attitude towards the other sex. One very important factor that contributes to this attitude is the atmosphere in which the child lives at home. In this age, the groups are not as well organised and systematic as the groups of childhood and their purpose is mostly social. Important social activities of young men and women are dances, singing sessions, picnics, mountain climbing etc. In Western countries in all such outings the number of individuals from either sex is almost equal, so that every one has his companion. Some boys and girl do not participate in such a big group, but choose to develop relations with an individual of the other sex. But people who choose to live in big groups do not entertain a good opinion of such solitude lovers. One finds considerable loyalty in conflict and even physical violence. Members of a particular group have the same conversational style, dress, modes of conduct, etc., and they mostly prefer to be together. Adolescents talk incessantly of their school and college, but they also show considerable interest in philosophical issues, national and international matters, professions, games and other subjects of universal significance. But their greatest pleasure is derived from their conversation on the other sex. It is another matter that some individuals pretend to be revolted not only to talking of such matter but even upon hearing them mentioned in their presence for some or the other reason. In adolescence, young men and women take considerable interest in their appearance, behaviour and presentability, because they have great zest for living and enthusiasm for every project that is put to them. In matters of appearance and dress, they imitate others, particularly adult men and women, whom they try to emulate in every respect. Leaders of adolescent groups are chosen on the basis of health and energy, loyalty, enthusiasm, sportsman spirit, organisational skill, originality, sympathy and many other qualities of personality. Common interest and traits lead to the formation of very strong, staunch and intimate friendships in this age; such friendships sometimes last a life time. Such profound friendship between individuals of different sexes even results in matrimonial ties.

In the domestic sphere, young boys and girls of this age are often found contradicting their parents and thus causing conflicts. On the other hand, the parents contribute their little mite to this general communion by constantly interrupting and correcting the youngsters on some ground. Both sides are equally anxious and desirous of foisting their respective views upon the other, and each side is dissatisfied with the views of the other, although they unanimously resent any external interference in their differences of opinion. Besides these more or less common problems, the individual may have his own problems of adjustment that result in his disappointment anxiety and dejection. In this age, every individual wants that he or she should develop fully and beautifully into a man or women and is disgusted and worried if he does not. Not only does physical development satisfied him; he also wants mental and intellectual development so that he may appear intelligent and able to his friends. Thus, different individuals make their best effort to gain proficiency in many different spheres such as studies, dance, music, various kinds of games and arts, etc. Some of them gain their specific place in society through sympathetic, co-operative and benevolent behaviour. While on the one hand it is eminently undesirable to be completely indifferent to public opinion, it is equally futile and dangerous to be completely infatuated with the idea of winning public acclaim and being in the good books of every person. People of this kind make every effort to become leaders through reasonable and unreasonable means.

Occupational interests of the individual are also significant for his social development. In different societies, some specific professions are more respected and regarded than others so that most of the adolescents prefer to adopt these professions. Success and failure in such schemes has important influence upon their social development.

From the above description of social development during adolescence, it is apparent that in this age, individuals are in particular need or guidance and direction. Factors such as sexual desires, occupation, family adjustment in school or college and others pose such problems for the young immature person that he is incapable of solving, and in which the interference and advice of his elders, both parents and teachers, is very desirable.

Social Development and Education

In every stage of social development of the child, education contributes, much, but this education is not the literacy thrust upon the child through books and lectures. The real and incalculable factors that exert this influence are the extra curricular programmes, the school's atmosphere, rules of conduct in school, radio, cinema, newspapers and magazines, etc. Group camp almost invariably have a healthy influence upon the individual's social development or socialization. It helps to form his character and develop social qualities. He acquires good habits and develops the qualities of leadership, he also gets many opportunities for developing many kinds of skill. In the informal atmosphere of the camp, individuals can meet and mix with greater freedom and informality so that their social education is set in motion. In this manner, teachers and parents can cooperate to give adequate facilities and opportunities for the healthy social development of infants, children and adolescents.

SOCIAL DEVELOPMENT IN ADULTHOOD

Social development continues into adult age. In this period of his life, the person's social development is affected by such tangible and strong influences as the peace and calm of married life, permanent and suitable occupation, good social and economic position etc. From the social standpoint, signs of a developed adult are friendship, control over emotions, power of leadership, desire and ability to cooperate with others, economic independence, family independence, good tastes in respect of entertainment, social and moral level of a high order, cultured and pleasant mannerisms and good heterosexual relationships. Possession of these qualities help the individual to adjust properly in society, their absence depriving him of this essential capacity. Even his physical and mental development have important repercussions on his social development. In addition to these rather personal qualities other broader and more social factors that influence his social development are atmosphere in family and occupation, the general and cultural atmosphere of society. It is essential for the individual's happiness, and peace that he possesses social maturity life It would be no exaggeration to state that the lack of social maturity might make his well nigh impossible. Here it should be remembered that normally the individual develops completely, that is proper physical, mental and emotional development makes it imperative that his social development also be excellent. It is equally true that incomplete development in any of these aspects leads to incomplete social development. Education is an attempt at just this complete development of the individual, and it necessitates the cooperation of the teachers as well as the parents.

FAMILY AND SOCIAL DEVELOPMENT

Human personality develops in a social environment. In the childhood the personality of an individual is very susceptible to change and variation. He can be turned in practically any desired direction. The famous psychoanalyst Freud has contended that the personality of man is formed in his childhood and the period after that marks only its development. In view the fact that the experiences, habits, etc., acquired in childhood are so extremely important, the family situation also becomes important because the childhood of the individual is spent within the precincts of the home. The family situation can be regarded as comprehending three factors (1) Relation of parents to child, (2) Order of the child's birth and (3) Presence of brothers and sisters and other members in the family. The important role played by the family in the formation of the child's personality can be clearly realized after these three aspects have been studied.

Relation between Child and his Parents

Having affected a psychological analysis of the importance of the parent-child relationship the psychoanalysts have tried to show why the child is influenced to such a great extent by his parents and the relation in which he stands with them. According to Freud the parents are particularly present before the child as ideals. They are more powerful and strong and can perform all activities efficiently. The child effects an identification with his father unconsciously. He wants to become as his father. It is often seen that the young child dons the clothes of his father and imitates his manner of walking and talking. The child behaves precisely as do his mother and father. Besides identification, the second element in this is that of imitation. The child learns much by imitation. There are many activities that the child learns to perform merely by observing and imitating the older members of the family. For the child, the parents are as examples and it be very difficult to prevent children from indulging in activity in which the parents themselves indulge particularly when they do so in front of the child. This difficulty arises because he feels that what the parents are doing should be done. In this both identification and imitation are included. The child also receives suggestions from his mother and father. The activities in which the mother and father indulge automatically suggest themselves to the child. In this way, the process of identification is not the only process that is activated in the relationship between the child and the parents but is supplemented by the process of imitation, suggestion and sympathy. According to Freud, the viewpoints of the male and female child towards their parents are not identical. Freud believes that the sex instinct is innately given in the individual and is present at birth. In this opinion, the child does not suck his mother's breast merely because he is hungry but also because it gives him pleasure. His mother is not exclusively the source of his nourishment but also the basis of his feelings of pleasure. Freud has further postulated the instinct for heterosexuality in children. Accordingly the male child loves his mother more while the female child shows greater, attachments to the male parent. The mother is the boy's beloved. Hence, naturally the father becomes his opponent and sometimes he sees that he is deprived of his mother's love only because of his father's presence. Often his mother leaves him and goes to his father when the latter comes. Consequently, the boy regards his father as a rival. On the one hand, he respect the father because he is the ideal, on the other, the child also hates him in his capacity of opponent.

Criminal Tendency and the Parent-Child Relationship

The misbehaviour of the parents or their neglect of the children are important factors due to which children often become juvenile delinquents. According to the report of *Women of the Street*, an important research on the prostitutes of London, the problem of prostitution has its origin in the relationship between the child and the parents. Often, when the child is deprived of parental love and is sternly punished frequently he is filled with the desire to revolt and disgust so much so that he runs away from the home when he gets the opportunity to do so. Once away from the home he falls into criminal ways. If neglected by his parents the child feels helpless and alone as a result of which he develops many kinds of complexes. The child becomes a delinquent also when the parents try to conceal too much from him. For example, the children are very apt to ask their parents as to where they came from or where the younger child, came from and they are often misled. When they come to know of their true source from servants or from their friends they develop a sense of insecurity because they are deeply hurt when they come to know that their parents do many things that they would not have the children know. This sense of insecurity often lures children into sex crimes.

Need for Balance

In this way, both excessive neglect and excessive love and affection are not to be desired in the relationship between the child and parents. Both are the origin of difficulties concerning the personality and all kinds of problems take root in the mind of the child. Similarly, it is harmful both to place absolute control on the child as well as to leave him to his own mechanisms almost entirely. If the child is given too much freedom he dose not develop any respect for authority and cannot be governed. If he is placed under excessive control, his personality is not allowed to develop and he is obsessed with a sense of inferiority and sometimes even turns to crime. The truth of the matter is that if the child is to be disciplined and, educated a bitter pill must be swallowed. It is very difficult to bring up a child. In this connection it is necessary that there be much balance and understanding Then there can be no one universal rule that can apply to all children. Some children are amenable to greater control while others respond to a lighter degree of authority. On the other hand all children are not similarly influenced by authority just as all children do not react in the same manner to parental love or neglect. All that has been said before is true in a general way but it is also open to exceptions.

Influence of Discrimination

Sometimes parents discriminate between their children in behaving towards them. They have unlimited love and affection for one while another receives only scolding and punishment. Sometimes it is the beautiful child that is loved while the ugly one is neglected and disregarded. Whatever the reasons at the root discriminatory behaviour it is bad because it arouses feelings of hatred for each other among the children. When the child observes that his brother or sister is being loved more than he is becomes anxious to revenge this injustice. Sometimes he is even possessed of aggressive tendencies. He also tries to harm the other children in one way or the other. He, is seen to be disappointed, insecure, fearful, etc. But it is also possible that the child may try to win the admiration and love of others in society and at school by appearing to be better than others in order to make reparation for the deficiency in family love that has been accorded to it. Whatever the outcome it is completely undesirable and psychologically unjustified to indulge in this kind of discrimination between the children.

Effect of the Character of Parents

The personality of the child is also appreciably influenced by the moral thoughts and conduct of the parents because usually the child looks upon his parents as ideals on which to mould his life in order to inculcate morality in the children the parents should place an example before them in the form of their own exemplary behaviour. There are very few children who can mould their behaviour according to social values and conceptions even when they have seen their parents indulge in theft, sexual immorality, falsehood, deception and other form of misconduct. In Miss Eliott's study the parents in 67 per cent broken homes and 44 per cent unbroken homes were indulging in immoral behaviour. If the mother indulges in prostitution her daughters have no inhibition against it and they would have no difficulty in imitating her and proceeding towards immorality and corruption.

Effect of the Mutual Relation of Parents

The personality of the child is further open to another important influence *viz.*, the mutual relation between husband and wife. If the husband misbehaves towards the wife then the child, particularly the male child, takes exception to it and this increases his hatred for the father. This can, under certain circumstances, lead to terrible consequences. Similarly, if the wife misbehaves with husband, the female child in particular is likely to dislike it and hence she hates her mother. Constant conflict and quarrelling between husband and wife leads to the creation of an atmosphere of insecurity in the home which is not at all conductive to the development of the child's personality. If the relations between husband and wife are good the children have a good and encouraging ideal in front of themselves which they can imitate to good effect. They then try to be good themselves. It is only natural for the child to develop some personality defects if the relation between his parents is not good.

Effect of the Broken Family

When the relations between the husband and wife deteriorate, the family is reduced to a broken family. This is because the relations between no two members retain their original charm, and goodness. A broken family is one in which the family relations have been severed. Family does not mean the living together of some individuals but rather the intimate and profound relations that exist between them. In the absence of this intimacy the family is disbanded and in, the broken family juvenile delinquents are reared and brought up. In the broken family the children are not looked after or cared for. According to some specialists, the broken family tends to create the criminal tendency in the female children more than it does in the male child. In 1947 in Bombay there were 386 boys and 169 girls under the child care society. Of these two boys and two girls had their parents in jail serving sentence for some or the other crime while 2 boys and 5 girls were victims of harsh behaviour and 5 boys and 6 girls were victimised by immoral insecurity. In the broken family the relation between the husband-wife, parents-child and brother-sister do not remain healthy. Hence, it is natural for boys and girls to tread the path of mistakes, crime and degradation.

The personality of the child is susceptible to the influence not only of the relationship between itself and its parents but also by the personality of his brothers and sisters. This influence seems to be more pronounced in the case of girls because they are not quite as exposed to external influences as the boys are. If the older children in the family indulge in criminal activity the younger are very likely to follow suit or at least to be profoundly influenced. If the sister is a criminal or indulges in immoral acts, the younger sister will also imitate her or at least she is, likely to do so. The individual is socialised in the family. If the child finds other children in the family who are not much older or younger than it then the child finds a good atmosphere in the family. If there is only one child in the family then it does not find this social atmosphere which is so conductive to its development and its development is to some extent adversely affected. But this deficiency can be compensated if the parents play with the children.

Effect of the Financial Status

The financial condition of the family also influences the development of the child's personality. If the financial condition is good and the parents can adequately satisfy the needs of the children then the children are generally not possessed with the sense of inferiority and want and they do not turn to crime. But if the financial condition of the family is extremely bad then the personality of the child suffers. Merrill has written that if the income of the family is low the children also have to work and their education is thus left incomplete. The child's personality does not react very appreciably to the conditions of work. Many of the desires of the poor children are left unfulfilled in order to satisfy which they turn to criminal activity. Poverty induces feelings of dissatisfaction and inferiority. But this does not warrant the conclusion that the poverty of the family will inevitably have a harmful effect upon the child's personality. Sometimes the children, both male and female, become delinquent even though, and sometimes because the financial condition of the family is very good. On the other hand, the children of the poor learn the lesson of self-reliance from the very start.

From the foregoing description of the parent-child relationship and the effect of various family conditions on the personality of the child it is evident that they are very important. In fact, it is these elements that are responsible for the development of the main characteristics of the individual's personality.

Family has a Nuclear Situation

Family is the first institution in the history of man. In the ancient age men lived in small families, which lacked any kind of organisation or permanence. But they served to fulfil simple biological and psychological needs. Generally, the family consisted of husband and wife and their offspring. The powerful men possessed many wives and thus they lived in big families with their wives and children. When man became oriented in agriculture, many families formed a group and stayed permanently at some place for farming. When these people started partaking of each other's pain and happiness as neighbourly gestures, social relations increased and in this way many families formed a community and the next step was the creation of nation. In this way family is that primary group which slowly evolved into human nations.

Family is a fundamental unit of human society. Its foundations rest, upon man's biological and psychological needs. In the modern age, many functions of the family have shifted to other institutions but nevertheless, there are many biological and psychological needs which man cannot satiate without a family. Havelock Ellis in his penetrative essays, has shown that the importance of mother's milk for the child cannot be obtained in any other manner. Psychologists have proved that the absence of family affection has a serious impact upon the child's development. Sexual passions can be satisfied even outside the family but it can never be the source of emotional fulfilment. That man is a social animal implies that man cannot live without a family. Thus family is a fundamental unit of society.

The family has a nuclear situation in human society. In primitive societies the entire organisation is based on family units while the division of labour in society is also based on the family. In the complex structure which is society today, the family has lost some of its importance, but even today the activities of most members are for the family or contiguous to it. It is seen that people work and labour more for the comfort of their wives, children and other members of family than even for personal comforts. Thus, even now the family is the nucleus of a major part of man's activities.

Society depends upon Family

Proper social organisation depends upon proper organisation of families. If the families disintegrate in some society, then the society will never be safe. One major cause of social disorganisation is family disorganisation. Families develop the characters of the members of society. Freud and other psychologists have proved that a child, when a man, exhibits the same character and mental tendencies which he acquires in the family. In the opinion of Adler, a man's role in the family determines his role in society.

Family socializes Individual

In this way, a person is socialised in the family. Defining family, Merrill writes, "Family is an enduring association of parent and offspring whose primary functions are the socialisation of the child and the satisfaction of the members." According to Dewey and Tufts the family is a social agency for the education and protection of the race. It is in the family that, the child acquires such important qualities as sincerity, sympathy, self-submission and realising responsibility etc. It is the character developed in the family which helps the child in becoming an important and responsible member of society. Wright was quite correct in stating that in every family, the child gets an opportunity for free expression of thoughts and developing his entire personality. Psychologists have incontestably proved that the proper development of the child is impossible, without a good environment in the family. The tendencies and habits which he acquires in the family, he finds impossible to shed later on. According to Freud, the viewpoint of a child towards the senior in the family determines his attitude and viewpoint towards the elders in society. The child's first is his home and family. According to Prof. Collingwood, the child's, education should be in the hands of the parents in family. The parents should participate in all the child's activities. A child, learns much by imitating his superiors. Mahatma Gandhi and such thinkers paid personal attention to the development of their children. It is the family which imparts practical education to the child concerning the customs in society, conduct, other important elements of culture, preservation of health, love, sympathy, cooperation etc.

It is evident from the above account that family is the primary and fundamental unit. Confucious remarked quite correctly that if you want to improve society improve its families. Society will improve automatically when the families improve.

Family is the Conveyor of Traditions

The family moulds the character and personality of the individual. It is through the family that society imparts its culture to the individual. Thus, the family is very important in the form of socializing agency. In the essay, *The Family Conveyance of Tradition*, Paul Schreker wrote that a particular function of the family is to sanction children. Like marriage, the institution of family is constituted by different elements of culture. It is due to this reason that it has religious, judicial, political, artistic and linguistic aspects. Whenever a new thought impresses itself on an age the family takes a new form in order that the upbringing and mental tendencies may be harmonious to that thought. Politics and law were dominant in Rome, so the family organisation there was such as to ensure the upbringing of children in harmony with the culture. Today, the economic order is predominating. So the family has changed its form, it makes the mental tendencies concur with the new culture. In this way, the family makes individual harmonious with the culture of society. In the family, the child acquires knowledge about the current customs, mores, traditions etc.

Social Control Through the Family

A social life is a web of relationships. In order to maintain these relations properly a system of rights and duties is organised which will avoid any conflict between the members of society and allow them to develop as complements to each other. In order to avoid any breach of this harmony between the individuals in society, the society applies numerous kinds of control on the individual. They are taught to obey the elders, have sympathy for the young and for others. A strict control over sex relationships is necessary for maintaining the social order, otherwise disintegration will spread over the complex social life of today. Relationships between men and women will lose their solidarity. Illegitimate children will be born with no one to look after them. Although the anthropologists Mead and Malinowski have discovered societies where control over sex relations is inordinately lax without disturbing the social order but such an order is completely contradictory to the thinking of today's cultured person. It is the family which does this work of controlling sex passions for society. In all cultures, the families exercise some degree of control over the unmarried members till they attain the matrimonial state. In the same way, the family acts as a preventive to, individual in keeping him from bad habits and crimes like drinking, theft etc. Not many parents could like their children to embark on careers of crime. Even the worst person tries to prevent his children from adopting similar habits and consequently any objectionable behaviour on the part of children is punished and laudable effort suitably rewarded. They thus drop bad habits and learn good things. In this way the making of a good citizen in society depends upon the parents.

In every society some values and ideals are regarded as high and, signs of culture. Whichever person exhibits these in greater measure is respected in society. For example, Indian society treats religious and spiritual qualities as supreme and a person who is possessed of them is appropriately respected everywhere. Besides, in India, pre-marital and extra-marital sexual relations are controlled as a necessary measure. The responsibility of creating these values in the individual, which are treated highly in society, lies with the family. It is true that the character of every person is different from any other by nature but the family environment also has a big hand in forming them. Most of the famous religious persons of the world like Gandhi were deeply influenced by some one religious person in their respective families. In the making of great men the mothers have always had a major part to play. The differences in the ideals of people related to different cultures are born in their families.

Mother Tongue in the Family

In every society the culture, conduct and values are very strongly related to the language spoken. Literature is the mirror of culture in society and literature is based on language which plays by no means a mean part in man's socialization. The credit for the complex order of human society must go to man's linguistic superiority over other animals and the language one picks up in the family. Human children brought up by animals in the forest are seen completely ignorant in matters of language. They communicate their wishes by signs in animal language, walk on all fours, eat raw meat and exhibit the least signs of humanity. A child brought up in an animal family grows like an animal as a child brought tip in a human family grows into a human being. To go even further, a child developing in a cultured family is cultured while one brought up in baser circumstances is coarse. The child is first taught language in the family. This is his mother tongue through the medium of which he exchanges thoughts. If some Indian child is brought up in some English family, English will become his mother tongue. Thus, the major element in the child's socialization in-the form of language comes to him in his mother's lap.

Besides the above mentioned elements, an individual receives a number of other things from his family. Not unusually, even the person's occupation in society is decided by his family. Even in the modern age many people carry on the paternal business and occupation for which they are trained in the family from the start. It is in no uncommon occurrence that a jeweller's child shows interest in the same business from his infancy and becomes able very soon.

Thus, in brief, the family educates the individual in culture, conduct, behaviour, customs, tradition, religion, laws of thinking, ideals, values, occupations, obedience of duties and proper use of authority, etc. It would be no exaggeration to say that the family is the most important institution in man's moral development.

SCHOOL AND SOCIAL DEVELOPMENT

A child's pesonality is influenced by his school, where he comes into contact with his teachers and his colleagues. At home the child's ideals are his parents and in school he forms his ideals around his teachers. A child hates a teacher who is cruel and uses the stick. He tries to revenge himself on such a teacher, but if the teacher is kind and considerate the child loves and worships him. Both the personality of the teacher and his behaviour toward the child influence the child's personality. A teacher is bigger than the child in size as well as in mental stature and he can make many demands upon the child. For this reason the child likes the idea of developing to the same size as the teacher. At home the child identifies himself with his parents while in school he identifies himself with his teacher but only when the teacher has a magnetic pesonality. If the teacher's own personality is not very strong he does not have much influence upon the child. On the other hand the teacher's, way of thinking and moral conduct influence the child's thinking and behaviour. The teacher's standard of living, modes of behaviour, conduct, etc., all affect student. Putting it briefly, every quality, good or bad, of the teacher that is manifest in his behaviour towards the child, leaves some influence upon the child's mind.

Influence of Playmates and Class-fellows

Normally, the child's class-fellows in school are his playmates and friends, though, sometimes, the child makes friends with children belonging to other classes. A child studying in a higher class normally behaves in a highhanded manner towards the child of a lower class. The same thing happens when two children of different age levels come into contact. An older child's behaviour towards his junior may be either loving or cruel, for in any case the younger child treats the older with fear and respect. Another factor is the competition in matters of study that occurs between children, for it can, on the one hand, induce the child to develop emotions of jealousy, hatred and disgust, while on the other it may inspire him to greater effort and independence.

Influence of Group on the Child

Individual influences do count but the most important influence upon the child in school is the influence of the group of his colleagues in the playground. Children tend to form groups with those boys and girls either with whom they play or the ones with whom they indulge in mischief. These groups compete with each other, while within the group there are always wrangles for leadership. Within each group, each particular child occupies a definite place and plays a distinct role. Each group has a complement of recognised members and an entourage of those who attach themselves to the group. There is a leader within the group whose intimate friends form the inner circle of the group. It is the function of the leader to look after the functioning of the gang, to do the thinking for the gang and to be its mainstay and its moral support. In certain groups the brain is provided by one child and the action by another. It is for the brain to draw up the, plans and for the dare devil to carry them out. Another common feature of such groups is the comedian or jester whose sole function is to play the fool and to keep his group amused. It is possible for such groups to have one child playing the role of the scape-goat. Functions within the group are allocated according to the ability or the capacity of each individual child. In fighting gangs the strongest, boy automatically assumes the mantle of leadership while in mischievous groups the most intelligent boy becomes the leader. A child's function in any such group coincides with his, personality, while the performing of this function influences his personality.

Growth of Community Sentiment

Modern psychology does not credit the existence of any group mind distinct from the mind of the individual, but in group situations the laws of group behaviour are freely employed. A college is a psychological group. Qualities such as discipline and cooperation can, be evolved in the students only after some community feeling has been injected into them. William Mcdougall has pointed out several conditions that are necessary for the development of a group mind. They can be put to good use in developing community sentiment in colleges. They are:

(1) **Permanence of the Group.** A college, in its role as a group, should possess certain degree of permanence or physical stability. Naturally, some students join the college every year while others leave it, and some change is always going on in the shape of additional buildings, staff members changing their colleges, etc. But despite this change there is some permanence for the average student who spends two to four years in one college while in exceptional cases this period even extends from ten to twelve years. If the teachers in a school are not unnecessarily changed at a rapid rate and some of the college rules are maintained, the students derive a sense of permanence and the realisation that the college has a distinct nature. This can help them to develop a community feeling, which is part of their greater community feeling comprehending their society as a whole.

(2) **Study of the Form of the Group by Members and the Member's Understanding of its Duties and Functions.** Each student is a member of the college group. He can have community feeling for it only if he learns to regard it as a group, realises the duties that he has to perform as a student, and has knowledge of the

college's rules and methods of working. For this reason it is desirable for the teachers to introduce their new students every year to the institution as it is, what it stands for, how things are run in it and what is expected of the newcomers. It is only in these circumstances that each student will be able to play his role in achieving the ideals of the college.

(3) **Contact with Other Groups.** Community feeling does not develop only by taking part in the functions of one's own group. It is necessary that members of different groups should intermingle. Occasions for such contact can be developed by, organising debates, discussions, dramatic performances, games and sports. But on all such occasions it is necessary that, the feeling of the contestants for each other should be those of friendliness and respect. Should these feelings be lacking, the healthy development of any community feeling is not easy. In all such programmes students come to regard themselves as representatives of a particular college, with which they identify themselves. It is for the honour of this institution that they have to fight. Community feelings will inevitably result.

(4) **Development of Community Tradition.** In a college, as in, every other group, the members keep on changing every year but the community life of the group can be maintained for years at a time if a community tradition is developed. Old students who keep up their contact with their old college play an important role. Old Boys Associations can perform a useful function by renewing contact with the newer generation of students and by holding meetings and thus keeping alive the traditions of the colleges. Many colleges and universities are famous for some particular tradition. Some colleges can boast of a fine tradition of discipline while another college may be producing the best students. If the old students and teachers are successful in keeping up these traditions every year the newcomers are encouraged to do their best. In this manner the communal life of the college runs smoothly.

(5) **Division of Labour among Members.** In every group different individuals are entrusted with the performance of different duties. Without this division of labour the life of the group cannot run smoothly. In a school or college, in particular, it is desirable that individual students should be entrusted with the task of looking after the discipline, the gardens and lawns, the classrooms, the library and the reading room, etc., and of organising cultural programmes. If the student is compelled to

perform such functions he learns to shoulder responsibility and to take decisions on his own. Besides, he feels some personal interest in the functioning of the college and this gives vitality to his understanding of the community spirit.

In addition to the above factors pointed out by McDougall, certain other means can be adopted for the development of a group mind in students. If meetings of the entire college are held from time to time, the students develop sense of identity. If the students' parents are invited to cultural programmes healthy atmosphere is generated in the college. Teachers of literature, music and art can contribute to the life of the college by making their teaching more colourful. Another way of improving community life is to have community prayer in the morning before teaching work begins and parades in the evening. When students are encouraged to participate in the celebration of a national day, prize distributions and the selection of different committees, they feel part of the college. The tone of the college has very great influence in this respect. And a good tone can be developed only when the life of the college is disciplined, marked by cooperation, law and order high moral level and an advanced level of mutual relations. This happens only when the teachers themselves set high standards and do not hold themselves aloof from their students. Teachers are the leaders of students and for that reason the responsibility of presenting the students with desirable ideals devolves upon them.

SOCIAL ISOLATES

Because of some physiological or psychological shortcomings some children find it impossible to mix with other children of their own age or to make friends with them. Hence, in their social life, such children tend to be isolated, and this isolation has the worst effect upon their mental, social and moral development. They tend to exaggerate their feelings of inferiority and to dress their sense of self-respect and self-confidence. The development of their character suffers in the process.

There can be many causes of social isolation. Physical handicap can be one cause. Defects of hand, foot, eye or of speaking can hinder the child. Feeble children also tend to avoid other children. Abnormality, physiological or mental, obstructs the socialization of the child and prevents him from mixing in the group.

A social isolate is the child who cannot make his own friends in society. For this he has to depend upon his parents or teachers. And such help should be forthcoming. He should be introduced to other children who can accept him into their group, but even then care should be taken that these children should not indulge in any activity which should make the isolate wish to run away. Such children are extremely emotional and even the slightest misbehaviour of disturbs them considerably. If the child suffers from no physiological or mental abnormality but is still an isolate then his isolation arises from emotional causes, the majority of which have their origin in the family, environment. The family environment may be made unbearable if the parents are extremely excitable, destructive, vicious or corrupt. A healthy family environment is the first requirement for the healthy social development of the child.

SOCIAL STRATIFICATON AND EQUAL DEVELOPMENT

Social stratification is a common feature in every social group, for different individuals occupy different social groups. In some societies these groups are based on social prestige, as is the case in India, where there are caste groups. In other societies they may be based an the economic status in which case there will be the low income, middle income and high income brackets. Generally speaking, the child is not conscious of the group to which he belongs, and it is seen that if children from different groups are allowed to mix informally they do not give any indications about their groups. However, in almost every case one finds the influence of the parent's group on the child. Parents themselves constantly tell their children about the groups and the relation in which they stand to each one of them. People belonging to the poor group tell their children to stay away from the children not belonging to their income brackets. In India individuals belonging to the higher castes do not allow their children to mix with the children of the lower castes, or the so called untouchables. It is, putting it briefly, the parents who are responsible for developing class consciousness in their children, and later on this, has a very profound influence upon the socialization of the children. In America it has been found that while many white children do not feel the least inhibition in playing with negro children, their parents instill into them various kinds of fear associated with the negroes, Thus a deep-rooted prejudice against the negroes is created in the children's minds. Similar tendency can be seen among the Hindu and Muslim communities in the country. It is now apparent that children are influenced by social stratification only because of their parent's teaching.

ROLE OF COMPETITION

Competition is an important factor among the various stimuli that encourage the child to work. This stimuli does not function for children less than two years of age. By the age of six the workings of this stimulus can be seen clearly. In this manner, the child's earliest behaviour pattern shows objectivity but later on he develops the tendencies of competition and cooperation. In the early stages this competition is limited to winning the love, and attention of the parents. It can occur when the child wants toys and other things to play with. Before the age of three this tendency does not play an important role in fashioning the child's pattern of behaviour. During this period the child is kept occupied with his toys and has little patience with what other children are doing. Gradually, he develops a feeling of competition. This occurs in most cultures, but in certain cultures where this tendency in children is looked down upon, the child does not develop it to any great extent. Obviously, the tendency to competition is the result of social and cultural environments. Besides, even in one culture the same child may show a spirit of competition on one occasion but not on another. Or, one child may have a deep desire to compete while another may be indifferent. There can be many factors responsible for this variation, among them the child's order of birth in family, the behaviour towards him of his parents and other relatives result in any competitive activity.

The spirit of competition plays an important role in the child's development. In individual competition the child exerts all his energies in getting ahead of the other child, and this improves the rate of his development. When the child is a member of a group competing with another, his energies are directed at securing victory for his own group. This improves his community spirit. It has been observed in a series of experiments that wherever there is scope for comparison with other's performance the child improves his own performance owing to competition. If the spirit of competition can be intelligently employed, it will yield positive results. But this can be done if the difference between the competitors is not very large, because if one is far more powerful and accomplished than the other, then inferior competitor is likely to lose his self confidence in the process of competing. It is this factor which controls the independent child's choice of competitors. Left to himself the child will move among children of his age and capacity so that he can compete with them. It is essential for the parents and teachers to remember that healthy competition can take place only within a group with a small range of individual differences.

Competition must necessarily be healthy. In healthy competition the child is inspired to work more than he is accustomed to and to do better than the others in his group. For this he has no need to employ dishonest means, so long as the competitor is not much better than he is healthy competition does not contradict cooperation: in fact it encourages cooperative enterprise. It is, then, best to encourage healthy competition rather than to stop or to increase it. Parents and teachers can create circumstances in which the child can compete. Care must be taken to ensure that competition does not rise to a level where the child is forced to adopt improper means.

ROLE OF DISCIPLINE, REWARD AND PUNISHMENT

There can be no two opinions about the importance of discipline in an organisation but the definition of the term discipline itself has raised some problems. Educationists differ in their opinion of it. It becomes important, therefore, to be sure of what discipline means. An unscientific definition of discipline would normally include such activities as obeying the rules of the college, respecting the teachers, arriving in the class on time, abstaining from conversation during lectures, not damaging college property, doing all work required by the teacher, not quarrelling with one's juniors, avoiding the use of unfair means during an examination, non stealing, etc. And in fact, each of the above activities is directly concerned with maintaining the organisation of the college in its normal condition.

Difference between Discipline and Order

There is subtle but distinct difference between discipline and order because no discipline can exist without an order. Discipline on the other hand, comprehends much more than order. In the words of T.P. Nunn, "Discipline is not an external thing like order but something that touches the in most springs of conduct. It consists in the submission of one's impulses and powers to a regulation which imposes form upon the chaos, and brings efficiency and economy where there would otherwise be ineffectiveness and waste." Real or actual discipline, is therefore, seen to rest on character. Training in order is the training of character. Outlining the difference between discipline and order Rusk, the educationist, has pointed out that while order denotes the child's behaviour at home or in school, discipline is taken to mean the training of character, which is far more comprehensive than order.

Object of Discipline

In the words of Welton, "The aim of all true discipline is the training of conscience which consists in cultivation of the good-will and development of moral insight." Training in discipline is given to develop a man's moral insight. And training of insight, implies the development of a goodwill in the child. Discipline children accept good work and avoid bad. If the insight develops the child's moral insight also develops and be learns to judge what he should do and what he should not. A disciplined child does not have to be told to do this and not to do that, whether he is at home, in the school, in society or anywhere. He can judge for himself and he does what is right and avoids that which is bad. Discipline aims at underlining the importance of morality in education. Herbert, another educationist, has remarked that the objective of education is morality, meaning that education aims at making the child moral. And this aim can be achieved only when the child develops a sense of morality.

Discipline in the Classroom

Some people think that the teacher who has the quietest class maintains discipline most effectively. There is no doubt that a disciplined class in not noisy but the mere fact of absence of noise does not make a class disciplined. Discipline is not merely staying quiet, for it comprehends many other things. Some teachers have recourse to suppression to maintain quiet in the class. There may be quiet in the class but it cannot be said, to be discipline. The following methods can be adopted to maintain discipline in the class:

(1) **Interesting Method of Teaching.** It is desirable for the teacher to teach even the most arid subject in such a manner as to make it interesting for the students. If this does not happen, the students soon get tied up, they yawn in the class and if possible make a lot of noise. If the mode of teaching is effective, the students take a natural interest in the subject and discipline is automatically maintained.

(2) **Alertness.** Discipline also depends upon the degree to which the teacher is alert. If the teacher is himself inclined to sleep or yawn in the class, there is little possibility of his maintaining interest and discipline among the students. When he is himself wide awake the student's tend to behave because they are conscious of his eyes upon them and they realise that he will object to any undesirable activity on their part. If there is real discipline the students behave not because they are afraid of being punished but because they want to cooperate with the teacher.

(3) **Definite Rules of Behaviour in the Class.** If discipline is to be maintained, there must be definite rules of behaviour in the class of which, the students should be made cognizant on the first possible opportunity. It sometime happens that the student does things he should not, only because he is not conscious of these rules. If for example, the teacher has pointed out that students should raise their hands and attract his attention if there is any

difficulty the students will, do so and there will be no disturbance during his teaching. Neither will the students feel that their difficulty has not been explained to them. After he has framed the rules the teacher should see whether the rules are being obeyed. If he finds any students disregarding the rules he should advise the students to change their mode of behaviour. This forces the students to realise that there are some rules of behaviour in the classroom and that decorum must be maintained.

(4) **Creating a Sense of Responsibility in the Students.** Self discipline is based on the sense of responsibility. Hence in order to maintain discipline in the class the students should be encouraged to be responsible. It should be made clear to them that keeping peace in the class, following the rule, keeping the furniture in order, etc., are all their responsibility. The task of keeping order and peace in the classroom should be left to the students so that they can create discipline themselves.

(5) **Impartial Behaviour.** Some teachers are partial to some students in the obedience to rules, and where they would punish some students they let others go scot free. This partiality is very dangerous because there can be no discipline if the teacher behaves inconsistently. Both the student who is discriminated against and the one who is discriminated in favour tend to get out of hand because in either of them the attitude towards the teacher takes an undesirable turn.

(6) **Training in Discipline.** Finally, students should be told about the advantages of discipline and order in the class. It helps to maintain discipline. The students should also be told how orders or laws should be obeyed. It is at times desirable to ask the students to make their suggestions about improving discipline in the class. This will make them feel that establishing discipline is their own task and they will be encouraged to cooperate with their teacher.

Methods of Discipline

Norman Macmunn has analysed the different ways of maintaining discipline in the class in his work *The Child's Path of Freedom*. The main methods are the following:

(1) **Repression.** In the past, repression was used to create discipline in schools the world over. Gradually, psychologists raised their voices against this treatment with the result that this method is looked down upon everywhere.

(2) **Impression.** In this method of establishing discipline the teacher makes use of his personal impression instead of punishment. He treats the children with love, in return for which he gets their affection and respect. Children behave themselves with such a teacher.

(3) **Emancipation.** Another method which differs from methods of repression and impression, is that of emancipation. In this method the child is left to himself and is allowed to see for himself which actions are desirable and which are not. If this is done he will naturally learn to distinguish between right and wrong, and will avoid undesirable activity. Proponents of this method have hinted at the mode of teaching discipline through nature. If the child puts his hand in the fire it is immediately burnt by the fire. Nature punishes without warning.

ROLE OF REWARDS

Meaning of Reward

Reward literally means that which is given to an individual in return for what be has done. Under this definition even punishment would become a negative reward. But more usually reward is not interpreted in such a liberal manner and is taken to mean only positive award. Reward, therefore, is the good and proper consequence of good and desirable actions. It can take the form of some concrete physical prize or even merely psychological satisfaction at having done a thing well.

Kinds of Rewards

Reward can take almost any form, but the more common ones are the following:

(1) **Oral Reward.** Oral rewards are given in the form of praise. The praise may even take the form of a certificate, a medal or a shield. It can also be praise, done individually or in public.

(2) **Physical Reward.** Schools and colleges have a tradition of giving things as reward. Such useful objects as books, sports, equipment, clothes, hair-oil, soap, comb, are normally given.

Each of the two above forms of reward have their own significance. Oral reward or recognition has the effect of satisfying the self-respect of the child and of encouraging him to repeats activity in future. Its drawback that words of kindness are forgotten, sooner or later. On the other hand if the words of praise are rendered concrete in the form of a cup or shield or some other form of reward, they will continue to encourage the child in his future life. In this connection books have their own significance because they not only impart knowledge to the child but can be retained by him for long periods. Sports equipment is the next best choice because it is liked by almost all children and also helps to enhance his prestige in the eyes of his friends. He can also derive pleasure by using this equipment and can also thereby improve his health. Equipment meant for outdoor games is better than that for indoor games. In fact, anything that has utility can serve as a reward, but that which has durability also is better than another which can be used up quickly.

Aim of Reward

The aim of giving a reward can be judged from the significance that such an act has. These aims are:

(1) **Encouraging Correct and Proper Activity.** Education aims at directing the child's activity towards a desirable end and preventing it from turning towards the undesirable. Prevention is affected through the medium of punishment and encouragement for good activity through the medium of reward. Rewards delight the child for the moment, but they also serve as an incentive for repeating the activity which brought about the reward. Rewards help to instill the right habits in a child and to improve his character.

(2) **Recognition of Desirable Activity.** It is only natural for a child to be recognised as the author of some desirable action after he has done it. He desires such recognition from the teacher or parent. Rewards are the token of this recognition, and once recognition is granted the child can hardly wait to do it again. Recognition is directly linked with self expression. A child desires to express himself and also to have this self-expression recognised by his teachers.

(3) **Setting Good Examples to other Students.** As a normal rule, rewards and awards in colleges are presented in a big gathering in which all students are present. Sometimes the parents of the students are also invited to join in the celebration. When the child goes forward to receive his cup, shield or certificate while his friends, parents and well-wishers look on, he feels delighted and very pleased with himself. At the same time the other students are also spurred on to do something which will put them in a similar position.

(4) **Encouraging Healthy Competition.** Healthy competition is an important factor in communal life. Students try to do better than their neighbours and they do better than they would otherwise

if the concrete result of this competition is present before them. It is often seen that the bright students in a class compete hard for the first position because of the prize that goes with this position. They also exert themselves in the sports field because, they are aware that the winner will receive a prize and a lot of cheers. Awards have played an important role in encouraging healthy competition in studies and in game. Besides, awards can be given not only for mental and physical excellence but also for moral excellence, for if a tradition for giving an award for the best behaved student is established in the college it will encourage the students to make a good job of it. Awards can help the child's development of character by encouraging him to excel in all walks of life.

(5) **Encouraging Hard Work.** If a child wants to win some award it is necessary for him to put in a lot of hard work. Hence, when there is some reward, the child tends to work hard in every sphere, the mental, physical and the ethical or moral.

Principles for giving Awards

If benefit is to be derived from the giving away of prizes it is desirable that some system should be followed. It is essential to take care of the following aspects:

(1) **Reward based on Ability.** In the first place, the reward should be directly proportionate to the student's ability and the student should realise that he unquestionably deserves the reward being given.

(2) **Limited Number of Awards.** If almost every student in the school or college can win one prize or the other the entire system of prizes loses its value, for it then fails to stimulate competition. Prizes therefore should not exceed five in number.

(3) **Prize Subsequent upon Effort.** It is never proper to give a prize for some quality acquired by birth. Prizes, should be given for things which involve effort and hard work, and the prize should be given for the maximum effort shown. It should also be realised that winning a prize entails effort as well as talent.

(4) **Three or Four Prize Distributions in a Year.** If primary and secondary schools have three or four prize distributions in a year it will help to maintain the enthusiasm of the students at a high pitch during the entire year. They will continue to compete with each other and their effort will not flag due to lack of encouragement. This will help the teaching and the maintenance of standard.

(5) **Prizes for Least Interesting Work.** If prizes are allocated to activities in which every one naturally takes interest nothing useful is achieved for the incentive is already there. It is desirable to keep prizes for subjects which are important in their own right but which normally do not arouse interest in the student.

(6) **Prize should not have High Exchange Value.** It is not desirable to have a prize which is itself worth a lot of money. A student should not desire to obtain the prize merely because it is valuable in terms of money. But at the same time the prize should not be so cheap as to arouse no enthusiasm in the student.

(7) **Encouraging Healthy Competition.** In making arrangements for prizes the teachers should take care that this should not lead to jealousy, hatred, formation of rival groups and other undesirable associations. The aim of having awards is to create a spirit of healthy not unhealthy competition.

(8) **Prizes should be Announced Well in Advance.** Before the competition begins students should have sufficient notice of the fact that there is a prize. This will provide them with sufficient time to work and will also keep them organised and hard at work for a longer period.

(9) **Impartiality in awarding a Prize.** It is absolutely essential that the person or persons entrusted with awarding the prize are completely impartial. If some partiality or discrimination takes place it not only robs the prize of its importance but creates ill feeling among the students.

(10) **Prizes should coincide with Individual and Communal Feeling.** Prizes should be such as to arouse the individual and communal interest of the student. It is for this reason that some awards are set aside not for individual performance but for the performance of a team as a whole, whether it is a sports team or a class Inter-school and Inter-college competitions help to develop a healthy community spirit.

ROLE OF PUNISHMENT

Punishment means the pain and suffering caused to students with a view to improving administration and curing ills. Punishment can also take two forms-physical and mental. Physical punishment is given through the medium of causing pain to the body. This pain may be mild or severe. Milder forms of physical punishment are asking the student to stand on his seat or in a corner, forcing him to run around a field twice and similar punishments which do not cause too much suffering. Severe physical punishments can take almost any form, but among the better known are pulling the ears, beating with a stick, slapping, pinching, punching, or even giving a severe thrashing in the presence of the entire school. Mental punishment can be given by admonishing, criticising demeaning, or a variety of other methods. At times, this mental or physical punishment is further supplemented by economic punishment in the form of fines.

Objectives of Punishment

As a general rule punishment can have three main objectives— taking revenge, curing a fault or improving, or setting an example for other people so that they may not do such a thing. Punishment, meted out in the college may have any one or even more of these three motives behind it. At times the students who disturb the discipline of the college are punished in front of an assembly of all students so that other students may be discouraged from following their footsteps. Punishments of this kind are often severe for they have far-reaching consequences, and without severity they lose their meaning. At the school level it is quite common for the headmaster to call a meeting of the entire school and then to proceed to thrash the recalcitrant students severely. The very sight of this is often enough to deter most of the other students from such activity. In the present day, however, almost all punishment aims at improving the student and curing him of his bad habits. Mental punishment in any case has no other objectives, because it can neither serve as an example to others nor can it be used for revenge. Many teachers inflict mental or physical punishment upon their students when they feet that they have been insulted. Such activity is absolutely improper and an individual capable of it has no right to be a teacher. There can be no doubt that students have been known to injure the dignity of the teacher, and it is only natural for the teacher to feel infuriated. But although he may desire to get a little of his own back by pushing the student, such a desire can hardly be said to be proper. Punishment should be meted out only when the student can be improved by it, or when such punishment will set an example before the other students and guide them along the right path.

Excessive Use of Punishment

During the middle ages punishment was a common thing while in India even today excessive punishment is not unknown. In rural areas in particular it is common. If a student fails to turn up at school three or four boys are sent to bring him there, and they do so by dragging or beating him. When he finally does arrive he is then set upon by the teacher who literally makes a pulp out of him. He is then forced to stand in the corner in a bent position with a brick balanced on his back. Many schools follow a standard procedure for convincing the students that punctuality is the king of virtues. The headmaster closes all approaches to the school and takes up his position at the gate with a thick rod in his hand. All students arriving late are welcome at the gate by the headmaster, given a sound thrashing and then allowed to proceed to the class, with a hefty kick to speed them on their way. After this few students would dare to be late again, and if he is there is every chance of his playing truant from school rather than risking the punishment. This tradition of inconsiderate punishment is not restricted only to primary and secondary schools but even to high schools and intermediate colleges. Besides, the tradition is not peculiar to India, because worse examples of excess in this direction can be found in the history of education in many western nations. Prof. Cubberley has written of a schoolmaster named Haubberley who appears to have had a Teutonic taste for a variety of things. This master has recorded that in his 51 years and seven months of teaching life he administered 9,11,527 strokes with the cane, 1,24,010 strokes with a stick, 20,989 strokrs with a ruler or a piece of rope, 1,36,715 strokes with the hand, 10,235 strokes on the face, 7,905 ear boxings and 11,15,800 slaps on the head. In addition to this he had a vocabulary of 2000 abusive terms some two-thirds of which were taken from the German language while the rest had been invented by the teacher himself. This example proves the extent to which mental and physical punishment was inflicted upon the students. Excessive punishment is normally inflicted when there is a desire to suppress the individual punished. It is taken for grant that the individual is by nature, a cheat and bounder and that if he can be prevented from doing his dark deeds it is only through the fear of punishment.

Consequences of Excessive Punishment

There can be many consequences of excessive punishment, almost the only desirable one being that it may frighten the individual into submission. It may result in permanent injury or even, in some extreme cases, in death. There can be no doubt that when other children see punishment of this order being given, they are inspired to stick to the straight and narrow path of virtue. Mental punishment is no less harmful than physical punishment. It has been seen that students commit suicide after they have been criticised and ridiculed beyond edurance by their teachers. And, on the other hand, it has also been observed that if the teacher limits himself to criticism and ridicule, the students imagine that he is either a fool or incapable of administering physical punishment. In such cases they become even more unmanageable.

Propriety of Excessive Punishment

Generally speaking, it may be said that excessive punishment can never be justified, particularly if it is physical punishment. It should, therefore, never be used to excess. Among its consequences are impaired hearing, loss of limbs and even death. Further, it can only succeed in creating feelings of hatred and revenge against the teacher in the student's mind. There have been cases where a student has been compelled to revenge himself upon the teacher and to bring about the latter's death. Such reactions can have no value and they reflect upon the system of education as a whole. Even the students who are deterred from antisocial activity when they see another student being punished, do not have any feelings of love or respect for the teacher. They are inspired only by fear and disgust.

Similar consideration applies, to the subject of excessive mental punishment. If the student commits a mistake he should not be ridiculed or criticised, so severely that he may be compelled to seek revenge or that he may develop a permanent inferiority complex. This can only have a bad effect upon his character and all such influences only serve to encourage indiscipline, not to discourage it.

These considerations should not create the feeling that punishment should be given up. Adequate punishment is desirable and at times even necessary. There are some students who, if they are not thrashed, grow impudent and feel that nothing can happen to them whatever they may do. This confidence leads them to do things which are completely undesirable. Such students must necessarily be taught that there is a divinity that shapes our end, even if the divinity takes the form of a ruler or cane. If students who disturb the discipline of the college go unpunished, the rules and regulations of the college lose their meaning for such students. If the importance of the rules is to be brought home to the erring students it is necessary that there should be provision for punishment. What is important is that this punishment should then be administered without discrimination.

Principles Underlying Punishment

Punishment should be administered only on principle so that it may not lose its meaning. The following things should be kept in mind:

(1) Punishment should be such as to improve the erring student.
(2) Punishment should be example to other students so that they may be deterred from following the same path.
(3) Punishment should never be excessive.

(4) Punishment should be in direct proportion to the magnitude of the misdemeanour.

(5) Physical punishment should be administered by the headmaster, but this individual should not display any anger. Punishment should be an act of justice.

(6) Punishment should not take the form of ridiculing or insulting a student.

(7) Punishment meted out to the student should be recorded in his report book and sent to the parent.

(8) There should be no discrimination while punishing a student.

(9) For all violations of discipline there should be fixed punishment. In all such violations the punishment must be inflicted upon the culprit. When the punishment is fixed the student either accepts the inevitable or decides to behave himself.

Finally, it can be said that if the above points are kept in mind in framing punishment in the college, the students will definitely improve. Good examples will be set to the other students. The success of all punishment depends to a great degree upon the psychological insight and intelligence of the teacher.

QUESTIONS FOR EXERCISE

1. What do you understand by discipline? Why is it needed? When is punishment the most effective method of disciplining the child?
2. How will you define discipline? Discuss the role of reward and punishment in inculcating discipline among children.
3. Discuss in brief the elements of good discipline. What are the effective rewards for children?
4. Discuss in brief the good educational practice in discipline. What cautions should be observed in educating for discipline?

15

Instincts and their Transformation

MCDOUGALL'S THEORY OF INSTINCTS

The most famous and scientific theory about instincts, however, is that of William McDougall. Defining instinct, McDougall calls it "an inherited or innate psycho-physical disposition which determines its possessor to perceive, and to pay attention to, objects of a certain class, to experience an emotional excitement of a particular quality upon perceiving such an object, and to act in regard to it in a particular manner, or at least, to experience an impulse to such an action."[1] As has been pointed out in the above definition, instinctive behaviour tends to concentrate a person's attention on some particular class of objects. There are, therefore, three stages in instinctive action — Cognitive, Affective and Conative. With every instinct a particular emotional excitement is felt. To quote McDougall, "We seem justified in believing that each kind of instinctive behaviour is always attended by some such emotional excitement, however faint, which in each case is specific or peculiar to that kind of behaviour."[2] The following are the instincts and the related emotions:

MAJOR INSTINCTS

	Instincts	*Emotion*
1.	Escap	Fear
2.	Repulsion	Disgust
3.	Curiosity	Wonder
4.	Pugnacity	Anger
5.	Self Assertion	Positive self feeling
6.	Self Abasement	Subjection
7.	Parental	Tender Emotion

1. Wm. McDougall. *An Outline of Psychology*, p. 10.
2. Wm. McDougall. *An Introduction to Social Psychology*, pp. 25-28.

Besides the above mentioned major instincts, McDougall mentioned some more of them in which the related emotional feeling is not quite as obvious. They are as follows:

MINOR INSTINCT

8.	Gregariousness	Loneliness
9.	Acquisitiveness	Feeling of Ownership
10.	Constructiveness	Feeling of Creativeness
11.	Food seeking	Appetite
12.	Sex	Lust
13.	Appeal	Distress
14.	Laughter	Amusement

With the exception of laughter, all the above mentioned instincts are found equally in human beings and animals. Among them, the acquired motives such as self assertion, self abasement, parental and gregariousness are not universal. Sex, escape, curiosity and laughter etc., are practically universal and innate. Food seeking instinct is found in all animals because all of them seek food. Similarly, the constructive instinct is found in man as well as animals. To acquisitiveness, the quality of universality cannot be attributed, though it is found in quite a number of living beings. Calling for help in times of danger and seeking help has its own biological importance and is a tendency possessed by most of the animals. As a result of this, the members of the society or the family come to the assistance of the victim. The tendency to avoid an undesired and detested object and to have a repulsion for it, is obvious in almost all the animals.

Criticism of McDougall's Theory

Although McDougall's theory of instincts was welcomed very enthusiastically, it also gave rise to a lot of severe criticism. J.R. Kantor, a contemporary of McDougall went to the extent of saying that "Nothing worse than McDougall's conception of instincts has ever been conceived in the field of psychology."[1] But the theory of instincts cannot be refuted with such ease. To arrive at any conclusion it is necessary to study the experiments in this field, from McDougall's times to the present day. Psychology being the science of behaviour, the theory of instincts can be accepted only if it helps in some way, to explain the behaviour of living beings meaning there by that they help to show some specific innate, internal organisation to be the cause of behaviour. The following are the main objections against McDougall's theory of instincts:

---

1. Kantor, J.R., *Principles of Psychology,* Vol. 3. Alfred A. Knopf Inc., New York : 1924.

(1) McDougall has himself accepted that experience does make very substantial alterations in the instincts. The environment and conditions cause a big change in the behaviour of animals and human beings.
(2) McDougall did, of course formulate the definition of instinct but he did not point out that at which level the instinct may be seen in its purest, and unaltered form in accordance with the definition. Neither he took the trouble of giving a detailed description of the conditions which may arouse an instinct and nor did he make any mention of the related emotions and their physiological and mental signs.
(3) McDougall has given a general description of the stimulating conditions for instincts and the corresponding emotions but no such general description can be of help in the understanding of the working of instinct in living beings because the different types of animals differ in respect of their physiological structure and nervous systems. A different description of each class of animals will have to be made if this purpose is to be fulfilled.
(4) McDougall maintains that every instinct has a definite neurological basis. He however did not disclose what the neurological basis was, which was precisely the most important and perplexing problem. He failed to supply details of it since experiments on this basis were necessary for every class of animals. They were to be comprehensive experiments.
(5) McDougall did relate different emotions to instincts and he also accepted different nervous basis for each of them but there were insufficient experimental data to support his hypothesis.

Sherman in 1927, Pratt in 1930, Irvin in 1932 and Taylor in 1934 all studied the reactions of children under controlled circumstances but they failed to prove anything thereby. Mostly people thought that there was only one central agency or energy which directed all the instincts. Freud's studies in 1925 and Burtt's in 1939 upheld this view. When the distinctions in emotional aspect could not be proved, attention was directed towards the cognitive distinctions in instincts. Every instinct has a specific internal structure which compels its possessor to observe or to pay attention to a particular class of objects. The same difficulty arose in the recognition of these structure because they became modified by experience or the effect of the circumstances so that it becomes difficult to distinguish between one and the other. Though McDougall did believe that the instincts had the tendency of adaptation he also gave credence to the idea that their internal patterns may vary. Some experiments revealed that some animals like the hen reacted to some specific stimuli in controlled conditions but they failed to pay attention to objects which they had been taught to pay attention to. This proved the hypothesis that there may be an internal perceptual system. But then, Lashley's experiments proved that many alterations are possible in objects, which aroused certain specific excitement. These experiments were carried out in 1938. These made the distinction of instinct difficult. In 1942, in a symposium Burtt came to the conclusion that "Along with lower animals human beings have some inherited tendencies, the more obvious of which are fighting, fear and sex, and perhaps there are others more difficult to ascertain." Even when the instincts were so limited in number, G.W. Allport in a symposium in 1946 refused to accept this declaration.

Thus, though many psychologists believe the existence of instincts in human beings, they give to them an importance far less than the one accredited to acquired motives. In elucidating human behaviour more emphasis is laid on his life history or his family or social conditions than on instincts. Some psychologists seem to believe that McDougall's theory of instincts may be of greater help in understanding the behaviour in animals but it is not very helpful to understand the human behaviour.

Experiments carried out in recent past upon the subject of instincts make it clear that the theory of instincts cannot be dispensed with such consummate ease. In 1951, Tinbergen conducted many experiments in which the unacquired and innate reactions of birds and animals to special kinds of stimuli, were noted. Experiments by other psychologists indicated that there are some innate mechanisms in various animals which are directed specific stimuli. But it is possible that future experiments may show different patterns of specific behaviour in different classes of living beings which may lead to the establishment of some neurological basis. Experiments in connection with learning have thrown light upon this. Some experiments are providing proof for the specific behaviour patterns. To conclude, in its present state, nothing can be said with certainty about the theory of instincts. But one thing is definite that enough evidence is not available to prove the theory of instincts baseless.

INSTINCTS AND EDUCATION

In modern educational psychology every possible effort is made to base the education of the child on its instincts. Modern education aims at the excitation of one or the other instinct in a child in order to make any and every kind of education, natural and normal. Various instincts in a child are useful in education in the following ways:

(1) **Escape.** In a child one finds the instinct of escape joined to the emotion of fear. The intelligent teacher arouses fear and a disgust towards bad things in the child'. He also tries to prevent fear and escape from acting in many unnecessary cases. Meaningless fears are thus eliminated.

(2) **Pugnacity.** The instinct of pugnacity or combat is a universal motive. The most important fact that accelerates or excites it is restraint. A child whose means of locomotion are stopped by the simple expedient of being placed under restraint will go red in the face and cry at the top of its voice. Conflict starts the moment one removes a chick from the hen, or makes fun of an irritable individual or prevents an animal from fulfilling and satisfying its instincts. The activity of conflict starts when some motive remains dissatisfied through some external agency.

The object or animal turning pugnacious is to remove the obstacle preventing its progress or to defeat the obstacle. As long as the individual fails to defeat the obstacle or to remove it from his path, his internal, physiological and psychological disturbance continues. The pattern of pugnacity or combat is not the same in all animals or individuals nor are the implements common to all. Animals having long nails or teeth use them in warfare. In most animals it is the male who is pugnacious. He combats the animals of different species, and other, males of his own species for supremacy over the females or for food. It is possible that the instinct of pugnacity is somewhat depressed by the female hormones. Human beings and some other animals are known to threaten before actually attacking. Proverbially it is the monkey who is the best showing their teeth, others, by making offensive noises while others show their ungentlemanly instincts by hanging on their chests. Forms of pugnacity are modified by age, intelligence, social and cultural influences and social behaviour. The pugnacious instinct of cultured individual finds expression in more indirect manner. His animosity continues over the years, and his vengeance is achieved in many devious and indirect ways. Litigation is only a form of conflict and it is very common in cultured societies. In fact, it is difficult to believe that pugnacity is only an instinct or an internal motive whose single object is conflict or fight. The instinct to competition may be innate but the pugnacious instinct is activated only when the fulfilment of a motive is obstructed. Anger results in conflict but sometimes anger finds expression in more devious and uncommon ways. An employee who has been severely reproved by his employer is in no position to answer him back in strong language as he goes in fear of losing his job, but as an alternative he lets off his pent up feeling of anger on his wife and children. Sometimes our pugnacious instinct is satisfied when we see others fighting. The tension of conflict is also released and relieved when one plays games or sees others playing or fighting going on the film screen. Within the family the parents prevent many of the child's instinctive actions so that he develops feelings of animosity for them. Children worry the parents so that the latter become angered. Children compete among themselves for the love of their parents. Similarly, some sort of conflict is usually found to exist between the best adjusted pair. In order to protect the household from the painful and often dangerous results of these conflicts, it is essential that harmless means of venting these tensions should be found and applied. Among children, games are the best outlet. Grown ups should be given a chance to get their pent up emotions off their chest once in a while. This is a useful expedient.

(3) **Repulsion.** The intelligent teacher does his best to develop motive of repulsion in the child for unsavoury and undesirable things.

(4) **Parental instinct.** To this instinct is conjoined the emotion of pity. This instinct finds its expression in the older child's love for his younger counterpart and for other living beings.

(5) **Sex.** Sex instinct of a person may be turned into more acceptable outlets such as dancing, music, art etc., by the teacher. And, particularly in the adolescent stage this instinct can be restricted and moulded to provide the desirable development in the adolescent.

(6) **Curiosity.** Curiosity is the most important instinct from the educational viewpoint. It is a fundamental instinct without any definite biological basis. When any living being is confronted with any new or unrecognised object, it is natural for it to desire a complete knowledge or understanding of it. Curiosity in human beings is accompanied by the sense of surprise. Almost all individuals are desirous of knowing new things and new places. When a child is handed something it has not seen before, it will immediately turn it over and explore it to the best of its ability. The child is always ready with an unending list of questions. He never tires of asking questions even if the parent tires of answering them till he is forced to rebuff the child. If the child's curiosity is not suppressed, it continues its exploration and questioning till it finally comes to know its surrounding to its own satisfaction. It is such

children who turn into the best investigators and scientists when they maintain their curiosity intact in their adult circumstances.

Teachers who fail to arouse curiosity in their students regarding the subjects of study fail to achieve even a semblance of order and administration in their classes. To curiosity is conjoined the emotion of surprise. An object or thing that surprises the child also arouse curiosity in him. Hence, if a teacher is intelligent he will create surprise in the child regarding the subject he, wants to reach with the result that the child will become curious. Once this is achieved more than half the battle is won, since the child starts studying on his own once his curiosity is aroused. Besides arousing the curiosity of the child, the teacher also has to turn it in the required direction. For a child to develop curiosity regarding detective novels or matters or sex may be harmful to him as well as to his normal course of studies. Hence, the teacher must see to it that the child's curiosity takes desirable paths, such as good books and subjects. Being curious about the subject, the child will find, interest in its perusal. Thus, he progresses on the path of education without any external instigation. Modern psychologists are thus justified in emphasizing the fact that teachers should arouse curiosity regarding a subject they intend to teach in the class before actually engaging in teaching it.

(7) **Self-submission.** Of course, the instinct of self submission may prove to be a hindrance in the child's development but the sensible teacher can turn it towards himself and arouse feelings of respect for the teacher and a healthy regard for discipline in the child. Students are prone to accept teacher's mandate with questioning so that success in education becomes possible.

(8) **Self Assertion.** The instinct of self assertion occupies an important place in the child's character. To it is conjoined the sentiment of self respect which helps the child steer clear of all undesirable activity and to concentrate only on the desirable one. In order to develop self respect in the child, the teacher must put before him examples taken from the child's own environment. If instead of punishing a child for his mistake, the teacher tells them that such foolishness is not expected of him or from one of his up bringing then the child will abstain from repeating it. He will also be remorseful. Once the instinct of self assertion is fully developed, the individual makes his own efforts to progress in life, since he does not want to live the life of insect but wants to hold his head high in society.

(9) **Gregariousness.** A child is gregarious by instinct and he naturally wants to remain with the group of friends. A child does not desire solitude. The teacher can make the best of this instinct and help in the social development of the child. The teacher should keep an eye on the various group tensions that develop within the school and also try to evolve healthy competition, cooperation and team spirit in the children. Blind faith in small groups may be turned to more productive channels when it is turned to love of country and philanthropy. In this way, the child becomes socially mature.

(10) **Food Seeking.** The food seeking instincts may be put to much fruitful if indirect use by the teacher as he can instigate the student to greater effort in his study by inspiring him with visions of success in his future livelihood. Young men are seen to work very hard as they are afraid for their bread at a latter stage. The instinct of self assertion also contributes to this process.

(11) **Acquisitiveness.** A child instinctively collects many odds and ends about him and takes great pleasure in doing it. It gives him a feeling of possession and pride. In their tender age children are often seen collecting stamps, match boxes, cigarette boxes, and are often seen fighting to the better end for them. Within the bounds of the school, this innate tendency of acquisition can be put to constructive use. They can be guided to collect stamps, photographs, old coins and books etc. But in this process it is essential to see to it that the child does not resort to undesirable methods of augmenting his collection. In the school, the child's acquisitive tendency can be adequately exploited to create a small library or a collection of odd bits, in which the child can retain possession over them and yet allow them to be used by all his colleagues. Children belonging to very rich families, particularly young children, can be inspired to develop their own libraries, laboratories, etc.

(12) **Constructiveness.** It is due to the instinct of constructiveness that the child is seen making and breaking many things. The teacher can teach the children to make many small objects of various kinds with clay, colours, wood, stones and small mechanical objects. This has the effect of inspiring to children to much greater creative effort when they grow up so that they become scientists and engineers.

(13) **Laughter.** The instinct to laughter is accompanied by the emotion of enjoyment and relief. If the children are made to laugh in class they are more inclined to accept the teacher's suggestions. Hence, the sensible teacher can get the children to perform different tasks by arousing laughter and enjoyment.

Transformation of Instincts

Earlier in this chapter after instincts have been described, it is mentioned that instincts can be changed or transformed. And from an account of the possibilities implicit in the transformation of instincts it is obvious that the teacher can do much in this direction. Psychologists have established and proved beyond doubt that the instincts with which an individual is born cannot be removed or eliminated out of his system. Hence, it is entirely futile to try to put an end to such instincts as curiosity, sex, constructiveness, etc. in human beings. At the same time, it is not expeditious to leave them in their animal and unrefined state to find their own mode of expression and satisfaction. In every society, certain customs and patterns of approved behaviour become obstructions to the fulfilment of the individual's instincts. Hence, transformation and sublimation of instincts becomes something of a necessity, otherwise it is not possible to achieve adjustment between society and individual. Many and varied are the methods that are observed in this connection:

(1) **Law of Hedonic Selection.** According to the law of hedonic selection human being, by his very nature, selects objects and activities that are pleasurable, and avoids unpleasant and painful objects and activities. Hence, heeding this natural principle, teachers award the desirable instinct-motivated behaviour of children and punish other instinctive behaviour that is not desirable. But according to educational psychologists, this method, being negative, is harmful for the child's development, and it should not be employed as far as is possible.

(2) **Law of Inhibition.** Believers of this law contend that if the instinct does not get a chance to find expression, it is destroyed. It will gradually cease to exist. The psychologist William James used to believe this law.

MEANS OF TRANSFORMING INSTINCTS

Modern educational psychologists are not inclined to grant complete and unqualified approval to either of the two above laws concerning instincts. Many different studies and experiments have served to create the conviction that no one instinct can be completely destroyed. In the case of people who try to supress these instincts, they find new outlets and satisfy themselves in various unusual and patently abnormal ways. Hence, the transformation of instincts is attempted through the medium of the process of education. Generally speaking, the following five methods are adopted for the transformation and variation of instincts in human behaviour:

(1) Through repression
(2) Through inhibition
(3) Through contradiction
(4) Through redirection
(5) Through sublimation

Detailed consideration upon these various methods of transformation of instincts, and a careful evaluation of their advantages as well as their disadvantages, will make it possible to decide upon the one that can be included in the educational process for achieving this end.

(1) **Through Repression.** As a general rule, no member of any human society has the facility of expressing and manifesting his instincts in a completely uninhibited and unchanged form, because such a condition would lead to serious conflict and crisis with the other members of society, the organisation of which would immediately be ended. Maintenance of reasonable, organisation within society entails the use of such instruments of social control as customs, traditions mores, etc., and many of the individual activities are obstructed in favour of general social warfare. Hence, it is understandable that the individual may be endowed with many such instincts the unbridled manifestation and satisfaction of which may not be palatable to society. It must be kept in mind, of course, that the society does not regard any individual instinct as bad or undesirable, and neither does it insist upon its exclusion from the body or being. Society only objects to certain specific modes of expression of some instincts for the sample reason that it obstructs and hinders in independence and freedom of other members of society. One example that readily comes to mind, is that of the sex instinct that is not, and in fact cannot be, considered bad or undesirable by any society, but every society has its own modes of satisfying this instinct that it can considerable. If the instinct is allowed to find some other form of expression then society is compelled to hinder and punish the individuals concerned. In Indian society, particularly in the rural background, premarital sexual relations between men and women are not considered very healthy, though there are not restricting on sex relations between individuals when they are husband and wife. Obviously, it must be essential for the younger generation of the country to keep some semblance of control on their passions as long as they remain unmarried. In much the same manner it renders control on the specific expression and manifestation of individual instincts.

The most prevalent method of controlling or, transforming instincts is that of repression. Normally if men and women find that some particular instinct is not considered desirable, in society, and its satisfaction is not to be sought or is not possible even through devious and mysterious, ways, they have recourse to its repression. In other words, they suppress that instinct. As the psychoanalysts have pointed out, when instincts are repressed, they disappear out of the conscious mind, but they are forced into the unconscious mind where they assume such a deceptive form for manifestation that the super ego of the conscious mind cannot find any objection to it. It is a common experience that our repressed, instincts are manifested in dreams, day dreams, or through the creative medium of art and literature. So far, there is no harm in repressing instincts, but the continued and constant repression of a particular instinct may endanger the mental balance of the individual. Hence, the transformation or control of instincts through repression is a method open to many shortcomings, the major ones being the following :

(A) Explosion of Repressed Desires. As has been pointed out earlier, a person's repressed desires leave the conscious mind and take up their abode in the unconscious from which they emerge in greatly transformed shape and form. There is not much harm in the repression of weak desires, but the repression of a very strong instinct we desire can only lead to great increase in tension within the unconscious mind. If even then this repression is carried to its final extreme, tension may increase to such an extent that the repressed desires may explode, as a consequence of which the person may become a mental patient or may even become insane. Even normally, repression has some adverse effect on the individual by disturbing his mental balance.

(B) Destruction of Creative Energy. Many psychologists have pointed out that the satisfaction of instinctive desires provides the individual with energy for creative purposes. For example, the normal and healthy satisfaction of the sex instinct creates in man tremendous energy for creative work. If, now, these instincts are denied satisfaction and condemned to repression, obviously, the individual will be deprived of these creative powers or energy. The energy that could have been utilised towards much constructive and creative expression of the individual is uselessly expended in reducing mental tension caused by repression.

In India, because the young boys and girls are not able to form a correct opinion of the expediency of celibacy or continence, they are forced into unnatural repression of the sexual urge, with the result that the energy that should have gone into study and development is consumed in self-denial. The main reason behind this is that they are not aware of the proper method of transforming desires that arise from the sex and various other instincts.

(C) **Emergence of Undesirable Characteristics.** Extreme repression of instincts prevents the normal development of the person's personality and character, and he manifests many undesirable and harmful mental symptoms. For example, it is seen that boys and girls, or grown up people for the matter of that, who are involved in excessive repression of their own sex instinct are prone to view the activities of others with suspicion and that their outlook is condemnably narrow. They show a vain pride in themselves, are very much averse to criticism at the hands of others, and pay unnecessary attention to the character of others. They show a lack of benevolence and natural piety. As a result of all this, their social adjustment is marred. Sometimes even men and women of sterling character are not able to find adjustment and contentment in their practical life. On the other hand people who do not repress their sexual or other instinct, normally exhibit better adjustment. When without good characters they have all the best things of life, including respect, they are shocked, and their faith is undermined. In such circumstances, many people develop anti-social tendencies. Hence, it becomes obvious that the formation and development of character requires that the transformation of instincts in the formation of character be affected through more desirable and proper means than repression.

(D) **Obstacle to progress.** It has been mentioned earlier that the excessive repression of desires originating in instincts leads to the destruction or wastage of much creative energy. Obviously then, repression can prove to be a very big obstacle in the path of a person's progress. The main cause of this is that repression obviates the normal development of personality, character and mind, makes possible very great harm and denies progress and development.

The above account of the defects involved in repression should not create the impression that repression is absolutely bad. The day to day small desires are things that a person is compelled to repress. There is no doubting the fact that if a person does not allow improper desires to arise, and thereby eliminates the necessity of repressing them it is much better but this is not quite possible, even in the case of most sterling characters. The environment in which man lives presents many kinds of enticements and attractions, the only way of avoiding falling for them being repression. Thus repression cannot summarily be abandoned. If its defects are to be avoided, one should avoid carrying it to its extreme. Proper habits reduce occasions of repression and forcible control. If bad habits are not formed, the individual finds that opportunities or repression are greatly reduced, hence he should try to avoid situations in which he may be aroused and have to resort to repression. This does not involve an escapist attitude in which the individual seeks to avoid the environment. It is easy to generate good qualities and habits by placing oneself in a good environment, but it is neither easy to live in unfavourable circumstances and continuously fight it, nor particularly desirable. The Christians very temperately beg of their Lord, "lure us not into temptation." To say that we will remain true to our ideals and never lose sight of the path we are required to pursue however hard be the circumstances, is not very psychological. It shows a lack of psychological acumen. Hence, it is best for the teachers to guide their wards into good circumstances and to help them avoid all circumstances that are likely to prove difficult to tolerance.

(2) **Inhibition.** In this process of transforming instincts, it attempted to place the growing child in circumstances that deny or retard the growth of instincts. For example, in ancient India, brahamchari or celibate students were forbidden to look upon the face of woman. When they went to the villages to beg, they were ordered to keep their eyes lowered, and even then their visits were infrequent. Dressing elaborately, using hair and other oils or ornamental objects were considered anathema to retaining their celibacy and hence completely denied. The day to day routine of this classic celibacy was rather strenuous. It was believed that such measures would either prevent the very origination of the

sexual desires in the celibates or kill it as soon as it manifests. Its expediency in this respect is a matter of controversy with modern sex psychology and educational psychology. But this method involves one serious drawback, and that is, that it weakens the instincts. According to many psychologists, inhibition does not kill instincts as they leave the domain of the conscious mind but that they continue to exist in the unconscious world, with the result that while the individual is apparently of a very high moral characters unconsciously he is a potential immoralist. Hence, inhibition as a method is not looked with any favour in the modern age. One very salient illustration of this fact is that many of the members of a recently formed committee, constituted to look into the growing indiscipline among students in Indian Universities, suggested that the colleges and universities, should provide greater opportunities for mixing between the sexes—in order to solve the problem of indiscipline.

(3) **Contradiction.** Indian educational psychology holds contradiction to be a good method of transforming instincts. For example, in order to be saved from the complexities and intrigues of sex, people are advised to develop brotherly or affectionate feelings for members of the other sex, particularly those who are in no way related to one by ties of blood. If such feelings of commiseration and love developed, the sexual urge will not assert its particularly in respect of those individuals for which this feeling is created. In much the same way, the combative instinct can be controlled and reduced considerably if one evolves feelings of universal brotherhood. Such a feeling must be made part of the normal ethos of a group. The basic tenet in advocating the use contradiction as a method of transforming instinct is that if the contradictory feeling is developed, the one that we want to avoid will not have a chance to create trouble. For example, if sickness is to be avoided, it is best to develop the conviction that one is healthy and certain to remain so. The feeling of contradiction strengthens the self-confidence of the individual, and helps to reduce the negative tendencies and conflict.

(4) **Redirection.** One good method of transforming instincts is that of redirection. In this, the mode of manifesting the instinct is completely altered. For example, instead of allowing the combative instinct to waste its energy in unnecessary struggle and destruction, it can be constructively and successfully employed in extricating the oppressed, and guarding the weak. Similarly, the passion or instinct for collection, called acquisitiveness, can be

put to good use in the making of libraries and other collections. In redirection, the individual's instinct is turned to benefit the society. It results in the following advantages:

(1) In this, like in the case of inhibition, instincts are not weakened; they maintain their strength.
(2) In this, there is no danger of the explosion of instincts as is ever present in the case of repression.
(3) In this, because the person's instincts are turned to good account, his complete development is healthy and desirable.
(4) In this, neither the individual nor society suffers, and both are properly synthesized and adjusted.
(5) Through this the emotion can also be desirably altered. For example, the emotion of fear can be turned into fear of Gods wrath on evil.

(5) **Sublimation.** One big difficulty in the method of redirection is that fundamentally the function of the instinct cannot be altered. On the other hand, sublimation not only alters the mode of its manifestation but also its fundamental and basic form of nature. According to Freud, "Sublimation is an unconscious deflection of libido into other more socially accepted channels."

In this manner sublimation can lead to preventing of sex tendencies from expressing themselves in an undesirable manner and transforming them into specially acceptable behavioural patterns. Stressing the importance of changing the basic nature or form of the instinct through sublimation McDougall, in his book *Introduction to Social Psychology*, defines it thus: "Sublimation is a process by which the energies of our instinctive nature are utilized on higher planes of action than the instinctive." In this way, sublimation helps to divert the instinct from its normal and accustomed expression to a superior moral direction, a direction that is better regarded by society. For example, in the sphere of art one can find many poets and artists who originally evinced a very strong hetro-sexual tendency, but which was later turned to the expression of beauty and art. Kalidas and Tulsidas are examples of this fact. According to the psychoanalysts, the God-worship of many great priests and Saints mystics and preachers, evinces a sublimated sexual instinct.

Sublimation is universally accepted to be the best of all methods of transforming instincts. It helps to run instincts and emotions to socially accepted and creative uses, while they retain their original natural urge and strength. For example, the sex instinct is sublimated through various kinds of plays, games, literature and art, all of which act as a medium. But in the case of every instinct sublimation can be carried to a certain extent, following which sublimation becomes difficult and can even prove injurious to the individual. Hence, in this respect, too, it is essential that a balanced outlook be maintained.

EDUCATION AND THE TRANSFORMATION OF INSTINCTS

Education is profoundly influenced by and is interested in the transformation of instincts. A teacher has to transform the instincts of the students in such a manner that they loose none of their natural urgency and that they should be expressed and manifested in a socially accepted and creative manner. It is only natural that the processes of transformation, redirection and sublimation should prove to be the teacher's best friends. The main burden of transforming his instincts falls mainly on the student himself, but the teacher can assist him in many ways. In this respect the following means of assisting him are important:

(1) **Creating Healthy Atmosphere for Students.** In order to transform instincts it is desirable to have a healthy atmosphere in the colleges. The task of maintaining discipline in the college should be entrusted to the students themselves. This will help in maintaining a desirable atmosphere in the institution. In a good atmosphere, the students find a desirable mode of expressing their instincts.

(2) **Extra-curricular Activities.** The instincts of students are sublimated if they are allowed and encouraged to indulge in such extra-curricular programmes as dramatic representation, music, art, discussion, celebration, meetings, picnics, visits to places of historical importance, mutual felicitation, etc.

(3) **Catharsis.** Catharsis implies providing an opportunity for the instinctive or emotional force in man to find its outlet. Despite redirection and sublimation there remain in an individual certain instinctive urges that have to be manifested in order to ensure his healthy development. It is seen that sometimes scientists and even old teachers try to relieve the atmosphere by cracking indecent jokes, and such practice cannot be condemned. This, helps in the catharsis or relieving of repressed tendencies. Colleges should not be very strictly administered and students should be given adequate freedom and opportunity to meet each other. If they sometimes indulge into foolery of a harmless nature even if it involves one of the teachers it should not be frowned down upon with necessary severity. Community singing and dancing is another method of achieving catharsis of instincts. When the atmosphere in celebrations and informal meetings is

kept free students get an opportunity to express themselves, and the catharsis of these tendencies helps to reduce tension.

Briefly, in order to achieve the transformation of his students' instincts the teacher should mix with them, keep an eye on their tendencies and provide them with situations where their instincts can be sublimated or can attain to a certain catharsis.

QUESTIONS FOR EXERCISE

1. Examine critically McDougall's theory of instincts.
2. Explain the nature of instincts and state how can they be modified.
3. Write short note on Methods of modifying innate tendencies.

16

General Tendencies: Suggestion, Imitation and Sympathy

SUGGESTION

The, word suggestion does not imply precisely the sense in which it is usually employed in colloquial usage. Suggestion is a mental process in which the thoughts or thought processes of one individual influence and mould those of another. To take a common example, many people will attack any individual if they see a crowd attacking him even if they are not aware of any animosity towards the individuals. If two bulls happen to fight in the middle of the road, or if a baton charge is made or even if some people happen to run in some direction without any particular cause they are soon emulated. The main cause at the root of such conduct is suggestion.

Definitions of suggestion

It is necessary to turn to some of the definitions of suggestion so that it may be understood more completely and precisely. Some main definitions are the following:

(1) **McDougall's View.** "Suggestion is a process of communication resulting in the acceptance with conviction of the communicated proposition in the absence of logically adequate grounds for its acceptance."[1] As has been pointed out in the foregoing example of hypnotism there is no logical ground or basis for accepting the suggestion given concerning the drinking of water and taking of dinner at the time they were made in view of the fact that these objects were not present at that time. And yet, the persons casually accepted the suggestions and even implemented them. In

1. W. McDougall. *An Introduction to Social Psychology*, p. 83.

the crowd that is motivated by fear most people are seen running about worriedly and anxiously even when they are not aware of the reason for this anxiety. The reason for this is the suggestion inherent in the mob behaviour. Suggestion is the process of communicating information. The hypnotist employs this power to communicate his desire to others and in this way he manages to induce other people to behave in the manner that he wishes. The utterances of the great leaders and the militarists have the some power of suggestion and the person who hears them finds it be young his control to resist them.

(2) **Kimball Young's Opinion.** "We may define suggestion a form of symbol, communicated by words, pictures or some similar medium for including acceptance of the symbol without any self evident or logical ground for its acceptance."[1] like McDougall, Young has placed emphasis on the fact that the suggestion communicated has no logical or self evident basis.

(3) **Thouless's View.** "The word suggestion is now commonly used for the process by which an attitude towards a system of idea is communicated from one person to another by a process other than that of the rational persuasion."[2]

Characteristics of Suggestion

The three foregoing definitions of suggestion point to the following characteristics that are to be found in suggestion:

(1) Through the medium of suggestion, some idea is communicated from one individual to another.
(2) There is no evidence or logic to support suggestion.
(3) Suggestion can be conveyed though any symbolical medium such as language, pictures, etc.
(4) Suggestion involves mental images.

In defining suggestion, in view of its fore mentioned, characteristics, it can be said that suggestion is a mental process in which an idea, which does not have any evidence or logical basis, is conveyed from one person to another through any symbolical medium such as words, pictures, etc.

Suggestion in Education

Many functions are performed in school life because of suggestibility. If we glance at all at the occurrences that take place all around us, we shall visualise the importance of suggestion in education. Suggestion influences

1. Young, K. *Handbook of Social Psychology,* p. 10.
2. Thouless, R.H. *General and Social Psychology* (1951), p. 247.

not only behaviour with others but also one's own private and individual behaviour. Some students are conversely affected by suggestion, *i.e.,* they act in contradiction to the suggestion that is conveyed them. Suggestion is sometimes direct. In the first case the individual is aware of the fact that a suggestion is being made to him while in the second case there is no such awareness. In addition to these, in education one sees the influence of prestige suggestions almost everywhere. The. behaviour of the students in a mob situation is an example of collective suggestion. It would be of help to glance individually at the various forms of suggestion in education, the main among which are the following:

1. Ideo-Motor suggestion
2. Prestige suggestion
3. Auto-suggestion
4. Mass suggestion
5. Negative suggestion
6. Direct suggestion
7. Indirect suggestion
8. Positive suggestion
9. Negative suggestion

(1) **Ideo-Motor Suggestion.** As is evident from the name given to it, there is no discrimination here between thoughts and actions, *i.e.,* action takes place almost immediately the thought arises. Hence, in this there is no time to think or to discuss. Generally, in suggestions of this kind the mind almost unconsciously accepts and adopts suggestions given to it. The famous psychologist Alfred Binet conducted important experiments in connection with ideo-motor suggestion.

(2) **Prestige Suggestion.** The advice of people is accepted in the fields in which they are considered to be specialists. A book of a famous author sells easily even if it is not particularly good. The ideas expressed by the famous scholars and leaders are casually uncritically accepted by young men. In any political discussion if any person mentions the name of Mahatma Gandhi as supporting the contention that he has put forward, then in all probability his view is accepted by many without further preamble. All these are examples of prestige suggestion. An experiment was conducted by P.A. Sorokin and J.W. Bodyreff in connection with the effect of prestige suggestion. In this experiment 1484 high school students formed the audience for two recorded songs, one of which was said to be the work of a great artist while the singer of the second was said to be a commonplace artist whereas in fact both were sung by good artists. Because of the prestige suggestion inherent in the name 96 per cent students pronounced the first song to be good while the second they unanimously rejected as second rate. After this, the examiner pointed out that there was no difference

between the records. Consequent upon this, 51 per cent immediately expressed acceptance, 16 per cent contradicted this view while 21 per cent abstained from expressing any opinion. It should be remembered that only 4 per cent of the students had originally pronounced the records to be the same and these were the only ones to use their intelligence in judging. All the other had been deceived by the suggestion.

(3) **Auto-Suggestion.** Much stress has been placed by Indian thinkers upon the importance of auto-suggestion in the development of character. The character that an individual develops depends upon his thinking, and thoughts that he entertains. Thought has power of suggestion. If you are always engrossed in thinking that you are not intelligent and can never score a good division in the examination, then how can you hope to study properly? The doctor always advises the patient to have faith in his cure, because the fact of this belief helps to influence the health of the patient and supplements to some extent the medicine that is being administered to him. The famous psychologist Emile Cone cured some patients of mental diseases on the basis of auto-suggestion. By studying the biographies and autobiographies of great individuals one can see that they always placed the highest ideals before themselves to pursue and even in the time of extreme adversity they reassured themselves that in the end they would be victorious and successful. In this way, auto-suggestion has important influence upon the mental and physical condition, behaviour and even success of the individual.

(4) **Mass Suggestion.** Why is it that the behaviour of the, individual undergoes considerable change when he is in a group situation? The reason why the most balanced and sane individuals who are the very essence of propriety in their private life become almost insane and exhibit animosity and pugnacity in a crowd is that they fall prey to mass suggestion. In one of his studies H.T. Moore has pointed out that students are more susceptible to mass suggestion than prestige suggestion. It is for this reason that one only too often comes across striking students who, pay no heed to the uttering of the Vice-Chancellor of the University let alone the poor professor, and victims of mass suggestion that they are, they precipitate the most awful gaffs and do things that cannot be expected of them. By his experiments, C.H. Marple has proved that there is a ratio of 4 : 3 between mass suggestion and prestige, suggestion.

(5) **Contra Suggestion.** It is often seen that people will indulge in the very activity that they have been warned against. This is particularly true of children who will inevitably touch anything that they have been prevented from touching or that they have been ordered to stay away from, or in other words, the order of abstaining from touching the object gives a contra suggestion.

(6) **Direct Suggestion.** Some suggestions are of a direct nature, i.e., the individual who is accepting the suggestion is aware that a suggestion is being made to him. Often the teachers use direct suggestions to improve the work of the educands, and the educands also accept them.

(7) **Indirect Suggestion.** But some suggestions are not quite so apparent and bizarre, and the intention of the person suggesting is concealed. He puts forward his suggestions but he does not indicate his intention in doing it. Suggestions of this kind make a greater impression upon the educand.

(8) **Positive Suggestion.** The suggestions that are made for the implementation of some order or for accepting some statement are said to be positive suggestions.

(9) **Negative Suggestion.** The suggestions that are made for rejecting some order or for abstaining from some particular course of action are said to be negative suggestions.

The degree to which suggestions are important in education is evident by the above description of the various kinds of suggestions, teachers acquainted with psychological facts make use of suggestion to have their ideas and notions accepted by the students and to have the latter behave according to their wishes. Whether we like it, or not we are influenced by suggestions of others at one time or another. And, even otherwise, suggestions can be employed not only to influence others but also for self development.

IMITATION

When a child attempts to walk impressively like his father, swinging a stick the while, he is imitating. Mead has characterised imitation as the conscious emulation of the behaviour and conduct of others. He writes, "Imitation is self-conscious assumption of another's acts or roles."[1]

Process of Imitation

From the psychological view point, the process of imitation is seen to possess the following characteristics:

1. Mead, C.H. Quoted by K. Young. *A Handbook of Social Psychology,* p. 110.

(1) The individual imitating does not indulge in thoughts or trial and error before he imitates but immediately becomes involved in the activity of imitation.
(2) The person imitating does not show any previous acquaintance with the activity imitated.
(3) In the process of imitation the person imitating performs exactly the same activity as the one being performed before him.

Imitation in Education

The activity of imitation possesses much importance for education. In fact, it would be no misnomer to say that a major part of the education of the children is given through imitation. It is by indulging in imitation that the child can make adequate use of the behaviour of others around him. It is imitation which provides him behavioural patterns whereby he conducts himself in the presence of others. It is only through the medium of imitation that customs, traditions, and mores act in society and are maintained intact in their passage from one generation to the next. The human child possesses a great capacity for imitation. Language plays a major part in this imitation and language and pronunciation is, acquired by the child only through imitation. In society many forms of behaviour such as dress, etiquette or manners, conversational modes, food, etc., are adopted by imitation. Every educator makes use of the tendency of imitation. The education of social behaviour is based primarily on imitation, it is trenchantly often remarked that one is known by the company he keeps. It is often seen that the students try to imitate and adopt the behaviour thoughts, ideals and mannerisms of their teachers and because of this a good teacher succeeds in moulding the conduct of the students on the desired lines. It also usually happens that people estimate the behaviour of the children according to the knowledge that they have of their family. It is commonly believed, and in most cases also taken for granted, that the offspring of cultured and well mannered parents will be of a similarly cultured nature while the children of quarrelling parents will be obstinate and quarrelsome. At the root of all these notions is the element of imitation. By making adequate use of the tendency to imitation that the human child possesses in great quantity, an able teacher can succeed in moulding the behaviour of his students on cultured lines. It is because of the tendency to imitation that children are so susceptible to the influences of their parents and friends whose behaviour they imitate indiscriminately. It is only because this importance of imitation has been understood that now great emphasis is laid, in every sphere of education, on the concrete presentation of the ideals before the individual that are to be inculcated into him. And particularly, in the various spheres of cultural life such as dancing, music, art, etc., demonstration and its imitation are of great importance.

SYMPATHY

The Meaning of Sympathy

In the words of Woodworth, sympathy means, "Experiencing with another." When one individual shares the pain of other and also shares in their joys then it is said that he is sympathetic towards others. This is common experience that when we meet a person who is smiling we also smile. In a serious atmosphere have to maintain the serious nature of the atmosphere while we feel almost compelled to feel joyful and happy in a colourful and gay atmosphere. In this way, the play of sympathy can always be seen in day to day experience and behaviour.

Sympathy in Education

Sympathy plays a very important role in the education of child. The child learns easily if he is taught sympathetically. While solving the problems concerning the development of the children, their character, personality, learning and discipline etc., the teacher, to be successful, must behave sympathetically. The child should be taught to behave sympathetically with his younger and equals. This will help in his social and emotional development. Though sympathy is very much innate in the child, it can be also taught by examples. Passive sympathy helps in the study of literature and in aesthetic development. Active sympathy is the foundation stone of moral development. Thus, sympathy plays a valuable role in every aspect of the child's development.

QUESTIONS FOR EXERCISE

1. Write a Short note on Suggestion.
2. What is suggestion? Describe the various kinds of suggestions. What part does it play in the development of child?
3. What is sympathy? How does sympathy differ from pity? What is the role of sympathy in the education of child?
4. Write a short note on Sympathy.

17

Play

What is Play?

According to the famous psychologist McDougall, play is a normal innate tendency similar to suggestion and imitation. Though the definition to play varies from psychologist to psychologist, most of them believe that it is an innate tendency. The following definitions of the term will make it possible to understand it better:

(1) **Valentine's View.** According to Valentine, "Play is a kind of amusement in the work." This definition emphasizes an indispensable element in play, *viz.*, amusement. Play is indulged in by people because it yields amusement but such a definition cannot, explain all games it fails to analyse some kinds of play. A simple instance is of the child who plays from morning to evening. In his case, one can hardly be justified in saying that he plays for amusement.

(2) **Stern's View.** "Play is a kind of voluntary, self constrained activity." This particular definition lays stress on two important elements of play. In the first place, play depends upon the wishes of the individual, and secondly, it is the player participating who himself controls it. If these two conditions are to be found in learning, it too, becomes play. This definition gives a good explanation of the play way method in learning. But it falls short in as much as it neglects the element of amusement inherent in play. In addition to being volitional and self controlled, play invariably includes the feeling of pleasure and amusement.

(3) **Gluek's Opinion.** "Play is what we do when we are free to do what we will." It is the volitional and independent nature of play that is stressed in this definition. It need hardly be pointed out that the definition is one sided and incomplete.

(4) **Thomson's View.** "Play is the impulse to, carryout certain instinctive actions." This particular definition of the term lays stress on its instinctive nature. In the play the human individual gives expression to those instincts which do not find any manifestation and outlet in his normal life. This particular definition is applicable to the playing of both young children as well as grown ups. But this definition lacks comprehension as it neglects such other characteristics of play as naturality, independence, amusement, etc.

(5) **Sir T.P. Nunn's View.** "Play is a profound manifestation of creative activities." According to this definition, play gives expression to the creative and positive tendencies of the individual. This definition of the term is particularly apt for describing the playful activities of children. Putting it briefly play is volitional, autonomous, instinctive and creative, or an activity that manifests these activities, and which gives amusement and pleasure to the Individual.

KINDS OF PLAY

Children are seen indulging in different games as they progress from infancy to adulthood. The games peculiar to the different stage infancy, childhood, adolescence and adulthood, are different. Types of play have been classified in various ways. Karl Gross, for example, he classified games in the following ways:

(1) **Experimental Play.** In these games, the children are seen examining and breaking up the objects that are within their reach. It is their method of examining and becoming acquainted with things.

(2) **Movement Play.** This classification includes the movements of the hand and feet, running about, jumping, making peculiar sounds etc., that are characteristic of infancy and childhood. It is a natural stage in the development of the child, any interruption in which can have only the worst effect on his development. Till the child attains the important age of two, such games as these form his chief occupation.

(3) **Constructive Play.** In playing with objects, the child can either destroy them or construct other things. His earlier efforts are marked by destruction and in his wake he leaves a long trail of smashed things but later on he breaks things only to make others. In fact destructive and constructive activity has close relationship. Children play both kinds of games. They make houses only to break them with all the unconcern of an engineer gone berserk.

Constructive games are played both individually and collectively and girls are seen caricaturing the life of their adults in making houses, marrying off their dolls and cooking. The tendency to constructive play is seen in the child from the age of three or four. According to Stern, boys are more blessed with this tendency than girls. Consequently, boys are of an inventive and ingenious turn of mind whereas girls are more imitative in nature.

(4) **Fighting Play.** Games of fighting are decided by winning or losing. The object is gaining ascendancy over the opponents. Hockey, cricket and table tennis are examples of individual games. Boxing and wrestling are games of apparent hostility and fighting. Previously, such games were confined to the males but now the females have invaded their province in all games except those in which physical combat is unavoidable.

(5) **Intellectual Play.** In modern civilised societies people also play such games as chess and cards that depend mainly on the use of brain. Word building and puzzle solving belong to the same category.

Play in Different Age Levels

In addition to the above games, there are some other kinds. There are imitative games in which the participant puts on different disguises and imitates the original. Then, there are inventive games in which the child attempts the invention of different new objects emotive games such as wishful thinking; volitional games in which the artist tells jokes though the audience is not allowed to laugh, or two people making faces and at each other, the one to laugh first being adjudged the loser. After the description of the various, kinds of plays or games, we now have the kinds of games that are played in different age groups:

(1) **Birth to Three Year.** From his birth till he attains the age of three, the infant is seen playing games that involve emotional, perceptive and biological motions. He is interested in playing with gaily coloured objects which he throws around breaks them and puts them in his mouth. Of all toys, those capable of locomotion are the most attractive to the infant. The very small infant is capable only of throwing his arms and feet about. The infants in his age group also play with coloured charts, paint and brushes, etc. They take keen interest in listening to stories and studying pictures in books. Playing with dolls and making sand edifices is an equally engaging occupation for them. As they continue to grow they also develop the capacity of continuous concentrations and attention. The retention and widening of attention is open to many influences.

A child of two can attend to any game from one to seven and a half minutes, a child of three from one to twelve minutes while a child of four can attend to a game from one and seven minutes to fourteen minutes. Basing his statement on his experiments, Van Alystyne has pointed out that the attention in play increases by two minutes with each age level. He found no difference in the games of male and female infants.

(2) **From 4 to 7 Years.** In this age group, the number of boys, increases along with their variety. The child of four to seven prefers the more active games of driving a baby motor car, riding a try-cycle, playing in sand and water, running and jumping, digging and flinging things about. He likes to make different patterns by putting together colourful pictures of wooden blocks. Individual and group games are particularly desired once the child has attained the age of five, a peculiar feature being the desire to play under the supervision of a teacher. The child also takes interest in music, dancing and tales of animals and fairies. Development of mental and creative activities is manifest in the constructive and imitative games indulged in by the growing child. And such games also help in the further mental development of the child. His aesthetic and cultural development progresses further through stories, poetry, acting, music, dancing, painting, etc.

(3) **7 to 10 Years.** In this age group, the child is primarily inclined to collective games, so that he plays group games much more than individual games. Games such as hockey, cricket and football are played in accordance with some definite rules and this restriction adds to the child's enjoyment of them. Besides playing these games, the child also takes avid interest in watching matches between more accomplished artists of this craft. The desire to collect odds and ends is another passion peculiar to this stage in life. Using the check list technique in 1923-26, Lehman and Witty studied the pattern of play among children between the ages of eight and one half years and ten years, finding the following characteristics, peculiar to them:

(a) pleasurable physical activities, particularly rhythmic movement;
(b) activities of hiding and seeking;
(c) activities of imitating and caricaturing the adult;
(d) activities of skill;
(e) constructive activity;
(f) activities providing pleasure through the excitation of sense organs;

(g) playing with ropes;
(h) plays of music and dancing (particularly among girls).

The participation of the child in group games in this period results in an increase in his social knowledge, in his emotional development and in an increase in mental capacity. Hence, it is all the more desirable that the teacher should organise collective activity as far as possible.

(4) **10 to 13 Years.** Having attained the age of ten the children come to love even more organised and systematic games. They develop team spirit and it is a matter of pleasure for them to play in the team. Some team games involving intellect are also found to interest the youngsters of this age group. Many children in this age develop an astonishing interest in reading stories, and in fact become voracious readers. It is at this stage that definite differentiation between male and female games is apparent. It is the first stage of adolescence. In this age, the female species tends more to constructive and inactive games such as knitting, stitching, painting, etc., rather than to violently active games of running and roaming all over the place. Taking advantage of their desire to be more ladylike in their occupation, the young ladies can be taught all the functions of a housewife. Any knowledgable teacher can help the child's development by developing in him such characteristics as sociability and discipline, and interest in study and other intellectual pursuits.

(5) **13 to 19 Years.** In this age, the adolescent has grown considerably, and the love of imitative and imaginative games is replaced by an attraction towards more active, collective and courageous games such as hockey, cricket, etc. It is at this stage that the young boy begins to take interest in adventurous tours and journeys. Other more common games teach him discipline, communal spirit, team spirit, etc. His mind and imagination are both fairly well developed. The adolescent tends more to research, constructive games and acting, with the accent on physical exertion of a high order. The girls, on the other hand, drop physically active pursuits and settle down to such domestic activities as knitting, dancing, music, painting, etc. It need hardly be pointed out that this difference in the play interests of young boys and girls is due to the pattern of their respective future, roles.

Factors Influencing Play

Of the many factors that influence play among children, the most important are the following:

(1) **Age.** Age is one of the most important factors influencing play. As the child progresses from infancy towards adulthood, his plays gain in complexity and from haphazard movements become organised games. Growing older, the child comes to appreciate group and collective games in addition to the individual games to which he has been accustomed. Growing much older, passing from adolescence into unmistakable adulthood, the erstwhile child comes to love intellectual games more than physical play. He stops going to the playground and substitutes it in his life by the club where he plays mentally relaxing games.

(2) **Sex Differences.** Many detailed studies have definitely indicated that the games played by boys and girls in their infancy and childhood are the same. Most of the time they even play together. Nevertheless, despite this fact one does come across some difference in the playing of boys and girls of this age group. Girls are more partial to dolls while the boys are tendencious towards games that call for exertion and a certain degree of toughness. A sharp differentiation between male and female games is apparent only when the age of 8 or 10 is reached, when boys prefer to play with boys and girls with girls. Boys who persist in playing with girls are usually teased by their friends on account of the implied femininity of the boys who do so, and as this trait is not desirable. At the same time, the differences in sex lead to differences in the nature of games played by the two sexes. Boys play with ball, while girls play with dolls. The influence of sex on the form of play is even more pronounced when adolescence is reached. Boys choose to play more courageous, organised and active games, while the young ladies prefer comparatively inactive games involving less strenuous, if any, exercise. Many studies in this direction, have indicated that this difference in the games played by boys and girls is not due so much to the physiological differences as to such cultural factors as social tradition and custom, mores and accepted behaviour patterns. In many cultures, both boys and girls play equally challenging games of a physical nature. Even in Indian societies in families in which the education of boys and girls is not sufficiently differentiated, the girls are equally interested in riding, swimming, tennis, badminton and other physical games. The difference that is attributed to difference in sex is due to the fact that parents do not like girls after a certain age level to play with boys or play the games boys play.

(3) **Mental Differences.** The researches of Lehman and Witty indicate that normally and generally, differences in mental levels do not exert any significant influence on the kind of play. In other words, the games played by very intelligent, average and feebleminded will not differ widely, if at all. But the fact remains, that the games of intelligent boys are more varied and complex than those of their less fortunate brothers; particularly, in the case of games based on intellectual ability, a certain minimum level of intelligence is indispensable. Among students, some take more interest in their studies than in games, but there is no definite trend regarding this behaviour. Children who spend most of their time with books have little time to devote to collective games.

(4) **Environmental Differences.** In addition to the above factors, environment exerts an important influence. This term includes all sort of things such as climate, geographical location, fellow students and friends, traditions and social mores, etc. The form of play is affected if these change. Definite and pronounced differences between the games of children belonging to rural and urban areas, hot and cold climates, plains and mountainous regions are to be noticed. Boys and girls of urban areas frequent cinema houses while their rural counterparts show greater interest in kabaddi and domestic chores.

THEORIES OF PLAY

Thinkers differ on the psychological basis of play. It has been elucidated by different thinkers in different ways and has thus resulted in many different theories. The psychological elements in play can be understood by a study of these theories. The following are the main theories:

(1) **Theory of Surplus Energy.** In the opinion of Schiller, a famous German poet, play is the, expression or consummation of our surplus energy. The theory finds the support of philosopher Herbert Spencer. It is also called the Schiller Spencer theory. It is conceived that children do not consume their entire stock of energy in their normal routine of the day, and they play in order to consume the surplus energy created. Among the adult population, individuals engaged in hard and tiring work during the day do not indulge in play as they have no surplus of energy. On the other hand, those who lead a soft life or whose work is confined to less tiring pursuits, feel the need of physical exertion in play. Reasoning in this vein, the theory further suggests that play is a kind of safety valve for people through which the

excessive energy is exhausted. If this surplus were not to be consumed through the medium of play, the further development of the body could possibly be hindered and obstructed.

This particular theory of play fails to analyse and explain some definite kinds of play. It does succeed in explaining certain aimless activities of the child such, as flinging its arms and feet about, but it fails to provide satisfactory answers to many questions, some of which are:

(a) Why do people continue to play even when they are tired?
(b) Why does play always have a definite pattern?
(c) Why do the games of different animals differ?
(d) How does play help in the development of the child while the surplus steam that is exhausted from a system engine is completely wasted?

(2) **Recreation Theory.** According to the German Lazares and the English Lord Kames, an Individual regains the energy in play that he has lost or consumed elsewhere. This explanation of play has been supported by G.T.W. Patrick. It is opined that people indulge in play as it affords amusement and amusement refreshes the individual whereby he repossesses the lost energy. It is for this reason that one sees among the individual playing even those who have been exhausted during their vocational pursuits. They find amusement in play.

This principle succeeds in elucidating the role of amusement in play and is applicable almost exclusively to the exertions of grown up people. It fails to explain how or why children play as there can be no question of their being so exhausted as to need recuperation through amusement. Then, again, there are some old people who spend an entire day in playing chess and checkers. Does this pattern of behaviour conform to the view that people play in order to regain energy consumed? In fact this continued indulgence in play leads more to exhaustion than to freshness or energetic condition.

(3) **Anticipatory Theory.** Melbranche was the first to propound this theory, but it was elucidated at length by Carl Gross. Having made a minute study of the play of many different living beings Gross came to the conclusion that in play living beings practice the activities that will be required of them in their adulthood. Pups fight because when they become dogs they will have to fight for their life. A kitten runs after a ball and rips it apart in the manner cats are seen doing with mice. Similarly, the babies of reindeer are seen moving with long and swift strides. The same phenomenon is

observed in the case of human children. Female children rehearse their later married life in their childhood games of playing with dolls, making houses and marrying off their dolls. On the other hand, the male child usually rehearses his future life in playing at being a professor, engineer, shopkeeper or the like. According to Carl Gross, the more developed the life of a species, the greater will be the variety of games their off-springs are seen playing. In the same proportion the playing period in life will continue to a later stage. Being the most developed living being, man suffers his issue to continue in the playing stage for a longer time than other animals. On the other hand, among the undeveloped animals and insects such as bees and lizards, the baby engages in its business of life immediately it comes into possession of a fully developed body. But one sees play in the comparatively developed animals such as cats, dogs, monkeys, reindeer, etc. In man, almost one-third of his entire life span is spent in playing, and among the more civilized of his race the games played are so varied that one would require a veritable volume to describe all of them in detail. The games played in civilized societies are more numerous than in comparatively uncivilized tribes. Similarly, children belonging to a higher social circle play more games and play them for a longer period than do children who belong to a lower strata of society. The variety of games increases with developments in the nervous system. Accepting the anticipatory theory of play as superior to the theory of surplus energy, Sir T.P. Nunn has remarked astutely, "Nature invented play not merely as a means of disposing harmlessly of the young animal's superfluous energy but as a device for using that energy to prepare him, for serious business of life."

It cannot be doubted that the principle propounded by Carl Gross does succeed in explaining many kinds of play, bringing to light, by implication, the reasons why play is adopted as a method of teaching. It also elucidates the psychological basis of play yet one can object that all play is not rehearsal or anticipation of the serious business of life. In particular it can be objected that the theory fails to offer any explanation of adult play. Then again, in what sense is playing cards a preparation for future life and there can be no denying that children do in fact play cards?

(4) **Recapitulatory Theory.** Stanley Hall, a famous American Scientist put forward the recapitulatory theory of play in refuting anticipatory theory. According to Stanley Hall, "Anticipatory

theory is very partial, superficial and perverse since it ignores the past where lies the key to all play activities."

In the opinion of Stanley Hall, the reasons for the child's play should be looked for in his past, rather than in his future. "The heart of youth goes out into play as into nothing else, as if in it men remembered a lost paradise."[1] It is the view of Stanley Hall that every tribe or race passes through many varied stages in its development and evolution, the impressions of which are to be found in its children at their birth. The stages, through which the human race has passed in its development over a period of some thousand years are present in children in the form of minute and significant impressions, and these are the impressions that are recalled by them in their playing. This recollection is the essence of Nature. For example, the embryo within the mother's womb passes through all the prominent stages of evolution of all, animals before it enters the specifically human stage. In this way, the child relives the uncivilised and aboriginal stage of the human race in its play. Hunting and playing, hide and seek are not the anticipations of any future life. In the words of Ross, "Hide and seek, chasing, hunting and fishing, stone throwing, the building of, houses and shelters, especially in trees, the fascination of caves, all remind us strongly of the youth of the race."[2] In this way, most of our play patterns are a recollection or reproduction of the activities of man in his uncivilised stages.

Stanley Hall's theory does explain some particular kinds of play such as hunting, climbing mountains, roaming etc. but it cannot claim to explain all kinds of play. Studies conducted by Lehmen and Witty have contributed to reduce the impact of this theory as they show that the various forms of play are not reminiscent of the various stages of the being's development as these forms are subject to variations caused by seasons, place and sex. Secondly, modern scientists do not subscribe to the view that the qualities acquired by the human race are present in children in the form of impressions.

(5) **Cathartic Theory.** Aristotle used the word catharsis to explain or elucidate the effect of tragedy in drama. It means purification or purgation. Just as some medicines purge the body of its undesirable poisons, the tragic drama also purges the human soul of its suppressed desires and pent up emotions. The principle, of catharsis also influences the causes of those of human games that

---

1. Stanley Hall, *Adolescence*, p. 211.
2. Ross, E. A. *Groundwork of Educational Psychology*, p. 104.

are reminiscent of the aboriginal or tribal man. Hunting, war, wandering or travelling all over the globe, are expressions of those suppressed tendencies in man that have been present in him since his undeveloped and uncivilised state. These tendencies do not find expression in the normal social progress, in civilised society. In this way, play is a cathartic process. A somewhat similar explanation of the phenomenon has been offered by Freud and other psycho-analysts. In the words of Sir T.P. Nunn, "Men cannot shed altogether the ancient tendencies to cruelty and vice but play is at once a means by which the mischief may be taken out of them and a means by which they may be transformed into impulse of ethical value."

Despite its wide application, the principle of catharsis does not explain the causes of all kinds of play. Nevertheless, it is an important theory. Its reality and rationality has been acceded to by Sir T.P. Nunn.

Concerning the above theories of play, one can safely concur with Sir T.P. Nunn that they are mutually complementary rather than contradictory. The various theories succeed in explaining some particular form of play, but they all prove inadequate if they are required to explain all the various forms. While some kinds of play are an anticipation or rehearsal of the future life, other forms give the impression of being recollections of man's activity in his tribal and uncivilised state. Some games are an outlet for the individual's excess energy that he cannot put to better use, but there are some forms of play which yield him pleasure and amusement. And almost all forms of play are cathartic in one respector the other. Apart from this, there are some kinds of play that are a mixture or compound of the amusing, recollecting and cathartic games. In this manner, the psychological basis of play is a composite of consumption of surplus energy, amusement, rehearsal or anticipation of future life, recollection of the functions of man in his primal state, and the catharsis through manifestation of many tendencies that cannot be expressed in the normal daily routine of an individual's social life.

IMPORTANCE OF PLAY

Plays contribute considerably to the development of children. They help in the child's physical, mental, emotional, aesthetic and character development. They not only afford it pleasure, but also provide a means of expression for many instincts. Play is one of the media through which the child can easily give expression to his general and common tendencies. In this sphere he is completely free of restriction and he turns to many kinds of play through internal inspiration. Although the guidance of the teacher can be of much advantage even in the sphere of play, yet it is desirable that there should be no unnecessary interference on his part. However, systematised and regularised the game may be, it must never be allowed to lose its natural spirit. It should never be permitted to become as serious as a vocation usually is. The importance of play can be guaged when it is studied from the following points of view:

(1) **Physical or Biological Importance.** As has been pointed out, and is itself fairly evident, play helps in the physical development of the child. And in infancy there are many games that are in fact indicative of the child's biological growth. Games give sturdiness to the limbs of the child. Many waste products of the body are released when the blood circulation is accelerated and when the child breaths rapidly or deeply. The heart and the lungs benefit by the exercise involved in playing games. Without this physical exertion these parts of the body will not develop properly. The body is further benefited by the enjoyment that the child and even the grown ups derive from games. After play people are seen embued with a new energy and freshness. Many forms of play prepare the child physically for the battles of life ahead of him. In this way, most of the outdoor games are beneficial to the physical development and well being of the child and the psychological well being of his parents.

(2) **Mental Importance.** The physical importance of games is itself indicative of their importance from the mental viewpoint also. Physical well being is always conductive to the proper mental development and health of an individual. Different games provide opportunities for the exercise of different powers and capabilities present in the child. Some games may compel him to enjoy his imagination while others may require making decisions by the child yet another may call for memory excellence while in a different game he may have to call upon his patience and concentration. These opportunities help in the development of the various mental capacities called into play. In games the individual has to confront and win over different and ever changing circumstances and eventualities with the result that he develops resource and courage. It also leads to his mental maturity. Play also assists in the child's attaining some mental balance.

(3) **Emotional Significance.** Play helps in the revelation and expression of many repressed emotions so that the individual is purgated of them. In the process of playing he learns to express

control and sublimate or transfer his emotions. Games help the individual get rid of destructive emotions such as feeling of futility, irritability, the tendency to quarrel without any reason, fear and anxiety. The more desirable emotions are developed to take their place. Emotional stability is attained through games and the individual develops the tendency to realistic, thinking rather than day dreaming.

(4) **Social Importance.** It is through games that the individual dual develops such qualities as discipline, co-operation, sympathy, benevolence, law-abiding and leadership. When children belonging to different social levels come together in the play ground, the main distinguishing and dividing features and barriers present between them are lost and they come much closer to each other, than they can in other social and economic spheres. In this way, play is of the important means of removing the sense of social discrimination and distinction between classes. In the collective or group games, the child is motivated by the interest of the entire group rather than by any individual motive. Such a realization of the community of interests leads to the development of sacrifice and team-spirit. Collective games help in the development of social and community consciousness.

(5) **Educational Importance.** The above elucidation of the importance of games is not intended to convey the impression that the teacher has no role to play in the process. This is not any where near the truth. The truth of the matter is that if the phenomenon of play is to yield all its physiological, emotional and social benefits it is indispensable that the teacher should come forward with constructive suggestion from time to time. Further, he should be present at game time in order to direct and guide the children. Modern primary education techniques make use of play in teaching children of a very tender age. In these techniques, games combine with teaching to develop the child. It is not only in the stages of infancy and childhood that games can be utilised to develop the child, but they be employed even in the education of adolescents and adults who can be made into well developed and ideal citizens of the nation through the simple expedient of being, allowed to play the games that they desire. Men and women should play games that harmonize with the tasks and vocations that they have chosen for their future lives. And these games will vary from adolescence to adulthood. It is fallacious to think that girls have less need of playing than boys,

but it is very essential in their case that the games they play are such that help them in the preparation for their lives.

Cure through Play

Nowadays plays are also utilized to get rid of many mental problems and character difficulties of children. The reason behind this is catharatic power of play. The emotions that the child is unable to express, due to the necessity of social life and general conformity and is forced to repress, cause many abnormalities in his personality and behaviour. Many methods based on play have been evolved to free the mind of the child of these abnormalities. The most significant gain in the use of play as a cure is that the child is not aware that be is undergoing treatment with the result that the treatment becomes natural and efficacious. Secondly, in cases of these abnormalities and maladies according to Meleniklein, children express their problems symbolically in their play. The analysis of these symbols of abnormalities can help in their cure. It is for this reason that Meleniklein has supported the cure of mental disorders through the medium of play. Play therapy methods are based on different kinds of play, but the basic principle common to all of them is that the child is to be placed in an environment in which he can facilely and freely give expression to his internal feelings and conditions. In plays oriented to this end, social circumstances and conditions are created in which many of repressed tendencies of the child's behaviour can find ready expression. Among therapeutic methods and games, the important ones are recreation therapy, finger painting, psychodrama etc.

(1) **Recreation Therapy.** Recreation therapy is the most natural method of psychological treatment. One important cause of juvenile delinquency is that the creative faculties and tendencies of the child are not afforded any opportunity of natural expression. The result is that they burst out in a destructive torrent and the adolescent becomes a criminal and delinquent. Recreation therapy provides the child with adequate means and opportunity for developing his creative faculty. He is allowed to make houses, castless etc. The main object behind these games is not the imparting of any knowledge to them, but of providing children the chance to manifest their mental tendencies and predilections. This satisfies the children and they avoid the danger of becoming abnormal. One major advantage of play is that it develops social qualities in children. The children come to possess feelings of brotherhood and cooperation, which preclude the development of anti-social feelings. Recreation therapy makes use of both individual as well as collective games.

(2) **Finger Painting.** The second important method of psychological cure through play is that of finger painting. In this method, the child draws by his fingers, lie is provided with many colours and a sheet of white paper. The child is directed to draw, any figure that he pleases with his fingers in any colour that takes his fancy from among the colours provided to him. Of course, the real object behind this is not to have the child draw some figure with skill but to give him the chance to get rid of his emotional tension, the figure acting as a medium of excuse. The child often spreads much colour on the paper, and even spreads on some parts of his own body and clothing. In this manner whereas he is given the chance to do as he wishes much of his emotional tension destroyed, and he again becomes a healthy child.

(3) **Psycho-drama.** Another method of mental therapy through play is that of psycho-drama. It was invented by the psychologist Moreno. In this method the child is invited to take part in an imaginary drama. This acting is psychological. The purpose, of this acting is not to teach him the art of acting but to pursuade him to give expression to his feelings. Even the role to be acted is chosen by the child himself, and it is through his own desire that he chooses to express feelings of anger, pleasure, hatred and conflict. The child becomes so engrossed and lost in, his acting that he has no compunction in expressing any emotion. Evidently, through his acting he manifests his repressed emotions and attains a peace of mind. In this manner, psychological acting leads to emotional catharsis and a balanced frame of mind. Psychological acting is indulged in both individually as well as within a group. Group acting is so conducted that the individual child has his choice of roles and he selects the one he finds suitable. Most often, in this connection the role chosen involves winning castle or overcoming a giant. Through the medium of role, the child gives expression to and gains relief from his aggressive and destructive tendencies.

PLAY AND WORK

Some people say that play should be treated as work and work as play. What they mean is that one should play with the same interest with which one works and work should be made to yield the same pleasure that play does. Play as you work, and work as you play, certainly, but do not forget that the two are distinct. Such proverbs are characteristically misleading as they seem to suggest that work and play are the same. Such a notion is psychologically wrong and indefensible. Work and play differ mainly in the following respects:

(1) **Difference of Objectives.** When you see a child playing, you may be inclined to enquire of him as to what he is doing and why, and normally the answer would be that he is playing, and that he is playing for the sake of play. In this way, play is a normal and common tendency, an objective and aim in itself. Play is indulged in of its own occord, rather than from any external motivation. Usually it is seen as the contradiction of work, with the result that all children more interested in games are considered lazy. Many young students run away from school and spend their entire time in playing and roaming about. If one enquires the reason of things from a card player, the almost inevitable response is that one may play and see for oneself. The pleasure resulting from it constitutes the reason why it is played. Now to take up the cudgels on behalf of work, one immediately perceives that no work is done without any motive and definite, objective. All the hundreds and thousands of vocations peculiar to the human animal, including study and labour, are pursued with some objective in view. The actual aim may be accumulation of wealth or the achievement of fame, or any other conceivable aim, but no work can be aimless. Work is not its own objective; one does not work for the sake of working. It is the thought of fruit to come in the future that infuses courage and enthusiasm in the worker labouring in the present. But while playing a game, every moment brings its own fresh pleasures and amusements, there are no future fruits to be considered. Its pleasure is in the moment. Of course, one may astutely object that one ever present motive in play is the desire to defeat and overcome the opponent. Then how can objective or aim be used to distinguish between games and work? But in answer to this question, one were to ask what the winner gains in defeating his adversary and what the latter loses in being deated, then it would have to be admitted that there is nothing concrete involved. In fact, as Drever has pointed out, the objectives and aims of play belong to the world of imagination while the aim in working belongs to the essential reality and concreteness of the world and everyday life. One often finds that work carries with it the letters of compulsion while no such feeling accompanies play.

(2) **The Meaning of Play is within the Act of Playing while that of Work lies Outside.** According to Drever, "in play the value and significance of the activity is found in the activity itself, whereas in work the value and significance of activity is found in an end beyond the activity." In this way, every moment spent in

play brings its own rewards in terms of pleasure and amusement, whereas work is accompanied by no such pleasure. Usually it is the opposite, as work is attended by pain and effort. It attains fruition long time after it itself has been completed.

(3) **Play gives Immediate and Work Remote Pleasure.** Man is by nature an epicurean who turns towards things that bring him pleasure and instinctively turns from objects that bring him pain and misery. Hence, in both work and play the aim and object of the child is obtaining pleasure but while play yields its pleasures immediately and in the present, the pleasures to be had of work are slower in coming. It sometimes never comes at all even in the future, and sometimes even brings pain and suffering.

(4) **Play creates Energy while Work Consumes It.** All work and no play makes the proverbial Jack, a dull boy. Play is a kind of recreation. It takes away the individual's fatigue and brings him balmy rest. It is for this reason that young and old, none are averse to playing. But this does not mean that play does not result in physical exhaustion. But the fatigue that results out of playing differs in nature from the fatigue that originates in hard work. The fatigue of play is health giving. Of course, excessive practice in competitive games may harm physical acts as a tonic both for the body and the mind, provided games are not played in excess of the body's energy. Such a condition can be easily recognised if one observes the physical condition after play. The individual should be refreshed and enthusiastic about the work before him, and should have the energy to perform it. In physical games the blood circulates rapidly through the body so that many undesirable elements present in the body are eliminated and the individual feels lighter and more energetic. After the day's tiring routine most people feel the need for some form of recreation and enjoyment. Play is one form of it. On the other hand, work reduces the efficiency of the individual. Hence games and work should be rationally synthesized.

(5) **Difference in Mental Attitudes.** Play and work differ in respect of their accompanying mental attitudes. Play is independently indulged in without any hint of compulsion whereas work is associated with the feeling of necessity and inevitability. The necessity may be due to some external compulsion such as the order of a superior or it may be imposed on the self from within. Man naturally engages in and concentrates upon play, but where

work is concerned, concentration is a matter of conscious effort rather, than one of effortless ease. The feeling of responsibility is conspicuously absent when one is playing, he is not answerable to anyone and he has nothing much to loose if he makes a mistake as nothing valuable is at stake. But on the other hand, in work the individual is conscious of a certain burden, and he is answerable to certain other individuals if he fails to perform his functions efficiently. He is responsible for the work he is allotted, and he is very likely to become a prey to boredom easily. It is for these, reasons that the child, in his infancy and childhood, is allotted little work and more play. Even the things that he is taught are presented in such a manner that he treats them as child's play. But when he attains adolescence and adulthood, he is entrusted with work involving greater and greater responsibility. He even comes to perform such responsible functions avidly and enthusiastically.

Despite the above superficial points of difference between work and play, there is little if any fundamental dissimilarity between them. There can be a sharp and precise dividing line that demarcates the two and divides them into water tight, compartments. The child learns both from play and work, in both he finds material that helps to develop his character, and both are essential and beneficial to him. Then, every individual can obtain some pleasure from the work he is engaged in by orientation and conscious effort. And in the case of very efficient and capable individuals, it is said that work is child's play for them. The ease and comfort with which famous authors compose voluminous works appears play to them. In fact, the ability with which an individual introduces the pleasure of play into his work depends upon the efficiency with which he can perform that work. To quote Sir T.P. Nunn, "An agent thinks of his activity as play if he can take it up or lay it down at choice or vary at will the condition of its exercise; he thinks of it as work if it is imposed on him by unavoidable necessity, or if he is held to it by a sense of duty or vocation." The person who approaches his work with the idea of duty or vocation soon fires of it, and achieves very little. The person who looks upon it as play and accepts it willingly and freely excels in it both quantitatively and qualitatively. To take a simple example, the gardener engaged in the gardening can choose to look upon his job as play or as a vocation. In the first instance, the work will afford him much pleasure whereas if he chooses to treat it as a vocation he will be depriving himself of considerable pleasure.

PLAY WAY OF EDUCATION

It is the intimate relation between play and work that has led to the useful employment of play in the field of education. Modern educational psychologists are inclined to lay stress on the play-way method in the education of infants and children Caldwell Cook is credited with introducing play way education of children. Cook observed that children play truants and run away from schools, show a lack of interest in studying and invent all sorts of excuses to play uninterruptedly. He conceived the idea that if some sort of amusement is created in education, then the children would take as much interest in school as they take in the playground. Accordingly then, the intention of the play-way method is to make education natural, free, amusing and interesting. It was Sir T.P. Nunn who pointed out that play also achieves the objectives of education in as much as both play and education lead to the individual and personal development of the child. "It is hardly extravagant to say that in the understanding of play lies the key to most of the practical problems of education." The adoption of this conception led to the development, perfection and adaptation of many play way methods and techniques A somewhat cursory study of these play way methods will lead to an insight into the importance of play in the process of education. The main methods of this kind are the following:

(1) **Kindergarten.** The kindergarten method of infants was evolved by the German educationist Froebel. The word kindergarten implies the garden of children. At its root is the principle that just as flowers and plants flourish in the free and unrestricted atmosphere of the garden while the gardener only looks after them, in a similar manner children should be allowed free and independent development in schools while, the teachers only occasionally interfere to look after them and to ensure that desirable conditions are maintained. And the fundamental activity for independent development is play because a child naturally indulges in playful activity. Such qualities as independence, dynamicity and effort, can be imbued in the child through play and these qualities can be made the foundation of his character. Hence Froebel emphasized the imparting of such subjects as gardening, natural science, mathematics, language, religion, and physical training through the play way. And for the play way, Froebel also evolved many instruments and objects. These objects of play can also be called gifts. He created gifts pertaining to many categories or levels. The first category contains six balls of different colours, the second has material figures in the shapes

of cubes, cones and circles. The fourth, fifth, and sixth categories contain gift of tabloid, stick and ring, respectively. These gifts impart knowledge of colour, lines and points, surface, forms, etc., to the child. In the kindergarten method, the children play various games with these gifts, the games being occupations. The education of the children takes place through these occupations.

(2) **Montessory Method.** This method of play way education was evolved by Doctor Maria Montessory of Italy, and it has gained fame in her own name. It is based on principles similar to the kindergarten method of child education. In this method, too, it is play that is the basis of education but it differs from it in respect of the fewer number of things and apparatus for education. It is the personal independence and self-dependence of the child that is more stressed in this method. In it, the responsibility of education is thrown on the children themselves in order that they may develop spontaneously. The mental bases of child development are freedom, self-education, discipline or training of sense organs, and the practice and training of useful practical activities. Various games and toys are used to acquaint the child with the forms and sizes of objects, and to develop his sense organs. The Montessory method of education has no provision for any control and administration, so that the question of any physical punishment does not arise. Predetermined curricula and a fixed time table are not insisted upon in this method of education.

(3) **Project Method**[1]. Another method of play way education that has been evolved in America is called the project method. It is a fairly recent innovation. In this method, the children are given different projects to perform and complete such as cooking, stitching knitting, making chairs and tables, setting up shops and organising markets, etc. It must of course be remembered that all the projects that they are required to perform have some connection with their needs. Education thus becomes purposeful. All the work to be performed in these projects is left to the children, the teacher's only function being guidance and general superintendence. These activities of the children savour of naturalness, independence, freedom and activity. They are part and parcel of play.

(4) **Dalton Method**[2]. This method of play-way education was developed by Mrs. Parkhurst. This method has three distinct

---

1. Kilpatrick, W.H., *Foundation of Educational Method,* The Macmillan Co., New York, 1925.
2. Parkhurst, H., *Education on the Dalton Plan,* E.P. Dutton & Co., New York, 1922.

parts—independence, society and individual performance. It is characterised by a lack of any systematic time table. The classrooms are called laboratories. And the laboratory for each subject is separate. In these laboratories the children work according to their own inclinations and inform the teacher to look after them and to assist them. Education takes on the appearance of play and becomes more palatable.

(5) **Heuristic Method.** The originator of this education method was Armstrong. In this method the children are, from the very start, induced to do research and invention. Knowledge imparted to them is through the inductive method, in the forms of questions and answers, Direction and assistance of the children is the teacher's function.

(6) **Scouting.** Sir Baden Povell is responsible for this method of play way education for children. Scouting helps in the social, emotional and character development of the child, but more often it is not rekoned to be a complete method of education, being employed as a complement to some other method of teaching in a school. Secondary importance is more usually I attached to it. Students take part in it very enthusiastically and in the camp and community life learn such qualities as self-dependence, co-operation, socialization, administration, leadership etc., which fit him for ideal citizenship. Such is the importance of the institution and the children are invited to do works of social welfare in crowds and organized meetings. Social development of the child is thus of a high order. Scouts often go out on long tours with the result that, their knowledge of natural things is extensive. As a method of education scouting has proved most useful in the case of adolescents rather than infants. Nowadays, in Europe and even in India, youth organisations similiar to scouting are being organised for male and female adults.

(7) **Dramatic Method and Appreciation Lesson.** It is dramatic method that is in vogue for the teaching of languages, of history and geography in schools. In a way, this method, too, is a play way method of education. Children appreciate and enjoy the literature, art and music that they are studying. Its efficacy lies in the expression of the child's own sentiments and feelings, as well as in the development of his aesthetic sense. In this manner, the dramatic method and appreciation lesson help in making a course of study as interesting and engrossing, as play.

From the foregoing cursory survey of the modern educational methods, it is evident that modern educational psychology lays much stress on education being imparted through the media of play. The plays utilised in education are both group plays and individual ones. The use of the play way method in education has proved useful in the infant and childhood states, but not so much when adolescence is attained. An adolescent is inclined to look upon himself as an adult, with the commensurate realization of responsibility, and secondly' by this time it is essential that he be acquainted with the grim realities and problems of life besides being fitted to solve them.

QUESTIONS FOR EXERCISE

1. What do you understand by play? Describe the various theories of play.
2. Point out the value of play in child life and discuss the main theories of play.
3. Explain any two theories of play. How can play be distinguished from work?
4. Delineate the importance of play in the development of personality during childhood.
5. Describe briefly the function of play in children and discuss the various theories of play.
6. How will you differentiate between play and work? Cite examples to illustrate the following cases:
   (a) When play becomes a work.
   (b) When work becomes a play.
   (c) When play can be effectively combined with work.
7. Explain any two of the following:
   (a) Play and work.
   (b) Characteristics of play.
   (c) Importance of play.

18

Learning, Maturation and Manual Skills

You are proceeding on a road and a dog follows. You give the dog something to eat. Now whenever you happen to traverse the road, the dog follows you. To take another example, a little girl being indisposed, is taken to the doctor. The doctor prepares the syringe while the little girl looks on with interest or indifferently, depending on her nature. The doctor injects the medicine and the girl feels pain. When the little girl is taken to the doctor next day her indifference is no longer there because she starts screaming the moment the doctor lays his hand on the syringe. Why this change in reaction? She did not react in this manner on first occasion. The answer would be that she had learnt by experience that injections are painful. In this way learning brings or causes changes in her behaviour.

WHAT IS LEARNING?

The following are some definitions of learning which should make it clear:

1. **Learning is Change in Behaviour.** In J.P. Guilford's opinion, "We may define the term very broadly by saying that learning is any change in behaviour, resulting from behaviour."[1] In this definition a distinction between change in behaviour due to maturity and change in behaviour due to learning is not clear though both these activities occur simultaneously. In the words of Wordworth, "Typically learning consists in doing something new, provided this something new is retained by the individual and reappears in his later activities."[2]

1. Guilford, J.P., *General Psychology* (1956), p. 343.
2. Woodworth, R.S. and Marquis, D.G., *Psychology,* Methuen & Co. Ltd. London, 1949, p. 491.

2. **Learning is an Organisation of Behaviour.** According to Garrett, "Learning is that activity by virtue of which we organise our response with new habits."[1] Thus the element or organisation in learning is very much important. Guilford too, maintains that learning involves organisation of behaviour. Thus in learning to ride a cycle we have to organise the activities of turning the pedal, balancing the handle, etc. in order to be reasonably safe with the vehicle. It is another matter that a person does not learn this organisation at the outset and that he may take much longer time to learn to balance the handle than the time he may take to learn to turn the pedel. But his learning of the activity of cycling will be complete only when he accomplishes this organisation.
3. **Learning is the Reinforcement of a New Activity.** R.S. Woodworth maintained that the learning of a new act is, an addition to the person's store of experiences. Clarifying the statement further, Woodworth says that reinforcement, too, is an indispensable element in the act of learning because it helps forming only successful responses and weeding out the unsuccessful ones. To quote Woodworth "An activity may be called learning in so far as it develops the individual in any way, good or bad and makes his environment and experiences different from what it would otherwise have been."[2]

   The psychologists who stress external behaviour consider learning to be a change of behaviour while those who lay emphasis on internal changes are convinced that learning is change in the perception of the individual. Combining these two views, Murphy writes, "From this point of view it would be legitimate to regard learning as a modification both of behaviour and of the way of perceiving."[3] The following definition of learning given by Hilgard is an essence of all the foregoing definitions offered by other psychologists, "Learning is the process by which an activity originates or is changed through reacting to an encountered situation, provided that the characteristics of the change in activity cannot be explained on the basis of native response tendencies, maturity or temporary status of the organism."[4]

---

1. Garret, H.E., Great *Experiments in Psychology* (Rev. ed.) New York: Appleton Century, 1941.
2. *Ibid,* p. 532.
3. Murphy, G., *An Introduction to Psychology,* 1951, p. 248.
4. Hilgard, E.R., *Theories of Learning,* Methuen, 1959, p. 13.

LEARNING AND MATURATION

Learning changes behaviour and so does maturation. Thus, sometimes it becomes difficult to say definitely as to which of the subject's activities are the result of learning and which are the consequences of maturation. Automatic activity, random acts, reflexes and instincts and sudden expression of emotion can be accepted as unlearned actions and the result of maturation, but in most of the activities of human beings it is difficult to decide whether these activities result from maturation or learning. In fact, these activities develop both due to learning and maturation. Take the example of learning language. It is true, of course, that a child is manifestly incapable of learning language until he reaches a certain stage or age in maturation, but it is also equally true that he does not learn the language just because he attains that stage. The language is taught to him.

An experiment on co-twins indicates the extent of the changes in behaviour caused by maturation and the extent to which changes may be affected by learning.[1] The purpose of the experiment was measure the extent of advantage of learning in such activities climbing the stairs. Two twins were chosen for the experiment because due to the similarity in heredity, the speed of maturation is the same and any changes which may occur may be attributed to climb the stairs from her forty sixth week. On examination this twin 'T' failed to climb at all at the age of 46 weeks and had to lid aided up all the 5 stairs. In the space of four weeks she climbed all the stairs in 26 seconds.

When 'S' was placed on the stairs at-the age of 53 weeks she climbed all the five stairs unaided but it took her some 45 seconds. After two weeks of practice 'S', at the age of 55 weeks, traversed the distance in 10 seconds. In this way, at this age 'S' was, ahead of 'T' who, at a younger age had practised three times as much. 'S' was three weeks older than 'T'. Thus, in spite of all kinds of learning, T was left behind due to a lack of maturity.

This experiment proves that learning plays an insignificant part in reflex and other physiological activities peculiar to one's species. Those activities which appear in all human beings at a certain age, are due to maturity. Those activities which do not inevitably appear in every person are affected by maturation to the extent that they can be learnt with ease at the age of maturity. Some examples of this type of activities are swimming, horse riding, climbing trees etc. The learning of these activities is made more facile by motor, sensory and neural maturation.

The above exposition on the relation of learning and maturation provides some very practical suggestions for learning and training. It is

---

1. Extracted from a treatise, 'Maturation of Behaviour, by M.B. McGraw published in Carmichaels' book *A Manual of Child Psychology.*

not useful to make an attempt to teach a child forcibly before he matures. Many parents try to precipitate their children into higher classes with the help of coaching, at a young age. This coaching cannot have a lasting or permanent effect and the children become weak in senior classes. The teaching of the proper job at a specific age depends on many factors two of which are the child's mental and physiological development. But-a general age for the beginning of the teaching of various subjects can be established. For example, it is comparatively easier to study Algebra at 15 or 16 than it is at 11 or 12. This relation between maturation and training justifies the suggestion for the fixing of a minimum age limit for admission to universities.

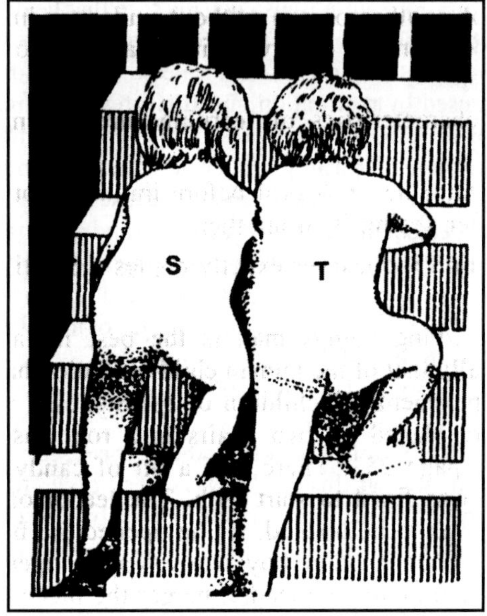

Fig. 14

PRINCIPAL FORMS AND METHODS OF LEARNING

The principal forms or methods of learning are, learning through imitation, learning through conditioned response, learning through trial and error and learning through insight. All these four forms are equally utilised by animals as well as human beings.

Imitation

Learning through imitation is one of the most important forms of learning. The human child learns mostly through imitation. It is a common place observation that children imitate the behaviour, habits, manners and ways of adults. In imitation the learner exactly copies the behaviour of another person without understanding or thinking. Whenever this copying is observed, it is said that one has learned through imitation.

The main characteristics of learning through imitation are as follows:

(1) The imitator never does it before imitation, but performs the activity only after seeing it in another.

(2) In imitation the learner exactly copies the activity performed before him.

Among the living beings man is the best imitator. In human learning, especially that of the human child, imitation has an important place. In an experiment, 42 children of 1st Standard were selected.[1] Two boxes were placed on two chairs in a room as shown in the figure given on page 253. There was a bit of candy in one of the boxes. A place was fixed to start with. The leader of the boys was told which box was to be opened. As he opened the box, he found a piece of candy. Then another boy was asked to open either of the boxes. If this boy imitated the leader, he got the piece of candy. If he did not imitate he got no reward. In every experiment both boys were made to stand on the start. In the first experiment both boys were told that "Here are two boxes here and there. There is a piece of candy in a box. You have to find the piece of candy. He will get first chance, then you will get chance. If you could not get in the first chance, you will get another chance." The leader was always given first chance. The piece of candy was not always kept in the same box, 22% of the boys imitated in the first chance. The rest 78% boys did not imitate. These boys might have reasoned that because the leader has already taken out the piece of candy from the box so it could not be there. On an average, in one out of 3 experiments every second boy imitated the first boy. When the, situation was changed and four boxes were placed on the four corners of an imagined square, 75% of the children imitated. This shows that the tendency of imitation learned in the first situation was generalised or transferred into an individual direction. In other, experiments the children were rewarded for not imitating the leader. This tendency of not imitating the leader was cent-per-cent transferred to new situation. It is important to note in this experiment that the children were asked to imitate an activity, which they could easily do, *e.g.*, all of them could reach the box, open it and take out things from it. In the complex activities this point is even more important.

---

1. Miller, N. and Dollard, J. *Social Learning and Imitation*, New Haven, Yale University Press, 1949, p. 124.

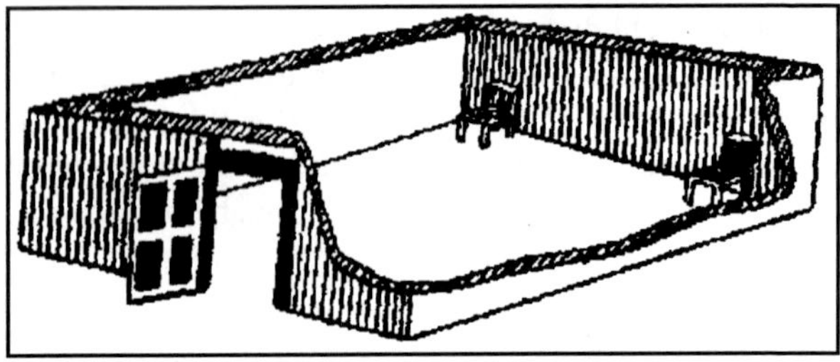

Fig. 15

The process of imitation is very important in learning. The teachers make a wide use of this fact. Education becomes easier and more perfect by demonstration. In the teaching of dance, music, etc., demonstration is very important since imitation has an important role in them. The efficient teachers generally demonstrate whenever it is possible and encourage, the students often to imitate the manners, ways, methods and habits etc., of the teachers. Thus, by presenting good ideals himself, the teacher can easily create the, same among the students.

Conditioned Response

As a general rule the higher the species of the animal, the more easily conditioning of response is achieved. Thus, conditioning should be easiest in the case of human beings. But man is a complex animal and hence the factors which distract his attention are larger in number than in the case of other animals. However, inspite of these distracting elements in conditioning of responses it certainly remains one of the most important methods of learning, especially in the case of children. In childhood many of the responses of the child are conditioned to particular objects and even when the individual becomes an adult, his conditioned response continues *e.g.*, if a man behaves wrongly with us, we develop a kind of fear, abhorrence or hatred with every person resembling him.

Modern psychology does not admit the view that all learning is conditioning, but no psychologist denies that conditioned response is an important method of learning both in the case of animals as well as of human beings. A person can find hundreds, of examples of conditioning of response in his daily life. In the case of the tamed animals the conditioning process is very much used to teach so many activities. The conditioning of response as it is established can also be extinguished. In the establishment of the conditioning the stimuli has to be repeated while in its extinction the stimuli is not repeated. Thus in the example of Pavlov's dog, if the dog's response has been conditioned by the ringing of the bell, it will be de-conditioned if food is not served inspite of the ringing of the bell or food is served without ringing the bell. Similar examples of de-conditioning process can be found in the case of human beings. Suppose a person is used to get out for a walk to a bridge with a certain friend, he will always remember his friend when he is absent. The sight of the bridge will make him recall his friend, because he always used to come with him to bridge. Thus the bridge and the presence of his friend have been linked. Now if the friend is absent and returns after a long time and the man has to go alone for a walk, he will forget his friend gradually and the sight of the bridge will no more awake the memory of him. In this example one finds de-conditioning of a certain response to a particular stimulus. Just as a response can be de-conditioned, it is also re-conditioned. Conditioning, de-conditioning and re-conditioning of the response are governed by the same fundamental principles.

TRIAL AND ERROR

The method of trial and error is used in the following circumstances:

(1) This method is used when the learner, is completely motivated and can see the goal clearly. If the cat is not hungry she will not try to come out of the cage or leave the attempt after trying it without success for some time. The cat tries to come out of the cage simply because she is hungry and knows that there is food outside the cage. In the absence of the food outside the cage, the cat will not try to come out of it. Thus it is clear that motivation as well as the presence of the goal is necessary for awakening the response in learning through trial and error.

(2) The method of trial and error is used when perception alone or learned activities are not sufficient. If the cat could come out of the cage by merely moving in some direction, there was hardly any need of several trials and errors.

(3) The method of trial and error is used when the learner fails to find the solution of the problem. In Thorndike's experiment the cat used trial and error method simply because she did not know how to come out of the cage. In the case of human beings in such situations, if the subject knows the solution of the problem, there is hardly any question of trial and error. It is only when he fails to find out the solution of the problem that he proceeds blindly, tries in various directions, commits errors, eliminates, them and finally arrives at the successful response.

Thus, the method of trial and error is widely used both by animals as well as by human beings. In the case of human beings however, this process is somewhat different, because man has better powers of perception, understanding, intelligence and language etc. Man uses the method of trial and error, but he also takes the help of language and other instruments in the process of learning.

INSIGHT

Insight is an important constituent in the solution of problems, and is found in the higher class of animals and human beings. It is the best method among the methods of learning.

According to the gestalt psychologists, a person can deduce the solution by insight if he perceives the situation as a whole. A German gestatist, Kohler, prepared some simple problems for experiments with dogs, hens, monkeys, and chimpanzees. In an experiment a hungry animal as released from the house while some food was placed behind the fence adjoining the wall. Both, the dog and the hen trotted around in the vicinity of the wall but as soon as they found the way out they made their exit and reached the food. This perception of the change in the meaning of the wall is insight. Before the insight the wall was an insuperable obstacle, but after insight it was no longer an obstacle but an object necessitating circumvention. The result of insight is the understanding of new relations, the discovery of new patterns and the formation of new organisations.

The most famous experiments conducted, by Kohler, in relation to insight were those that were carried out on chimpanzees. Some bananas were placed outside the cage of a chimp called Sultan, who was then given two sticks so constructed that they could be fitted together. Sultan tried to pull the bananas with the sticks, an effort which he kept up for an hour, but he got tired of the attempt and gave it up for playing. While playing he brought the two ends together and suddenly he got an idea which resulted in his fitting the smaller stick in the hole of the bigger one. He then used the two together to draw the banana inward. The two sticks disintegrated but he fitted them together again. He then pulled in everything within reach as if he were trying out his discovery. The next day be took far less time to fit the two together. It is a peculiarity of insight that once the solution is leant, it is not forgotten though its memory may becomes hazy with the passage of time.

The above experiments make it quite obvious that learning by insight has certain characteristics of its own. They are briefly as follows:

1. Insight is sudden.
2. Insight alters perception.

3. Old objects appear in new patterns and organisation by virtue of insight.
4. Insight is relative to the intellectual level. The higher species of animals including human beings have more insight than the members of lower species.
5. In insight understanding is more useful than dexterity of hands.
6. In Woodworth's opinion, insight is sometimes hindsight and at others it is foresight. To quote him "Foresight is seeing the way to the goal before taking it or perceiving the uselessness of a certain lead without trying it and hind-sight is observing that a lead is good or bad after trying it. When the whole situation is clear and above-board, there is a good chance for foresight, but when important characteristics of the situation have to be discovered by exploration and manipulation, hindsight is the best we can expect."[1]
7. Previous experience is of assistance in insight, though the excess of previous experience does not necessarily increase insight because organised perception too is an essential factor in learning.
8. Maturity also effects insight as evidenced by the smoother working of insight in older age than in adolescence.
9. If the pieces essential for the solution of the puzzle are present together when perceived, insight comes about earlier.
10. Some psychologists say that learning by insight is associative learning. Insight appears suddenly after the manipulation of thoughts or objects for a small though significant length of time.
11. The insight gained in particular circumstances is of assistance in other circumstances. A verbal formula is generally extracted by people learning by insight and this formula is capable of facile application to other circumstances.

The above mentioned characteristics of learning through insight apply both to the human and animal learning. The solitary difference is the fact that a human being by virtue of his superior capacities of experiencing and understanding observes relation between various objects quickly and sees the patterns concealed in them with alacrity. He is assisted in this by language. As a matter of fact insight occurs only when the learner perceives the related link hidden in the activity. The learning curve is altered suddenly due to insight. Insight is impossible in an extremely unfamiliar problem, because familiarity is very necessary for insight. A student of literature will have no insight in any scientific problem because he does not know even the a b c of science. When the

[1] Woodworth, R.S. and Marquis, D.G., *Psychology,* Methuen & Co. Ltd. London, 1959, p. 507.

subject of study becomes a part of life, insight becomes easier. History can be made alive by exhibitions, Geography by travelling, and Arithmetic by shop accounts. Familiarity is also important besides the theoretical study.

One example of human learning by insight will suffice. A student of Arithmetic tries hard to solve a difficult problem of Arithmetic. He tries many methods but fails to secure a solution. He gives up and lays it aside or goes to sleep. After some time suddenly or when he is awakened the solution suggests itself and he notes it down in his note-book. When he is confronted with similar problems in the future, he will have no difficult in solving them.

The insight method is superior to imitation or conditioned response because both the latter methods take more time.

Trial and error emphasizes the acquisition of motor skill but in insight mental effort is stressed upon.

While insight depends upon perception, trial and error depends upon sensory motor co-ordination.

The person keeps an eye on the goal, in trial and error and activity is goal-directed but insight is in the unconscious mind which exerts the most while the conscious activities are either very few or aimless.

Every new problem has to be tackled from the very beginning if the trial and error method is used. On the other band, both generalisation and differentiation are present in insight, which adds to the possibilities of transfer of learning and the use of old insight in the solution of novel problems.

Students will be permanently helped by the use of the insight, method of learning in place of the trial and error method in their study and other daily activities. They will also be able to conserve their energy. Suppose that a person has to arrange furniture in a room. An average person will determine the position of the table by using the trial and error method and shifting the table from place to place. An intelligent person will take up a position from where the whole room is visible, and imagine all the possible positions of the pieces of furniture in an imagined frame work of the room and then place the respective pieces accordingly. But this does not mean that trial and error method is not meant for the intelligent. By no means is this so. In many novel situations progress is not possible without it. An intelligent person should use, both these methods according to the needs of the situation.

LEARNING MANUAL SKILLS

Manual skill means proficiency in different type of activities which require the use of hand. The child holds a thing, turns it over, puts it here and there and throws it away. He requires manual skill in eating, putting on clothes, writing, playing, swimming, cycling and hundreds of other activities. This manual skill is gradually developed according to development of age. The psychologists have arrived at very important conclusions on the basis of their observations and experiments concerning manual skill. It has been found that a more or less definite pattern of the development of manual skill can be observed in childhood, though some individual differences also play their role.

The development of manual skill very much depends upon the development of sense organs, specially eyes and touch. The child uses his thumb at the age of five months. At 9 months he tries to hold things with the help of fingers and thumbs. At the age of 16 weeks the child looks towards an object but does not try to catch hold of it, a child of 20 weeks tries to pull it towards him. After 24 weeks of age the child definitely tries to handle things manually. At the age of 1 year, he can hold a pencil or take off his cap. He can also hold a cup or spoon. He can use a fork at the age of 2 years and pour milk in the cup. He can open a box and a bottle, turn the pages of a book, build different types of structures by means of wooden blocks, colour a paper, draw different types of sketches on it and cut it by scissors. At the age of 3 he becomes very much self-dependent in manual skills. He can eat, bathe and put on clothes all by himself. He can take utensils here and there and wash them. He can draw by means of chalk and pencil on the paper. At the age of 4 he can draw the sketch of house or man on the paper. At the age of 5, he can mould paper to form a triangle or square and draw these figures on the paper. He can put the toys in the box, wash his face and hands, cut something by scissors and draw a figure of man which can be easily recognized. At the age of 6 years, he can write very well and it is easy and normal for him. He can mould clay to make toys and use wood to make different types of things. He can also sew and knit and help in various household activities. At the age of 12 years, he can use his fingers, arms and shoulders in anyway he likes. His style of writing gets established and he can also learn to play various types of musical instrument.

By an observation of the development of various types of manual skills at different ages, the psychologists have formulated a general pattern of the development of manual skills. Some important manual skills and their development is as follows:

(1) **Throwing the Ball.** According to Gassel an infant of 6 months can throw a ball. At the age of 12 months, he can throw it in a definite direction. At the age of 2 years the child takes much interest in playing with the ball. In the beginning the child uses both the

hands in throwing the ball while later on he learns to throw it by using one hand only.

(2) **Catching the Ball.** Catching the ball is more difficult than throwing it. Therefore this manual skill is not possible for all children even at the age of 4 years. At the 6 years, 2/3 of the children can catch a ball thrown towards them. This skill is more advanced among girls as compared with the boys. In catching the ball also the child initially uses both the hands, but gradually learns to do so by one hand only.

(3) **Eating and Drinking.** An infant of 8 months cannot hold the glass, cup or bottle by his hand. At the age of 9 months he can put the bottle in his mouth and also take it out. At the age of 1 year, he can use a spoon for drinking milk. While using a utensil he initially uses both the hands, but gradually learns to do so by one hand only. In the beginning when he uses his hand for eating, he spills much food on his person. At the age of 2 years, he can eat more carefully. At 3 years of age he can very easily eat by himself. Most of the children learn eating and drinking by the age of seven and eight years.

(4) **Putting on and taking off Clothes.** Before learning to put on clothes the child learns to take them off because this activity is easier. From the age of 1-1/2 years upto the age of 3-1/2 years, the child learns to put on and take off clothes. In this manual skill also the girls excel the boys. At the age of 5 and 6 years, the children can easily put on and take off clothes.

(5) **Writing.** The child begins to hold pencil at the age of, 1 year. Within 6 months after it he uses the pencil on paper. At the age of 2 to 3 years, he can draw different types of sketches on the paper. At the age of four years he can draw the figure of man, house and birds and beasts. At the age of 6, he can write very well and at the age of 12 years, he has his own style of writing.

Thus, it can be seen from the survey of different types of manual skills given above that the process of the development of manual skill becomes complete at the age of 12.

HANDEDNESS

Handedness means that one hand is used more often as compared with the other. Thus handedness is of two types, right handedness in which the right hand is mostly used, and left handedness which involves the use of left hand. The right handedness is most common among children because they see the adults using right hand. Handedness, however, is not clearly right from the beginning, though at the age of one year the child makes more use of some one hand in different types of activities. Right or left handedness is determined at the age of 3 or 4 years. The psychologists have explored the causes of left-handedness as it is found in exceptional cases.

As has been already pointed out, the pattern of handedness is not clear at the age of one year. Henceforward because the child observes human beings around him using right hand mostly, he develops right-handedhess. Right-handedness therefore is not a hereditary trait. In fact handedness has no concern with heredity. Studies about handedness have shown various causes. According to one view as the left hemisphere of the brain is more active than the right, the right hand is more often used because it is connected with the left hemisphere. Another cause of right-handedness has been found in the structural strength and efficiency of the right hand as compared with the left. But according to most of the psychological observations and experiments, right-handedness is the result of learning through imitation in family. Thus it is a result of the process of socialization. According to Hurlock, man needed more use of one hand than the other in working with the mechanical tools. He therefore developed handedness. In civilized societies children have to use several tools and instruments for various purposes. They therefore invariably develop handedness. It has been estimated that 95% children have right-handedness while left-handedness is observed in bare 5%. Among left-handed children the number of males is much more than the number of girls. Sometimes effort is made to restrain left-handedness forcibly. On the other hand, right-handedness is very much encouraged. In fact the development of handedness is necessary for efficiency because if this is not there, the person cannot decide as to which hand should be handed on a particular occasion. Thus handedness improves efficiency. If it is delayed for a considerable time, the child becomes obstinate and full of tensions. His studies suffer and so also his manual skill. He therefore develops inferiority complex. His activities lack speed, power and accuracy and there is more danger of accidents with him.

Therefore, efforts must be made to develop handedness in the child. The guardians and teachers should teach the child to use right hand. But if the child is left-handed no haste should be made to make him right-handed. If he adopts right handedness by persuasion and practice, it is so far so good, but if he fails to do so, it is not a cause of too much worry. The childs should be left on his own to develop his handedness freely.

QUESTIONS FOR EXERCISE

1. Distinguish between learning of maturation. What is the place of maturation in learning?
2. Elucidate the role of maturation in human development by citing experiment on maturation and learning.

3. Describe the process of learning manual skill by children.
4. Explain the nature of learning and describe the development process of motor skill of a child.
5. To what extent is left handedness an innate characteristic? What should be done about it?
6. Explain with reasons whether the following statement is right or wrong :
   Left handedness is a kind of abnormality.
7. Discuss whether handedness in children is hereditary or a product of training.

19

Senses and Sense Training

The first response towards the environment from a child is in the form of sensation. This sensation is received through some sense organ. Different sense organs receive different types of sensations. These sensations are closely interconnected.

Some spontaneous responses have been observed in an infant when he is stimulated internally or externally. Different sensations are gradually differentiated. The infant knows his environment only through sensations particularly those of vision, hearing, touch, taste and smell. The sense organs must work properly if the child has to gain knowledge of the environment. Much of this is the result of maturity and development, but some learning is also helpful. This requires sense training.

The sense organs develop in the womb, therefore a neonate has almost all the sense organs. In the embryonic period the embryo reacts to light. The infant cannot understand anything in his environment before experience. As he gathers experience he gradually learns to distinguish between different types of sensations. The just born infant is seen to react towards sound and taste. While he prefers sweet solutions he dislikes different types of saline things. He cannot distinguish between smells, but he gradually learns to do so. He experiences the sensations of heat and cold, hunger and thirst, pain and pressure. He can express the feelings of pleasure and pain towards sensations. These feelings can be seen in his physical activities and facial expressions. In the beginning the stimulus affects his total body, but gradually different sensations affect different sense organs. As the child achieves maturity and receives various types of sensations from the environment, he learns to react towards them. He begins to understand meanings of the gestures of his mother. He can distinguish between various persons. He recognizes different types of food. Thus, gradually, he learns to distinguish between various types of sensations and understand their meanings.

1. **Visual Training.** As the infant is seven or nine days of age he is seen reacting differently to different colours. The blue colour is more impressed than red colour gets the minimum. The girls are more impressed by colours than boys. Some boys are colourblind and they have no sensation of the red colour. The infant reacts to light within three hours of his birth. Intense light unfavourably affects the eyes.

   For visual training the child is given objects of different colours and different forms. While he plays with them he learns, to distinguish between different colours and forms. At the kindergarten stage the child learns the use of vision while playing with different types of balls. In the kindergarten method he is given woollen balls of different colours and forms by which he learns to distinguish between colours and forms. The flowers are also used for this purpose. In the Montessory system of education different types of toys are given to the child to play with. In advanced classes the children are shown different types of films, flowers, plants, animals and things. The child learns to distinguish among these and thus trains his Vision.
2. **Auditory Training.** Immediately after few hours of birth the infant's ear reacts to sounds. This sense organ, however, is least developed at the time of birth. Some infants cannot hear anything even for several days. Normally, the infant begins to hear within one or two weeks of his birth. The auditory training, starts right now. Different types of mechanical toys can be used to produce different types of sounds and the child gradually learns to distinguish among them. He is very much interested in different types of musical instruments and loves to hear songs. These can be utilized for his auditory training. In kindergarten schools several types of musical instruments are utilized, to train the child's sense of sounds. Similar is the procedure in Montessory schools. The child gradually learns to distinguish between the voices of different animals. Auditory training is necessary for the development of correct pronunciations of words.
3. **Training of Smell.** The just born infant distinguishes between different smells within few hours of birth. This sense organ acts all the time unless the person is unconscious. Smell is trained by means of providing different type of smells to the child.
4. **Training of Taste.** The just born infant has a developed capacity of taste. At the age of one week he is seen reacting differently to different type of tastes. While he likes sweet tastes he rejects same and better tastes. He can also distinguish between edible and

non-edible things on the basis of smell. The sense of taste can be trained by providing the child with fruits and other edible things of different taste.

5. **Training of Touch.** The just born infant shows reactions towards heat and cold, touch and pressure. These reactions are observed in the whole body and yet some organs are more sensitive towards touch. For example, the infant's lips are found to be most sensitive. The sense of touch can be trained by providing different type of touch sensations to the child, such as heat and cold, pain and pressure etc. In Montessory schools the child is provided with pieces of muslin, silk and other types of cloth. He learns to distinguish between different types of touch through these.

The above discussion regarding the training of different sense organs shows that the main technique of training a sense organ is to provide suitable stimuli to the child. Thus toys of different forms, touch, colour, etc., are given to the child. He learns to distinguish between different types of sensations while playing with the toys. As the child knows his environment by the sense organs, sense training is necessary for his proper adjustment with the physical environment. It is the ground of his mental development. Therefore, in modern systems of education, such as kindergarten, Montessory and others, sense training has been given an important place in child's education.

QUESTION FOR EXERCISE

1. What do you understand by sense training? What is its educative importance?

20

Perceptual Development

When the child is born all his sense organs are complete and begin their work within a short time. The child begins to react to light within few weeks. It takes-some time to begin to hear. He responds towards sound within few weeks. Gradually, he learns to understand the meaning of the gestures made by his mother. He gradually learns to distinguish between various sensations by seeing various types of objects, hearing different types of sound, tasting different types of food and touching different types of surfaces.

The child's perception develops after the establishment of sensations. Perception starts mental process. It involves sensations. As the child gets more and more experience his perceptual capacities develop. He begins to understand the meaning of different sensations. The just born infant cannot understand the meaning of his experiences in the environment. By his contact with persons and things he gradually learns to distinguish between them. Sense training plays an important part in this process. It clarifies the perceptions of the child and improves his field of knowledge.

CHARACTERISTICS OF PERCEPTUAL DEVELOPMENT

In comparison with the perceptions of the adults, the child's, perceptions show some peculiarities. His perceptions are influenced by the acuity of his sense organs, stimuli received from sensations, his past experience, his interest and attention. The interest and attention of the child change very fast. His early perceptions are therefore not very clear. As his experience increases he begins to recognize special characteristics of different things. In short, the following are the chief characteristics of child's perceptual development:

1. **From Whole to the Part.** The child's perceptions proceed from whole to part. In the beginning he has a general perception of the whole thing. Gradually, his synthetic knowledge becomes

analytic and be comes to recognize peculiar characteristics of different things. Thus, as his experience increases his knowledge becomes analytic. The perceptions of the adults, on the other hand, are directly analytic. The adult can immediately see flowers and leaves separately. The child, on the other hand, first sees them together and then distinguishes between flowers and leaves.

2. **From Particular to General.** The child develops the capacity of generalization by gradual practice. Therefore, his early perceptions, are the perceptions of particulars. For him every thing or person is particular. If he uses a particular glass to drink milk, he wants to have the same glass and distinguish it from others. This is the reason why children are found insisting upon taking some particular object and do not agree to take similar thing. The adult perception, on the other hand, is more general. He can use any cup to drink, because he knows that cups do not make much difference. It is because of his perception of the particulars that the child cannot understand the definition which the adult-can understand. The child gradually arrives from particular to general perception in the due course of development.

3. **Illusory and False Perception.** According to Dumville many of the perceptions of the child are illusory and false. While on the one hand he dances with glee at the site of burning flames, on the other hand he is terrified by seeing fire-fighting engine. The adult persons, on the other hand, are terrified by seeing flames, and become happy at the site of fire-fighting engine. In this example the child and adult have seen the same things in different meanings. But on the other hand, sometimes sonic perceptions of very young children are much more real than the perceptions of adult persons. In fact the child's perception is more illusory and false because he lacks experience and cannot understand the meaning of things. The required training and experience is given at school and in the family. As the child gets more and more experience, his perceptions become real.

4. **Gross Perception.** The child tends to perceive gross things and cannot perceive subtle qualities as the adults do. Thus perception develops from gross to subtle. The child's ability of subtle perceptions increases with his development.

5. **Influence of Immediate Interest.** The child's perceptions are very much influenced by immediate interest. It is because of these interests that he perceives different objects. These are also, related with attention. If the child is hungry he attends to food

and perceives it easily. The colour, smell and other qualities of the food attract him and he immediately perceives them. The interests of the adult, on the other hand, are far reaching and indirect, and his perceptions are not so much coloured by them.

6. **Perception of the Intense Stimuli.** The child is much more influenced by the intensity of the stimulus as compared with the adults. He immediately perceives attractive colour, bring light and other intense stimuli. The adults, on the other hand, sometimes give much more attention to less intense stimuli, because of different purposes.
7. **Narrow Span of Perception.** The child's span of perception as well as attention is narrower as compared with that of the adults. He, therefore, perceives much less things as compared with the adult.

The above characteristics of the child's perception are not equally found on all the occasions. Secondly, one finds individual differences among children regarding their capacity of perception. This difference is mainly because of the difference in mental capacities and the capacities of the sense organs. Sex distinction is also a cause of distinction in the perception of the children. According to Crow and Crow, while the girls tend to see things as a whole the boys pay more attention to peculiarities. In primary schools, the girls are found to have more capacity of the perception of size, and colour. Perception of the child is also influenced by the environment of the home and school. All these factors create differences among the perceptions of various children.

PERCEPTUAL DEVELOPMENT

At the age of three years, the child, achieves maximum activity of his sense. His experience also increases. Therefore, at this age one finds sufficiently clear perceptions in him. Before this age he cannot easily understand the meaning of stimuli and often misunderstands them. The child normally perceives those things which are of immediate interest to him. He finds that some, things are edible, some things produce sounds, some produce light, and some things are movable. He learns to distinguish between different types of food according to their form, colour, smell and taste. Whenever he commits a mistake, it is due to absence of interest and attention. His experiences also play an important part in perception. For example, if the child has enjoyed eating ice-cream, he will easily locate it anywhere.

In the beginning the children perceive only those things which are directly presented to their sense organs. They perceive these things in their gross and whole form and do not understand their subtle meanings.

The studies of the child's interpretation of pictures have revealed that they first of all recognize those things which are already known to them. They perceive those things in which they are interested or about which they have some experience. After some time they perceive different activities and interpret them according to their interest and experience. As the child becomes mature he begins to interpret things according to his own interests. In fact, the influence of interest on perception is found even among the adults, though they are more objective as compared with the children. The social factors also play an important part in the child's perception. They lead to a refinement in his perceptions.

The above discussion shows that the perception and understanding or meanings in the child improve with maturity and development. This fact can be easily observed in the child's perception of persons. A very young infant cannot distinguish between different persons. With the development of age, he learns to distinguish between different persons and their characteristics. This knowledge helps in his social adjustment.

INFLUENCE ON LOGICAL REASONING

Logical reasoning involves perception of the relationship in the given material. In the absence of this capacity, a person cannot reason out the particular from the general and general from the particular. Thus, the capacity of reasoning is very much related with the development of perception. Before sufficient development of perception, the child's perception is from whole to part, particular to general, gross to subtle and influenced by immediate, interest. After gradual development the child learns to perceive the parts, the general concepts, subtle qualities and mild stimuli. He can now perceive relationship among different incidents. He now understands that many things and incidents which appear to be outwardly related are not really so. He can distinguish between different incidents and their causes. He finds that several dissimilar incidents are due to similar causes. Thus the development of perception leads to the development of the capacity of reasoning. In fact, the child's mental and intellectual development progresses as a whole in which perception and logical reasoning develop side by side.

ADJUSTIVE FACTORS

The process of the development of the child involves his continued adjustment with the environment. Education also help's in this process. Adjustment with the environment requires development of innate tendencies. The child's perceptions and reactions should adjust to the needs of the environment. In particular social, geographical and psychological environment, the individual has to behave in a particular way to achieve adjustment. For example, cold and hot climates require different types of efforts to adjust with the temperature. In the social environment also the individual is required to behave according to particular social norms. He is to adjust according to his own culture. Thus it is clear that social adjustment acquires the adjustment of perceptions and reactions of the children to the demands of their environment. In the primitive society the child is left on his own to adjust according to circumstances. In the civilized society, however, a complicated process of education has been developed for this purpose.

QUESTIONS FOR EXERCISE

1. Mention the sensational and perceptional capacities of the infant.
2. What are the chief characteristics of the perceptional development of the child?
3. How do perception and development of meaning take place in children?
4. What are the major landmarks in the development of a child's perception?
5. Write short note on child's perception of person.
6. Discuss the factors that tend to make perception and reactions of children more adjustive to demands of their environment.

21

Thinking and Reasoning

According to Warren, "Thinking is an ideational activity, symbolic in character, initiated by a problem or task the individual is facing, involving some trial and error but under directing influence of the problem set and ultimately leading to a conclusion or solution of the problem." Thus thinking starts from some problem and it culminates in the solution of it. The children have to exercise thinking in order to solve their own problems. The child's thinking, however, can be distinguished from that of adults by the following characteristics:

CHARACTERISTICS OF CHILD THINKING

1. **From Gross to Subtle Concepts.** The process of the development of the concepts in the child proceeds from gross to subtle. The child's concepts are generally more gross than that of the adults.
2. **Ambiguity of Concepts.** The child's concepts are more ambiguous and indistinct as compared with the adult's concepts. With the child's mental development, the clarity of the concepts increases.
3. **Indefiniteness of the Concepts.** As compared with the concepts of the adults, the child's concepts are more indefinite. They, become definite as he advances in mental development.
4. **Simplicity of the Concepts.** As compared with the concepts of the adults, the child's concepts are more simple. He begins to understand the concept of man at the age of 27 months and knows that both male and female are human beings. At the age of 42 months he has the concept of fruit including mango, banana and other fruits. The child knows that brinjals, carrots, etc., are all vegetables. Thus as he becomes more and more mature the concepts in the child's mind become more and more complex.
5. **Concepts of the Whole.** As the child perceives the whole thing and does not attend to parts, he first forms the concept of the

whole and later on that of the part. In thinking he first understands the general meaning and then arrives at the particular meaning.

6. **Wrong Concepts.** In comparison with the adults many of the concepts of the child are wrong. He develops right concepts by means of education. The false concepts lead to maladjustment and therefore they must be replaced by right type of concepts through education. There are several reasons of child's forming wrong concepts. In the first the child is given much false information regarding many things. The adults do not care to tell him the truth. Secondly, the child's experiences are very much limited and therefore lead to the formation of wrong concepts. Several superstitions prevalent in the family of the child also lead to false concepts. Besides some wrong habits, false expectations and defects of the sense organs also result in the formation of wrong concepts.

The concepts of the child can be improved by means of education at home and in the school. This is necessary for the development of the child's thinking.

FACTORS OF CONCEPTUAL DEVELOPMENT

Concept means a general symbol representing some particular experience. Thus the child develops different concepts at different stages of development. The concepts multiply with the increase of experience. In the beginning they are simple because the nervous system and sense organs of the child are undeveloped. In the beginning many of the child's concepts are illusory and wrong. It is difficult for the child to form right concepts unless he has attained sufficient experience. The development of concepts in the child depends on the following factors:

1. **Interest and Attention.** Upto the age of 3 years, the child cannot concentrate for more than 6 seconds. At the age of 5 years this limit is increased upto 13 seconds. It is after this age that the child can attend to a thing for some time. He can now attend to complex problems. The duration and span of his attention increase. These are intimately related with his interest. Besides, the motives also affect attention.
2. **Physical Adjustment.** As the child manipulates different things in his environment his physical adjustment increases. This adjustment leads to such experiences which cannot be attained by means of sense organs only. For example, he learns to distinguish between different qualities concerning the sensation of touch.
3. **Questions of the Children.** The child tries to understand his environment by asking questions to his adults. This trend starts

at the age of 3 years and continues upto the age of 6 years. The answers which he gets to his questions lead to the formation of various concepts. It is, therefore, necessary that the child should be given correct answers to his questions, otherwise he will form wrong concepts about different things. Most of the questions of the child are concerning what and where. After the age of 4 years the child asks about why, how and when. The answers to the child's questions must be simple so that he can understand them. He should be given answers in terms of his own experience, because if anything has not been experienced by the child he will not understand it. In the beginning the child's questions are mostly concerning the immediate incidence and concrete things. Gradually he asks questions about abstract relationships and far off things. As he begins to read he searches answers to his questions in the books.

FACTORS INFLUENCING THE CHILD'S CONCEPT

The formation of concepts in the child is influenced by several factors. The important factors influencing the child's concepts are as follows:

1. **Defects of the Sense Organs.** The child attains experience by means of his sense organs. The defects of the sense organs therefore influence his concepts. For example, the deaf children do not develop the concept of sound while the colour blind children have no concept of colour.
2. **Intellectual Ability.** The intellectual ability plays an important role in the development of child's concept. The conceptual knowledge of the child increases in proportion to his intellectual ability. This in its turn leads to the formation of new concepts.
3. **Opportunities of Learning.** The concepts in the child's, mind develop in proportion to the opportunities of learning which he gets. Thus as the child learns more and more he forms new concepts of different things.
4. **Experience.** Both direct and indirect experience helps in the formation of concepts. It is hence that the child's concepts are less accurate in comparison with the concepts of the adults. The experience increases with age. It also increases through education particularly through the extra-curricular activities. It is hence that the child's mental development is influenced by his socio-economic status.
5. **Influence of Class.** The conceptual development of the child develops with the rise in socio-economic class. It is because in

the higher socio-economic status the child comes into contact of more thing and gets more varied type of experiences.

DEVELOPMENT OF SOME IMPORTANT CONCEPTS

An analysis of the development of some important concepts in the child's mind will give an idea about his conceptual development.

1. **The concept of Self.** The infant develops some type of concept of self at the early age of 6 months, though he cannot put it in language. He plays with his own physical organs and smiles at his reflection in the mirror. After gradual learning he distinguishes between different sense organs and physical parts of the body. At the age of $2^1/_2$ years he can recognize different parts of the doll's body. According to Termann a child of three years can tell his name and knows about his sex. Between 3 and 4 years of age, the child pays very much attention to himself. The young girl tries to make up imitating her mother and admires herself in the mirror. At the age of 4 years the child recognises himself as an individual distinct from other children. On the one hand he forms concepts regarding his body, form and complexion, while on the other hand he forms concepts concerning his internal feelings, attitudes and ideas. All these are concerned with his inner life. Sometimes the child fails to distinguish between these two aspects of his self. It is only after gradual development that the child becomes a social being in which both these aspects of self are synthesised.
2. **Concept of Space.** The concept of space plays an important role in perception and conception. Even a small infant can distinguish between here and there. He gradually learns to distinguish between right and left, forward and backward and different directions. A child who passes most of his time at home, finds it difficult to move outside. But as soon as he succeeds in finding out his way he does not like to be led by others. He finds that outside his house and in the neighbourhood there are many places of interest. This is more so when the child gets opportunity to visit far off places with his parents. By these experiences he forms a concept of large distances. The distance is inferred by means of experience. By the experience the child knows that there are many wards in the city and each ward consists of several streets and lanes in every street he finds many houses and locates his own house. In the beginning he recognizes length by demonstration from others. It is only after going to school that he knows about meter and centimeter. At the High School stage the child does not really understand a

kilometer's distance though he may know the number of meters in a mile.

3 **Concept of Time.** The child lives in the present. Before the age of 3 years, tomorrow has no meaning for him. It is only after it that he begins to distinguish between now and then. He gradually distinguishes between yesterday and tomorrow. Before going to school he learns the names of different days in the week. Though he has no knowledge of months in a year it is at the age of 8 years that he can accurately tell days and months. The child has to learn to see the watch and tell the time. Before the age of 12 years he cannot understand the relation between different times and units of long duration.

4. **Concept of Form and Colour.** A child below the age of 3 years can recognize forms and colours. From 3 to 6 years of age he can combine colours. At the age of 6 years he can combine different forms. In the beginning the child cannot distinguish his parents from other males and females, but he very soon begins to recognize them. At the kindergarten stage the child is influenced by the different types of colours and forms. This also helps in the formation of the concept of space. Playing with the toys helps in the formation of the concepts of forms and colours.

5. **Concept of Number.** A child I can recite numbers between 2 to 3 years of age. According to Termann and Merrill, a child of 4 years can count two things, while a child of 5 years can count four and that of 6 years can count 12 things. A child of 6 years can count numbers upto 100. At the age of 7 years he can add and subtract numbers and solve simple questions of multiplication and division. At the age of 9 years, the child develops numeral concepts upto 1000.

6. **Concept of Weight.** In the beginning the child connects weights with size and things bigger things to have more weight. Gradually he learns to distinguish between size and weight and knows that the weight of a thing cannot be determined unless it is taken up by hand.

7. **Concepts of Currency.** The concept of currency develops only when the child starts using it. He now learns to distinguish between different coins and they become meaningful for him. Even before going to school some children collect coins given to them. After going to school they learn to spend them. At the age of 6 years the child can recognize different coins separately. A child of five years of age does not know the relationship between

coins and cost. Within 2 years he understands that be can secure many things and services in exchange of coins.

8. **Concept of Causation.** At a very early age the child knows that he has to behave differently with different persons. At the age of 2 to 4 years he knows what type of behaviour is expected of him towards different persons. He knows which cause leads to a particular result. By using different things, clothes, etc., and experiencing the consequences the child forms the concept of causation. These concepts, however, are concrete. The child cannot think of abstract causation.

DEVELOPMENT OF REASONING

The child starts reasoning at a very early age, but his reasoning is different from that of the adult persons. Reasoning means inference of unknown things on the basis of known facts. It may be deductive *i.e.,* from general to particular or inductive *i.e.,* from particular to general. Both these types of reasoning can be seen in the child's thinking.

Reasoning in a child starts at the age of 2 years. From two to four years of age, he begins to generalise about individuals and things in his environment. At the age of 6 years, his reasoning is very much the same as it is at the age of 11 years. According to Piaget, the child cannot reason out properly even at the age of 7 and 8 years. He can do so only at the age of 11 and 12 years. An important cause of the deficiency of reasoning in child's thinking is the inadequacy of experience. The child mostly lives in the world of imagination. He does not pay much attention to actual facts. Studies have, however, revealed that the child can reason about causation at the kindergarten age. As he develops in age he improves the capacity of deductive reasoning. The power of reasoning is intimately connected with the development of concept. It increases along with conceptual development. This can be helped by the parents and teachers.

CHARACTERISTICS OF CHILD REASONING

The following are the important characteristics of reasoning process of the child as compared with the adults:

(1) **Imaginary Reasoning.** As compared with the adults, the child generally lives in the world of imagination. He takes imaginary things to be real and cannot distinguish them from the real things. The adult persons, on the other hand, mostly live in the real world. It is hence that the concepts of the adult persons are more real than the concepts of the child. The child's concepts on the other hand are more imaginary.

(2) **Less Subtle Reasoning.** The child's knowledge and experience is very much limited as compared with that of the adults. Therefore, his reasoning ability is also much less developed. His concepts are more ambiguous and false and his reasoning power is much less than that of the adults. The adults can understand subtle relationships between different facts and incidents. Therefore, their reasoning is much more subtle than that of the child, conversely, a child's reasoning is less subtle than that of adults.

(3) **Reasoning by Trial and Error.** Solution of a problem requires insight in it. The child does not have this insight and, therefore, his reasoning proceeds by trial and error. According to Jersild even in the problems in which the adults follow some definite solutions, the child mostly takes recourse to trial and error. He cannot have much patience in thinking and therefore commits more errors and has less insight.

(4) **Reasoning according to Desire.** The child has no knowledge of the rules of reasoning. He therefore reasons according to his desire. Sometimes when he asks for a thing and he is told that it is not available in the house he argues that it must be in the house because he needs it. According to Jersild, a child of $2^1/2$ years does not believe factual statement because the most important reason before him is the fulfilment of his desire. He therefore does not pay any attention to facts in his reasoning. He twists facts according to his own wish to which he gives all importance. He will do the same thing for which he has been forbidden. He will pluck a flower and if he is asked to explain the reason he will immediately say that is because he had a desire to do so. This tendency gradually decreases with the increase of age. The child now understands reasoning. If he asks for sweets and he is told that the shop is closed he does not insist on getting sweets right at the moment. Thus, the elder child and the adolescent can be persuaded to understand facts, In this way with the increase of age, the child does not argue according to adjusts according to real situation.

QUESTIONS FOR EXERCISE

1. Define thinking. In what way does the process of thinking of a child differ from that of an adult?
2. Describe the nature of thinking in children. How do the concept develop?

3. Write notes on—
   (a) Characteristics of children thinking.
   (b) Difference between the thinking of children and adults.
4. What are the characteristics of children's concept. Describe how the concepts of causality develop in the child.
5. What is meant by concept? Discuss the process of concept formation.
6. Describe the characteristics of reasoning process in children. Give some examples from your own experience of child reasoning.
7. Explain the process of reasoning and thinking in the children and show how these differ from those of the adults.

22

Imagination

WHAT IS IMAGINATION?

Imagination is mental manipulation. Suppose that a person has to decorate a room with furniture. One way of doing it is to move every individual piece of furniture all over the room and to find a suitable place for it. This will only mean a wastage of a lot of time, and there is little possibility of success because the correct place for a piece of furniture can be defined only in the background of the rest of furniture. We cannot know the most suitable place, for a chair in an empty room. The question of its most suitable position arises only when other pieces of furniture have also to be placed. Decoration by physical manipulation is bound to be tedious and it is, therefore, better to turn to imagination. If now the person takes up a strategic position in the room, from where the whole room is visible, he can picture the room in his mind and decide the location of the various pieces of furniture by moving them around in his mind. This involves mental manipulation as a substitute for physical manipulation. It is thus an example of imagination.

CLASSIFICATION OF IMAGINATION

Imagination has been classified in a number of ways, the most general classification being Reproductive and Creative.

(1) **Reproductive Imagination.** Reproductive imagination is, directed by external suggestions. Students of history, to take a common example, are able to imagine incidents which took place some thousands of year ago. The vividness of this imagination will be more or less according to the vividness or otherwise of the description. Similarly, when a person loses himself in some novel which he is reading he feels, for some time at least, that he is seeing everything with his own eyes. Even when people are

moving around in historical places, incidents related to them present themselves to the spectators through their imagination. In all these examples, the basis of imagination is external, the imagination being a mere reproduction of external objects and not an individual or original construction. These are therefore, examples of reproductive imagination.

(2) **Creative Imagination.** But, if some person writes a story, poem or drama it is not merely a reproduction of external happenings but it has an additional element of original imagination. Creation is not the same thing as reproduction. The difference between creative and reproductive imagination is the same as that between an author and his reader. The poet, author, artist and the like depict their emotions and feelings through the medium of creative imagination.

Creative imagination, too, has been divided into two classes Passive creative imagination and Active creative imagination. These types of imagination are described as follows:

(a) **Passive Creative Imagination.** Sometimes, and as a matter of fact quite often, when a person's brain is unoccupied, imaginative ideas flit through the mind one after the other. The person has to make no effort in their coming or going. This is called passive creative imagination because in this state the mind is passive. Among instances of passive imagination are included dreams, day dreams and other imagination of the type. Some sports are also included in this class, due to the passivity of imagination in their case, but most of the other organised games cannot be classified under this heading. Now chess, for example, calls for active imagination. Imagination is passive in dreams and daydreams. The aim of the day dream is fulfilment of desires through the imagination instead of effort. The person imagines himself to be the hero of his day-dream. The conquering hero fulfils his desire through victory while the suffering hero does the same through suffering. Adler attributed these desires to power while Freud considered them to be related to sex. These day-dreams are useful to man in as much that they fulfil unfulfilled desires and restore a balance in personality. In fact, every person has day-dreams some time or the other but if it becomes abnormal and an excuse to escape from the realities of life, it causes grave harm to the individual. The dream, too, is a similar passive creative imagination.

Freud maintains that dreams fulfil unsatisfied sex desires. According to other psychologists external psychological factors also influence dreams.

(b) **Active Creative Imagination.** In the case of active creative imagination the subject imagining various things has predetermined goal in view. The reality and reasoning are not disregarded. From the view point of aim or goal, active creative imagination can be classed as: (1) Pragmatic and (2) Aesthetic Imagination.

(1) **Pragmatic Imagination.** The making of a plan for a big bridge or canal, deducing of a mathematical theory of the exercise of the faculty of imagination for an invention are all examples of pragmatic imagination. In these cases imagination was guided by some particular objects in view. Pragmatic imagination, as is implied in the name, has a particular end in view. Pragmatic imagination, in its turn, can be divided into two classes as follows:

(i) *Theoretical Imagination:* Imagination which helps in the proof or clarification of some theory is theoretical imagination. This is the type of imagination employed in scientific theories.

(ii) *Practical Imagination:* The construction of a plan for a bridge or a canal are examples of this type of imagination. Practical imagination is the imagination which helps us in constructing something useful and not to prove some theory.

(2) **Aesthetic Imagination.** On the one hand, the aim of the pragmatic imagination is to find something advantageous while on the other, aesthetic imagination aims simply at the creation of beauty. This is the type of imagination employed in literature, music and art. A poem, created by a poet, aims only at the creation of beauty and not any other practical aim. It is not necessary to include all literature, music and art in the class but it is undoubtedly true that these are the creations of beauty. Aesthetic imagination is of two types—artistic and fantastic.

(i) *Artistic Imagination:* In the artistic aesthetic imagination, beauty has a specific pattern and its description in literature or painting is attempted. Thus, even though artistic, aesthetic imagination is as free from the limitations of the external world as possible, it. is directed towards the fulfilment of some predetermined aim of the artist. In the writing of a story the imagination of the author does create beauty but even then some aim and pattern is concealed in it. It works within a predetermined framework.

(ii) *Fantastic Imagination:* As Opposed to artistic imagination fantastic imagination has no direction, pattern or aim and everything depends on the fantasy of the individual. Fairy tales and fantastic poems are examples of this type of imagination. Though this too, results in some advantage to the society or the individual yet as in the case of artistic imagination, fantastic imagination has no pre-determined end in view.

CHARACTERISTICS OF CHILD'S IMAGINATION

Imagination grows in the child alongwith the growth of his other mental capacities. Without the growth of imagination the child cannot express all his needs, desires, expectations and fears. Imagination helps him in the expression of many of his desires and needs. It is not definite as to when the power of imagination starts developing in the child but it appears that imagination develops side by side with the development of speed. According to Jersild a child of 10 months can imagine conversation while playing with the toy. Similarly, a child of 1 year can indulge into imaginative activities while playing with the toys. Before the age of 3 years, the children can be observed imagining, talking with the animals, and playing with the toys and extinguishing the fire etc. After some time they are found imagining and copying the actions of blind, deaf and old persons. The following are the important distinctions in the imagination of the children from that of the adults:

(1) **Distinction in Images.** As compared with the adults, the images in the child's mind are more lively. Secondly, while the, child's imagery includes more visual images, the adult imagery includes auditory images. The auditory images gradually develop in the child Thirdly, there is more use of symbols in the images in the child's imagination, while this is not the case with the adults. Fourthly, the image in the child's mind changes as he grows in age. Fifthly, the images of child's imagination are rather gross, while those in the adult's mind are more sublte.

(2) **Imaginations concerned with Imaginary World.** The child's imaginations are generally not concerned with the actual world, but with the world of imagination. For example, while an adult person imagines marriage ceremony of some real persons, the child dose so in the case of toys in which imaginary persons participate and imaginary things are served in the feast.

(3) **Imaginations are taken as Actual.** The child and the adult both take recourse to imagination now and then but while the adult persons can distinguish imagination from reality, the child cannot do so. Thus even the toy train is taken as the actual railway train by him.

(4) **Full satisfaction with Imagination.** As the child does not distinguish between imagination and reality so he derives complete satisfaction by means of imagination. On the other hand since the adult individual does not consider imaginary things as real, he is not satisfied purely by imagination. He does not indulge into imagination for satisfaction but for repairing some future plan. The child is sometimes satisfied by imaginary explanations. For example, if he asks about the dead man he is told that the man has gone to God, and he is satisfied with the reply. The adult persons, on the other hand, cannot be satisfied by such imaginary explanations.

(5) **Imaginary Thinking.** While the adult persons sometimes use imagination in thinking, the child's thinking is mostly imaginary. The adult and the child both utilize imagination for thinking about the future.

(6) **Losing Balance in Imagination.** As the child considers imagination to be real, he sometimes almost forgets the real world in the world of imagination. Thus while imagining some pleasant scene, he begins to dance with glee, and while imagining some painful incident, he begins to weep bitterly. An adult person while somewhat influenced by imagination distinguishes between imagination and reality and therefore he is not so much moved by mere imagination.

MEMORY AND IMAGINATION

Memory is closely related with imagination. The material of imagination is generally borrowed from man's past experience which is kept safe in his mind in the form of memory. It is on the basis of memory that a man imagines about his future. Thus the form of imagination depends upon the type of memories a man has in his mind, though the material supplied by memory is moulded in the new forms by means of imagination.

Imagination plays a vital role in the child's life. The child plays for hours together with the toys and derives much happiness by living in the world of imagination. The child's capacity to act is much less developed than that of the adults, he fulfills deficiency by means of imagination. Different types of imaginative plays are played by the children at different ages. At the age of 3 years they imagine themselves to be the adult men and women and emulate their activities. At the age of 5 and 6 years, they imagine themselves to be different type of animals and emulate their voice. At the age of 8 and 9 years, they are very much interested in imaginary stories of Gods and Goddesses, giants and fairies. The children literature everywhere is fall of such imaginary tales. These stories also help in the development of the imagination of the child especially when they give him some practical lesson. At the age of 11 and 12 years, children are very much interested in reading stories of courage and bravery, because by means of imaginary identification with the hero of the story, they undergo all the experience of his activities. At the age 12 and 13 years most of the adolescent boys and girls pass much of their time in the world of imagination, where they have not to face the hard realities life.

It has been observed that the imagination in childhood takes the form of ambition in the adult age and the individual tries to realize his imaginations in the actual world. It is hence that children should be given biographies of great men to read. Besides influencing ambition, imagination also influences physical and mental health. If a child often imagines about his diseases and death, this tendency results in adverse effect on his health. Such imaginations are the result of hardships in the child's life at home or at school. The children should not be told stories involving much fearful scenes because these stories create fearful imaginations in their minds. Because of imagination children sometimes tell many false stories and circulate rumours. At the age of 4 to 9 years they can be observed playing and talking with imaginary friends. Unless this tendency becomes excessive, it is not harmful for the child's development.

FACTORS HELPING IN IMAGINATION

Factors helping in imagination can be used for the development of child's imagination. Some important factors are:

(1) **Knowledge of Language.** Language plays an important role in the development of imagination. The richness of imaginations is correlated with the richness of vocabulary. The vocabulary of the child can be developed by means of radio, television, and other forms of communication. The child's vocabulary grows very rapidly after he learns reading and writing.

(2) **Stories.** The stories are the best medium of the development of imagination in the child. It is hence that in almost every culture on finds very old traditions of interesting children stories for example, Alif Laila tales of Iran, Aesop's fables of Europe and the

Panchtantra; Hitopadesha and Jataka stories in India. In children's literature the stories of Gods and Goddesses, fairies and giants, are given a prominent place. These stories tell the tales of magic, bravery and courage, humour, pleasure and pain. These stories are told not only at home but also at the school. They have been given an important place in Kindergarten stage of children's education. The children should not be told stories involving immoral deeds, fear, prejudice, hatred and superstition. On the other hand, they should be told stories involving high qualities in the hero. The stories in language and subject matter should be according to the age of the child.

(3) **Acting.** Acting is a very important means to the development of imagination. While imitating voice and actions of different types of individuals and animals, the child receives different types of experiences and his constructive imagination develops. Imitation plays an important role in acting and the child can be taught many important things through acting.

(4) **Play.** The most important simple and natural media of the development of imagination in the child are different types of plays. In these plays the child has to adopt different roles at different times, which require different types of qualities in him. Thus while playing different types of plays, the child develops many qualities such as qualities of leadership, team work, responsibility, etc. Some plays are natural to the children, while other plays, can be taught to them. These plays should help in the formation of good character in the child alongwith recreation. The plays involving team work develop valuable social qualities in the children.

(5) **Poetry.** Poems are based on imagination. The child is naturally interested in hearing and reciting poem. This interest, can also be cultivated and developed. The child can be given poems to learn by heart and encouraged to recite them before a group of children. In the adolescent age, boys and girls tend to make poems and the teachers can help them in developing this talent.

(6) **Art.** Art is an important medium for the expression of imagination in human beings. Very small children mould clay in the form of different types of toys. They can also draw on the paper by different colours. Painting and drawing give much pleasure to the child while it develops his power of imagination. It is hence that in the elementary classes, children are given to do clay work and drawing. The child learns the relation of form and matter by means of artistic creation. He also distinguishes

between different colours and forms. He develops his taste in learning different types of fine art. Thus, the artistic tendency of the child should be developed in the home and at school.

QUESTIONS FOR EXERCISE

1. Write a short note on Imagination.
2. Define Imagination and describe its various kinds. How can we develop children's power of imagination?
3. In what ways does children's imagination differ from the imagination of adults? Give examples.
4. Write short note on children's imagination.
5. What role do day dreams and fantasies play in the development of a child?
6. Discuss the relationship between memory and imagination. What will you do to develop the power of imagination of a child?

23

Memory and Association

The conscious level of the human mind is not the solitary level of mental activity. The impressions of various experiences become permanent at the subconscious stage and they come to the conscious level whenever they are needed or whenever there is that relevant context. Experiences are not obliterated from the mind with the passage of time, but rather, they remain in the mind permanently in the form of memory and can be recalled with effort and recognised. But, it is common experience that people do not remember, their experience completely and a major part is not even remembered. Thus remembering and forgetting are matters of everyday experience. Memory is a general word which includes several mental activities like recall, recognition and retention. A person experiences ease in relearning an activity which he had learnt previously but had forgotton. This proves very obviously that the previous learning had not been wiped out completely but had left an impression on the mind or a change in the nerves which facilitated relearning. People do not completely forget the story of any movie they have seen but recount it with ease when they are requested to do so. If someone else takes on the tedious task of telling the, story of the same film, they affirm it because they are reminded of it, and if they hear any song from the film played anywhere they are easily reminded of that too. Thus there is retention, recall and recognition in the memory of an experience, which makes it a complex activity.

WHAT IS MEMORY?

Bentley and his followers maintained that experience acquired by a person leaves impressions or marks on the brain in the form of memory traces. These form the basis of memory as a functional tendency, because retention ends when these traces are wiped off. These psychologists have established that retention is a psychological process. But Bartlett,

Piron, Gibson and some other psychologists have attempted to show that memory is a mental activity independent of memory traces. They have proved by examples of stories, pictures, etc., that memory depends more on mental states like interests, motivation, bias etc., than on repetition of experiences. This makes memory a mental activity. But just as every mental activity has a physiological basis, so is the case of memory. Briefly, memory is a psychological activity.

Processes in Memory

Memory is preceded by learning and, therefore, memory involves four processes or activities in general. They are as follows:

1. Learning,
2. Retention,
3. Recall,
4. Recognition.

Two of these four activities namely learning and retention are essential in memory. Recall succeeds learning but there may be no recognition. Sometimes retention is followed by recognition without any recall. Besides learning and retention both recall and recognition are necessary for complete memory. Sometimes it is recall which takes place first to be followed by recognition but equally often the order of the two activities is reversed.

1. **Learning.** It will be quite in keeping with the context to give a brief description of each of these activities. As has been mentioned above the first step or activity in memory is learning. If learning is good, memory will also be good. Thus the methods which assist learning do the same for memory. Learning creates memory traces on the mind on the basis of which recollection is effected.
2. **Retention.** The second activity in memory is retention, which means retaining of the residues of experience. The residues of experience are left on the mind in the form of memory traces where they are safe though they are acted upon by interest etc. The proofs of retention are recollection, recognition and relearning. Though recollection is a proof of memory, its absence is not the proof of the absence of memory because a person often remembers something at a later date which had eluded him at the earlier occasion. Same is the case with recognition because while its presence indicates memory its absence is no proof of the absence of memory. If we come face to face with a long-separated friend and find ourselves unable to recognise him, we cannot take this to mean that all the experiences related to that person have

been obliterated from the memory because the next moment we might succeed in recognising him. The most convincing proof of retention is furnished by relearning. If there is no progress in relearning it will be concluded that there was no retention.

Retention, as has been mentioned above, is the retaining of the residues of experiences. The different forms taken by these remains of experiences indicate that there are different levels of retention. Something remains on the fringe of consciousness and can be recalled into consciousness effortlessly. About some things we feel as if these had been experienced yesterday and can be recalled at will. The same cannot be said of others which we forget and can remember only when some one reminds us of them or when some new event takes place. In this way, efforts have to be made in order to recall impressions in the conscious and sub-conscious levels. The experiences in the unconscious cannot be remembered and can be recovered only by word association, dream analysis and other techniques.

3. **Recall.** Another activity in memory is that of recall. This is the activity by which the residues of experiences are brought back to the conscious level. A student studies for his examination all the year round and a major part of his learning is present in a permanent and healthy condition in the mind. While answering the question paper in the examination hall he recalls this learning existing in the memory and puts it down in black and white. Though this recollection cannot be identical with the original learning, its matter resembles the original and a significant part of the learning can be remembered in the same form if suitable efforts are made. Actually, recall is not a mere reproduction of the past experience or perception. In spite of the fact that it depends on retention, recall is not fashioned entirely by it. It is not necessary that if retention is good the recall will also be good.

Ebbinghaus experimented to see whether recall is creative or reproductive, *i.e.,* whether the person concerned puts something alien with the, recollection or does he make a faithful reproduction, Ebbinghaus taught some senseless stanzas to some people and asked them to recall these stanzas after different time intervals. From the results he concluded that recall is reproductive. Bartlett and his followers did not agree with this view and to prove their point they experimented with the recollection of a story. A student was made to read a story with care and was asked to recall it fifteen minutes later. This reproduced story was given to another student to read and he too was asked to recall it. In this way, students were made to recall a story by this chain method and it was found that in the last recall, the conclusion and even names of the characters had been changed.

4. **Recognition.** The last step in mamory is recognition. Sometimes recall comes after recognition as, for example, when we recognise an old friend the moment we set eyes on him and then we are reminded of many things about him. On other occasions, it is recall which precedes recognition. Suppose that I am travelling in a train and I am confronted with the embarassing situation of someone asking me whether I had recognised him. I apologise doubtfully and confess my inability to recognise him. The person says, "When ten years ago we lived in Civil Lines, Meerut, we were neighbours". And this statement starts a reaction, reminding me of my experience of ten years ago. I then recognise the person, shake hands and start talking of this and that. This example shows that recognition sometimes follows recall.

   Recognition may either be definite or indefinite. A person recognises a friend as soon as he sees him and is perfectly aware of everything about this person, this being an example of definite recognition. An example of indefinite recognition would inability of a person to remember the time, place and context in which he first heard a story which has just been related to him in spite of the fact that he recognises it.

   In recognition, the recognised person or subject is separated from other people. When a person recognises a friend in a crowd, he distinguishes his friend from the rest. This distinction has a lot of significance in recognition and the more acute it is the better will be the recognition. And recognition is impossible in the absence of distinction. Recognition means literally cognising again, and it is therefore the cognition of some subject cognised before. Thus recognition comes after cognition.

MEMORY OF THE CHILD

The child's and the adult's memories can be distinguished in the following respects:

1. **Distinction in Immediate Memory.** It has been observed by many studies that the immediate memory grows along with the growth of age. The rate of growth is slow upto the age of 13 but from 13 to 16 it grows at a faster pace and reaches its culmination at the age of 25 after which it may some what decline. Thus immediate memory develops rapidly in adolescents. Besides, individual differences can be observed regarding immediate

memory in different children. According to Ross, the immediate memory of adults and adolescents is more intense than that of the children.

2. **Remote Memory.** While the immediate memory of the child is weaker than that of the adult, his remote memory is stronger. It is hence that the childhood experiences are remembered for almost the whole life. It is necessary that the child should be given rich and pleasant experiences in childhood, so that their memories may enrich his mind in later age. Many things taught in childhood are remembered in later life. Thus the child's capacity of retention is much more than that of the adult. In other words, childhood is a favourable age for retention. It is a very formative period in the development of the child. The childhood impressions cannot be eliminated in later life. They form the basis of the adult's mental and emotional development.
3. **Development.** The memory grows along with the general development of the child. The child's memory therefore is much less developed than that of the adult. An important cause of this distinction is that the adult person has more experiences and ideas The memory begins to function in infancy and can be seen in the child's capacity to recognize things and persons.
4. **Effect of purpose.** In comparison with the adult person the child has very few purposes to achieve through his actions. Generally, his only purpose is to avoid pain and satisfy his physical needs. He remembers things which give him pleasant experience. On the other hand, he also remembers things which give him painful experience, because he knows the value of avoiding them. He can remember the facts and incidents which have created indifferent feelings. The adult person, on the other hand, has many purposes to realize and therefore sometimes very well remembers facts which are uninteresting to him.
5. **Interests.** In comparison with the adult person the child's interests are very much limited. This in its turn limits his field of memory. Thus the field of memory grows along with the field of interests. While the adult's interests involve immediate as well as remote things, the children are interested in immediate things.

QUESTIONS FOR EXERCISE

1. Describe fully the various factors on which memory depends. How does the memory of the children differ from that of adult?
2. Describe the process of memory and imagination in a child. Compare these with that of adults.

24

Attention and Interest

MEANING OF ATTENTION

Attention is a motivated process. Man lives in an environment. The stimuli from the, environment are always affecting him. But these stimuli do not affect him equally. It is a common place observation that some stimuli affect us more than others. This shows that man selects out of environmental stimuli. The tendency of selection shows that there is a motivational process in him which is known as attention. This attention is affected by interest, attitudes and set. It is a selective process which includes motivation, set and selection. The cat will not attend to the mouse unless it is hungry. Among several animals present before a cat, the cat will attend to the mouse. As a cat is attending to the mouse, one can see a definite set in it. This set is both physical as well as mental. To take example from human beings, if a student is not motivated, he will not attend to the class lecture. Again, while a professor is delivering a lecture in the class, there are several other sounds being made in other rooms and the surroundings. The student who hears the lecture selects professor's voice out of the noise in the surroundings. While a student is attentively hearing the lecture, one can very well note his physical set which is also symbolic of his mental set. Receptor adjustment, bodily adjustment, postural adjustment, muscle attention and central nervous adjustment are typical of bodily attitudes in attention. Thus, in brief, attention can be defined as a process which compels the individual to select some particular stimulus according to his interest and attitude out of the multiplicity of stimuli present in the environment.

CONDITIONS OF ATTENTION

As a selective act of the mind, attention depends upon several conditions. These conditions, may be of two types — External or Objective and

Internal or Subjective. External or objective conditions are related with the environment. In the environment or surrounding of the individual there are several stimuli, but he does not attend to all of them at the same time, because some stimuli are stronger than others. The factors making these stimuli more than others, are known as external determinants of attention. Besides the external conditions, the mental conditions, culture and heredity, also influence attention. Due to these internal conditions some objects attract our attention more than others. These internal factors are internal determinants of attention. The methods of achieving attention are based upon these external and internal determinants of attention.

External Determinants

The following are the most important external determinants of attention:

1. **Nature of Stimulus.** Nature of stimulus means its type, *i.e.,* whether it is visual, gustatory, auditory, Olfactory or factual stimulus. It has been found by experiments that in comparison with other sensations, form, colour and sound attract more attention. Among the pictures, the pictures of human beings attract more attention than those of animals or objects. Among the pictures of human beings those of beautiful women attract more attention. Besides these, the coloured pictures attract more attention than colourless ones. All these factors are important in advertisement. In the auditory stimulus, the melodious voice attracts more attention than other voices.
2. **Intensity of the Stimulus.** The intensity of the stimulus is a helpful condition in attention. In comparison with the weak stimuli the intense stimulus attracts more attention of the organism. High sound, excessive pressures and acute pain attract our attention. In the market there is always some buzzing sound and yet the pedestrians hear the horn of the motor car, since the sound of the horn is louder than other sounds. But it is not always necessary that one should attend to the intensity of stimulus. Sometimes while walking on the road, calling of our name attracts so much attention that we fail to hear even the loud sound of the motor horn. As a matter of fact the attraction of the attention does not depend on any single factor but on several factors inter-connected with one another. Hence, it can be said that other things, being the same, the more intense stimulus will attract more attention.
3. **Size of the Stimulus.** In the visual stimuli, the size of stimulus is also a determinant of attention. As a general rule, the bigger size

attracts more attention, but a small advertisement of a very wide background also attracts attention. Thus the attraction of an object does not depend upon its size alone, but also on its background. To illustrate a big black spot on a black face will not attract so much attention as a very small black spot on a white face.

4. **Location of the Stimulus.** The location of the stimulus also affects attention. In the visual stimuli, the most effective location is just in front of the eyes. The role of different pages in the newspaper or the magazine and the different places on the same page, is important in advertisement. It has been found by experiments that advertisement given on the front page or on the upper half of any page attracts more attention.
5. **Contrast of the Stimulus.** The contrast of the stimulus is also an important determinant of attention, *e.g.*, the presence of a woman among men and that of a man among women definitely attracts more attention.
6. **Change of the Stimulus.** Attention cannot be concentrated for a long time on some particular object. Hence the change of the stimulus. The advertisers change their advertisements from time to time lest it may cease to be attractive.
7. **Isolation of the Stimulus.** A man sitting alone in some corner of the park, hotel or club attracts more attention than others. A student sitting alone at the far corner of the class, is seen first. Thus, isolation is an important external determinant of attention. This fact is based upon the reason that the isolated individual is not mixed with other individuals and hence seen separately in his own background. By experiments in advertisement it has been found that only the fact of isolation attracts 30% more attention. In the British, Journal of Educational Psychology of August 1951, D.B. Berlyne pointed out the following principles based upon latest experiments :
   (a) In comparison with the unchanged stimulus the stimulus changed in the near past has more possibility of attracting attention.
   (b) The effect of the change goes on diminishing with the passage of time.
   (c) Whenever stimuli are changed together and in which one is left unchanged, the effect of change is not noticeable.
   (d) If changes goes on in the changed stimuli, the process of attention is rather permanent and strong.

   The modes of change also influence the process of attention. If there is a change absolutely opposite to the present stimulus, it will definitely attract more attention. While studying one does not hear the sound of the clock or that of electric fan but if either of these suddenly stops, one cannot fail to attend to it. Man becomes used to regular changes and does not pay much attention to them. But if some irregular change or any sudden change occurs, it at once draws attention.

8. **Duration of the Stimulus.** As a general rule, the stimulus having more duration, attracts more attention. Thus duration of the stimulus is an important determinant of the attention. But sometimes the smallest flashing of a movement attracts more attention than the bigger stimuli *e.g.*, a sudden flash of light for several seconds will attract more attention in a dark night than the continuously burning lamp.
9. **Repetition of the Stimulus.** Along with duration, repetition of the stimulus is also an important determinant of attention. It is a common place observation that when the teacher has to attract the attention of students towards a particular phenomenon, he repeats it several times. But sometimes, man ceases to attend a phenomenon simply because it is repeated many times *e.g.* If a man says something about him, we take interest in it once or twice, but if we find that he always repeats the same thing, we cease to pay attention to it.
10. **Movement in the Stimulus.** In comparison with the static the moving stimuli attract more attention. The position of stimulus changes due to movements. An object lying in some corner of the room will not attract our attention, but even if there is some illusion of movement in it, we cannot help attending to it. The influence of movement in stimulus is widely used by the shop-keepers and businessmen, who advertise through moving electric lights.

Internal Determinants

The conditions of attention as described so far are the external determinants of attention. They can also be called external laws of attention. The presence of these conditions in the environment is helpful for attention. Besides these external conditions, some internal conditions are also helpful in drawing attention. These conditions are related with motives. As a matter of fact the influence of conditions depends on these internal conditions to a very great extent. The hungry man will attend to the form and stimuli of the food. A man with a full belly will not attend to food, however nice it might appear. In the advertisement those demonstrating the naked organs of the woman have the maximum power of attraction of attention. Those interested in cinema look to the advertisements of cinema at first sight. It is difficult to describe all the internal conditions helpful in attention. Hence, only the most important will be enumerated here:

1. **Interest.** Innate and acquired interests draw the individual's attention to a particular object. Doctors, engineers, professors, all attend to the objects of their own interests. Even among the professors an object attracting the attention of a professor of geology need not attract the attention of a professor of philosophy as well. Thus the innumerable differences in interests create innumerable determinants of attention in different men. The stimuli influencing innate tendencies attract more attention than those influencing acquired interest.
2. **Basic Drives.** The basic drives or instincts of the individual are also important in drawing his attention. The animal attends to a particular stimulus when driven by the basic drives of hunger, thirst, sex etc., *e.g.*, a normal man motivated by sex will naturally attend to individuals of opposite sex. We all know by experience that when hungry we may attend to even a distasteful object. But while our belly is full, we may not attend to even the most tasteful food. Among the instincts, fear has got a definite influence upon attention. All men who fear snake will attend to all things resembling the snake. Like fear, curiosity also influences attention. We attend to even the smallest details of the object about which we have curiosity.

   Innate need also is very important in attention. The influence of sexual need in attention is very much exploited in the advertisements. Normally, the sexual need in human beings can be easily evoked. Hunger, thirst etc., are felt occasionally and the means to satisfy them are also readily available, but neither the sexual need is ever fully satisfied nor are the means of satisfying it available to all persons, all the time. Hence most of the advertisements draw attention by stimulating the sexual need in human beings.
3. **Mental Set.** Mental set is one of the most important internal determinants of attention. Mental set means the tendency or attitude of the mind. A man will attend to those objects towards which his mind is set. In the days of examinations, the mental set of students is generally towards the examination and hence even the smallest thing concerning the examination will attract their attention.

4. **Aim.** Aim also influences attention. Every man has some immediate and some ultimate aims *e.g.*, the immediate aim of the student is to pass the examination while the ultimate aim may be to get a job to earn living or any thing else. The man whose aim is not to pass the examination will not be concerned with text books or notes etc., but one who has the aim to pass the examination will at once attend to them.
5. **Meaning.** In comparison with meaningless things, meaningful things and talks attract more attention. A man will not attend to a thing which has no meaning for him. Men do not like to hear meaningless talk. If some persons are talking in Tamil, the Punjabi will not like to hear it since for him it has no meaning.
6. **Habit.** Habit is also an important determinant of attention. If a man is habituated to rising early and winding his clock early in the morning, he must attend to the clock as soon as he gets up. It has been rightly pointed out that man learns as to which object he should attend to and to which he, should not, and thus develops habits of attending and not attending to things. Thus habit has two aspects in relation to attention. On the one side man develops a habit of attending to necessary desirable things and on the other side he develops the habit of not attending to unnecessary and undesirable things. Both these kinds of habits help man in his daily routine.
7. **Disposition and Temperament.** Both disposition and temperament are important internal determinants of attention *e.g.*, a man having religious disposition and spiritual temperament will attend to religious matters, while another person having a sexual disposition and criminal temperament will attend to matters concerning sex or crimes etc. William James has rightly pointed out that it is our tendency to take interest in particular things, a result of our innate disposition and mental development., that determines which among the crowd of situations, should attract our attention.
8. **Past Experience.** Past experience also affects attention. If we know it by our past experience that a particular person is sincere towards us, we shall pay attention to whatever he advises us. If we know by experience that he is not sincere to us, we shall not attend even to his most serious advices.
9. **Emotion.** Emotion is also an important determinant of attention. It is a matter of every day experience that we attend even to the smallest fault of a person whom we hate while we do not attend even to the greatest blunder of a person whom we love.

The mother seldom finds faults with her child. The lovers find the whole world singing and dancing and immersed in romance.

10. **Social Motives.** Social motives are very important determinants of attention. In advertisements the human figures attract more attention than figures of animals and things. The reason is that man is guided by his social motives. The news about altruism, bravery and saving another's life by putting one self in danger, attracts our attention because we praise these qualities. Men attend to things concerning their duties due to social motives.

Besides the conditions described above, many other factors influence attention. Heredity, education and training have a wide influence on attention. The family, school, club, class and society of which an individual is a member, do have some influence on his attention. The physical condition, desire, purpose of the person concerned also affect his attention. Thus all the factors affecting the personality of a man affect his attention as well. As a matter of fact it is difficult to describe all direct and indirect determinants of attention. The description given here, however, includes the most important of such factors.

ATTENTION AND INTEREST

Attention is a selective act of the mind. To attend to a thing is to concentrate on it by removing attention from other things. The mind can attend on one thing at a time. Hence mind has to select. In the selection it is natural that the mind should select such objects in which it is interested. This is amply demonstrated in our daily life. The boy whose interest is in playing will attend to play while one who is interested in studying will attend, to study. Hence, one cannot attend to the studies by forcibly sitting for it. One can attend to the studies only when one is interested in it. Hence the successful teacher tries to make the students interested in their studies.

Interest is affective disposition which evokes attention and maintains it. Interest is not activity. It is a permanent tendency or a mental structure which supplies sufficient motivating power to motor activity. Interest is sometimes innate and sometimes acquired. In the fulfilment of instinctive needs, the animal naturally shows interest. Thus the individuals of different sexes are naturally interested in each other. The herbivorous animals are interested in grass while the carnivorous are interested in meat. Lion is interested in goat while goat is interested in green leaves Besides the instinctive interest there are some acquired interests as well *e.g.*, the scientist is interested in the instruments of his laboratory while they are of no interest to the ordinary layman. Thus, the individuals develop different interests according to their disposition, attention, economic, social and political status etc. Attitudes towards those things are mostly acquired. The acquired interest depends upon experience. The interest is directly related with the emotions and desires. The thing or the individual in which we are interested finds a place in our inner life and we develop it through our emotions towards it. It is not necessary that the interest should be permanent. Things which do not fulfil any permanent need evoke only temporary interest. As the need is fulfilled, the individual ceases to take interest in such objects *e.g.*, if a man has to cross a river, he will be very much interested in the boat, but after he crosses the river his interest in the boat will also come to an end. Permanent interests are related with emotions and sentiments. They are permanent mental conditions. According to Drever, interest is a disposition in its dynamic aspect. Interest is not an affective experience, but affective tendency. It is not mental process but mental structure. According to McDougall, "Interest is latent attention, attention is interest in action." As it has already been pointed out, interest is mental structure and it is expressed through attention. When the individual is not attending to a particular object, his interest in it is in a dormant form.

QUESTION FOR EXERCISE

1. Show the relationship of attention and interest.

25

Personality

Ordinarily, personality is taken as the external appearance of individual. In philosophy the meaning of personality has been interpreted in the sense of the self. But in psychology neither is the personality the external appearance nor is it the self, but it includes both and much more. The word personality has been derived from the Latin word *persona.* The word persona was used for the cover, utilised by the actors to change their appearance, but in the Roman times it was taken as the particular character itself. The second meaning has been taken in the word personality, Thus, personality is not a fixed state, but a dynamic totality which is continuously changing due to interaction with the environment, Personality is known by the conduct, behaviour, activities, movements and everything else concerning the individual. The way in which an individual adjusts which the external environment is personality. In the words of Munn, "Personality may be defined as the most characteristic integration of an individual's structure, modes of behaviour interests, attitudes, capacities, abilities and aptitudes."[1] Behaviour requires integration. This integration of various traits is found differently in different persons. As a general rule every normal individual has some sort of integration. The peculiar forms of integration in a particular individual are his personality traits. Thus, personality is the characteristic integration of an individual's traits. It is personality which makes distinction in one man and another. In the words of Gordon Allport, "Personality is the dynamic organisation within the individual of those psycho-physical systems that determine his unique adjustment to his environment."[2] The personality is the organisation of the internal and external activities. It includes the external appearance, abilities, aptitudes and capacities etc. It is not a collection of

1. Munn, N.L., *Psychology.* George G. Harrap & Co., London, p. 569.
2. Allport, G.W., *Personality, A Psychological interpretation,* New York, Holt, 1937.

the traits, but a particular organisation of them. It is the total quality of the individual's behaviour. Individual affects other individuals through his personality. Thus personality manifests in his various activities. In short, personality is the total quality of the attitudes, interests, capacities and behaviour patterns which are manifested in the individual's relation with the environment.

BIOLOGICAL FACTORS AFFECTING PERSONALITY

For some time there was a discussion among the psychologists about the relation of heredity and environment in the development of personality. In this discussion arguments were given from both sides and data were gathered on the basis of observation and experimentation. It was found by this data that the development of personality depends upon both heredity and environment in the factors influencing personality.

The factors affecting personality can be divided into two classes: (1) Biological and (2) Social. The biological factors affecting the development of personality are three (1) Ductless Glands, (2) Physique and (3) Nervous system.

Ductless Glands

Ductless glands send their secretions directly to the blood without ducts. Their secretions are called hormones. These hormones are responsible for many changes in the personality. Each gland secrets one or more type of hormones. A description of the effect of some of the ductless gland will show the extent to which personality is influenced by them.

1. **Pancreas.** Pancreas send insulin to the blood. The amount of sugar in the blood depends upon the amount of insulin in it. When the deficiency of insulin, *i.e.*, sugar, is in the body the mental capacities are weakened and the personality of the individual seems less balanced. His mood is changed temperament becomes irritated and fear increases.
2. **Thyroid.** Thyroid gland has a very important function in the development of physical structures as well as mental development. If it is absent since the very birth, body and mind of the child do not develop. Cretins, imbeciles etc. are the result of the absence of thyroid gland. Its destruction causes a disease known as myxoedema. This disease creates laziness in man. The activities of the mind as well as those of muscles are slackened. The memory becomes weak, concentration and thinking becomes difficult. In the period of development the excess of the activity of thyroid gland results in rapid physical growth, specially the development

of, height. An excessive activity of this gland results in tension irritation, worry and instability in man. Thus, with the increase or deficiency in the activity of thyroid gland, the activity of the body as well as of the mind also increases and decreases. But this does not mean that the increase and decrease of the activity in the body is always due to the effect of thyroid gland. Occasionally it might be due to the other causes as well, but thyroid gland does play an important art in them.

3. **Adrenal.** Adrenal gland secrets adrenaline. Adrenaline has an important influence upon personality. Its excess creates hyper sexual traits in men or women. Its deficiency in woman is responsible for the absence of the rounded contours and feminine voice. It mobilises the capacities in the time of emergency. The excess of adrenaline causes rapid heart-beat, high blood pressure and the postponement of the activity of the intestines. The individual having less adrenaline feels relaxation in the muscles, more sweat and the pupils of the eye are extended. An entire absence of adrenaline, results in the disease known as Addison's disease. In this disease one feels weakness and lethargy in the body, the power of resisting disease is lessened, the interest in sex activity disappears and metabolism becomes slow, the skin becomes black, the power of resisting heat and cold is lessened and behaviour becomes irritable.
4. **Gonads.** The secretion of the gonads *i.e.*, sex hormones is an important factor influencing personality. In adolescence there is a special increment in sex hormones. Hence changes are observed in the individuals according to their sex. In the body one finds the appearance of masculine characteristics such as beard, moustaches, high pitch in voice etc., while in the girl there is development of mammary glands and appearance of other womanly traits. The processes concerning pregnancy *e.g.*, mensus, pregnancy, the bearing of the child and maternal behaviour is very much influenced by the sex hormones.
5. **Pituitary.** The hormones secreted, by the pituitary glands control other glands. The hormones secreted by the front part of the pituitary gland increase the activity of other glands as well. The hormones secreted by the back part of the pituitary glands control the blood pressure and the metabolism of water in the body. These hormones also effect physical growth. In the time of physical growth the bones and muscles of the individual grow speedily due to the activity of these glands. In its excess, the height can go even upto 7 to 9 feet. But because after excessive

activity this gland becomes very much inactive, these very tall persons die at an early age. If the activity of the pituitary gland is very much deficient during the period of development, the individual remains a midget, though his intellect is normal and the physical structure is not unattractive. If the activity of this gland is normal during the development period and becomes excessive afterwards, the hand, feet, nose, and lower jaw etc., become broad. This state is known as acromegaly.

The effect of the hormones is influenced as well as the environmental factors. But still the excess or deficiency in their activity creates some changes quite apparent in the personality of the individual. It is not necessary that the excess of the secretion of any one of the particular gland should always show some special influence in the body *e.g.,* the excess of sex tendency should not always be supposed as due to the excess of secretion of the sex gland, since different glands also interact upon each other due to which the activity of some is increased while that of others is decreased. The sex behaviour, for example, is very influenced by social norms, customs, circumstances, habits and many other things. Hence, inspite of the deficiency of the sex by the hereditary hormones, the individual may appear to be very much interested in sex activities. On the other hand, inspite of the excess of the sex hormones, the individual may not appear to be interested in sexual activities.

Physique

Another important biological factor affecting personality physical structure. It is sometimes observed in daily life that the fat men are easy going and social, while the thin persons are self controlled, irritated and un-social. Thus the physical structure has some relation with the temperament. But even the instances contrary to this rule are not lacking. Hence, the relation of physical structure and temperament has not been definitely established. More studies are required in this direction. The studies conducted so far have been mostly on college students. Before one arrives at some definite conclusion, studies must be conducted on adult, persons as well. But even after that, the problem of the basis of correlation remains up-answered. Similarly, by correlation between temperament and physique the former cannot be taken to be the result of the latter. It should also be remembered in this context that physical structure makes a difference in other's behaviour towards a particular person. It is observed that our behaviour towards different individuals is modified, to some extent, according to their physical structure. This difference in our behaviour makes a change in their personality. Hence, a particular difference should not be supposed to be due to physical structure alone but also due to other's behaviour towards the particular person, though the former may be more important.

Body Chemistry

Another important biological factor effecting personality is body chemistry. In ancient times, the differences of temperament were supposed to be due to differences of chemical elements in different men. Thus the nervous personality was taken as the result of excess of nervous fluid. It was supposed that the sanguine persons have an excess of blood, the choleric persons an excess of bile, phlegmatic persons an excess of phlegam and the melancholic persons, an excess of spleen. This principle is not accepted in modern psychology, but still no psychologist denies the relation of personality with the proportion of chemical elements in the body. These chemical elements are of two types. Some reach the body from outside while some are created in the body itself. Thus, the drugs have sufficient effect on personality. The behaviour of the drunkard is an example of such effect. Different types of intoxicating drugs have a clear influence upon the personality of the individual. The deficiency of different vitamins also causes some change in the personality. With the increase or decrease of the quantity of sugar in the body, the physical and mental state of the man is very much changed. In convalescence one finds a difference in the individual's personality. Difference is also noticed after a long illness.

Besides the above-mentioned biological factors many other factors influence personality, *e.g.*, sex, intelligence and nervous system etc. The difference in the sex of male and female creates a difference in their personality, though it has been established that much of this difference is caused by social and cultural environment Galton and Goddard believed that intellect is absolutely hereditary. The modern psychologists do not agree with this view though the influence of heredity is not denied. The environment affects intellect, but, the development of intellect is ultimately limited. The influence of specific abilities, as that of music, mathematics etc., on human personality is very well known. Like the intelligence, the abilities are also generally hereditary. According to Kempf, the author of *The autonomic function and personality,* the nervous system is one of the important determinants of personality.

SOCIAL FACTORS INFLUENCING PERSONALITY

The environments of different individuals are very much different from one another and so also their effects, but the influence of environment on personality can be roughly classified into that of home, school and society. All these three play an important part in the development of personality.

Influence of Home on Personality

The environment of the home has a comprehensive influence on the development of personality. This influence, as a general rule is according to the patterns found in a particular culture. In the family the relation of child with the parents is the most intimate. The cultural development of the child is very much influenced by the behaviour of the parents, *e.g.*, a child brought up in Indian family will be very much different in his behaviour than another brought up in a Western home. But even in the same culture much difference can be observed in the parent-child relationship in different families *e.g.*, generally the child has a respectable place in Indian family, but all Indian parents do not sufficiently love and sympathise with the child. In such circumstances much repression is observed in child's behaviour. He becomes an introvert and often enjoys in his dreams, day dreams and imaginations things which are denied to him by his parents. The influence of the presence of the parental love is again not the same in the case of all children. A child may become aggressive while another may become submissive in the same circumstances. On the other hand, if the parents show excessive affection towards the child, the child may become an extremist and excessively dependent upon the parents. A child excessively ignored show's different types of conflicts in his personality. Children brought in the psychological clinics for the cure of defects of personality showed that an important cause of their defects was the behaviour of their parents, towards, them. According to Sigmound Freud, the tendency to depend upon the parents in the childhood is manifested in the tendency to depend upon the leader in the adult age. If the child is allowed freedom in the matters concerning his belongings, food, clothes, books etc., he will develop a habit of freewill and if all these are decided by his parents, he will not get an opportunity to utilise his judgement and so becomes over dependant or, submissive.

Parents are more powerful and efficient than the child. Hence they are the ideals before him. The child wants to become like his parents. Thus he establishes his identification with either of the parent and tries to follow his manners, ways and behaviour. The child also fulfills his frustrated desires through this identification. It has been observed that the little boy wears the big shirt of the father and walks proudly like him with a stick in his hand. This identification with the parents in the childhood is later on converted into the identification of the individual with the leader. By the identification with the leader the individual is happy in leader's achievements and sorry for his failures.

In the absence of affection and sympathy, the child often turns criminal. While discussing the causes of criminal tendencies, Hearly and Bronner have emphasized three factors *viz.* the effort to get rid of the painful circumstances, the tendency to revenge for the misbehaviour of his father, the effort to satisfy the frustrating desires. Often the child has the curiosity as to where from the younger brother and sister have come. The answer to this question by the parents has an important effect on his personality. The child has a natural curiosity towards the sex tendency. Often the parents try to suppress his curiosity towards sex or they just rebuke when he asks such questions. But the child is not silenced by this. He tries to enquire from the servants or friends in the house. But this leads to guilt conscience. The reactions in the parents about the every day matters in the family and the relation of the mother and father among themselves also affect the personality of the child. In short, the behaviour of parents and the circumstances in family affect the personality of the child.

It has been observed that the behaviour of the eldest and the youngest, the elder or the younger is not the same in the family. Similarly, it has been found that the parents' behaviour toward them is not also the same. This has led the psychologist Alfred Adler to emphasize the importance of birth order in the development of personality. The birth order of the child fixes his status in the family which decides his roles which affect his personality. The youngest child is treated with affection, by everyone, hence he becomes over-dependant. The eldest child becomes self-sufficient and tyrant, because being, the only child for some time he does not share his rights and things with others. The birth of another child in the family has an important influence on the first child, since it takes away his monopoly in affection and sometimes he is neglected altogether. Hence he feels jealous with the younger child and tries to regain his rights. On the other hand, the new child is anxious to make his place in his family. The above description of the child's problems based upon the conception of birth order has not been conclusively proved. The researchers have found similar conflicts in different birth order. Adler has truly said that the individual develops his style of life from the pattern of his early life in the family, but there are no grounds to suppose that this style of life remains unchanged in future. It cannot be denied that the environment in the childhood is one of the most important factors determining personality but it is difficult to believe with Freud and Adler that the personality of an individual is completely determined in childhood.

INFLUENCE OF SCHOOL ON PERSONALITY

School also has an important influence on the personality of the child. In school both the teachers and class fellows mould personality. Just as in the family the parents are ideals before the child so are teachers in the school. The child hates the cruel and strict teacher. On the other hand, he respects good and sympathetic teachers. The personality of the teacher and his behaviour towards the child both exercise important influence on the child's personality. The child tends to identify himself with the teacher and tries to imitate his ways, manners and personality traits. This is only with the influential teachers and not with everyone. Thus, teachers mould the personality of the child by their example.

Besides the teacher, the classmates and playmates exercise important influence on the personality of the child. These constitute a group in which every child has his own particular status and roles corresponding to it. One can see the leader, the dare devil and the scapegoat child in the group. The leader is the mind of the group. He plans adventures and games. The dare devil executes them while the scapegoat is left to receive the blame and consequent punishment. In different types of groups of children, different traits of leadership are required according to the purpose. Thus sometimes the intelligent child leads while at other times the leader is the dare devil. This particular role in the group determines the future role of the individual in a society. This however, is not without exceptions. The development of the personality is a complex process and serious changes are affected in new circumstances which the individual has to face.

INFLUENCE OF SOCIETY ON PERSONALITY

Society is a web of social relationships. These social relationships connect men and women with one another. These interpersonal relations influence and mould the personality of the individual. In the society each individual has some peculiar status and roles corresponding to them. For example, in Hindu community, members of different castes have different social status in society. The roles and functions of an individual are determined by his status. This mechanism controls the behaviour of the individuals. Social control is further exercised by mores, traditions, myths, legends, customs etc. These determine the style of life of the individual. The individual cannot behave in the society as he likes. Society punishes the individual who breaks its norms. The fear of society is often more powerful than even the fear of heaven and hell or punishment by the state. Therefore, social norms influence even the ways and attitudes of the individuals. This ultimately influences his personality. The individual adopts the prevalent patterns of social behaviour. This is why one notices so much difference in the behaviour and personality of members of different societies. This however, does not mean that there are no individual differences in the same society. In fact, in every society one can find men and women who scarcely care for the social norms. But in every case, personality is affected by the social environment. Individuality is an outcome of the process of socialisation which is impossible without society. There is constant interaction between the individual and society and this interaction moulds the personality of the individual.

MEASUREMENT OF PERSONALITY

Psychologists employ a number of methods to measure personality, *e.g.*, situation test, psycho-analytic test and projective method etc. Besides these, the case history method, interview and questionnaire land rating methods have their own importance. Briefly, the methods of measuring personality are:

1. Case History Method
2. Interview Method
3. Questionnaire Method
4. Performance Method
5. Rating Method
6. Situation Test
7. Psycho-Analytic Test
8. Projection Techniques

Among the above mentioned methods, the projection techniques are the most popular. A brief description of the other methods, before we make a detailed description of this specific one, would be quite in keeping with the context.

1. **Case History Method.** In the case history method, as the name obviously indicates, the facts concerning the life of the subject are collected. This case history supplies all the facts related to man's environment and heredity. This method can be employed to study both normal and abnormal personality but it needs experienced testers.
2. **Interview Method.** The interview method is the most common of all the methods for the study of personality. It is the method widely used in the selection of people for government, semi-government and private services. In this, the subject and the tester sit facing each other and the former answers questions asked by the latter. Besides the answers which the subject offers,

his personality is indicated by his expression. This method, like the case history method, needs very experienced testers who ask questions which may probe the correct thing and enable the subject to express himself without any apprehension. Thus the interview method depends as much on the tester as it does subject.

3. **Questionnaire Method.** Questionnaires have been used extensively in the investigation of personality. The name suggests that it is a list of selected questions the answers to which throw light upon different traits of personality. 'Yes' and 'No' are written in front of these questions. The subject either strikes out the wrong answer, or indicates the correct one. Questionnaires are used to gain knowledge of traits like self-confidence, sociability, introversion or extroversion, tendency to dominate or be dominated etc.

   There are some difficulties in the questionnaire method. It has the following limitations:

   1. Often the subjects conceal the facts an give wrong answers.
   2. Sometimes the framing of the questions is such that the tester takes them to mean one thing and the subject another.
   3. Usually the subjects write the answer without an adequate amount of thinking thus leaving possibility of mistakes.

   In spite of these difficulties, the questionnaire method has proved to be of tremendous value. Allport and Minnesota etc., have formed questionnaires which help in the study of some subtle traits of personality. It affords a lot of assistance to comparative study because of the various answers of the subjects to the same questions. The conclusions based on these questionnaires are comparative as well as numerical. They also facilitate wide study because a number of people can be studied simultaneously.

4. **Performance Method.** The performance method was developed by May and Hartshorne. In this method the subject is given a variety of specific jobs to be performed and the particular trait of his personality is examined. For example in order to test the honesty of children some weights with little difference between them, were presented to them. The exact weight of each was written under it and the children were told to place them in the correct order. The honest children experienced great difficulty while the dishonest read the weights under them, and placed them in order promptly. A very simple method of judging the honesty of the students in the class could be something like this. Some piece should be

dictated and the copies are collected and examined. The mistakes of each should be secretly noted without any marking on the copy, following which the copies should be returned with the direction that the mistakes are to be noted and marks allocated. The dictation should be written on the black board. The honest will mark their mistakes while the dishonest will quietly correct them. The honesty of the students can be judged by comparing these with the mistakes previously noted.

5. **Rating Method.** Another method of measuring personality is the rating method, in which the procedure is of two types. One, the subject is asked to answer questions related to traits of personality. The answers which the subject offers or selects exhibit his personality. Another way of applying the rating method is to, place the subject in real situations and then study his behaviour and reactions. For example, in order to judge personality traits a person is given a variety of jobs to perform.

   As it is, the rating method is very simple. But it needs more skillful testers. Roughly speaking, it presents the following difficulties:

   1. Much skill and capability are essential in the tester.
   2. The possibility of prejudice is very great.
   3. It is very difficult to enumerate or evaluate the subtle traits. Mistakes are often made in this.

   In spite of the above difficulties both social and industrial psychologists make much use of this method. As has been pointed out previously too, it can be made useful to a large extent if the tester is very skillful.

6. **Situation Test.** As usual the name suggests the nature of the method. In it, the subject is placed in some specific situations and the traits of his personality are ascertained. Actually, it resembles the performance method, the difference lying in the fact that in this case the person is placed in a situation while in the performance method he is given some work to do.

7. **Psycho-analytic Method.** In the psycho-analytic method of measurement of personality two types of tests are more popular, Free Association and Dream Analysis. Both these tests show the traits of the personality in its unconscious aspect. In dream analysis, the subject describes his dream and without using reasoning associates freely the dream objects and activities. Because of the absence of reasoning the truth of the unconscious mind is expressed by this association, by which-the psycho-analyst

discovers many characteristics of personality. The psychoanalytic method is mostly used in discovering the personality traits and mental ailments of abnormal people. Its main condition lies in the need for a skilled and experienced psycho-analyst. Often the psychoanalyst has to analyse his own mind in order to remove the possibility of any prejudice.

8. **Projective technique.** The most popular of all the methods for the investigation of personality is the projective method. Its name, suggests the fact that it is founded upon the element of projection. The Taj Mahal, to take an example, is a marble building many people go to see. Different people find in it different things in keeping with the peculiarities of their personalities. An emotional person sees it in the form of a formal symbol of emotions while to the person who gives importance to political and economic questions, it may be a symbol of exploitation. This is an example of a material object but it does make clear the fact that human being method does not see an object as it is but also projects the traits of his own personality upon it. Many peculiarities of the personality are investigated by an analysis of this projection and a comparison it with the projections affected by others.

   Two tests in the projective techniques are more widely used:

   1. Rorschach ink blot test.
   2. Murray's Thematic Apperception Test, known in brief as T.A.T. They are extensively used in the investigation of personality. These will, therefore, be described briefly here.

1. **Rorschach Ink Blot Test.** This Test was developed by the Swiss scientist Herman Rorschach. He used 10 original ink blot cards which are still in use today. There is no picture made in these blots. Five of these are black, two black and red and the other three multicoloured. To investigate personality, they are exhibited before the subject one after the other and he is asked to describe everything he sees in the blot. These are shown for a definite interval of time. Then they are shown to the subject for a second time and he is asked to point out the location, of whatever he had seen, on the blot. In order to establish the meaning of the subject's reaction to the blots, the psychologist analyses the location, determining factors and the object. The analysis of the location serves to indicate whether the subject reacted to some particular spot on the blot or towards the blot as a whole. As a general rule, it is believed that the person who reacts more completely is more principled. The analysis of the determining factors is an attempt to find out whether the reaction of the subject is towards the share

of the blot or to the colour or motion in the blot. As to the object, the analysis shows whether the subject sees in it the figure of a man or an animal or anything else.

Besides the above analysis, facts like the time taken by the subject to react to the whole blot, the number of activities which he did and whether he did them normally or not, are also noted and observed. All these things tend to help in the analysis and investigation of the conscious peculiarities of the subject.

The difficulty in the ink blot test is that the description of the subject's reaction becomes quite subjective, which conceals to some extent the correct personality traits of the subject. But efforts are being made to make this test more objective.

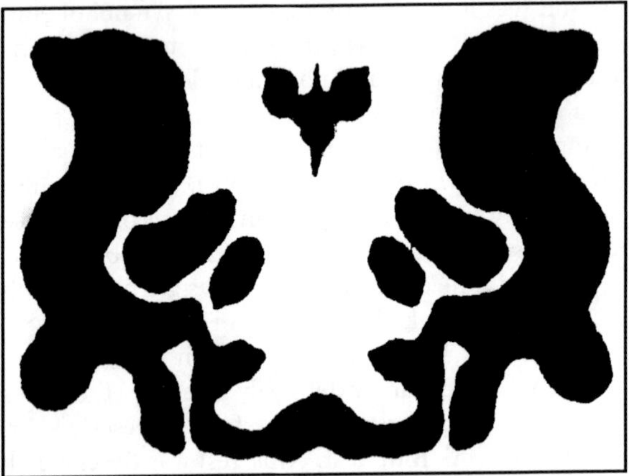

Fig. 16

2. **Murray's thematic apperception test.** The founder of this test, Murray investigated the personality traits with the help of some pictures. These pictures are still considered to be standard. Observing these pictures, the subject by projection, identifies himself with the person in the picture and expresses his innate dispositions.

STAGES OF PERSONALITY DEVELOPMENT

The different conditions of infancy, adolescence, youth and old age are very clearly depicted in the psychological development of the men. The speed and direction of psychological development differs from one stage to another. In the different stages of the development of personality, different changes are visible in the personality of the individual. In some stages these changes are faster and more comprehensive while in other stages the change is comparatively less. This change shows a change in the personality too.

(1) The First Six Years. Freud and many other psychologists give great importance to infancy in an individual's life. Some psychologists have claimed the development of personality to start during pregnancy. In Rank's view the development of personality starts in the mother's womb. The opinion says further that the very activity of its conception affects the child's personality, the presence or absence of difficulties in it making a difference in the personality. But it has not been possible to prove this theory by experimentation. In Freud's opinion, whatever incidents take place in the first three years of a child's life permanently mould his character, the rest being a mere development of these peculiarities; suckling, weaning, loving, fondling, scolding, beating, toilet training etc., all effect the child's personality. The love or affection of the parents has a very significant effect upon the child. Excessive love and affection make a child stubborn and inconsistent. Lack of affection stunts the development of his emotions while proper love gives him emotional stability.

Besides love and affection, suckling also impresses the personality of the child. Experiments indicate that even when the child is not hungry, he does not want to release the breasts. Actually, suckling is not merely a mode of satisfying hunger but also a symbol of the mother's love for the child and consequently weaning also affects the child's personality because it sometimes expresses the indifference of the mother directed at the child. If the child is suckled for a long time he becomes dependent and comfortable. Early

Fig. 17. An Indianised Picture from T.A.T.

weaning may lead to the development of the tendencies of pessimism and morbidity. An interesting experiment was carried out on college students in this context. They asked their mother about the ages at which weaning had been carried out, and they were subsequently tested for their feelings of security or insecurity, this experiment indicated an important correlation between weaning and the feelings of security and insecurity. Those who had been weaned at an age of 6 to 9 months; scored less points in security than those suckled for over 9 months but those who had not been suckled at all or only for about three months, showed no sense of insecurity whatsoever. This strange result was seen in the light of the fact that in the cultural group from among which these students have been chosen, the cause of weaning was not desire but the inability to continue suckling. This study indicates that weaning does not have as great an effect as indifference on the part of the mother. The effect of weaning which is felt is the effect of the mother's indifference. In the first six years, the child learns the adjustment of his needs with the environment. His relations with his mother during this adjustment leave a permanent mark on development of his personality. The development of a feeling of insecurity at this age leads to mental conflict making a child frightened and depressed and aggressive and naughty. Even toilet training affect the child. If, in the teaching of cleanliness, of which parents and other members partake, excessive hardness and resolutions are applied, the child may develop many compulsions. The birth order, and the birth of a new infant, all have an effect on the child. The relation of the parents among themselves, the social and financial status of the family, both leave an indelible mark on his personality. The outlook and reaction of the family members towards the sexual tendencies also tend to affect the child's personality. Unnecessary fear develops a criminal tendency in the child. The intelligent, satisfaction of his curiosity has a good effect on his development.

Traits of personality become apparent at a very early age of the child. The difference of will power, friendliness, determination and impressing others etc., between children appear at the age of two or three. By the time a child is five he starts expressing competitiveness. It has been seen from experiments that qualities or traits like mobile adjustment, self-dependence, love for the family, humour, emotional adjustment and reaction to resistance etc., of the personality appear at the age of seven and stay permanent even after adolescence. But some qualities show some change. Actually there is a lot of truth in the fact that the foundation of the peculiarities in the personality of a person are laid in childhood.

(2) **Pre-pubertal childhood.** The second stage in the development of human personality continues till the oncoming of puberty and it is accordingly entitled the Pre-Puberty stage, the conditions of the school start affecting the development of his personality because commonly, by now, he has started attending school and playing with other children. The child is given a particular place in the family, whereas he has to acquire for himself a position among his colleagues. He thus learns the lesson of equality and justice. His mother does not afford him security in the school, whereby he learns the qualities of independence and self dependence and these changes are also felt in the family. The child enters his own age group and acquires a role according to his personality and by living in a group learns the patterns of his future grown up life. It is at this stage that he learns the lesson of leadership, friendship, sympathy and social adaptation. His success or failure in the group develops many good and bad qualities in the child. A child extremely dependent on some one member of the family, has difficulty in adjusting to the group, a state which generally results in the origination of a feeling of inferiority. The practices which a child adopts are the ones which, have brought him success in his attempts at the adjustment within his group. If obstinacy and self assertion or aggression are more advantageous he will develop them and if escape is more successful the child will become an escapist.

(3) **Puberty and Adolescence.** The next stage in the development of human personality is the stage of puberty and adolescence. Puberty is a physiological condition, in which the maturation of sexual activities takes place. It is the link between childhood and adulthood. Adolescence as a psychological stage is generally characterised by extensive disturbance.

Puberty does affect personality. After puberty, the interest in sexual activities becomes specific and developed. Many studies have made it known that the social behaviour of girls and boys registers a maturation after puberty. This may be caused by an awareness of the physiological condition in puberty leading to a feeling of adulthood. In this stage the boys and girls want to identify themselves with adulthood, their interests becoming adult. Immediately before puberty, there is extensive physiological development and immediately after it the boys and girls start exhibiting the respective physical signs of their sexes. The girls start having menstrual cyclesand their organs acquire rot contours. Boys grow beards and moustaches and their voices become heavy. In this stage mental development, too is maximum. Puberty takes place two years earlier in girls than the boys, this being the reason for their earlier exhibition of pubertal changes.

The psychological state of adolescence affects personality in no small measure. The girls and boys start taking an interest in persons of the opposite sex. They also experience an increase in the feeling of independence. The adjustment of adolescence is a problem which differs with culture. The disturbance of an adolescent in civilised societies is not found in the people of Samoa. In their society, unlike the civilised societies, there are restrictions of sexual behaviour and the individual becomes self dependent at an early age. The disturbance of the adolescent stage is due to those mental conflicts through which a civilised person has to pass. These conflicts arise from many social problems like independence from the parents, sexual adjustment, self-dependence, choice of profession, etc. In this age, if the parents still look on the young as a child he will either make a strange revolt against it or submit to it, the latter course leading to a stop in the development of his personality. The indifference to sex education makes these adolescent problems even more intricate. In India, there is more sex education and less sex restrictions in primitive tribes than there is in the Urban Society. Thus, the transition from adolescence to adulthood is easier for the tribal youths than the Urban youths. Absence of the means of satisfying sexual curiosities and a social feeling of evil related to them increase the guilt conscience and anxiety of the adolescent, and this does not allow the proper development of his personality. It is a baseless idea that there is a complete reorganization of his entire personality. Adolescence is a stage in the development of personality and - development is a continuous process in which infancy affects adolescence and adolescence affects adulthood.

THE ONLY CHILD

The status of the child in the family is very much important for the development of his personality. This importance is very much realized in the case of the only child. Being the only child he is the centre of attention of the whole family. There is no one to share his things and he is given all opportunities to do whatever he likes. The parents fulfil most of his desires and therefore he becomes self centred and other dependent. His social qualities do not develop and his personality does not develop normally. When he becomes an adult he cannot mix up with his fellow beings. It has been seen that such a child, when he becomes adult, fails to adjust in his material and social life. A sound development of personality requires child's playing with other children of his age. If he, is the only child, he should be given an opportunity to mix up with the children of neighbourhood and at school so that he may achieve proper social development. It is because of the adverse effect of the status of the only child that it is advised that in the family there should be more than one child.

PERSONALITY TRAITS IN CHILDHOOD

Personality traits of different children can be found to be different at a very early age. This is because of the different families in which they are brought up. But even in the same family different personality traits can be observed in different children because of their different status and roles. The child's personality is very much influenced by his birth order and style of life in the family. The habits of behaviour formed in infancy lay the foundation stone of the future development of character and personality. Besides the social and cultural factors, child's personality is influenced by biological factors, such as the endocrine secretions and body chemistry. The parents play the most important role in the child's development of personality in the family. Among the parents the influence of mother is even more important. Besides, brothers and, sisters and all other relatives present in the family also exercise their influence. All these factors create different personality traits in different children.

The child should be encouraged to develop sociability, balanced emotions, good habits and friendly behaviour. This can, be encouraged at home by the parents in the child's behaviour towards his brothers and sisters. At school the teacher can utilize various procedures such as group plays and other group activities for the development of favourable personality traits. In the adolescent age, homo and heterosexual relationships play an important role in the development, of personality traits. The adolescents can be given elementary sex education. They should be taught to pay attention to their physical and mental development and proper behaviour with others. A suitable communal atmosphere in the school will help in the development of social traits of friendship, team work and good behaviour in the boys and girls. They cannot be taught anything by means of force but mostly they should be encouraged to imitate good behaviour and personality traits of their elders at home and in the school. Thus, the parents and the teachers should present good examples so that the boys and girls may emulate them in fostering good personality traits.

QUESTIONS FOR EXERCISE

1. What personality traits should be fostered in early childhood and what procedures have been found satisfactory for developing them?
2. Write short note on the only child.

26

Individual Differences

Meaning of Individual Differences

In education, even since the most ancient times, students have been differentiated on the basis of age as difference in age levels entitles the children to differing levels of education. As the child's age gradually increases, the subjects of his education can be made more complex and difficult. In addition to differences in age, another factor that was partly taken into consideration is the difference in levels of intelligence. Besides this, educational attainments were also considered to be important. In this manner, during the ancient and the medieval periods, individual difference was believed to be the capacity of attaining skills in a particular subject. In modern schools, other kinds of skills and abilities, and peculiarities of personality in individuals are also taken into consideration. According to Skinner, "Today we think of individual differences as including any measurable aspect of the total personality." From this definition of individual differences it is evident that it comprehends every aspect of the human personality, albeit all aspects that are in some manner measurable. Aspects of this nature can be many such as variability, conformity, difference in the rate of learning and development of mutual relationship between the various characteristics of personality, etc. In this manner, various individual differences of physical and mental development, nature, rate of learning ability, specific abilities, interest and personality, etc.

TYPES OF INDIVIDUAL DIFFERENCES

1. **Average Intelligence.** The following brief description may serve to make individual differences a simple concept that can easily be grasped. Individuals are seen differing in considerable measure in respect of their general intelligence. It is not possible

to send to schools children with an intelligence quotient of below 50. Children with intelligence quotients between 50 and 70 can learn only the very simplest tasks. Even the small schools trouble children whose intelligence quotient varies between 70 and 80. Children between 75 and 90 I.Q. are considered morons and they have considerable difficulty in progressing along with other children in their learning. Generally, 40 to 60 per cent of the children in schools have I.Q.s varying between 95 and 105, being the children with average intelligence who form the basis for the formulation of the syllabus and curriculum as well as the method of teaching. Children who are either above or below this level of intelligence require special educational methods and conditions. Children with intelligence quotients varying between 115 and 120 are considered brilliant or intelligent. The following facts have come to light concerning individual differences of intelligence in children:

(a) However good and beneficial the environment and the method of education, the moron invariably reaches his highest level of learning before the average or the intelligent child.
(b) In favourable circumstances the average child generally gives a good account of himself in his academic pursuits.
(c) If the circumstances are favourable, the intelligent child shows great alacrity in the process of learning.
(d) Adverse circumstances have the worst effect on all children, and their learning activities are hindered.

2. **Special Abilities.** During the junior high school as well as the college stage, the individual's differences in respect of special abilities, in addition to the general intelligence, are also important since special professions and specialised fields of vocation all need certain specific abilities. Abilities of this kind are concerned with mental, artistic, personality or motor ability.
3. **Differences of Background.** In school the differences that the children exhibit are the outcome of their different families and their communities. Attitudes towards education and authority differ in each family, culture and class. Some of these attitudes are favourable while others are unfavourable to education. In either condition, the differences of attitudes results in differences among children. Besides these attitudes, the child's emotional, social, aesthetic and moral development is influenced by his

family and the neighbourhood. Hence differences of background are also manifest in individual differences.

4. **Alacrity in Learning.** Difference in the quickness or alacrity in learning is visible not only in children of different ages but also among children in the same age group. This difference is dependent upon their maturity and educational background. Differences in the alacrity of learning result in benefits accruing from formal education.
5. **Mental Age.** Children of differing ages as well as children of the same age show differences in their respective mental ages. Generally speaking, all students studying in the same class differ according to their mental ages. It has been observed that in the age of 6, differences in mental age range up to 5 years. Mental age and education are intimately related. The child's level of education is determined according to his mental age.
6. **Motor Ability.** The individual's movements of the hand and feet and other physical abilities are seen to be very individual, as they do not resemble another's to any great extent. Till the individual attains adulthood, his manual dexterity, rate of muscular movement and resistance to fatigue develops continually. In this manner, the same individual in different ages and different individuals in the same age group manifest considerable differences in manual dexterity.
7. **Sex Differences.** Makneimer and Terman discovered the following differences between men and women on the basis of some studies:
   (a) Women have greater skill in memory while men have greater motor ability.
   (b) Female handwriting is superior while men excel in mathematical logic.
   (c) Women show greater skill in making sensory distinctions of taste, pain, smell, etc., while men show greater reaction and consciousness of size-weight illusion.
   (d) Possessing greater linguistic ability women are superior to men in languages, similitudes, word building, compositions and use of long sentences etc. On the other hand, men are superior in physics and chemistry.
   (e) Women are better than men in mirror drawing. Faults of speech etc., in men were found to be three times of such faults in women.
   (f) Women are more susceptible to suggestion while there are three times as many colour-blind men as there are women.

(g) Young girls take interest in stories of love, fairy tales, stories of the school and home and day-dreaming and show various levels in their play. On the other hand, boys take interest in stories of bravery, science, war and scouting, stories of games and sports, scouts stories and games of occupation and skill.

8. **Racial Differences.** Many scientific studies have indicated the presence of various kinds of differences between individuals of different races, although differences of environment are a normal factor in causing these differences. Karl Brigham has composed the following list on the basis of differences in level of intelligence among people who have migrated to United States from other countries. These differences have been calculated by the Stanford Binet tests:

Country	*Mental age*	*Country*	*Mental age*
England	14.2	Belgium	12.56
Scotland	13.77	Ireland	12.2
Holland	13.75	Austria	12.16
Germany	13.41	Turkey	11.96
America	13.32	Greece	11.88
Denmark	13.26	Russia	11.45
Canada	13.25	Italy	11.42
Sweden	12.16	Poland	10.96
Norway	12.75	Negro America	10.71

On the basis of these average differences between the races, the mental age of a particular individual of a definite race cannot be calculated since this difference is based on environment.

9. **Nationality.** Many studies have led to the conclusion that individuals of different nations differ in respect of nature, physical and mental traits, interest and personality, etc. Such a difference is only natural since their cultural and geographic environment is distinctive.

10. **Economic Situation.** Economic differences are seen causing differences in the children's interests, tendencies and character, etc.

11. **Differences Relating to Learning.** In respect of learning, children manifest such differences as past experience and learning, ability in the use of various kinds of apparatus rate of learning, interest in learning, etc.

12. **Difference in Respect of Development.** Difference in development is in evidence not only in individuals of different age groups but also between individuals of the same age.

13. **Difference of Interests.** As has been pointed out, the difference in sex leads to a difference in interests. Similarly, factors such as family background, level of development, differences of nationality and race, etc. cause difference of interests.

14. **Personality.** Differences in respect of personality have led psychologists to much study, and on the basis of this study individuals have been classified into many groups. Jung, for example, has divided individuals into three groups: (a) Introvert, (b) Extrovert and (c) Ambivert. This is, the, psychological classification of people. Stephenson has divided human beings into two categories – preservator and non-preservator. In this division, people of the first group are very sensitive and susceptible to experience while people of the second group are not influenced by it to quite that extent. Cattell has put people into the surgent and the surgeless or non-surgent classes. The former is similar to Jung's extrovert while the surgeless resembles his introvert individuals. Terman has put people into 9 classes according to their level of intelligence (a) Genius, (b) Near Genius, (c) Very superior intelligence, (d) Superior, (e) Average, (f) Backward, (g) Feeble minded, (h) Dull, (i) Idiot.

    Thorndike has divided people into four categories on the basis of thinking: (a) Abstract thinkers, (b) Ideational thinkers, (c) Objective thinkers, (d) Thinkers in whom sensory experience is predominant. These names indicate the peculiarities of thinking in these individuals.

    From the viewpoint of nature, personality has been divided into three classes (a) thought dominant, (b) emotion dominant, (c) action dominant.

    Concerning these classifications of the human personality, it should be remembered that although one specific person may exhibit the main broad characteristics of one class of personality, he cannot be said to belong to only that class of personality as the differences between various personalities are so subtle and minute that it is not scientifically feasible to divide them into classes.

Teacher's Advantage in knowing Individual Differences

The objective of modern education is the complete development of the child. In this connection, the teacher has the following advantage to derive from a knowledge of individual differences:

(1) This can help him to form the proper attitude towards the brilliant and the dull-witted students. It is only too evident that very good results cannot be expected from dull-witted or mediocre students.

(2) Any effort to bring all or a majority of the students in the class to the same level is futile since some 50 or odd percentage of them will invariably remaining below this level.

(3) Improvements in atmosphere, method of teaching, and the apparatus of education cannot lead to the satisfactory teaching of all students since their individual ability to learn differs widely.

(4) Knowing the presence of individual differences the teacher is not perturbed at the failure of some of his students since such failure are only to be expected from below-average students.

(5) The teacher does not come to expect successes that are impossible. Individual difference makes it clear that all aspects of the personality are mutually related and to develop any one aspect it is essential that all the aspects be developed.

INDIVIDUAL DIFFERENCES AND EDUCATION

By the above account of benefits that a teacher can derive from a knowledge of individual differences it is evident that lie can make use of it in education and teaching. The main features in this connection are the following:

1. **Curriculum.** In school, the curriculum should be modified to suit the needs of, the dull children. Failure to achieve this adversely affects the development of all three kinds of children. Whereas the backward student's start playing truant from school the brilliant children find the studies inadequate and turn their intellect to more perverses.
2. **Limited Size of the Class.** Keeping in mind the individual differences of the students, it is advisable that if they are to be taught properly a class should not include more than 20 students. With 50 or more students it is impossible to teach them keeping in mind their specific requirements.
3. **Method of Education.** It is never advisable or efficacious to use the same method of education in the case of all children. It should be varied to suit and conform to their individual differences and mental requirements.
4. **Educational Guidance.** Knowing the personal differences between his students the teacher can render them signal service by guiding them in their educational career. It is the teacher who can tell them the subjects they must choose to pursue in their higher studies if they are not to do violence to their natures.
5. **Vocational Guidance.** Different professions require some specific physical, mental and personality traits of the individual.

Hence, knowing their peculiar mental make up and their tendencies the teacher can guide the students in the vocation that they should adopt.

6. **Contribution of School, Family and Community in Education.** Knowledge of differences among children determines that education in school is not completely sufficient since many differences are due to the family and community. Hence, according to modern educational psychologists, to attain the objective of all round development of individuals, prescribed by modern education, the co-operation of school, family, community and the religious institutions is sought.

7. **Individual Training.** Having knowledge of individual differences, now many methods of individual training have been devised. In America, the Dalton plan, project method, Winnetka method, contract plan and activity programme methods have been devised for individual training. A brief resume of the various methods is given below:

   (a) *Dalton plan* : In this, children are not taught in class rooms. They are given subjects that suit their interests and they are given a project that covers a period of 15 days to a month. Such treatment leads to the development of naturality, independence, co-operation and sociability etc.

   (b) *Project method:* In this the children are required to do work of every day requirements, such as cooking, stitching, furniture making, etc. And in the process of this work, they are taught novel things.

   (c) *Winnetka system:* In this method, the student on his own tries to attain a certain definite objective and the teacher offers very little assistance. Later on, through some tests, the extent to which the student has attained his goal is discovered.

   (d) *Contract plan:* In this, similar to the Dalton method, the subjects of study are determined and similar to the Winnetka method the student's progress is measured through tests. In this manner it is a synthesis of the Dalton and Winnetka method.

   (e) *Activity programme:* In this method, keeping in mind the interests of the students, activities are prescribed in order to define the curriculum. These activities are based on democratic principles. This helps to develop democratic notion in the children.

It is evident from the foregoing description that modern, education makes proper arrangements for a child's education, keeping in view his peculiar nature and special abilities. In a democratic society every individual has the right to achieve a definite level of development. Hence, even more essential it is that individual differences be kept in mind while educating people of democratic countries.

Two facts emerge when human development is studied. One, that the development of separate individuals exhibits certain similarities. Two, that different individuals show differences from the biological and social viewpoint. Generally speaking, these differences are quantitative rather than qualitative. In other words, the same qualities are to be found in most individuals but it is the quantity or intensity of these qualities that differs in these individuals. And this difference leads to considerable differences in the education of different individuals. Hence, the teacher should keep in mind the differences between various boys and girls and he should make the necessary arrangements so that everyone be educated properly.

QUESTION FOR EXERCISE

1. Write short note on Individual Differences.

27

Problems of Backward, Problematic and Gifted Children

What is a Backward Child?

Generally speaking, no mother or father is easily prepared to accept that their child is mentally backward. But modern intelligence test techniques have indubitably established that some children are mentally backward. A backward child is more in need of assistance than one with average or above average intelligence, hence in modern school teachers are expected to pay particular attention to the weak students in the classes. A backward child, evidently, is one who has an intelligence quotient lower than the average child. In the words of Cyril Burt, "A backward child is one who, in the middle of the school career, is unable to do the work of the class below that which is normal for his age." In this way, the backward child falls far behind other children of his age in matters of study. In school, such children remain in the same class for many years, and fail to progress upward. Educational psychologists have no single opinion of the intelligence quotient below which a child can definitely be called backward. Yet generally, psychologists classify those children as backward whose intelligence quotient falls below 85.

PROBLEMS OF BACKWARD CHILDREN

Children who are backward have certain problems that are peculiarly their own Having a very low intelligence quotient, they require to be taught many things by others. A backward child cannot lead, he is more in a position to need the help and sympathy of friends and relatives. A child who is very feeble minded, having an intelligence quotient of 70 or less cannot obtain education in the ordinary schools, and has to be sent to special institutions. Emotional adjustment of the child is completely integrated if he fails in the same class time after time. In a class, teaching approximates to the average level of students. Hence, it is only natural for the backward child to meet with failure. Failure in school leads to the assumption that he will also be a failure in life. His ambitions are destroyed and he becomes hopeless.

Backward child also faces difficulties in social adjustment. In the group he does not easily grasp even the smallest thing and rules of play have to be repeated for his benefit. His colleagues naturally heckle him. It is possible that a spark of leadership may be ignited in him if he communicates with those younger than himself but on the same intelligence level. But there he is unwelcome since other children steer clear him because of his physical superiority. Adults pay him little or no attention, instead he is scolded from time to time. In adolescence and adulthood, too, the position of the child does not improve. He is made the butt of every joke. Activities of the group are usually on a higher level, so that he does not fit in them either.

CAUSES OF BACKWARDNESS

It is not even possible to recount all the various causes of backwardness, but the main causes are the following:

1. **Physical Causes.** Due to many physical defects and abnormalities, the child lags behind other average children. Such physical conditions would be weakness of eyes, deafness or being hard of hearing, stuttering, being weak or crippled, etc. This also has an adverse effect upon his social adjustment.
2. **Mental Defects.** It has been indicated earlier that the backward child has a very low intelligence quotient, as compared with that of an average child. Having a low intelligence, his other mental characteristics and abilities also do not compare favourably with the average child.
3. **Educational Immaturity.** Physical and mental shortcomings in the child result in educational immaturity: Putting it differently, he has not adequate maturity to grasp the teaching that is customary for his age level.
4. **Emotional Factors.** The child's social adjustment is detected by his mental and physical abnormalities, and he meets with successive failures. He meets with criticism on every account. Hence it is natural for him to manifest anxiety, tension, depression and other emotional factors. Sometimes, though every other, defect is absent the child is backward in his class for no better reason than these psychological or emotional factors.

5. **Atmosphere in the Home.** One reason of backwardness can also be the atmosphere in the home. Proper development of the child cannot occur in a virulent family atmosphere. Hence, he falls behind children of his age group. And among the factors that contribute to the defective atmosphere in the home are constant quarreling and fighting between parents and children, unbalanced diet, strict discipline, absence of all peace and calm, poverty etc.
6. **Lack of Interest.** Sometimes, even though the child is free from all the defects and shortcomings mentioned above and even those that have not been mentioned, the child falls behind the rest of the class for the simple reason that he cannot stir any interest in the various subjects being taught. This causes repeated failure.
7. **Factors concerning the Schools.** The school can be a veritable storehouse of factors that inhibit the child's development such as inadequate method of teaching, uneducated teachers, undesirable atmosphere, inadequate curriculum, defective time table, disgusting relations between students and teachers etc. All these causes conspire to make even the average child look backward.

Cyril Burt's Opinion

Different educational psychologists have stressed different factors present in the analysis of backward children and their causes. Different factors have been considered more or less important. Cyril Buit has allocated importance to the various factors in backwardness in the following proportions:

Cause	*Percentage*
Poverty	20%
Home atmosphere	16%
Educational causes	11%
Health	8%
Neighbourhood	3%

Even if this kind of guesses are not relied, upon, one can still say that backwardness is considerably aggravated through the contribution of physical and mental defects, atmosphere in the home, emotional causes, lack of interest in subjects of education, neighbourhood and school, etc.

SELECTION OF BACKWARD CHILDREN

Modern schools are led to believe that the backward children in a class should be specially attended to. Hence the teacher must know how to distinguish and recognise a backward child. This can be done in four steps:

1. **Discovering the Child's A.Q.** Tests in arithmetic, language and general knowledge can be used for discovering the child's A.Q.
2. **Discovering I.Q.** Selective children with an intelligent quotient of below 85 their exact I.Q. should then be calculated.
3. **Individual Intelligence Tests.** Now the result obtained from the group intelligence tests should, be examined for their reliability by obtaining results through individual intelligence tests and coinciding the two conclusions.
4. **Rating by Teachers.** Following this, rating by teachers should be sought concerning children who appear to be backward so that the results of tests are confirmed by educated insight.
5. **Case History.** After all the above tests have been completed, the child's detailed life history should be prepared.

Solution of the Problem of Backwardness

Most of the so-called backward children can be improved. In the case of children with intelligence quotients below 70, no improvement is possible through education in the ordinary schools since they need to be sent to specialised schools and institutions. In children with intelligence quotients between 70 and 85, considerable improvement is possible even in regular educational institutions. Many of these children can be raised to the level of average normality through cures so that they can find success in school and later life, if they are given some encouragement and are shown some success, they learn many simple activities. But this requires modification of the curriculum, the teacher's method of teaching, and separate educational establishments are not essential as they require only special attention and periodical expert examination. But with children of intelligence quotients below 70 separate arrangements are unavoidable.

1. **Curriculum.** Often many children fail repeatedly in the same class for the simple reason that the curriculum does not suit them. Consequently, the teacher must modify his curriculum to meet the requirements of backward children so that it contains only those subjects. The entire curriculum should be so fashioned that when the backward child completes his course, he should be fitted to adopt some particular profession. Basic education should be emphasized in the curriculum. Children can also be trained for some specific professions and vocations.
2. **Method of Teaching.** The sole quality of a teaching method is that student should grasp what it has to teach. Hence, there

should be different methods of teaching for students on different levels. It is evident that backward children will not gain much if they are taught by a method that is found suitable for average children. For them, there should be a special method of teaching with the following characteristics:

(a) Pace of teaching should be slow.
(b) Lesson should be repeated more than once.

PROBLEM CHILDREN

What is a Problem Child?

Problem children as is evident from the term applied to them, are children whose behaviour is not normal and it results in some or the other problem of adjustment being caused. In the words of Valentine, "Problem children is generally used to describe children whose behaviour or personality in something is seriously abnormal." In this manner the class of problem children includes all those juveniles whose character or personality shows some signs of abnormality. Some behavioural abnormalities that seem to indicate this condition are-stealing, lying, annoying children weaker and younger than themselves, not doing home assignments, running away from school, or arriving late at school. They can also be called defects or abnormalities concerning character or personality because conduct of this nature indicates shortcomings in both personality as well as character.

For an understanding of the psychology of problem children it is necessary that a detailed analysis of the behaviour be made and the problematic form of behaviour distinguished from the normal forms. It must here be recalled that the problem child is not a member of a group distinct from the normal child groups. There is no distinct line that distinguishes him from his more normal counterparts as to some extent, and at varying stages in childhood the behaviour of every child becomes problematic. Almost every child, at some stage or the other and for one reason or another tells a lie or steals something. Hence, it is not quite desirable to declare one completely problematic and another more or less completely normal. It has been seen that very often the child is prone to much naughtiness between the ages of two and five, and his conduct appears somewhat problematic and strange. But as he continues to grow older this naughtiness disappears and he no longer appears a problem child. It is for this reason that specialist have made very detailed studies into problem behaviour. In his book on educational psychology, Cronbach made a mention of an experiment or study by Richard Henderson which had revealed the symbols of problematic behaviour that were considered the most sure, signs of problematic trouble by the best trained and particularly intelligent research workers.

Causes of Problematic Behaviour

Problematic behaviour can have two kinds of causes: (1) hereditary and (2) environmental. Hereditary causes include physical, emotional or nervous defects, but sometimes these may also be the result of weakness. The environmental factors are the following:

(1) **Atmosphere of Home.** One major cause of problematic behaviour is the contaminated behaviour that exists in many homes. A large majority of problem children come from broken families of divorced persons. In a study conducted by Bannister and Rooder it became known that 66 per cent of the children come from homes that have an improper atmosphere. Certain other studies traced abnormal behaviour to such diverse causes as poverty, lack of recreation, absence of care, almost complete absence of affection and love, cruel behaviour of step-mothers or other relatives, too much cinema seeing, etc. Where the entire, family is compelled to live in a small house with only two rooms the child may have occasion witnessing of which has the worst influence upon his undeveloped mind and, leads him to forming bad sexual habits. Signs of problematic behaviour are also generated in children who come from homes the atmosphere in which is either strictly disciplinarian or completely lax and uninhibited. Much of what is said in the following chapter regarding juvenile delinquents is also true of the problematic children.

(2) **Bad Company.** Besides the family another agency plays an important role in developing signs of abnormal behaviour in the child is his companionship. Falling into bad company the best of children learn stealing, smoking, physical outrage, cruelty or sex habits of a bad nature.

(3) **Atmosphere in College.** Another important case of problematic behaviour is the defective and contaminated atmosphere of the college. It is only natural for children to show signs of abnormal behaviour when they are compelled to study in colleges or schools in which the teachers present improper and immoral ideals before them, the method of teaching is disgusting or uninteresting, and where there is absence of wholesome recreation, etc.

Cure of Problem Children

Hence, the cure of problematic, children demands the removal of all objectionable elements from the atmosphere, at home and in college as well as from the child's company. The main facts to be noted in this connection are the following:

(a) **Measures concerning the Family.** Valentine has made the following suggestions concerning the administration of discipline in the family:

(1) Discipline should not take the form of pressure or fear but should aim at ultimate self control in the child.

(2) Level of conduct should not be too high.

(3) The behaviour of parents should be benevolent and there should be every possible co-operation between the home and school.

(4) Discipline and rules should be relative.

(5) The child should never be allowed to feel that he is loved by anyone.

Following these suggestions it will be possible to improve the atmosphere in the family. Residences of families should normally be as far as possible from prostitution houses, gambling dens and factories, etc. Children should not be allowed to view very inflammatory or highly sexually arousing films. Parents should be affectionate and understanding in their behaviour, as the child's behaviour, character and personality depends upon these Corresponding elements in themselves. Thus, they must present the best ideals to the children, and should the child develop any undesirable symptoms it should be dealt with psychologically rather than having recourse to physical punishment.

(b) **Good Company.** The company that a student keeps outside the house, in the college or in the neighbourhood should be carefully studied and kept in mind. If he has had the misfortune of failing into bad company tactful methods should be employed to wean him of it and introduce him into better circle of friends. It is equally improper and unjustified to give the child too much pocket money or to give him none at all. There, should be adequate arrangement for his recreation.

(c) **Methods adopted by Schools.** Schools can adopt the following measure for the prevention or cure of problematic behaviour in the students:

(1) **Presentation of High Ideals by Teachers.** In the school the teacher is no less than an ideal to the student or child, hence it is essential that the teacher's character, personality and conduct should be of the highest order and exemplary so that the best ideals become personified in him.

(2) **Interesting Method of Education.** If the method of education, or teaching be not interesting the children run away from school and fall into very bad habits. If they are taught by more interesting methods they will be interested and thereby prevented or protected from many ill usages.

(3) **Proper use of Educational Apparatus.** In schools through the medium of libraries and reading rooms children and students should get healthy literature so that their thinking may take on a healthy hue and proper form.

(4) **Balanced Curriculum.** The curriculum in various classes for students should be so designed as not to strain the student too much, but at the same time provide him with a variety of knowledge.

(5) **Arrangement of Extra Curricular Programmes.** Where the question of preventing problematic behaviour in children is concerned, much more can be gained by extra curricular activities such as picnics, touring, camps, scouting, community, singing, dancing and debate, etc., than can be achieved through the formal curriculum.

(6) **Means of Healthy Recreation.** If the child is to be persuaded to avoid any unhealthy means of entertainment it is necessary that various kinds of games and means of recreation be available to him so that he can enjoy himself without injuring his development.

(7) **Self Discipline.** Discipline in the college should not be foisted upon the student but should take the form of autonomous or self discipline. This will help to increase a sense of responsibility without being a burden upon them.

(8) **Synthesis between Family and School.** In order to prevent or to cure problematic behaviour in the child it is essential that the teacher and parents should jointly endeavour to achieve it. Hence, family and school should be synthesized.

(9) **Guidance.** Children are often faced with problems the solution of which is beyond their own ability, and this results in difficulty that manifests itself in the form of symptoms of problematic behaviour. Hence, the school should provide for individual, educational as well as vocational guidance.

CHILD'S DEFECTS AND ABNORMALITIES

Children can have both defects and abnormalities. The general system of education is devised for the average and normally healthy children, as, a result of which it cannot incorporate the development of abnormal, children since they need special arrangements. One has to speak louder than when one is speaking to a normal reason if one wants to communicate with a deaf individual. A modern teacher is concerned not only with the development of a majority of average children, but also with the development of brilliant, backward, defective and abnormal children. Hence, the system of education should also provide for such individuals. Unfortunately many circumstances conspire to make provision of such facilities impossible in all schools. Nevertheless, the teacher should definitely be aware of the defects and abnormalities that mar the development of a child, or arise during its progress. Here these defects will be divided into various categories concerning physical, mental, character etc.

PHYSICAL DEFECTS AND ABNORMALITIES

Almost any and every organ of the body can be deformed through defects, and it is not possible to list all such defects. Secondly, all of them do not have any effect on education. Thus, the physical defects and abnormalities that are to be treated of here, are specifically those that are particularly important for the point of view of educational process.

(1) **Defects of the Head.** Of all the parts of the body, the head is most important since it houses the brain. Hence, removing defects of the head is most important thing. Common defects of the head are the presence of leeches, skin eruptions, pus, etc., that are mainly caused through the head being left unclean. A child cannot himself keep his head clean. Parents should keep an eye on its cleanliness. One definite measure that must be taken very regularly is that it should be cleaned with soap or other cleaning ingredient, and another is its regular massage with oil, and proper hair combing. It is always advisable for young students to keep hair short and trimmed. This both avoids putting much weight on the head and also makes for easier cleaning and maintenance. Oils that are used for lubricating the head should be those that have a good effect on the head and brain. Application of the oil itself should not involve mere smearing of it on the head but be more of the nature of massage so that the oil penetrates into the roots. There are a variety of oils available for the purpose, but only the best should invariably be preferred. If the child develops some disease of the skin on the, head or acquires leeches, his head should be shaved clean following which he should be submitted to expert medical advice and care. In the classroom, the, teacher

himself should see the extent to which his wards keep cleanliness. If they tend to be dirty, he should invite their parents, to school, and point out the desirability of cleanliness and personal hygiene.

(2) **Defects of the Eye.** Another organ of the body that has considerable importance from the educational viewpoint is the eye. It, too, is another organ that is prone to many defects in the case of children. Some defects are innate, and even hereditary, but many others are the result of excessive strain on the eye.

Schools should provide facilities for regular periodical checks of the children's eyes so that it should be possible to know of a defect as soon as possible. Besides making arrangements for having any such defects cured the teacher should also advise the student as to the proper mode of eye care. Power of the eyes can be maintained and increased through such expedients as splashing cold water on the eyes, standing facing the sun early in the morning with closed eyes, planning, deep breathing, consuming almonds, white pepper, etc., and other things that increase the power of the brain. Students should never be careless on this score since it is on this that their entire future is based. Finally, as has been pointed out earlier, teachers should read books published by Dr. Bates and other nature cure specialists, so they can acquaint their students with various exercises of eye that keep them in good health. One very useful book on this subject is Harry Benjamin's *Better Sight Without Glasses*.

(3) **Defects of the Ear.** After defects of the eye, come the defects of the ear that are no less harmful. Some children are born deaf, with the result that they also remain dumb since language cannot be learned without hearing. Being deaf, they cannot profit by studying in the normal kinds of schools. Special schools have now been provided for the education of such handicapped children where the deaf can learn many things that the normal people know. Consequently, they are also in a position to achieve a good status in society. Another defect that afflicts the ear is a difficulty to hear slight sounds. Their problem resembles the problems of the deaf to some extent. But in their case this shortcoming can either be cured or made less abnoxious through the use of some mechanical devices. Social adjustment is a problem for deaf children and for those who are hard of hearing. Teachers and other well-wishers must devote some of their attention to these problems. It usually happens that in large classes, teachers have no way of knowing the various physical ailments that are affecting their students. Hence,

it is for them to examine their students from time to time through tests, and advise their guardians of their condition periodically. It is as necessary to cure defects of the ear as it is to provide for their general care. Living continuously in an area that is very noisy may lead to serious additional consequences since such conditions can cause deafness. There have been definite cases of traffic policemen in big cities going deaf through being constantly in the centre of extreme noise. When the ear accumulates dirt, most people are in the habit of cleaning it with some sharp-edged instrument a practice that is most depreciable as it endangers the ear drum. If there is dirt within the ear then it should be removed in such a manner that it does not endanger ear drum. Itching in the ear can be cured or at least relieved by putting lukewarm castor oil or oil of neem in it. And even otherwise if some oil is put in the ear from time to time, it prevents extreme dryness of the ear. Too much dirt or any disease of the ear is a condition that only expert physician or ear specialist can treat. Considerable damage can result in such cases even from the least evidence of carelessness. Students who are hard of hearing should be given place in the front of the class so that they may not miss too much of what the teacher says.

(4) **Defects of the Teeth.** Dental care is as important as the care of any other part of the body. Usually, parents pay little attention to the care of the children's teeth. Carelessness can lead to serious diseases such as pyorreha, that can lead to serious general complications apart from irreparably damaging the teeth. This happens as food reaches the stomach through the teeth. It is for the teachers to arrange for periodical checking of children's teeth, and for instructing them and their careless parents in the care of teeth. Cleanliness of teeth can be achieved through very regular brushing with some good dental cream or delicate branches of the neem tree. Whenever something is eaten, it should be followed by a careful gargling of the mouth so that all residue that is embeded in the teeth is eliminated. Decay of teeth often results from children drinking sweetened milk at night immediately before going to sleep since they do not then wash their mouths. Even if every meal is not succeeded by brushing of the teeth, they should be cursorily cleaned by carefully running a finger over them and removing any matter that sticks between the teeth.

(5) **Defects of the Speech.** Some children are afflicted by defects of speech, such as stumbling over words, mispronunciation, etc. Many of these defects can be got rid of through the simple

expedient of regular practice. Demosthenes, a famous speaker of Greece, stuttered from birth. He made a habit of going to the seashore and speaking with pebbles in his mouth, a habit that finally cured him of the trouble after he had persisted with it for a long time. Children who falter and stutter are usually teased and laughed at by other children with the result that their social adjustment is considerably hindered. The child himself develops many undesirable attitudes. Presence of such defects makes it imperative that the advice of a good physician be sought in order to remove them. Sometimes a condition of stuttering is actually induced by parents who first imitate children because the child's faltering tongue is pleasant to listen to. And, they often try to remind children of the manner in which they used to speak. In fact, even when the child pronounces incorrectly, parents should encourage them patiently to speak correctly so that the wrong pronunciation should not become a habit. Defects of speech can be more easily corrected in childhood than at a later stage. Yet, it is not quite right to plunge the child into complexities very early, since such a method can affect his emotional development adversely. A child's pronunciation depends to a considerable extent upon the pronunciation of other family members. Hence, teachers and parents should take care to pronounce words correctly when speaking in the presence of children. If the child persists in stuttering and faltering, he should be sympathetically assisted rather than criticised or looked down upon. In this respect, family members are particularly responsible.

(6) **Defects of the Nose.** Concerning children, parents should also remember that cleaning of the nose is also important. Lack of proper care can lead to serious complications and consequences. A child himself cannot keep his nose properly clean, so that all responsibility for his hygiene is upon his parents. As soon as any disease of the nose or difficulty in breathing is discovered, the child should be submitted to the care of an expert.

(7) **Extreme Delicacy of the Body.** Another defect of the body is its extreme delicacy or weakness. A weak child finds social adjustment difficult since other children take advantage of his incapacity and bother him. General weakness of the child's body can normally be alleviated through proper food and exercise. Hence, parents should see to it that other children do not worry their weak friends, and at the same time to do their best to improve the general health and debility of the children.

(8) **Crippled Children.** Some children become crippled either through some accident or even in pregnancy. Some children experience difficulty in social adjustment and adaptation since other children are prone to make fun of the cripple. Some parents develop a habit of mentioning the child's crippled condition in front of him, and showing their disgust at it. This has the worst possible effect upon the child's mind. In fact, children of this kind should be treated with more love and care than normal children, though it should be remembered that he should not be reduced to complete helplessness and dependence where he can do nothing on his own, but needs the assistance of his parents. Sensible parents can help in the adjustment of their children. Becoming crippled, the child's education should, not be reduced in any measure as adequate and proper education can lead even cripples to considerable achievement and progress.

(9) **Other Physical Defects.** In order to preserve the children from normal defects, teachers should train them to walk, sit, read, write, etc. in the correct manner. Many physical defects can result if the child forms a habit of walking crookedly, siting in a doubled up position, or reading in a reclined position. Eyes can be adversely affected if the child develops a habit of reading with the book either too close or too far from the eyes. Furniture in the classroom should be comfortable and well-designed. Teachers should interrupt the students to point out defects and faults in their posture, their manner of reading, the angle of light, etc. Girls who do not know the way of carrying themselves gracefully, unwittingly deprive themselves of much of their natural charm and poise. The truth of the matter is that the right sort of carriage hides many defects while it brings into prominence all the good qualities of the individual.

Mental Defects and Abnormalities

Besides the physical defects and abnormalities, one also finds mental shortcomings and abnormalities in children. For example, some children have a very low intelligence quotient while those with below 20 are regarded as mentally retarded. On the other hand, some children show abnormal intelligence quotients, while those with scores of 130 and above are considered abnormal and gifted. Besides these variations within wide limits, children can also possess many kinds of mental aberrations. Mental complexes, inferiority complexes and superiority complexes are among the more normally found conditions of the mind in children, although their being found commonly does not reduce the ill effects that they have upon the personality. Some children are also subject to epileptic and other kinds of fits. Fainting fits also are not quite unknown. Some children are over-sexed in that the sexual urge is very intense in them. Other children give evidence of neuroses and psychoses. Such mental diseases can only be cured under expert medical advice and care. Sometimes, manifestations of mental diseases are misinterpreted as extreme obstinacy in the child, for which he is severely castigated and punished by parents and even teachers. This not only does not cure the child, but rather further precipitates the conditions of illness. If the child is to be protected from emotional complexes, it is essential that he be treated with sympathy, love and understanding, with a little bit of common sense being thrown in for good measure. His problems should be understood and be should be assisted in his efforts to overcome them. Every school curriculum should make the proper provision for education of back ward as well as exceptionally intelligent children. Extracurricular programmes should also be adequately modified to suit the needs of children.

Defects and Abnormalities of Character

Children exhibit defects and abnormalities concerning character, in addition to defects and complications in the physical and mental aspects of their being Development of child's character is an essential part of the educative process. Character is evident in conduct, and conduct is formed of habits that are acquired in childhood. Hence, proper care and attention to the child can save him from forming harmful habits that become permanent in the form of character elements. Faults of character usually have their origin in sex motivated activity. And in this much of the responsibility can be placed squarely upon the shoulders of teachers and parents. Actually speaking, it is the parents and not the children who are to be blamed for these bad habits since it is for them to satisfy the child's curiosity of all forms, to explain everything to him sympathetically rather than beating him to put an end to the string of questions, he puts forward, to create such a healthy and affectionate atmosphere in the home that healthy development of the child's character is almost ensured. Once the presence of some criminal streak in the child's character is discovered, it can be eliminated through some illuminated and sensible maneuvering. Once the sense of self-regard is developed in a child, his character then usually progresses in the right and desired direction.

STEALING

Some children start on a career of crime by stealing when they are only 5 or 6 years of age. They begin with stealing things from the house, stealing food and other domestic things. Then, gaining in confidence, they extend the sphere of their activity to the neighbourhood. Such children are often apprehended stealing books from other children when they go to school, with the result that their well-wishers and parents have sometimes to stand for much disgrace and embarrassment in front of strangers. Knowing of the child's activity, they give him a sound beating, but once the habit of stealing has set in, there is no gating rid of it, at least not so easily. Hence, what is more important is that they should not be given an opportunity to acquire any such habit in the first place. Yet, if he does form any such habit, it ia essential that efforts at destroying a habit should be very tactful and imaginative. In either condition, it is essential to divine the reason why any child steals. Modern educational psychologists have discovered why children steal, and in this connection have shed some light on the psychological factors involved. Knowledge of these elements will help teachers and parents to solve the problem of stealing by children.

Causes of Stealing

Main causes, why children steal, are the following:

(1) **Sense of Insecurity.** Children develop a sense of insecurity when the family is in turmoil, when children are indifferently treated by the parents or when they are frequently punished by them. If parents lie to their children and the children manage to find out that the parents have been misleading them, they feel insecure. And this sense of insecurity sometimes induces the child to steal. Hence, it is essential that the calm and peace of family life be maintained intact, children should be told the truth as far as is practicable and they should be treated with love.

(2) **Spoiling through Excessive Love.** Love and affection are, things for which the child rightly yearns, but too much of them can spoil him and make him very obstinate. A child who has his full of love and affection has far too many needs and while these needs can be satisfied in a family that is financially strong, in poor families this creates a problem. Descent from a strong financial position to an inferior level of income also creates a problem, and the child begins to steal. It is, of course, not inevitable that members of poor families steal. On the contrary, one finds habits of stealing in children who come from the richer families. Stealing or not is more positively concerned with the child being spoiled. Hence, it is essential that the child should be scolded if he does anything undesirable.

(3) **Strict Discipline.** Presence of extreme discipline in the family leads the child to complete repression of many of his tendencies. And repression leads to the formation of sentimental complexes that complicate his adjustment activity, for the fulfilment of which he turns to theft. Too much beating and punishing also instigates the child to stealing since this gives him a sense of independence. Hence, where discipline in the family is concerned, it is never desirable to wield the rod with a liberal hand.

(4) **Dissatisfaction of Needs.** The basic cause why a child steals is that his needs are not satisfied. If a child gets enough to eat, wear and play within the home he has no need for stealing. Generally, a child should also be given some pocket money when be goes to school. What actually happens is that when the child sees, other children spending money on all kinds of things, it is natural for him to want the same things. When he finds no resources to do so, he steals things from school and money from his own home. It should also be remembered that if all the child's demands are promptly met with, instead of breaking off the habit of stealing, there is every possibility that it will be intensified. Lack of control spoils the child so that he has no compunctions in stealing.

(5) **Sex Problems.** Psychological studies have revealed that a child steals because of an unconscious desire to satisfy his repressed sexual desires. Scolding and punishing the child if he enquires after his curiosity on matters of sex leads to the formation of a guilt complex in the child, and he learns stealing, lying and other bad habits.

(6) **Sense of Adventure.** Some children find stealing an adventure, and the excitement involved is the main consideration. Plucking flowers where it is prohibited gives them a sense of thrill.

(7) **Imitation.** Where children observe other members of the family stealing, it is comparatively more natural for them to adopt such activities. Some women surreptitiously remove money from their husband's pockets, some other children in the family are prone to stealing and the child imitates them.

Eliminating the Habit of Stealing

On the basis of the above mentioned causes of stealing, among children, the teacher can discover the cause of stealing in the case of an individual child with the parent's help. In fact, a child's stealing is less a crime but more a bad habit and defect of character. In order to kill this habit in the child, a teacher will advise the parents to maintain an atmosphere of peace and calm within the family, to love the child, to provide him with a reasonable amount of spending money, and to look after him carefully. Children who find stealing thrilling because of the adventure involved can be broken of the habit by being busied in games that involved adventure and require courage. Children who steal because of an unconscious desire arising out of the repression of sexual impulses can be guided into the right mode of behaviour by being told the healthy things about sex and by affectionate behaviour. Actually, within the family a system should be developed whereby the children should use only what is theirs and not to pickup anything belonging to any other family member. Such a step will develop his sense of possession over what is admittedly his and will also develop in him a habit of keeping his hands off things that do not belong to him. Scolding or punishing a child after his stealing has come to one's notice is not a very constructive measure, neither is there anything to be gained by ignoring theft, If such a condition is precipitated, the teacher can coolly discuss things with the parents and discover the causes that lead the child to crime, and will remove them before trying to break him of the habit.

LYING

Meaning and Kind of Lying

Conscious and willful saying of a thing that, is, known to be incorrect is called lying. If a child says something that is incorrect but is not aware of its invalidity, it is incorrect to call him a liar. He is a liar only when he has knowingly said something that is untenable. Habits of lying of this type must be removed. Lying can be of many kinds. The famous criminologist Cyril Burt has classified lying in the following manner:

1. **Playful Lies.** In infancy and childhood, sometimes the child tells a lie just for the fun of it. It is no crime, it is just wantonness.
2. **Lie of Confusion.** When something is in doubt, the child fails to distinguish between true and false, and says that which is false.
3. **Lie of Vanity.** Some children lie for the sake of false vanity. They talk of things that they have never done. Such lying satisfies their false vanity.
4. **Lie of Revenge.** Sometimes the child who has been defeated and has no means of wreaking revenge upon the winner, turns up spreading false gossip and creating all kinds of false information to manifest his superiority over his adversary.
5. **Selfish Lie.** Telling a deliberate lie in order to conceal some fault of one's own doing is called a selfish lie. For example, when some

children are caught being naughty, they invent all kinds of false reasons to escape the natural reckoning.

6. **Lie of Loyalty.** A child is very loyal to his group and tries to cover up its objectionable activities by telling lies.
7. **Pathological Lie.** Some lying is the result of many abnormalities and mental complexes in the individual. Such lies resulting from mental diseases can arise due to the following causes:
   (a) Overactive imagination,
   (b) Facility in the use of words,
   (c) To hide certain bad sex habits.

Cure of Lying

Once the child evinces the habit of telling lies, the teacher must endeavour to end it, since its persistence will adversely affect the, development of his character and leave incomplete the function of education. Hence, teachers who catch their students telling lies, use many ways of curing them. Some of the main methods are the following:

1. **Psychological Treatment.** In psychological treatment, the child is treated with love and affection in order to discover the causes of his lying. Having discovered them, the teacher tries to persuade the child and also causes such changes in his environments that the need for telling lies ceases to exist.
2. **Indirect Punishment.** According to modern educational psychologists, direct punishment of the child leads to development of feelings of hatred and revolt against his teacher, hence this mode of retribution is not desirable. As an alternative, some forms of indirect punishment can be used that often prove to be more effective even than direct punishment. Some such methods are not talking with the child, ignoring him, being indifferent towards him.
3. **Avoid Provocative Occasions.** Generally speaking, the teacher should always try to avoid all occasions that may provoke the child into lying. Testing the child by deliberate creation of such situations is not very expedient since there is no bad habit that the child is incapable of picking up. Hence, as far as is practically possible and feasible, one should avoid all occasions that provoke lying in children.
4. **Confession.** When a lie is detected the first time, one must try to make the child confess that he is in the wrong. This inspires him to repent, and the embarrassment involves acts, as a sufficient deterrent in case of future provocation. His self respect is injured, if he has to confess. Secondly, having confessed to his fault and

having promised not to repeat it, the child himself does his best to avoid all such occasions.

5. **Positive Instruction.** According to modern educational psychologists, a teacher should avoid negative instruction and direction as far as possible, and try to make his directive positive. It is more expedient to say always tell the truth than to order the student to avoid lying. Children have an almost natural tendency of contradicting all negative orders, being more prone to accepting positively worded requests and orders.
6. **Rational Attitude towards the Child's Imagination.** A child is naturally imaginative. He imagines all sorts of things by imaginatively putting himself in different situations. Sometimes he fails to do these things in the concrete, he boasts that he has done this or that, and that he has seen this or that plane. Hence, realising child's sensitivity with regard to imagination one should take the child to see new places, give him the independence and freedom to play all kinds of games, give him new things. When this is done, he will not tell lies among his friends for the simple reason that there will be no need to do it.

Finally, it can be said that successful elimination of the child's lying habits depends upon the teacher's psychological insight, patience and tactful behaviour. He can benefit in his efforts by the suggestions of educational psychologists.

Some children are prone to cause pain to other children junior to themselves. The teacher observes that one child is annoying a younger without any apparent reason. On the other hand, one student comes to him with the report that a class-fellow has beaten him up. Sometimes, reports of this kind are untrue and maliciously reported. But whether the report is a lie or a fact it is for the teacher to investigate and find out, as otherwise his wards are inclined to lose faith in him, and the discipline of the school is seriously jeopardized. The child making the complaint should be sympathetically treated and made to understand that this problem will be solved and in future he will not be molested. Now, the major problem that remains is how to prevent some children from annoying others without reason. Usually, teachers punish and thrash youngsters who do these wanton things with the result that the student is awed and under the influence he is not prone to repeat his exploits. Yet, though this helps to maintain the proper discipline in the class, it defeats the purpose of education. The teacher's object is not to prevent the children from being naughty but eliminating the causes that lead him to undesirable behaviour. Hence, if he is to completely cure the child of his habit of want only causing pain to his juniors, it is essential that he discovers the basic causes that originated the tendency.

Causes of Teasing Other Children

The tendency of teasing other children want only is one that reveals a streak of cruelty in the child and in this the environment in the family plays a large part. Main causes in this connection can be the following:

1. **Cruel Behaviour on the Part of Family Members.** The child has an invariable tendency to imitate the conduct of family members. If members of the family quarrel with each other and the stronger and older beat the youngsters in the family the I child will follow suit.
2. **Absence of Discipline in the Family.** Lack of discipline in the family permits the children to quarrel with each other, the seniors almost invariably triumphing over the juniors by beating them and many parents have not the strength of will to prevent such insane behaviour. Hence it can only be expected that children from such families will injure smaller children in school. It is sometimes seen that the parents take a hand in the punishing to stop their children behaving in this manner. This may create a state of enforced peace and acquiescence in the home, but when in school, the child will imitate his parents and injure and beat children younger and weaker than himself.
3. **Relations between Parents and Child.** If the relations between parents and children are not loving and confident, the child becomes irritable, quarrelsome and selfish. He will manifest these qualities in fighting children younger than himself. The tendency towards cruelty is further promoted by the prejudiced and base behaviour of parents towards their children.
4. **Lack of Discipline in Schools.** In schools where senior students are seen beating and overpowering youngsters, there is little or no discipline. Teachers must adopt psychological means to create an atmosphere of discipline and rational obedience in the school.

There can be some other reasons, besides those mentioned above, why big children may injure and worry smaller children. For example, being over sexed, some children tease their juniors. Whatever the situation, the teacher must try to discover the causes involved in the situation and then try to eliminate them. Acting on two fronts, the teacher must use love and affection to persuade the student while he tries to eliminate the causes that have led to the formation of such a habit in him. Half of his battle is won if he can convince the child's parents of the need of improving the atmosphere at home. He must also try to make the student realise that it is indecent to tease smaller children. Secondly, it is for him to train the children to cooperate and work in an atmosphere of mutual confidence, love and sympathy. Once such an atmosphere has been successfully created in the school, incidents of big boys worrying small ones will be reduced Teachers should keep an eye on such various tendencies as over sexuality, aggressiveness, false vanity, and criminal tendency that arise in children from time to time, and should also resort to tactful behaviour in trying to eliminate them.

AVOIDING TASKS ALLOCATED FOR HOME WORK

In most schools, teachers allot some work to the students complete a home. Sometimes, due to various causes that create unpredictable circumstances, the child fails to do this, but he is not to blame. But, if a child makes it a habit to avoid doing the allotted work, the teacher must do his best to break the child of such a habit. This habit can be caused by any one of the following:

1. **Improper Atmosphere in the Home.** The atmosphere some children's houses is not at all conducive to any sort of serious effort, as a consequence of too much noise and lack of any quiet corner.
2. **Lack of Interest and Enthusiasm.** Children who are not interested in academic pursuits and have no enthusiasm for it, usually do not complete the work allotted to them.
3. **Little Respect and Awe of Teacher.** If a child does not respect a particular teacher and holds him in no awe whatsoever, then that teacher's commands have no particular value for him. In fact, he does the very contrary of what is required of him. His neglecting the work allotted for completion at home is all that can be expected from the child under the circumstances.

(4) **Other Causes.** In addition to these above causes, there can be many other reasons why a student may fail to complete the work required of him. For example, if the child has failed to understand a particular lesson taught in school, how can he be expected to do any problems pertaining to it?

Solution and Cure

Keeping in mind these various causes, the teacher should see to it that students do the work that he allots to them as their home work. In this effort he can, on the one hand, request the children's parents to improve the atmosphere at home, and, on the other he can improve his own conduct in the classroom. He must be able to win the respect and admiration of his students. Having done this, it will be easy for him to have his orders obeyed. Nevertheless, if some student persists in disobeying the instructions of the teacher, then it becomes necessary to administer some indirect punishment to persuade the student to abandon his lax ways. Among them is indifference to the particular student, abstaining from holding conversations with him, and other means whereby the student himself should realise the teacher's displeasure. A teacher must invariably avoid any situation that may lead students to develop feelings of antipathy and hatred towards him or to feel that the work allocated for home is an unnecessary burden forced upon him. Proper methods of education and desirable behaviour on the teacher's part coupled with adequate interest and inspiration in the work cause students to do their home work enthusiastically and sometimes even go to the length of doing work on their own initiative if the teacher does not allot any, and showing it to him. Such children should be praised in front of the whole class. This will have the two-fold effect of adding to their already exuberant enthusiasm, as well as inspiring the other students to emulate them and win the teacher's admiration.

ABSCONDING FROM MATHS CLASS

Mathematics is one subject that has created aversion in more than one student and they all do their best to avoid it. Some of these children are enterprising enough to run away from the mathematics class. If this sort of truant behaviour is constantly noted, then the teacher is compelled to take note to solve it. He must first of all uncover the causes that induce the child to have such irresponsibility. Main causes could be from among the following:

(1) **Low Level of Maturity.** Mathematics is one subject that essentially requires the presence of a certain level of maturity in its students. At different levels of maturity, the curriculum relating to mathematics should be different.

(2) **Defects of Educational Method.** If the teacher takes, it upon himself to teach mathematics by a method that makes the subject appear easy to the student, he will not play truant from the class. Hence, sometimes, one of the reasons why students avoid the mathematics class could be a defective and unimaginative method of teaching.

(3) **Student's Personal Difficulties.** If the student has no interest in academic study, lacks enthusiasm and inspiration regarding

it, a subject as notoriously dry as mathematics is the least likely, to hold his attention. Repeated failure is another thing that may discourage him. There can be numerous other similar problems that may prompt the student to avoid the mathematics class and for this, attitudes, mental abilities and qualities of the personality have a special significance.

Solution and Cure

The teacher should try to discover the causes of a student's running away from the mathematics class, and having done so, should try to remove it. The child should constantly, practise in this difficult subject. Lessons should start with simple questions that are comparatively easy to solve. Success will increase his enthusiasm, and he will be eager to delve into more difficult problems. In teaching mathematics the teacher should adopt a method that makes it easy to grasp so that students achieve a kind of auto inspiration in learning it. Besides this, if the children are found avoiding these classes through some personality defects, then the, teacher should consult their parents, and through loving and affectionate behaviour, try to eliminate these shortcomings.

BEING LATE FOR SCHOOL

Causes

Being occasionally late for the class is nothing unusual. But if a student persists in being late for the school, the teacher has of necessity to investigate and find out the cause for it, since punctuality is an important asset and a part of personality development. There can be many causes why a Child is consistently late for the class, main ones among them being the following:

(1) **Parent's Carelessness.** Children can be punctual in reaching school only if their parents prepare them for school well in time. If they are careless in this respect, it is only natural that their children should be late for school.

(2) **Aimless Wandering.** Another reason why children, who, are prepared for school in time by their parents, teach the school late is that they fall into bad company and play on the wayside or roam around before reaching the school. Once a child falls into a company of vagrants it is only natural for him to develop a liking for wandering. It is a kind of wander lust.

(3) **Tendency to avoid Classes.** The fundamental reason the child is always late for school is that there is nothing in the class to

interest him, and he wants to avoid it, any way. Tendency to run away from classes can be inspired by many things, among them are uninteresting methods of teaching, strict discipline, level of education being higher than the child's level of mental development, bad atmosphere in the classroom very strict administration in school, etc.

(4) **Other Causes.** There cannot be the same reason for children being late for school. Due to different reasons and under different circumstances, children do this. It is quite possible that a child may have a special passion for some particular form of exhibition and that this exhibition may be situated on his way to school so that he may be tempted to spend a few minutes there everyday.

Cure and Solution. Whatever it may be, the teacher must begin his investigation to examining the reasons why a student is delayed on his way to school and then, efforts can be made to eliminate these causes, a venture that requires the cooperation of the parents. Parents and teachers can cooperate to punish the child indirectly and thus break him of his habit. Parents must do their bit by preparing the child for school with a good bit of time to spare. If the atmosphere in school and the method of teaching is defective, it can be removed and education made more interesting. It is the duty of his seniors to save the youngster from bad company. A child naturally likes to live in the group, be it a group of good children, or one of bad children. The sole method of having the child avoid bad company is that he be put in good company. Then, he will not try to go to bad company. Parents should communicate with the teacher at regular intervals to find out whether their child is reaching the school in time. If this is not done, it is upto the teacher to immediately inform them if he thinks it fit. Such co-operation and sensible behaviour can help to rid the child of this bad habit. Secondly, this problem can also be solved by teaching the child all the virtues of punctuality. Some people fail to see the significance of doing things at the time allotted for their doing. Punctuality is a quality that is developed both in school and at home. Having become habituated to having meals, getting up, going to sleep at appointed hour and doing many things by the clock will develop into such a strong habit that he will be instinctively compelled to get to school in time. Otherwise, he is apt to reason out the little difference it makes by being late for school. But, before inculcating the wisdom of punctuality in children, it is essential that the parents and teachers themselves be very punctual. Teachers who themselves are usually late for their class can hardly expect to convince their students that punctuality is a virtue. Punctuality is a thing that is best learned by imitating one's seniors. If parents and teachers themselves are very punctual, the child will drop the habit of being late for school.

GIFTED OR SUPERNORMAL CHILDREN

Who is a Gifted Child?

Many studies have indicated that the intelligence quotient of children differs, from one individual to another. This difference is seen not only among children of different ages but between children of the same age group also. On the basis of this children are classified into the average, the backward and the gifted group. All psychologists do not, agree about the level of intelligence required for a child to be considered gifted. Some psychologists believe that an intelligence quotient of 120 denotes exceptional gifts while others believe that the gifted child must have an, I.Q. of 140. Children with an intelligent quotient even higher than 140 can be accepted as exceptionally gifted. It has been calculated that only one out of 4,00 children belongs to this category. Such exceptionally gifted children have an intelligence quotient ranging between 140 and 190. But an I.Q. of 170 or more is rarely seen, while an I.Q. between 140 and 150 is more common.

Characteristics of the Gifted Child

The gifted child differs from the average child in other respects also, in addition to his greater intelligence. Physiologically, the gifted, child is frequently better built, emotionally better balanced than the average child. Leaving aside the exceptions, it is often seen that the child is gifted not only in terms of intelligence but also in terms of other individual qualities, in which he is more developed. Apparently, the gifted children enjoy the benefits of nature and environment. Most of such children are born into families with a fairly high social and economic level. They, therefore, belong to the more well-to-do group of families with the result that the care lavished on them, the food provided, the education, etc. are all considerably better than that enjoyed by the average child. Besides, they also get good training in controlling their habits and emotions, which helps in developing many exceptional qualities of character and personality.

Frequently, the gifted child is one to two inches taller and a few pounds heavier than the average child. At the time of joining school, such children are seen to be 4 or 5 pounds heavier than the others. At the age of 15, such children are 10 to 15 pounds heavier. In addition to this the gifted children do not normally suffer from headaches, they have clearer skins, they are less irritable, less inclined to exhaustion and less susceptible to such common maladies as cold. In one study a group of 220 successful and 170 unsuccessful candidates were compared, and it was found that the successful candidates suffered from fewer physical defects than the unsuccessful ones. In this case there was one exception, since the gifted competitors were found to suffer from a higher incidence of visual defects. One possible explanation of this may be their excessive use of the eyes in reading and study. But physiologically they were neither weak nor dwarfed. In fact, they were taller and heavier.

It should be remembered that all gifted children are not better than the average child in their physiological characteristics, emotional stability or social adjustment. In fact, quite a few of the gifted children are below the average in this respect. In actual fact, gifted children differ from each other very much in these respects. As a general rule, all that can be said is that defects lead to more defects while good qualities generate more good qualities, although this, too cannot be accepted as a universal rule. For this reason, it is desirable that each gifted child should be studied individually.

Problems of the Gifted Child

As in the case of the backward child, the gifted child is also unlike the average child. As a result, certain problems arise in his case also. These problems should also be tackled with the same care and attention as is accorded to the backward child, although it is now certain that the teacher identifies a backward child much, sooner than he can recognise the gifted one. It may also happen that the teacher may completely fail to observe the qualities of the gifted child, and may even consider him backward. Such a situation is extremely harmful because it binders the gifted child's proper development, and at the same time creates administrative problems for the school and the class. The future of any nation depends upon the proper development of all the gifted children born in it. Hence, school should make special provisions for their training. But the parents also must accept responsibility for their training and education.

The Education of Gifted Children

The following suggestions have been given for the education of gifted children:

1. **Selection.** The first step in their education is to find out which child is gifted. This selection can be made with the help of marks obtained at previous examinations the advice of the class teachers, the results of psychological tests and the reports given by parents.

2. **No Separate Classes.** Some psychologists have suggested that gifted children should be taught in separate classes set apart for them. But this is not a very good psychological suggestion for this may engender a feeling of vanity and superiority in them.
3. **Curriculum.** Many psychologists have suggested that the gifted child should be made to study some subjects in addition to the normal syllabi intended for the average class. This is a more practical suggestion because the gifted child's abilities can be better developed by the more comprehensive syllabus. It will also help to remove inactivity, social difficulties, and also create a better atmosphere in the class. But it must be remembered that the syllabus should never be so extensive as to become a burden on the child.
4. **Faster Promotions to Higher Classes.** It has also been suggested by some psychologists that the gifted child should be promoted to higher classes more rapidly than the other children. This will give them a chance to develop their minds and also save time. But from the standpoint of the child's social development, this may not prove very beneficial. He will tend to be handicapped by the fact that all the other children in his class will be older than him. It is therefore better if the gifted child is given some additional work, but without promoting him to the higher class.
5. **Individual Education.** Nowadays many psychologists are of the opinion that the gifted child should be educated individually with the teacher generally acting as a guide without undue interference. The child is given a particular task to perform within a fixed period. The teacher keeps an eye on his development and provides him with fresh programmes as he goes along. This method of education has proved the most useful in the case of gifted children.
6. **Extra Curricular Activities.** Another way of developing the qualities of the gifted child is to engage him in extra curricular activities such as games, music, dancing, other arts, practice for debates and sports competitions.
7. **Facilities and Apparatus.** Gifted children can also be given certain kinds of special facilities such as fee concessions, opportunity to do work of exceptional responsibility of importance, etc. The school should also provide many kinds of means for learning the arts, games and other activities. Very often the gifted child finds a good library as a very good aid.

It is clear from the above exposition that the teacher can play an important role in nation building by helping in the proper development to the gifted children tendered in his care. In actual fact, the proper development of the gifted child depends considerably more upon the intelligence, wisdom and the sense of responsibility of the teacher. He should try to make arrangements for developing special qualities in his more gifted children. But in this connection, the responsibility of the parents is not less than that of the teacher, because different means can be adopted for the child's development as effectively at home as in the school. The parents should also take special care of such children. If this is not done, their balanced development is retarded. Besides, they may even become very difficult problems for their parents. If a child shows some extraordinary skill at some particular work, he should be sent to a school in which he can be trained to exercise that particular skill. The government can also facilitate the development of gifted children by providing fee concessions and other kinds of monetary aid. Thus, an environment can be created in which the future leaders of the nation may develop and grow.

QUESTIONS FOR EXERCISE

1. Describe the defects and abnormalities in a child's development and point out its remedies.
2. What light has educational psychology thrown on the problem of (a) stealing, (b) lying among children? Give examples.
3. What should the teacher do in the following circumstances:
   (a) A child annoys smaller children without any reason.
   (b) A student does not do the home work allotted to him.
   (c) A student always absconds in the mathematics class.
   (d) A student invariably comes late to the class.
4. What is a backward child? What are the causes of backwardness and what remedies will you apply for them?
5. What do you understand by development irregularity? What are its causes?
6. Write short note on Mentally deficient children?
7. How will you define a gifted child? Describe the methods by which gifted children can be identified.
8. Write short note on Supernormal children.

28

Juvenile Delinquency

In modern civilised countries a criminal is not looked upon as a sinner or a bad person, but rather as a mentally diseased individual or one who has been victimised by circumstances. There was a time when even small children were severely punished if they committed some crime. But as psychologists proceeded to draw the attention of the civilized world to the causes of juvenile delinquency, the tradition of punishing children lost favour, to be replaced by efforts at improving and rehabilitating them. Now-a-days, in every nation efforts are made to correct the juvenile delinquent rather than to punish him. To take the deviant once again as a healthy and responsible citizen of society, efforts are made through reformatory schools, probation and other measures.

Legal Definition of Juvenile Delinquency

Legal definition of juvenile delinquency does not conform to its psychological definition, as, from the legal viewpoint, a juvenile delinquent is a person between the ages of 15 and 17 who indulges in anti-social activity. In U.S.A., the Ohio Code defines juvenile delinquency in some such manner as this: a Juvenile delinquent is one who breaks the law, is a vagrant, persists in disobeying orders, whose behaviour endangers his own moral life as well as the moral life of others or one who tries to marry without the consent of his parents. It may as well be pointed out that the age of the so-called juvenile delinquents has not been similarly determined in all countries. It varies from country to country but is within the usual limits of 16 and 20. Normally, it is the 17 year old adolescent who qualifies for this term, but in India, according to the prevalent laws, the maximum age of a juvenile delinquent is fixed at 16. Laws pertaining to this subject have been passed in U.P., M.P. Maharashtra, Tamil Nadu, Mysore, Delhi, West Bengal, Orissa, and East Punjab. In those states in which the juvenile acts have not been passed, the reformatory act of

1997 prevails. In these the maximum age of a juvenile delinquent has been determined at 15. In Maharashtra and Madhya Pradesh it is 16. According to reformatory act, the term Youth Offender will be appended to any individual below 15 who has been sentenced to life imprisonment or has been convicted of some crime.

Psychological Definition of Juvenile Delinquent

Differing from the legal definition of the controversial terms, psychologists lay much emphasis upon the causes of juvenile delinquency in defining it. From the legal viewpoint all those who are not apprehended are not criminals but from the psychological viewpoint all such offenders also are criminals. Consequently, the psychological definition of juvenile delinquency is more comprehensive than its legal definition. According to the psychologists, any and every child, of either sex, between the ages of 15 and 18, who commits a crime, irrespective of the fact that he is apprehended or not, is a juvenile delinquent. In this manner, juvenile delinquent is one who forcibly possesses the property of another or causes it damage, indulges in anti-social activity, creates danger to another's life or hinders the activities of others. Hence, a child who throws stones at a car and runs away, one who sets fire without cause, creates danger for the life of another just for the fun of it, are all juvenile delinquents, from the psychological viewpoint.

Defining Juvenile delinquency, Dr. Sethna has written, "Juvenile delinquency involves wrong doing by a child or a young person who is under an age specified by the law (for the time being in force) of the place concerned." Newmeyer puts the same idea in these words, "A delinquent is a person under age who is guilty of anti-social act and whose misconduct is an infraction of law."

CAUSES OF JUVENILE DELINQUENCY

According to the Novel approach and, concepts of modern criminology, the causes of juvenile delinquency have been divided into two classes-personal and social causes. In crime, two special factors are at work-internal and external. Internal factors include physical and psychological factors while the external factors consist of social elements. Criminals have been divided into two categories by the American criminologists: (1) social criminals, (2) personal criminals. Social criminals, in particular, are the result of social circumstances. Walter Recklace has pointed out two specific causes of crime: (1) constructive and (2) circumstantial. Some other criminologists have divided the various causes of crime into two parts: (1) sociogenic and (2) psychogenic. Here the causes of juvenile delinquency will be divided into three classes for convenient study:

(1) social causes, (2) psychological causes, (3) economic causes. Of these, we are only concerned with the second.

PSYCHOLOGICAL CAUSES OF DELINQUENCY

1. **Intellectual Weakness.** Dr. Goring advanced the theory that intellectual weakness is a cause of crime. Goddard was the main exponent of the notion that mental weakness is the cause of crime. In his book *Mental Efficiency and Levels of Intelligence,* he has written that the greatest single factor or cause of crime is mental weakness. After examining 4000 children for their intelligence, Healy and Bronner came to the conclusion that 13 percent of them had an intelligence quotient below 70. This conclusion is borne out by S.S. Glueck and E.T. Glueck in their book *Unraveling Juvenile Delinquency,* who studied 1000 criminal children in 1934 and came to the conclusion that 13 per cent children have an intelligent quotient of below 70.

   This contention has, been objected to on the ground that it is based on the study only of those juvenile delinquents who have been, produced before the courts. Naturally, the intelligent and shrewd, juvenile delinquents will be apprehended far less than the backward ones. In one of their studies, C.W. Mann and N.P. Mann have confirmed this view and shown that children with an intelligence quotient or less than 90 stand a far greater chance of being apprehended than brilliant children. They calculated the median of the intelligence quotient of 1061 criminals in which the boys were discovered to have an I.Q. of 94.88 and girls of 83.77. In 1947, Merrill, in his book, *Problems of Child Delinquency* calculated the average of the intelligence quotients of 50 criminal children, measured on the modified Binet scale. The average was 92.5. Examining 2904 healthy children for their intelligence level it was found that their average intelligence quotient was to 101.8. From both these enquiries Meirill concluded that a low level of intelligence cannot be accepted as a cause of crime since the low level of intelligence in juvenile delinquents is not distinctly different from that of healthy children. There can be no denying the fact that it is comparatively easier to mislead backward children, but intelligent and shrewd children are also liable to get involved in crime.

2. **Mental Diseases.** Other criminologists have tried to establish a definite relationship between, mental disease and crimer. In the many studies carried out upon criminals, some mentally diseased individuals were also found. According to this view, a criminal

is a kind of mentally, diseased, individual. Who is in as much need of treatment as need of punishment. Some psychiatrist and neurologist believe that the psychopathatic personality is a cause of crime. Psychopathic, children, are born in families where, there is almost complete absence of love, affection and control. Concerning psychopathic children Tappan has written that he is very unsocialised, irritable, cruel, obstinate, suspicious, selfcentred, lonely full of feelings of revenge, backward, and hypersexual or uncontrolled in his sexual behaviour. In an extremely advanced stage, he lacks the ability to sympathise, and is completely devoid of repentance over his own cruel doings and the pain or suffering of others. A psychopathic child, of his nature has the existence of an uninvited guest in his own house. He is never loved by any one, but is instead the butt of every criticism and abuse in the house. It is only natural that the child should react to such behaviour feelings of unhindered obstinacy and homicidal tendencies. In his book *Juvenile Delinquency* Tappan has described the case of a psychopathic child, Issac. He was a very intelligent child of 14, accused of theft, truency from school, unnatural sexual, practices and general indiscipline. He was a beautiful child who almost invariably impressed all strangers. He was the only child in the family, and his mother died while he was an infant. His father deserted him at the age of 2, following which he was disgustedly and disinterestedly cared for by one relative after another for short periods. Finally, he, was sent to an orphanage. All these causes led to the manifestation of many complexes and aberrations, in his childhood.

Issac never paid attention to daily routine and showed no respect for authority, always giving evidence of obstinacy and bitterness in his conduct. He put forward all kinds of impossible and unrelated demands. His behaviour towards the two individuals whom he loved very much did not differ from his general behaviour. These two individuals, a farmer and a social, worker, did their best to cure the child. Generally, he was made aware of the folly of his ways and the nature of his behaviour. His interest in agriculture was encouraged. As a result of sympathetic behaviour over a considerable period, these two individuals came very close to Issac, consequently becoming his ideals that went so far as to assume the form of his Self-consciousness and awakening, feeling of disgust with his, previous ways was aroused in him and then came to seek their advice whatever he did. When Issac manifested this tendency towards better adjustment, ideals, of better behaviour were gradually put, before him. Due to the self confidence and persistence of the two individuals, Issac succeeded in reorganising his future, to be selected in the United States Air Force in 1941 at the age of 21.

Some psychologists and criminologists have criticised the conclusions reached by the study of psychopathic criminals. Sutherland writes that a neurologist studied the prisoners in Illinois prison. And studying the symptoms he found that among 98 per cent prisoners in the same prisons they found only 5 per cent of them to be psychopathic. Actually, this term has been used in so many varied senses and on the basis of so varied symptoms by different psychologists and psychiatrists that it has been left with, no specific meaning that can be used to elucidate scientific facts.

(3) **Characteristics of Personality.** Tendency to crime also found to have close relationship with characteristics of the personality. Personality is the method of an individual's adaptation to environment. Criminal children resort to illegal modes of such adaptation. Hence, juvenile delinquents have been found to process some characteristic features of the personality that shed light on causes of their delinquency. In his book *Unraveling Juvenile Delinquency,* Glueck pointed out that the degree of freedom, irresponsibility, revolts, homicidal tendency, suspicion, lack of control, some forms of sadism, emotional and social maladjustment, extrovert behaviour etc., in juvenile delinquents is much higher than in normal children. Immaturity in sentiment and lack of emotional balance were found to be some eight times more than in normal child. A normal child is comparatively well-behaved, less explosive, peaceable, obedient and social. The juvenile delinquent, on the contrary, is found to be naughty, explosive, anything but peaceful, disobedient and unsocial. Glueck also, discovered considerable difference between the general interests and forms and recreation of normal and abnormal children. Delinquent child was found to take much interest in works of an adventurous and dangerous nature. They were found to take considerable interest in seeing pictures and films. Among his interests and modes of recreation were found such practices as cigarette smoking, gambling, staying away from home, breaking things and travelling without tickets, etc. He is often the member of one or the other gang. On the contrary,

normal healthy children were found engaging in games. In some study it has been proved that female juvenile delinquents exhibited considerable emotional instability and immaturity.

(4) **Emotional Instability.** In this way, emotional instability is one of the most important causes of crime. A child's personality is rendered unbalanced through lack of love and affection, emotional, insecurity, very strict discipline, feeling of insufficiency and inferiority and reaction of revolt. Such a state of mind inspires the child to criminal behaviour. In their studies, Healy and Bronner saw that 93 per cent of all juvenile delinquents manifest symptoms of emotional imbalance. A detailed analysis of these juvenile delinquents presented the following emotional patterns and influences:

(a) 46 prisoners or criminals showed that feelings of insecurity, lack of acceptability, extreme discrimination of an unfavourable nature, inferiority and not being properly understood existed in their minds.

(b) In 28 criminals, lack of affection had led to suppression of their normal and abnormal desires.

(c) 54 criminals showed that they felt inferior or inadequate in school life, family life, in the friend circle or in play.

(d) 34 criminals showed signs of emotional imbalance as a result of bad behaviour of the parents conditions of family life mistakes of parents and lack of proportion in the family.

(e) In 31 criminals, feelings of extreme hatred and jealousy towards fellow mates were very strong.

(f) In 17 criminals, illusions or an unhappy life, based possibly on past experience, were found existing.

(g) 9 criminals clearly evinced the presence of self-condemnation and awareness of having committed crime due to some past criminal behaviour. These feelings were both conscious and unconscious.

REFORM OF JUVENILE DELINQUENTS

Modern welfare states aim at reforming the juvenile delinquents so that they may become responsible citizens when they grow old. The following are the most important methods to realise this objective:

(1) **Probation.** In this method the juvenile delinquent is kept under the supervision of a probation officer whose job is to look after the delinquent, to help him in getting established in normal life and to see that the delinquent observes the rules of bail bond.

Thus the delinquent not only gets a chance to reform himself but also Lets advise and concrete help for the purpose.

(2) **Reformatory Institutions.** Institutions such as reformatory schools, certified schools, auxiliary homes and borstal schools are devised to reform inmate delinquents. These institutions aim at all round progress of the delinquent.

(3) **Psychological Techniques.** Whereas the above measures are adopted by the state, the teachers may adopt psychological techniques for the reform of juvenile delinquents. Of these the important ones are the following:

(i) *Play Therapy* : In this technique the delinquent children are given opportunities to participate in such plays as give expression to their repressed motives and help in the development of creative energy. In play therapy individual as well as group play are utilised.

(ii) *Finger Painting* : In this method the child is given plain papers and some colours. He is allowed to paint in his own way, by means of his fingers. The purpose is not painting but expression of repressed motives in the child, which leaves him serene and healthy.

(iii) *Psycho Drama* : In this technique the child is allowed to participate in different roles in group drama and thereby manifest his repressed motives.

Besides the above mentioned specific techniques, the teacher can reform delinquents by creating healthy atmosphere in the school and by providing adequate and healthy recreation. Finally, cure of juvenile delinquency requires co-ordinated and concentrated efforts of teachers, guardians and the government.

QUESTIONS FOR EXERCISE

1. Write a short note on Delinquency.
2. Discuss the form and causes of juvenile delinquency. How can the child guidance clinic help in this matter?
3. What is delinquency? Describe its causes and methods of treatment.
4. What are the main causes of delinquency? How can delinquents be helped?
5. Why does the child become delinquent? How can such a child be relieved of his delinquency?
6. Examine the causes of child delinquency. Give some techniques to cure it.
7. How do children develop criminal tendencies? How can these be treated?

29

Adjustment and Mental Hygiene

Human situation is a constantly changing one. New conditions and problems are constantly be setting the individual right from his infancy to his death-bed and he is invariably engaged in trying to find a satisfactory and pleasurable solution to them by employing his intelligence and other gifts of the mind and body. In other words, life is the name of unceasing process, the process of adjustment.

Meaning of Adjustment

What is adjustment? In the words of Laurence F. Shaffer, "Adjustment is the process by which a living organism maintains a balance between its needs and the circumstances that influence the satisfaction of these needs." Accordingly, the process of adjustment has two primary or main elements: one, the needs of the living organism and two, the conditions or circumstances that influence these needs. These needs can be bio-genic, originating in society, personal or communal, or arising from any other conceivable source. On the other hand, the circumstances influencing these needs also can either be inside the individual or outside him. Factors within the individual that influence these needs are his physical and mental states, capacity, attitudes, interests etc. For example, most, weakly constituted individuals cannot fulfil their own psychological motives, and thus, their, needs, are definitely effected by their lack of strength. Factors arising within the environment are usually geographical conditions, political and cultural influence. And, these conditions and circumstances can help as well as deter the fulfilment of the individual's requirements. In this manner, the nature of influences upon the person's needs can be of two kinds—favourable and unfavourable. Positive or favourable influences help in the fulfilment of needs while unfavourable influences hinder their satisfaction.

Three Elements in Adjustment

An analysis of the process of adjustment will reveal the presence of three main elements:

1. **Motive.** The very process of adjustment in the living being is set in motion by the presence within him of some motive or need or requirement.
2. **Thwarting Conditions.** When the environment does present any features that tend to become obstacles in the fulfilment of these needs, then the adjustment is natural, facile and effortless, and no problem results. But if circumstances create obstacles in the path of such fulfilment, then the process of adjustment progresses further.
3. **Varied Responses.** Once the fulfilment of a need has been obstructed, the individual indulges in various actions which are a reaction to the obstacle. Such a reaction can be normal just as much as it can be abnormal.
4. **Solution.** As a result of these reactions and responses the individual achieves a degree of adjustment with the circumstances. The problem of adjustments is thereby solved.

Example of Adjustment

All these various component elements of adjustment can be well understood with the aid of a concrete example. A student is actuated by a strong desire to stand first in his class, and to do so by scoring very well. He works extremely hard but fails to achieve his objective because he has not the necessary mental equipment. Lack of the requisite intelligence forms an obstacle to the satisfaction or this motive, and hence, as a result, the student condescends to lower his aim somewhat by aiming at securing a, second division. In order to accommodate his change of objective the student changes his mode of study. A change of response, a suitable modification of the objective, and the means is achieved with satisfaction. The adjustment problem is also solved. Such a process of adjustment is an universal phenomenon, and is to be seen at every level of life, at various times and under most conditions.

MOTIVE AND ADJUSTMENT

Generally speaking, the process of adjustment can be set in, motion by any motive, for example, our physical needs are constantly being manifested in the form of adjustive behaviour patterns. But from our point of view these needs do not have much importance, for on the one hand they are easily satisfied, and, on the other, in the event of their dissatisfaction life itself ceases in the organism, thus, obviating all further adjustment activity. Hence, social motives and requirements have greater importance for the adjustment process. Social motives are developed within a cultural environment. Individuals of different cultures have different motives, and different cultures do not generate identical motives. For example, our society requires the development and encouragement of such motives as self-respect, self-realization, acceptance, security, love, sympathy, etc., and these social motives naturally have definite influences upon sex and other biological needs. Just as social motives have greater importance than physiological needs, in the same manner the process of adjustment places greater emphasis upon motives that are stronger than others. Strong motives, once they have been excited, can only be satisfied. Inability to satisfy them only leads to further dissatisfaction, and this tension is not ended till the objective has been attained.

THWARTING IN ADJUSTMENT

It has been remarked earlier that one important element in the process of adjustment is the presence of conditions that thwart the satisfaction of motives. Many are, the forms that this thwarting can take, and is known to take. One form is frustration. If, for example, a person fails to catch a train and reach his destination because his wrist watch is not functioning properly, then he has to face frustration that arises out of the environment. This frustration can also be present in the individual himself. Another form of thwarting or obstacles is conflict. A state of conflict is precipitated when the individual is actuated by more than one motive arising simultaneously. And in the throes of these various motives he cannot decide upon the direction of action that he should adopt. Among the classical example of a state of conflict and indecision is the state of the mind of Arjuna, described in the Gita, when he is divided between war and peace, between indecision and *attachment.* If, similarly, a student wants to continue his interest in game's while at the same time he does not want to neglect his academic pursuit, then his mind will be a battlefield of confrontation between these two desires. This state of conflict and tension will continue till the individual decides upon one particular motive and rejects the other. When conflict extends over a very long period of time, the individual shows signs of mental illness and other abnormalities of behaviour and conduct.

Frustration and conflict, the two forms of thwarting mentioned earlier, are closely related, Normally, when frustration results from some obstruction, the organism involved is seen adopting aggressive and violent behaviour towards the obstacle. Such aggressive behaviour can be direct as well as indirect. In children, and unintelligent people it takes a direct form while in the case of most adults and intelligent people it takes a more, indirect manifestation. Now, if the child's normal expression of aggression, and violence resulting from some form of frustration is curbed and restricted, then it is actually prevented, but at the same time it becomes repressed and gives rise to feelings of fear and insecurity. Thus, some people become violent on being faced with some frustrating feelings of fear and insecurity as a result of the curb on their aggressive behaviour. As to the mode of behaviour that should be adopted in dealing with obstacles that cause frustration, an individual learns through trial and error. Different situations and circumstances find him behaving differently, and the behaviour patterns of adjustment that satisfy him are repeated while the patterns that cause him displeasure are discarded and replaced and the various reactions concerning the adjustment to different frustrations gradually take on the form of habits. Hence, adult individuals display permanent individual differences in the patterns of adjustment.

MALADJUSTED REACTIONS

Any state that contradicts that of adjustment is called maladjustment. In this condition contradicting that of adjustment, the individual organisms fails to, maintain a balance between his needs and the circumstances that influence the satisfaction of them and, in this condition one observes reactions that are tendentious towards further imbalance. Reactions of this kind include all those behaviour patterns which can be called abnormal. For example, all kinds of mental illness will be cited as maladjustment reaction. Maladjustment will be the term to be applied to criminal, delinquent and anti-social behaviour. The maladjusted individual fails to attain to a state of adjustment with his circumstances, and, instead of trying to face up to the situation, tries to run away from it. Abnormal fears and mental formations be seen in the individual. Even his mistakes are construed as no mistakes, and he rationalises upon them. Instead of working to achieve something of his own accord, he identifies himself with the achievement of others and thereby satisfies himself. He has very little capacity to cooperate with others, and he finds it difficult to live with them. He prefers solitude and loves to wonder in an imaginary world. Extreme day dreaming is a maladjusted reaction. Another example of it is the projection of one's faults upon another and holding him responsible for one's own frustrations. Similarly, many apparently adult individuals are seen behaving in a markedly childish manner; this too is a form of maladjusted reaction. Briefly, maladjusted reactions include all such reactions that prove obstacles to adjustment.

CRITERIA OF PERSONALITY ADJUSTMENT

The implication of adjustment is the balance between an individual's needs and the circumstances that satisfy these needs. Hence, the evaluation of the adjustment achieved by a person will require the knowledge of two things. The first is the requirement of this person and second the conditions and circumstances that influence the satisfaction of his need. Once these two are known it will be necessary to find the balance that is struck between them. If the balance is good and desirable, then the individual can be said to be properly adjusted, but if the balance is disturbed then the person will be considered maladjusted. Evidently, this adjustment will differ from individual to individual, since, their needs and the conditions that satisfy them need not be common. In this manner, the criterion of personality adjustment is relative to the individuals requirements and the cultural and social complex of circumstances in which he lives. In other words, the criterion changes when these conditions change. For example, in a culture that encourages the combative and aggressive spirit men have greater need for this motive in their adjustment. On the other hand, in a culture that places very great stress upon amiability, the adjustment of personality will depend upon this motive, and it will have great influence upon the criterion of adjustment. Adjustment itself is relative to the individual and his circumstances. Thus, the qualitative traits that are required for adjustment to particular society and culture cannot be considered to be efficacious in every society and culture.

Despite the fact that the above limitations are operative everywhere, certain tentative and general criteria of adjustment can be established. Main criteria would be the following:

1. **Integration of Personality.** One criterion of adjustment is the integration of personality. Personality complex is a complex of all psycho physical traits. In this the various mental reactions and processes of intelligence and sentiment, desire and determination, etc., do not subsist in any disorder but rather in a proper organised system of functioning. Conflict is quite absent from them evidently, the proper integration of the personality is an ideal at which one and all should aim. It is only in such a state that persons can have internal peace and total welfare. The integrated personality is flexible, determined and organised. Mcdougall calls it the organisation of character and intelligence. The higher the degree of organisation in an individual's personality the better will be the degree of his adjustment, since in the absence of adjustment the personality cannot be integrated and organised. On the other hand, permanent adjustment is not

possible in the absence of personality integration. The individual with an adjusted and organised personality maintains a balanced and practical outlook on life. Failures and frustrations do not disturb him unduly, and he persists in looking calm and master of the situation. His emotions, needs, thinking and other mental activities are adequately balanced and systematic. On the other hand, the personality of a maladjusted person is disintegrated. His life is disturbed, without any peace, and he also tends to disturb the peace of everyone else.

2. **Reduction in Tension.** Another criterion of personality adjustment is the reduction or decrease in tension, a decrease that is consequent upon the fulfilment of this needs, irrespective of whether the fulfilment is achieved through socially acceptable or objectionable modes. It is a psychological fact that whenever some one, or the other need of a person remains dissatisfied it creates a state of tension and this tension is removed only when the object satisfying that need is obtained. Absence of adjustment results in the increase of tension while its increase helps in reducing tension. In other words, a person's adjustment can be evaluated in terms of tension existing in his mind.
3. **Harmony between Need and Environment.** As has been mentioned earlier, the adjusted personality can be recognised from a harmony between his needs and his environment. Greater the degree of such harmony, the better will be his adjustment, while on, the other hand his personality will be considered less adjusted if this harmony is not of a high order. An adjusted individual has the capacity and energy to accommodate his needs and motives according his environment, as also to mould this environment to suit his own needs and motives. In this manner, maximum satisfaction and pleasure is to be had in the mutual adjustment and harmony of both environment and requirement. Persons who fail to make an adjustment of their motives and needs to the environment in which they are placed cannot be happy even in the best of circumstances, and are always to be found complaining of the adversity of conditions. Failure of this kind also means that the individual who has not within him the power and capacity to mould conditions according to his own requirements, his usual condition is one of frustration and maladjustment. Problems are a part of everyone's life, but they also add spice to its otherwise dull fare. There is hardly any, if any at all, individual who is never, in this life called upon to face a situation that promises conflict, promises him frustration

and anger. If such conditions are present then the enterprising individual bends himself to varying and modifying them to suit his own requirements and thus achieves adjustments or otherwise makes changes in his own requirements and needs. For example, it is commonly noticed that some people succeed in making their ends meet very facilely even on a low income, and they give every appearance of being happy and contented. Contrary to such are people who are incessantly complaining of the extremity of their means even when they have a reasonable income. There is a condition of unhappiness, since there is a wide gap between their income and their expenditure, their needs are never even temporarily completely fulfilled. In such a condition the adjustment of personality is liable to be disturbed from two sides, first in case the needs of the person do not conform to the circumstances, and in the second case when the conditions are not propitious to the fulfilment of the needs. Hence, adjustment requires the balance between these two, even if modification and alteration is essential in both.

COMMON MODES OF REACTION TO DIFFICULTIES

Every individual has certain definite needs, and every individual lives in certain specific conditions. It is within these conditions that his needs are fulfilled. When the conditions are favourable no particular difficulty arises in such fulfilment, but for every individual this is not always possible. A condition that is, not propitious for the fulfilment of some need is common in the life of every individual, and such circumstances and conditions always prove obstacles in the satisfaction of that need, thus creating problems. Difficulties refer to the conditions that prove obstacles to the satisfactions of a person's needs. As it is, one finds great individual differences in the manner of reacting to these difficulties, but even then there are certain modes of reaction that can be seen in every pattern of reaction behaviour. These methods are roughly the following :

1. **Constructive Adjustment.** One very general form of reaction to difficulties is the mode of constructive adjustments and examples of this mode of behaviour are to be seen everywhere in life. Students in educational institutions are constantly faced with situations that become obstacles to the achievement of their educational and vocational objectives, praise and knowledge of self needs that are basic to them. Most students have recourse to constructive adjustments in order to overcome these situations, such as putting in longer hours of study or consulting numerous

books and teachers in order to overcome their academic obstacles. Similarly, when a trader is faced with some problem of his trade, he resorts to some constructive adjustment to solve that problem. If a person is in financial straits then the simplest constructive adjustment would be for him to exercise economy in his expenditure. In constructive adjustment the main feature to be remarked is that it offers a quality of facing the situation rather than running away from it, and making efforts that solve the problem instead of merely postponing it.

2. **Substitute Adjustments.** All individuals do not have the ready wit and wisdom to achieve constructive adjustment and thus retain their mental balance in the face of difficulties. A very large number of individuals have recourse to substitute adjustments when faced with difficult situations. This, also, is a common and usual method of reacting to difficulties. For example, in a large number of cases, when students fail to pass at an examination, then, instead of urging them to work harder, they take it upon themselves to blame the teachers in particular and the entire educational system in general, and they daydream themselves into success in future. Some students start avoiding school when they fail while other more enterprising though more censored are the ones who leave home. The question that now arises is whether these reactions are activities of adjustment, since they do not tend to solve the problem inherent in the situation. A close observation will reveal that even through such reactions the individual is trying to satisfy need that in other individuals are solved through constructive and positive adjustment activity. A student failing in an examination is usually defamed and this obstructs his social ambitions and motives. Tensions that are created through this obstruction he tries to end by his activity of running away or transferring the blame on the teachers or by day-dreaming of success. Thus, for this reason are these reactions to difficulties called substitute reactions. Even though no direct satisfaction is forthcoming from such activity, yet the unsatisfied motive is indirectly, and momentarily pacified, and in this manner adjustment is improved through decreases in, tension. It must be noticed that adjustment is not a question of successful results but one of satisfaction of motives, irrespective of the methods that are adopted, be they normal, originating in disease and mental deficiency. It is often remarked that weak, lean and thin individuals usually walk with a swagger and an imposing style. The psychological reason for this is that in weak

and lean individuals the motive of self-respect is suppressed, and in order to overcome this repression, instead of reasoning to some form of constructive adjustment, they walk with a swagger, thus saving their self-respect from injury and their mental balance from collapse. Here, it must be remarked that this should not be interpreted to mean that the satisfaction accorded to a motive by constructive adjustment is equal to the satisfaction caused by a substitute adjustment. The facts of the matter are other than this. Reactions of substitute adjustment usually win scorn and ridicule for the person practicing them from other members of society and this further causes suppression of the person's desire for social acceptance. A person running to solitude away from this life's ignoble strife can save his desire for competition from being frustrated, but then his motives of security and sociability are frustrated. Hence, it is evident that the substitute adjustment usually results only in more frustration and suppression. On the other hand, these modes of adjustment are also usually harmful for the individual. For example, certain normally ugly individuals are seen trying to attract female attention through undesirable activity since they cannot win it in the normal course, and this usually results in great inconvenience to other more reasonable members of society. One characteristic of proper and constructive adjustment is that not only the individual but entire society benefits from it, besides improving the individual's social relationships.

3. **Mental Mechanism.** Another mode of reacting to difficulties is that of mental mechanisms, main among them being projection, compensation, rationalization, etc. As a general rule the consequence of these mechanisms is not good either for the individual or for society. Yet, in some degree or other all or some of these mechanisms are to be found in every individual can be declared abnormal on their account. It is only when one of them develops out of proportion that symptoms of abnormality can be discovered. Normally a tendency to overlook one's owns fault and to blame others for one's failures is only naturally present in men, but if a person is observed in doing this all the time and unduly regarding everyone else his enemy, then his conduct will undoubtedly be classed as abnormal. These mechanisms are also called the tools of adjustment, since their objective is the attainment of adjustment through various methods.

MENTAL HYGIENE

What is Mental Hygiene?

Mental hygiene is the science that creates a personality in every individual in society that makes for good adjustment with the environment, that attains a proper synthesis between the intellectual, emotional and physical aspects, that is satisfied and optimistic, vividly in mind if he is to preserve mental health, prevent mental disturbance and promote mental health among his students:

1. **Discipline.** As has been pointed out earlier, discipline in the school has an important influence upon the mental health of students. But this discipline should never be very hard since such conditions will lead to mental ill health. Thus, discipline should be exercised not through creating fear of punishment but through arousing feelings of responsibility and the desire to be law-abiding among the students. True discipline is self-discipline. And discipline in college should be maintained by selecting its guardians from among the students themselves. It develops feelings of responsibility among the students.
2. **Affectionate Behaviour.** It is only too evident that affectionate behaviour towards students on the part of teachers has good effect on the former's mental health. It will inspire him to obey the teacher, respect him and do nothing that may incur his displeasure. A teacher should maintain the same loving attitude towards all his students. Any discrimination in this treatment injures the feeling of students.
3. **Play and Recreation.** Mental disturbances and imbalance is created by the repressed motives surging in a student's brain. They can be given opportunities for healthy expression through games and other forms of recreation play and recreation have, a cathartic effect.
4. **Sex Education.** In adolescence the morals of young boys and girls show alarming tendencies to proceed to degradation because of the sexual instinct, or alternately its repression leads to much mental distress. Teachers should make use of psychological weapons to remove any sexual deviations that may be embedded in the minds of students and for this, the best way is to provide young boys and girls with necessary elementary sex education. This will help them, on the one hand, to develop a healthy attitude towards sex and prevent them from forming harmful complexes, as well as assist in their physical, mental and emotional

development, on the other, they can then later on become well developed and integrated individuals.

5. **Educational Guidance.** In order to maintain a state of mental health, it is essential that they be given subject that conform to their requirements and abilities, their educational problems solved. Taking personal advice of a psychologist in this connection is called educational guidance.
6. **Personal Guidance.** Many of the problems that arise before the student are such that they cannot be solved by the student himself, hence he needs the personal guidance of the psychologist to solve them.
7. **Vocational Guidance.** Every individual is compelled to adopt some one or the other profession once his education is complete, and he begins to worry about it even while he is still engaged in his academic pursuit. The knowledgeable teacher can, help his students in their choice or a suitable career.
8. **Formation of Good Habits.** Mental health depends upon good habits. Hence, it is desirable for the teacher to help students in the formation of good habits regarding a regular life, balanced diet and exercise, good behaviour and high thinking, etc.
9. **Balanced Curriculum.** The curriculum in school should be such as to develop all aspects of the student's personality, to increase his fund of necessary knowledge, and to avoid all unnecessary strain on the mind. The integrated development of the students can be promoted through the organising of various kinds of extra curricular activities in the school and college.
10. **Balance Home Assignment.** It is improper to think that, if the child is given too much homework to, do, he will not have the time to indulge in destructive and naughty pranks as he will be too busy. Loading them with too much homework only leaves then worried and anxious, with the worst influence upon their mind. Hence, the homework required of them should be careful and sensibly formulated.

Finally, it may be stated that the prevention of mental imbalances is a problem of social and national importance. For this, efforts will have to be made to get rid of circumstances of social disorganisation, exploitation, corruption, various tensions and conflicts, crimes, alcoholic effects, etc. The defects of urban life in the form of excessive crowding, unhealthy small houses, promiscuous mixing of the sexes, and noise will have to be eliminated. Suitable and interesting work for all will have to be provided, in addition to opportunities of health and recreation. It is only through efforts at the national level that proper and effective prevention of mental maladies can take place and for this co-operative effort on the part of government, teachers, social workers and sensible people in the public will be necessary.

QUESTIONS FOR EXERCISE

1. Enumerate and explain the basic principles of Mental Hygiene.
2. Write short note on Mental Hygiene.
3. What do you understand by Mental Hygiene? Discuss its importance in the proper development of the child.

30

Psychological Testing

IMPORTANCE OF MENTAL TESTS

Psychological tests have been proved to possess great utility in many spheres. Briefly, the utility and importance of mental tests can be observed in the following spheres:

1. **Guidance.** As has been indicated earlier, psychological tests are indispensable in all forms of guidance.
2. **Appointments.** Psychological tests are now-a-days resorted to for the appointment of appropriate individuals to posts in offices factories and government services. It has the doubly beneficial effect of securing proper and desirable jobs for individuals according to their interests inclinations, intelligence and abilities, as well as ensuring that the highest level of efficiency is achieved by the right man being in the right job. In this way, both the employee as well as the employer are benefited.
3. **Selection of Training.** An individual can benefit from training for some particular job only if he is initially in possession of the requisite intelligence, abilities and qualities, besides the necessary interest in the work involved. It is evident, that the individual should be tested in respect of these qualities before any training is imparted to him. Hence, in all advanced nations of the world, all kinds of training institutes make use of psychological tests for selecting the required candidates. In India, for example, the recruitment to the Police Training Colleges, the Govt. Teacher's Training Colleges, and other technical institutions is done only on the basis of psychological tests. In public schools, the students who receive scholarships are selected on the basis of psychological tests in order to ensure that the scholarships are not wasted, as well they might be if they are provided to the wrong individuals.

Psychological tests are farther used for selection or candidates for the National Defence Academy in the country. Such use of psychological tests for the selection of personnel in training, schools is constantly on the increase.

4. **Classification according to Level of Intelligence.** Now-a-days, all educationists agree that the success of education depends upon the student being provided education of a kind that accords with his level of intelligence. Hence, individual students are classified and stratified according to their level of intelligence, and different curricular and extra-curricular programmes devised for the three categories of students, the brilliant, the average and the retarded. The classification is based on intelligence tests. It is not only in the, field of education but also in various vocations, armed forces and industries that intelligence tests are used to classify individuals so that they can be given the proper kind of work that is within their capacity to perform with reasonable success.
5. **Prediction.** The term indicates the forecasting of success in the case of an individual. While guiding the individual, psychologist can normally make fairly accurate predictions as to the degree of success that one is likely to achieve. The prediction is based upon psychological tests; the greater the capacity of a Psychological test to assist in prediction, the greater is its validity and its reliability.
6. **Diagnosis.** Before giving any guidance, the directing psychologists makes a diagnosis of the problem present before him. He gives suggestions for alleviating a certain condition only after he has decided upon a diagnosis, since it is only upon diagnosing some problem that he reaches the root causes and psychological tests are essential for diagnosis; without them a proper diagnosis cannot be achieved.
7. **Research.** Psychological tests are of use even in the field of psychological research. Intelligence tests, interest inventories, personality tests, tests of mental abilities and personality qualities he in research in these specific directions.

What are Mental Tests?

Importance of psychological tests is fairly evident from the preceding exposition of the subject. Before proceeding to a study of the various kinds of tests, it is essential to know the kinds of psychological tests that are in use, and the principal elements active in them. Defining psychological tests, Mursell writes, "A psychological test, then, is a pattern of stimuli selected and organised to elicit responses which will reveal certain psychological characteristics in the person who takes them."[1] In this way, psychological tests are an organisation of some stimuli. These stimuli are selected with some special objectives in view. The object is to discover some psychological characteristics of the person being tested. Stimuli present in psychological tests are called test items and they can be of several kinds — pictures, figures, wooden blocks, word groups, sentences and figures, etc. and the way in which these stimuli uncover psychological characteristics will be evident from a description of each of them.

Psychological Tests and Experimentation

What should here be kept well in mind is that psychological tests differ from psychological experimentation although in both cases some stimuli are given, and it is the reactions to them that are examined. But the main difference between the two is one of purpose. As has been pointed out, the object of psychological tests is to ascertain the psychological characteristics of the subject, while in the case of psychological experimentation, the object is more purely academic as they aim at discovering a mental process concerned with the particular experiment. In this manner, it is evident that while psychological tests lead to the discovery of abilities or capabilities, the psychological experiments discover and, confirm various mental processes. Nevertheless, the difference between the two is very subtle, since now-a-days, psychological tests are also being used for discovering and identifying mental processes.

Classification of Psychological Tests

Mental tests are of various kinds. They have been classified from various different standpoints. Classifications are as follows:

1. **Classification according to Method of Testing.** Tests have been divided into two classes, in this case classification is based on the method involved.
   (a) *Individual Tests:* These tests are administered to one individual at one time, as indicated by the term denoting them. They include performance tests. In addition to these, they also include tests that require linguistic ability. Some examples of these are Standford Binet intelligence test, Weshler Belleview intelligence tests, Kohez's block design test, Rorschach's ink blot test, and T.A.T. Test, etc. These tests are particularly appropriate for testing of individuals, but they are not financially suitable as they are expensive,

1. Mursell, J.L. : *Psychological Testing,* New York, Longmans Green (1953), p. 1.

in addition to requiring more expert training than in many other cases. Secondly, they are less objective than group tests.

(b) *Group tests :* In this category the tests included are performed upon a large number of people simultaneously. Some examples are the group intelligence tests to the Psychological Bureau of Uttar Pradesh, interests lists, vocational lists etc. They are more objective and less expensive requiring very little, if any, specialised training that may prove expensive. But in these tests no real rapport between the subject and the examiner is established. Hence, they are less useful for solving problems of individuals, than are the individuals tests. Nevertheless, they have proved really useful in the case of educational and vocational guidance requirements.

2. **Classification according to the Medium of Instruction.** In these tests, classification is based upon the medium of teaching of the subjects. The psychological tests, from this viewpoint, are divided into the following two classes:

(a) *Verbal Tests:* This classification comprehends tests in which questions are orally asked, linguistic and concerned abilities being essentially required. One of the best examples of verbal tests is Dr. Sohan Lal's intelligence test utilised at Uttar Pradesh Bureau of Psychology. These tests are not intended for and cannot be used in the case of illiterates, only slightly educated persons and small children, since such people lack linguistic ability.

(b) *Non-verbal Tests*: This classification includes tests that do not require the use of language, but substitute figures, pictures, blocks and other implements for it. Examples of it are Pidgon's non-verbal tests and Raven's progressive matrices. Their particular felicity lies in the fact that they can be applied to the testing of illiterates, very slightly educated individuals and very young children. This category includes all non-verbal tests.

3. **Classification according to the Objectives of Testing.** Division of tests oil the basis of their individual objective or aim leads them to be put into the following categories:

(a) *Intelligence Tests:* These help to test the intelligence in the form of both verbal and non-verbal tests. They can be administered both to the individual and to a large group.

(b) *Testing of Mental Abilities*: In this is included the various tests of mental abilities such as tests of spatial ability, artistic ability, mechanical ability etc.

(c) *Interest Tests:* These tests help to discover the interest of the individual, some examples of which are Strong's Vocational Interest Blank, and Cudor's vocational inventory. Both of them are described in detail at a later stage. Besides these, the vocational interest list devised by the Bureau of Psychology, Uttar Pradesh is also an effective test.

(d) *Aptitude Test*: These tests are devised by combining the different tests of mental abilities.

(e) *Personality Tests:* These help to find out the individual's personality traits or characteristics. The main methods of personality testing are Rorschach's Ink Boot test and T.A.T.

Characteristics of Good Tests

Good tests of a psychological nature bear the following features:

1. **Reliability.** The higher the degree of reliability that results of a test have the greater is considered the reliability of the test itself and the reliability of its conclusion means that if the same test is performed upon the same individual more than once, results obtained in each individual list should be the same or commensurate with the first one, if it is modified by changed circumstances.
2. **Validity.** The validity of a test is the fact that it, succeeds in testing the particular quality which it is designed to test. For example, intelligence tests can be valid only if they, in fact, test correctly the intelligence level of the individual subject.
3. **Objectivity.** A test can achieve a high level of objectivity only if the answer to each of its various questions is distinct and precise and if there is no difference of opinion, regarding it among the various examiners. Its efficacy lies in the fact that the conclusion or result is in no way influenced by the examiner's individual thoughts or opinions, so that the conclusions or results are obtained no matter what the number of examiners who examine the same subject.
4. **Comprehensiveness.** Another feature of a good test is its comprehensive nature. This feature involves inclusion of all features or qualities allied to the one in question. It will provide information on qualities, concerned with the one quality actually being tested. In this manner, in a comprehensive test, questions cover the quality in question as well as allied qualities so that no aspect of the measured or tested ability escapes attention.

5. **Discriminating power.** This term applies to, the ability which helps to distinguish between persons with greater or less ability so that they score more or less points or marks.
6. **Utility.** This feature concerns the extent to which a particular test can be used with facility. And for this it is essential that the questions asked should be simple, the method easy, the time involved less and the expenses negligible.

Of the above mentioned characteristics, the most important are validity and reliability. Hence, both these qualities will be described in detail here.

VALIDITY

What is Validity?

It is apparent from the description of intelligence tests that all tests do not have a common degree, of validity, it being completely dependent upon the extent to which any judgement based upon the test's result is objective. For example, validity in the case of intelligence tests can be attributed only to those tests that actually succeed in testing the individual's level of intelligence. A test can be accepted as valid only to that degree to which it can correctly gauge the intelligence of the subject. In this way, validity of a test is that quality on the basis of which the correctness or incorrectness of judgements based upon it is evaluated. For example, the validity of interest tests is less than the case of intelligence tests. Here there is a slight difficulty. Suppose, for the moment, that the intelligence of some students was measured by one particular method. Now the validity of the test will depend upon whether the students tested do in fact possess the intelligence that they are indicated as possessing. The problem that arises here is how can one ascertain whether the students do or do not possess the intelligence indicated by the above test. Evidently, there must be some independent criterion for deciding upon the validity of the particular test in question or tests in general. In this case of the intelligence level of students, the examination results can be the basis for measuring the validity of the test. Generally speaking, it can be said that if there is a correlation between marks obtained at an examination and the result of the test, then the test is valid.

Kinds of Validity

But as is evident from the foregoing description, validity is a relative term, as no test can have complete validity. Hence whenever a particular test is termed valid, or whenever the lack of validity of a test is in question, it is necessary to indicate the, sense in which it is considered valid or invalid. Apparently, validity is of many kinds. Psychologists have roughly accepted the following kinds of validity:

1. **Face Validity.** Face validity is concerned with the form of the test. Such a validity is attributed only to the test which provides an item or subject that appears valid.
2. **Content Validity.** Another kind of validity is content validity in which the validity of the test is based on the validity of its contents. In order to obtain this kind of validity in a particular test, it is essential that the items of a test should achieve the objective for which they are originally designed. For example, content validity in the case of an intelligence test will be attributed only in the event of its succeeding in discovering all factors concerned with intelligence.
3. **Factorial Validity.** This is inclusive or the validity of the factors in the test and in order to judge whether a test has factorial validity, it is examined by the method of factor analysis, and a correlation between this result and the evident factor resultant of tests is established.
4. **Predictive Validity.** This the ipost popular form of validity. In this, results are obtained on the basis of a particular criterion, and correlation between the scores and the criterion is established. In this, the choice of a criterion requires much care and attention. The coefficient obtained by this correlation between scores and criterion is called the validity coefficient. The validity coefficient varies between 0.5 and 0.8. A lower coefficient makes the test inapplicable and lacking in utility, while a higher coefficient is not normally obtained.
5. **Concurrent Validity.** It resembles the predictive validity since in it, too, a correlation between the test and some definite standard is established. But, despite these common features, there are also some definite variations.

From the above analysis of the various kinds of validity it is evident that validity exists in a particular context, or in other words, every test is valid for a particular objective and for a particular age group in individuals. It can just as well be invalid for a particular age group in individuals and in a particular context. Hence, to attribute validity to a test without qualification is completely unjustified and inaccurate. For the sentiment to have any value or meaning, it is essential to state the context and conditions in which it is applicable.

RELIABILITY

What is Reliability?

In addition to validity, it is essential that in every test there be a definite element of reliability. It is only then that the conclusions of the test can be considered reliable and worthy of trust. Reliability of a test consists in any quality, in the test that may inspire confidence and trust. And this quality can be attributed to only that test which provides the same score every time it is performed on the same individual. Now, if some intelligence test yields one score for an individual at one time, and another if it is applied to the same individual at a different time, it is only too evident that such a test cannot be considered reliable and his reliability of the test does not reside in any one part of it, but in its wholeness or completeness. Its reliability will considerably be weakened and decreased if even one part of it is injured in some respect. Hence, it is essential that the internal parts of a test possess internal consistency and uniformity. It is only on the basis of such a reliable test that guidance can be given.

Means of measuring Reliability

Reliability can be measured in the following four ways:

1. **Test Retest Method.** One method of gauging reliability is to perform the same test of the same group of individuals on two different occasions, and to test the scores or results obtained. One group of individuals can be subjected to the Binet intelligence test. Then later on the same group of individuals can again be subjected to the Binet intelligence test. If the results obtained in each case do not tally, then the tests cannot be considered reliable.
2. **Parallel form Method.** Another method of judging the reliability of a particular method is to prepare a method similar to the one being judged and examined. Now the same group can be examined through the basic and then through the modified or parallel methods. Finally, the results of the two can be compared to judge the reliability of the test. Gulliksen has suggested that more than one parallel method be devised for greater accuracy.
3. **Split half Method.** Another method of judging the reliability of a test is to divide the components of the test into even and odd times whose results can be individually obtained. Now the results can be compared to show the reliability of the test.
4. **Inter Item Consistency.** In this method of measuring the reliability of a psychological test only one method is applied at one time. The mutual relation between the scores obtained for

each specific item in the test is observed. At the same time the relation between the marks obtained for one specific question and the marks obtained for the whole test is also ascertained. As this method of measuring reliability involves considerable statistical skill in correlation, psychologists Cudor and Richardson, have devised some formulae for application in this method.

As has been indicated previously, the implication and meaning, of reliability also change the method of judging reliability. Hence, it is not sufficient to remark that a particular test is reliable. It is equally essential that the sense in which reliability is judged also be mentioned, or in other words mention must be made of the method by which its reliability has been established.

Of the above mentioned methods of judging reliability of psychological tests, the third is the most prevalent and useful, since it is the most easy. In this method, the necessity of collecting the same group of individuals more than once is obviated. Reliability is known from the coefficient of reliability, and this coefficient is known as the reliability coefficient.

In this manner, both reliability and validity are important qualities of tests. Validity is related to the scale or structure of the test while reliability is an attribute of its ability of testing.

The aim and object of education is the comprehensive, overall development of the child. This development and progress is gradual. Hence, it is essential to examine the child at regular intervals to find out the extent to which he has progressed. In the school, students study a number of subjects. To test one in respect of these subjects from time to time is essential as it makes clear the success with which be is studying and understanding them. It is the examination that makes it possible for one to know the child's achievements in terms of ability in learning these subjects. Hence, in almost all schools some mode of examining the children, in respect of their attainments in learning and retaining all that is taught to them, is present.

INTELLIGENCE TEST

Historical Outline

As the new individual dissimilarities came to light, psychologists tried to measure the various individual differences, and to this end, different tests were evolved. Among these tests, those devised to measure intelligence achieved a lot of fame. Near the close of the 19th century, Galton developed some tests to measure the function of the different organs. By these, Galton measured sensory discrimination, sensory perception and sensory acuity. Though these, measures are not directly related to intelligence they may be accepted as the forerunners of intelligence tests.

In 1880, Ebbinghaus prepared several tests to measure the differences in the intelligence of various individuals. In 1890, a famous American psychologist Cattell evolved some mental tests. On the basis of these, Cattell measured individual differences between some students of Columbia University in respect of the speed of reactions, sensory acuity, memory and some other simple mental activities.

But in fact, the first concrete step in the direction of intelligence tests was taken by a famous French psychologist Alfred Binet. Alfred Binet was conducting some research in the mental activities of school-going children. In the course of his research he observed that in order to give any useful education to the feeble-minded children it is essential to put them in special classes. In order to investigate this subject a committee headed by Binet was formed in 1904. The first difficulty, concerning the study of feeble-minded children, was need of a scale with which to measure the intelligence of children.

With Simon's assistance Binet developed and published a sea in 1905, known as the Binet-Simon Scale. In this scale, some 50 tasks, from the simplest to the most complex, were prescribed in a serial order. On the basis of experiments with the average and feeble-minded children carried out with the help of this scale Binet and Simon determined norms for various age levels. According to the Binet-Simon intelligence tests, if a five-year old child is capable of performing tasks which an average child of three can perform, his mental age will be rated as three years and if that child fails to perform more than the first five among the thirty tasks he will be classed as idiot.

Binet and Simon made revisions in this scale from time to time. The first revised scale was published in 1908. From the success of this revision, psychologists of other countries developed intelligence tests suitable to the environment of their own countries. Among them, Burt's London Revision and Termans Standford Revision are well known. The modern revised edition of the 2nd revision was published in 1937 under the name of Terman Merrill Scale.

In the Terman Merrill Scale which was a revision of the Stanford Binet Scale, some more subjects, related to intelligence tests were included. It now became usefiil for the age range of 2 to 18 years. In this scale, there were provisions for two types of tests, yearly and half yearly, for children belonging to the age group of two to four years. Many other subjects were included for the adult people. For every age group there were six to eight subjects. In this scale there are tests which enable the examiner to examine the intelligence of an individual in a very short time.

In Indian conditions, Binet's test was adopted for the first time by Dr. C. Herbert Rice. But its revised form is almost completely different from the Binet tests. These tests were compiled in Urdu and Punjabi. There are two types of scale in it, one having 10 tasks, the other 35 tasks, and it was the smaller scale of tests which proved dependable. In 1927, Dr. J. Munry of Christian College started verbal group tests in Urdu, English and Hindi. In 1933, Mr. Lajja Shankar developed group tests for children from 10 to 18, which adopted a revised and studied form of Terman group tests. Besides these, the group tests started by Dr. Jalota of Lahore, in Hindi, in Urdu and English proved very valuable. In Bihar, under the direction of Dr. S.M. Mohsin, a test battery was constructed to measure mental abilities and intelligence of participants in many group tests. In the non-verbal group tests, Menzel has created tests founded upon the ability of Indian children in drawing. Besides, Mr. I.R. Kumaria organised group tests for college students. The other important contributions in this direction have come from Dr. Lalit Kumar Shah, C.T. Philip, H.C. Banerjee, D.H. Roy, T.P. Bhowmick and H.P. Maiti. The above description makes it quite clear that not much work has been done in the direction of non-verbal tests. There is hope of development in this direction in the future.

Types of Intelligence Tests

Intelligence tests are classified as follows according to the activities prescribed in them:

1. Verbal Tests,
2. Non-Verbal Tests.

As the name itself suggests, verbal tests make use of language while the non-verbal tests include such activities which do not necessitate the use of language. Both these types are suitable for individual as well as group tests. Consequently, verbal and non verbal tests are further sub-divided into two classes-individual and group. Thus, finally, there are four types of intelligence tests:

1. Verbal Individual Intelligence Tests,
2. Non-Verbal Individual intelligence Tests,
3. Verbal Group Intelligence Tests,
4. Non-Verbal Group Intelligence Tests.

Verbal Individual Intelligence Tests

The very name verbal individual intelligence tests suggests that there are intelligence tests given to individuals or in other words they are meant to test the intelligence of individuals. Language finds adequate use in them. Binet-Simon tests and the various revisions are all included in this classification.

The State Manovigyanshala of Uttar Pradesh has made a Hindi version of the Terman Merrill Scale. This revision includes a variety of material, from solid object to difficult questions. The activities in the beginning are simple like constructing a bridge or tower of blocks or fitting in irregular wooden blocks in their proper place supplied for them. At the same time, at the end of the tests there are difficult questions which need considerable thinking. This test is divided into several age, groups. The higher groups use language and its use gradually declines with the age group. For example, the two year's group includes the following activities:

1. The form panel with three holes,
2. Recognising of objects by name,
3. Recognising the organs of the body,
4. Making a tower of blocks,
5. Naming an object from its pictures,
6. Word building.

Non-verbal Individual Intelligence Tests

It is quite apparent from the above example that in verbal test the child's knowledge of language is more in demand, and, therefore, the use of these tests is limited to students and literate persons But these verbal tests cannot be used in the case of illiterate individuals as these tests involve an extensive use of language which fails as a medium to measure the individual differences between the illiterates. Consequently, illiterate individuals are tested with the help of non- verbal individual intelligence tests. The name itself indicates the nature of these tests. These tests involve the least possible use of the linguistic ability and are similarly almost unaffected by knowledge derived from books. An example of these non-verbal tests is the Performance Intelligence Tests.

It would be in keeping with the context of our discussion to understand in detail the performance intelligence test as an example of the non-verbal individual intelligence tests. The word 'performance' is usually applied to tests which require a minimum use of understanding and language. Thus, these tests make use of items requiring performances and not language and these tests can be applied to children, illiterates, feeble-minded individuals as well as foreigners.

Merrill-Palmer Block building Tests

One of the most important of performance tests for children is Merrill-Palmer Block Building Test. Besides Seguin Form Board it includes Block building test as well. In the figure given here a four year old girl is making a structure by means of blocks as demonstrated by the tester.

FIg. 18

Pintner Paterson Performance Scale

An example of the performance intelligence tests is the Pintner-Paterson performance Scale. It was evolved by Pintner and Paterson in 1917. In this scale there are 15 types of tests, of which 4 are form boards, 6 picture completion, memory span and the rest picture puzzles and imitations etc.

Porteus Maze Test

Another example of the performance intelligence tests is the Porteus Maze Test. In it paper and pencil mazes are used. For his tests, Porteus created mazes for children from 3 to 14 years. It gets difficult, corresponding to the increase in age. The subject is allowed two chances and if he fails in the attempts then the conclusion is that his intelligence is not of that age level. Children of 12 to

FIg. 19

14 years are given four opportunities. These tests designed by Porteus not only measure intelligence, but they also reflect the temperament of the individual. It is distinguished from other tests in as much as that it includes some aspects ignored by such tests as the Stanford-Binet tests.

Form Board Test

A comparatively simple example of the performance intelligence test is the form board tests, among them the tests of Seguin and Goddard deserve special mention. In the form board test, there are numerous blocks and a board in which there are holes corresponding to this block. The subject as shown in Fig. 20 has to fit the blocks in these corresponding holes in the board, the time taken and mistakes committed being noted from which the score test is calculated.

Wechsler Bellevue Test

Another example of the performance intelligence tests is the Wechsler Bellevue test, evolved in 1939, meant for people from 10 to 60 years of age. In a modern clinic, these tests are included in Binet class, as one of the most important. In this way it is the most apt test for measuring the intelligence of adults. In this test there are five verbal tests and five performance tests. This test affords not only an index to mental abilities but also a profile of abilities.

Fig. 20

Bhatia's Battery of Performance Tests

The description of performance intelligence tests is incomplete without reference to Bhatia's Battery of performance tests. It is the battery created by the former director of Uttar Pradesh Manovigyanshala, Dr. Chandra Mohan Bhatia. It has the following 5 sub-tests:

1. **Kohez Block Design Test.** 10 items of tests out of the Kohez block design test have been included in the battery. There is one card on every subject upon which is depicted a colour design. The subject or the examinee sees this design and makes a similar one out of the blocks as shown in the Fig. 21. These designs become correspondingly more and more complex, having been simple at the start.

Fig. 21

2. **Alexander Pass Along Test.** The Bhatia battery also includes Alexander pass along test, in which, too, there are some designs. As shown in figure no. 22. the subject shifts coloured pieces in an open box and places them in similar design.

Fig. 22

3. **Pattern Drawing Test.** This test has been developed by Dr. Bhatia himself. In this there are eight cards on each of which there is a particular form. The subject draws a particular figure or pattern after seeing this form.
4. **Immediate Memory Test.** Some digits are recited, which are immediately repeated by the subject, this activity throwing some light on the immediate memory of the subject.
5. **Picture Construction Test.** In this sub test there are five subjects in which pictures relating to the rural life are fragmented into 2, 4, 6, 8 and 12 pieces respectively. At one time pieces of a picture are placed before the subject who puts them in order and constructs the picture.

Difficulties in the Individual Intelligence Tests

Some difficulties are faced in both the verbal and non-verbal types of individual intelligence tests. They are roughly as follows:

1. **The Difficulty of Time.** The individual intelligence test takes an hour usually and only one person can be tested at one time, Obviously, at this rate it would be essential to have a very big number of trained examiners and in spite of that it would be difficult to test all the people.
2. **Need for Experienced Examiners.** The second obstacle in the individual intelligence tests is the need for experienced examiners because the correct result cannot be arrived at if the examiners are inexperienced. At the same time, the availability of such a large number of trained personnel is almost impossible.

Notwithstanding these difficulties, in some circumstances the individual intelligence tests become unavoidable. This is because the level of accuracy reached by the individual intelligence tests, in the assessment of a person's intelligence, is beyond the reach of the group intelligence tests.

Verbal Group Intelligence Tests

The group intelligence tests owe their origin and development to the difficulties from which the individual tests suffer. As the name suggests, these tests are designed to test the intelligence of a group and not of an individual. All the people in the group are given the same directions and have to perform the same activities. Even the score of the result of group intelligence tests is calculated by machines thus dispensing with the necessity of skilled examiners, resulting in an economy of time.

Army Alpha and Beta Tests. An excellent example of group intelligence tests is afforded by the Army alpha and beta tests, which were evolved during the World War I in order to test the American soldiers. For example, it revealed separately the feebleminded, men capable of becoming skilled specialists, men capable of becoming officers, men needing some training, etc.

Naval and Army General Classification Tests. Due to the success which attended these tests, some group tests for classification of naval or army soldiers were evolved during the World War II. Of these two particular forms deserve mention. These two are: (1) Naval general classification tests and (2) Army general classification tests.

With the type of calculations made by Cruze, some one billion people were tested by the military general classification tests during the years 1941 to 1946. In these tests there are three subjects, *viz.*, those relating to vocabulary problems, relating to mathematics, and relating to problems of counting blocks.

From the above example, it is quite clear that these verbal group intelligence tests examine the reasoning ability, ability of comparing and contrasting sense of directions, ability in numerals and language, of the individuals who constitute the group. It is essential that the examiner should be fully acquainted with the test and he should also understand the corresponding directions. Thus, often the examiner examines himself to start with. At the same time, it is necessary for the examiner to have some knowledge of the mechanical aspects of the conditions of examination such as the proper seating arrangement of the examinees, the distribution of test blanks and the preparation of material related to tests, like pencils, etc.

Difficulties in the Verbal Group Intelligence Test

Even after taking all the precautions, some difficulties are discernible in the verbal group intelligence tests which can be eliminated only by reverting to the individual intelligence tests. It is due to these difficulties that the individual intelligence tests are considered more realistic than the group intelligence tests. The difficulties of the verbal group tests are fundamentally as follows:

1. **Difficulties relating to Co-operation in Tests.** In these tests it is difficult to judge whether the examinee is extending his full co-operation or not.
2. **Difficulties related to the Balance of the Subject.** In tests it is difficult to determine whether the physical and emotional balance of the examinee is even or disturbed.
3. **Difficulty related to the Ease of the Subject.** In the verbal group intelligence test it is difficult to ascertain if the examinee is feeling at ease and free or restrained.
4. **Possibility of Cheating by the Subject.** Another difficulty in these tests is that no one can testify whether the person has written the answer himself or copied it from his neighbour.

In spite of difficulties which arise in the verbal group intelligence tests, they have their own advantages due to which they are used comprehensively. As has been said before, the advantages are the same as the difficulties of the individual intelligence tests.

Non-verbal Group Intelligence Tests

As has been mentioned before, the verbal intelligence tests are meant only for the literates because of the requirement of linguistic ability. It is for this reason that the non-verbal group intelligence tests have been developed, the examinee making a minimum use of language but performing, instead, many activities. One example of the non-verbal intelligence test is Cattel's Culture Free test and the N.I.I.P. test. An example of the subjects given in these tests is as follows:

In the Fig. 23 there are 3 squares with some figures drawn in the three squares. On the left various figures are shown in five squares. In the given diagram, the fourth square has to be filled with one such figure from the five squares that its relation to the third square must be the same as the relation which the figure in the first square bears to the figure in the second square.

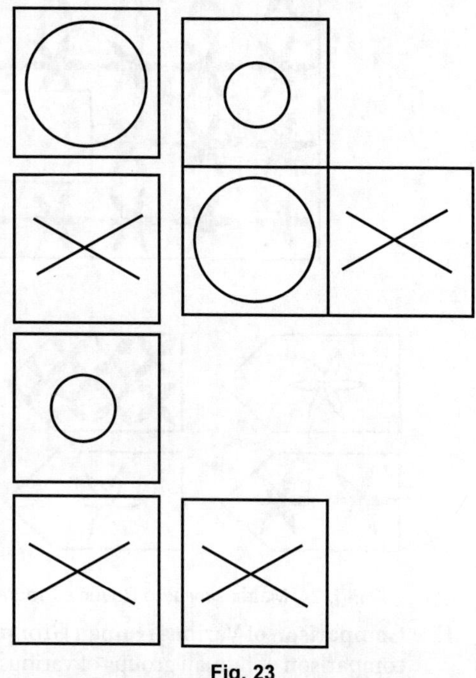

Fig. 23

In these non-verbal group intelligence tests the examiners have to explain to the examinees even the simplest directions which are also demonstrated as far as possible. All this is done to make least possible use of language. There are some performance tests in these group intelligence tests, in which the examinee draws some lines according to his abilities, fills in some empty spaces, draws some simple figures, or performs some simple activities. Some psychologists do not give credence to these non-verbal tests in their role of measuring intelligence of the subjects, while on the other hand some psychologists consider them to be better than verbal tests. For example in Alexander's opinion, "A complete performance battery will be a better measure than a complete verbal battery."

Characteristics of the Non-verbal Group Intelligence Tests

The truth is that even if non-verbal group intelligence tests are not more important than verbal tests, they are certainly not less important than these tests. Some of their characteristics are as follows:

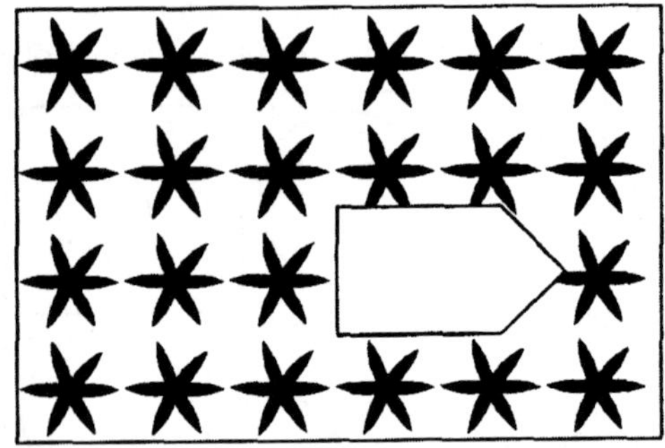

Fig. 24. Matrix similar to Raven's Progressive Matrices.

1. **Comparison of Various Human Groups.** The first obstacle in the comparison of human groups of various languages and cultures is the difference in their language. This obstacle can be over-come by non-verbal group intelligence tests and a comparison between different human groups is rendered possible.
2. **The Testing of Illiterate Soldiers.** The verbal group intelligence tests are manifestly inapplicable to illiterate soldiers for the testing of their intelligence. Consequently, the abilities of illiterate soldiers are assessed by employing the non-verbal group intelligence tests and the possibilities of learning are known.
3. **Intelligence Testing in Children.** The linguistic ability is very low in the case of children and consequently the verbal group intelligence tests cannot be given to them.

Reliability

The reliability of a test depends not on any one item in the test but on the test as a whole. The reliability of the test diminishes if any one item of the test is defective. This is why there must be a uniformity and internal consistency between the various items of the test. It is only on the basis of such a reliable test that correct directions can be given.

Reliability is investigated in three ways. These ways are as follows:

1. The test is applied to the same group under two different conditions and the results thus compiled are compared. Suppose, for example, the group is tested for its intelligence using the Binet test. Now, after sometime, the same group is tested employing the Binet-test. If the I.Q. resulting from both the tests is the same, the Binet tests will be accepted as reliable. If there are some differences between the I.Q. received from the two tests, they will be considered unreliable.
2. In a test in which there are many items, the results of the even and the odd items are compared, to examine its reliability.
3. Another method of examining reliability is to prepare a test parallel to the one whose reliability is under examination. Now a group should be tested by both the original and the transformed forms of the test. This is followed by a comparison of the two results and the reliability of the test is, in this way, examined. Gulliksen has advised the preparation of more than one parallel list.

Among the three methods of examination of reliability, the second is the most popular because it is also the easiest. This method does not necessitate the collection of the group time and again. Reliability is known from the coefficient of correlation which is known as the reliability coefficient.

Thus, both validity and reliability are essential qualities of tests, While validity is related to the scale or structure of the test, reliability is related to the capacity of the test.

MEASUREMENT OF PERSONALITY

Psychologists employ a number of methods to measure personality, *e.g.*, situation test, psycho-analytic test and projective method etc. Besides these, the case history method, interview and questionnaire and rating methods have their own importance. Briefly, the methods of measuring personality are:

1. Case history Method
2. Interview Method
3. Questionnaire Method
4. Performance Method
5. Rating Method
6. Situation Test
7. Psycho-Analytic Test
8. Projection Techniques

Among the above mentioned methods the projection techniques are the most popular. A, brief, description of the other methods, before we make a detailed description of this specific one, would be quite in keeping with the context.

1. **Case History Method.** In the case history method, as the name obviously indicates, the facts concerning the life of the *subject* are collected. This case history supplies all the facts related to man's environment and heredity. This method can be employed to study both normal and abnormal personality but it needs experienced testers.
2. **Interview Method.** The interview method is the most common of all the methods for the study of personality. It is the method widely used in the selection of people for government, semi-government and private services. In this the subject and the tester sit facing each other and the former answers questions asked by the latter. Besides the answers which the subject offers, his personality is indicated by his expression. This method, like the case history method, needs very experienced testers who ask questions which may probe the correct thing and enable the subject to express himself without any apprehension. Thus, the interview method depends as much on the tester as it does on the subject.
3. **Questionnaire Method.** Questionnaires have been used extensively in the investigation of personality. The name suggests that it is a list of selected questions the answers to which throw light upon different traits of personality. 'Yes' and 'No' are written in front of these questions. The subject either strikes out the wrong answer or indicates the correct one. Questionnaires are used to gain knowledge of traits like self-confidence, sociability, introversion or extroversion, tendency to dominate or be dominated etc.

   There are some difficulties in the questionnaire method. It has the following limitations:

   (a) Often the subjects conceal the facts and give wrong answers.
   (b) Sometimes the framing of the questions is such that the tester takes them to mean one thing and the subject another.
   (c) Usually the subjects write the answer without an adequate amount of thinking thus leaving possibility of mistakes.

   In spite of these difficulties, the questionnaire method has proved to be of tremendous value. Allport and Minnesota etc. have formed questionnaires which help in the study of some subtle traits of personality. It affords a lot of assistance to comparative study because of the various answers of the subjects to the same questions. The conclusions based on these questionnaires are comparative as well as numerical. They also facilitate wide study because a number of people can be studied simultaneously.

4. **Performance Method.** The performance method was developed by May and Hartshorne. In this method the subject is given a variety of specific jobs to be performed and the particular trait of his personality is examined. For example, in order to test the honesty of children some weights with little difference between them, were presented to them. The exact weight of each was written under it and the children were told to place them in the correct order. The honest children experienced great difficulty while the dishonest read the weights under them and placed them in order promptly. A very simple method of judging the honesty of the students in the class could be something like this. Some piece should be dictated and the copies collected and examined. The mistakes of each should be secretly noted without any markings on the copy, following which the copies should be returned with the direction that the mistakes are to be noted and marks allocated. The dictation should be written on the black board. The honest will mark their mistakes while the dishonest will quietly correct them. The honesty of the students can be judged by comparing these with the mistakes previously noted.

5. **Rating Method.** Another method of measuring personality is the rating method, in which the procedure is of two types. One the subject is asked to answer questions related to traits of personality. The answers which the subject offers or selects exhibit his personality. Another way of applying the rating method is to place the subject in real situations and then study his behaviour and reactions. For example, in order to judge personality traits a person is given a variety of jobs to perform.

As it is, the rating method is very simple. But it needs more skilful testers. Roughly speaking, it presents the following difficulties:

(a) Much skill and capability are essential in the tester.
(b) The possibility of prejudice is very great.
(c) It is very difficult to enumerate or evaluate the subtle traits. Mistakes are often made in this.

In spite of the above mentioned difficulties, both social and industrial, psychologists make much use of this method. As has been pointed out previously too it can be made useful to a large extent if the tester is very skilful.

6. **Situation Test.** As usual, the name suggests the nature of the method. In it, the subject is placed in some specific situations and the traits of his personality are ascertained. Actually, it resembles the performance method, the difference lying in the fact that in this case the person is placed in a situation while in the performance method he is given some work to do.
7. **Psycho-analytic Method.** In the psycho-analytic method of measurement of personality two types of tests are more popular—Free Association and Dream Analysis. Both these tests show the traits of the personality, in its unconscious aspect. In dream analysis, the subject describes his dream and without using reasoning, associates freely the dream objects and activities. Because of the absence of reasoning the truth of the unconscious mind is expressed by this association, by which the psycho-analyst discovers many characteristics of personality. The psycho-analytic method is mostly used in discovering the personality traits and mental ailments of abnormal people. Its main condition lies in the need for a skilled and experienced psycho-analyst. Often, the psycho-analyst has to analyse his own mind in order to remove the possibility of any prejudice
8. **Projective Techniques.** The most popular of all the methods for the investigation of personality is the projective method. Its name suggests the fact that it is founded upon the element of projection. The Taj Mahal, to take an example, is a marble building many people go to see. Different people find in it different things in keeping with the peculiarities of their personalities. An emotional person sees it in the form of a formal symbol of emotions while to the person who gives importance to political and economic questions it may be a symbol of exploitation. This is an example of a material object but it does make clear the fact that a human being does not see an object as it is but also projects the, traits of his own personality upon it. Many peculiarities of the personality are investigated by an analysis of this projection and a comparison of it with the projections affected by others.

   Two tests in the projective techniques are more widely used:

   1. Rorschach ink-blot test.
   2. Murrey's Thematic Apperception Test, known in brief as T.A.T.

   They are extensively used in the investigation of personality. These will, therefore, be described briefly here.

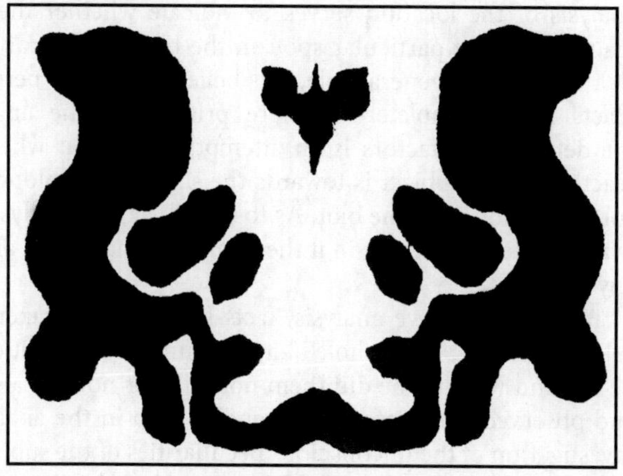

Fig. 25

1. **Rorschach Ink Blot Test.** This test was developed by the Swiss scientist Hermann Rorschach. He used 10 original ink blot cards which are still in use today. There is no picture made in these blots. Five of these are black, two black and red and the other three multicoloured. To investigate personality, they are exhibited before the subject one after the other and he is asked to describe everything he sees in the blot. These are shown for a definite interval of time. Then they are shown to the subject for a second time and he is asked to point out the location, of whatever he had seen, on the blot. In order to establish the meaning of the subject's reaction to the blots, the psychologist analyses the location, determining factors and the object. The

Fig. 26. An Indianised Picture from T.A.T.

analysis of the location serves to indicate whether the subject reacted to some particular spot on the blot or towards the blot as a whole. As a general rule, it is believed that the person who reacts more completely is more principled. The analysis of the determining factors is an attempt to find out whether the reaction of the subject is towards the share of the blot or to the colour or motion in the blot. As to the object, the analysis shows whether the subject sees in it the figure of a man or an animal or anything else.

Besides the above analysis, facts like the time taken by the subject to react to the whole blot, the number of activities which he did and whether he did them normally or not, are also noted and observed. All these things tend to help in the analysis and investigation of the unconscious peculiarities of the subject.

The difficulty in the ink blot test is that the description of the subject's reaction becomes quite subjective, which conceals to some extent the correct personality traits of the subject. But efforts are being made to make this test more objective.

2. **Murrey's Thematic Apperception Test.** The founder of this test, Murrey investigated the personality traits with the help of some pictures. These pictures are still considered to be standard. Observing these pictures, the subject, by projection, identifies himself with the characters in the picture. The pictures are presented one by one to the subject who has to compose a story on each of them within some fixed time period, say five minutes. Unknowingly, the subject expresses many of the peculiarities of his personality in these stories by projection. He does not get time to think. Therefore, the story expresses his natural desires, emotions, sentiments etc. On the basis of these stories, the psychologist analyses the personality of the subject and uncovers its traits.

   As in the Rorschach ink blot test, there is some difficulty in Murray's thematic apperception test, since the personality investigation done by it is not numerical but qualitative with possibility of mistakes. But there is no doubt that an experienced and skilful psychologist can use this method to uncover many hidden traits of the personality of the subject. This test helps in the discovery of many abnormalities of personality as well.

MEASUREMENT OF SPECIAL ABILITIES

Such problems as the profession an individual may adopt, or the course of study a student may profitably pursue are ones that need guidance and for this guidance it is essential that in addition to measuring the individual's level of intelligence, his special abilities are investigated. Hence, efforts have been made to devise tests to discover special mental abilities, and they are being extensively used.

Before going on to a description of the special mental testing of abilities, it is necessary to know the age in which these tests can be suitably administered. This question arises for the simple reason that in childhood, these special abilities are not distinctly present and psychologists are not unanimous in their opinions regarding the age in which these abilities become distinct and separate. According to some, man's special mental abilities can be separately distinguished at the age of 11, while in the opinion of Cyril Burt, it is at 13 that these abilities become distinct. Generally, it is the former opinion that is accepted. Accordingly, all educational guidance is rendered at the age of 11 or thereabouts.

Number of Special Mental Abilities

Having determined the age in which the special mental abilities become distinct, it is now essential that their number also be determined. In fact, it is very difficult to determine the exact number of special abilities, and there is no unanimity of opinion on this question. In 1938, Thurston and his associates fixed the number of special fundamental abilities at seven, calling them Primary Mental Abilities— verbal abilities or V, numerical ability or N, reasoning or R, memory or M, word fluency or W, and spatial ability or S, and perceptual speed or P. The Chicago primary mental abilities test has been based on these mental abilities. Another test battery formed on the same principle is used in the American Psychological Corporation. It contains the following seven tests:

(1) Verbal reasoning,
(2) Numerical ability,
(3) Abstract reasoning,
(4) Space relation,
(5) Mechanical reasoning,
(6) Clerical speed and accuracy,
(7) Language uses.

Now, we can go on to a slightly detailed account of some special abilities tests.

1. **Thurston's S.R.A. Tests of Primary Mental Abilities.** To repeat, Thurston has discovered the presence of seven fundamental abilities through his study. This conception of primary mental abilities wrought a great change in the field of guidance and counselling. Following this discovery in the field of guidance even more importance began to be attached to these abilities than

to intelligence, since mental abilities of different individuals with similar levels of intelligence were found to differ in the extreme. On the other hand, people with the same mental abilities were found to have different levels of intelligence. In fact, the choice of a course of study to be taken up by a student or the choice of a profession by a person requires a test of special abilities more than it requires intelligence tests since success in these fields depends more upon innate as well as acquired ability than upon intelligence. Hence, in England and America many tests of mental abilities were evolved, and they were combined to form test batteries. Then, these test batteries were used extensively in the field of education and professions.

Thurston constructed three batteries of tests for special abilities for various children in the following, three age divisions and used different test items in each of them:

1. **For Children between 5 and 7.** In the test battery for this division, he included tests of verbal reasoning, spatial ability, speed of perceptual knowledge tests of motor ability.
2. **For Children between 7 and 11.** Test battery for this classification includes tests of verbal ability, numerical ability, speed, of logic and perceptual knowledge.
3. **For Children between 11 and 17.** Test battery for this division includes tests of verbal ability, numerical ability, word fluency, spatial ability and power of abstract reasoning.

Tests for Individual Abilit

Test batteries devised by Thurston reveal the main mental abilities of children of different ages, but in addition to this there are individual tests for separate mental abilities. It would be in keeping with the context to describe them also.

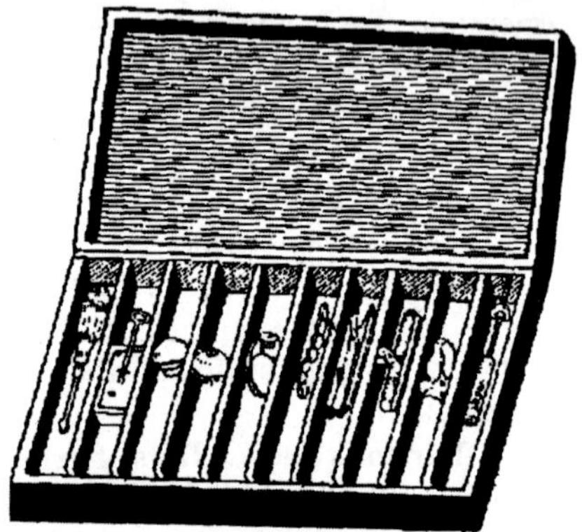

Fig. 27. Box of Minnesota Test.

1. **Spatial Ability Tests.** This reveals the person's spatial or form ability. One example of this is the N.I.I.P. from realtion test devised by the National Institute of Industrial Psychology,

London. It has been described earlier. The Psychological Bureau of Uttar Pradesh has been making use of it for quite some time; besides the Bureau has also formulated its own test for measuring spatial ability. Another example of such a test is the Minnesota Paper Form Board which includes 64 test items in which one has to combine various incomplete geometrical forms to complete figures. In the Minnesota Spatial Relation Test, there are four tests of the form board. Both these, tests have proved to be of immense value.

2. **Mechanical Ability Tests.** Through these tests, the person's ability of handling mechanical devices is measured. For this, some laboratories use paper and pencil while other use mechanical tools and objects. One example of this is the Minnesota Mechanical Assembly tests. In this there are three boxes that contain the various parts of some common mechanical device. In the test, these parts have to be put together to form the complete objects. Other test of mechanical ability that are famous are the Bennett Test of Mechanical Comprehension, and MacQuarrie Test for Mechanical ability.
3. **Motor Dexterity Tests.** In these tests, the motor ability of the hands and fingers is measured. Examples of such tests are Bennett Hand Tool Dexterity Test, Purdue Peg Board Steadiness Tester and O' Co-nor Tweezer Dexterity Test. Only the first two will be described here.

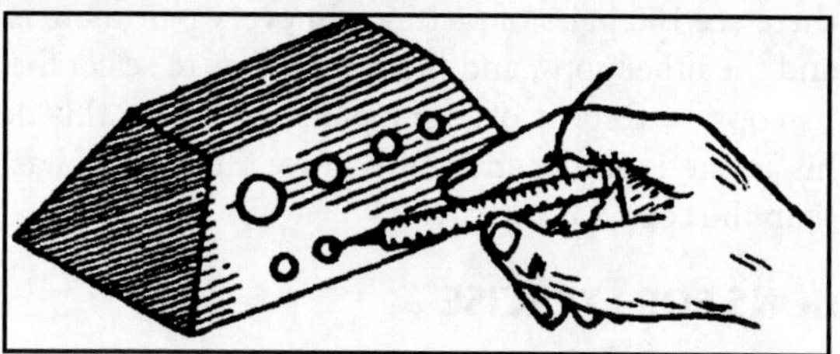

Fig. 28. Steadiness Tester.

(a) *Steadiness Tester:* This device examines the steadiness of the hand and the fingers. In this there is a box, on one side of which there are numerous holes arranged systematically so that they proceed from the widest to the smallest. The subject takes an instrument called the stylus into his hand and inserts it completely and draws it out of these holes successively. If in doing so the stylus touches any of the walls of the hole, a bell rings. The test consists in the ability to prevent the stylus touching the wall while inserting it into the hole and drawing it out. The hole in which the bell rings is tried thrice by the subject. This test helps to discover the individual's dexterity with his hand and fingers, and the extent to which he can handle minute instruments.

(b) *O' Conor's Tweezer Dexterity Test:* In this test, there are 100 small holes on a board, in rows of ten each. There are 100 pins placed by the side. The subject has to use a tweezer to place each of these pins in this board, one in each hole. He scores according to the short time that he takes to complete this task.

4. **Clerical Tests.** These tests measure the individual's ability concerning writing and composition. It is composed of tests in arithmetic, word groups, distinct reading and good writing, tests in direct knowledge, etc. One example of the clerical tests is the Minnesota Clerical test which has two parts. In one part there are pairs of numbers, the correct pair having to be marked in which both numbers are given. In the other part one has to point pairs of names that are similar.
5. **Artistic or Aesthetic Ability Test.** In these, the individual's ability concerning art is tested. One example of this is the McAdory Art Test. Sea Shore Measure of Musical Talent measures the individual's ability in respect of music. Meier Art Judgement Test is another test of artistic and aesthetic ability. In this test there are 100 pairs of pictures. In every pair there is one original and the other copy, and the student has to select the original and its copy in respect of every pair. Success in this depends upon his aesthetic ability and acuity since the original has more beauty than the copy.

QUESTIONS FOR EXERCISE

1. What is psychological testing? What are different types of mental tests?
2. How is intelligence measured? Give examples.
3. Give examples of some ability tests.

31

Child Guidance

Students are perpetually perplexed with the problem of selecting suitable subjects in the course of their study. It often happens that no care is taken in making such a selection, an ill-considered selection being made. A girl decides not to study mathematics because her sister happened to fail in that subject, while another boy takes up the study of music because he is under the illusion that it is easy to pass in this subject. Another has taken up the study of science because his parents have ordered him to do so. All such methods of selection and other modifications upon them are completely unscientific. No student should turn to the study of merely because it is an enduring passion with him to become an engineer. It is not at all essential that he may be possessed of the qualities of an engineer. Often the child endeavours to achieve that which appears glamorous or creditable to him. And on the basis of this interest or attraction nothing can be said of the success or failure with which he is likely to meet. It is totally wrong and irresponsible to select a subject either because he has been told to do so or for a variety of other equally ephemeral and meaningless reasons. The basis of the selection of subjects should be the child's individual tendencies and ability. And, these tendencies and abilities cannot be understood merely by observing them. For this, a systematic and scientific testing is required. There is no student whose life is totally devoid on any problem whatsoever; whether he is rich or poor, he must face some private troubles. Most students manage to cope with these problems in some or the other manner, but there are numerous other students who fall to achieve some solution on their own effort. In this manner, some students frequently need some or the other kind of psychological guidance while others have to have recourse to it occasionally. This psychological guidance is intended to help them solve their problems. These problems are involvements of behaviour, both internal and external. Educational psychology makes use of the principles of psychology for the synthesis of this very behaviour or conduct. Evidently, guidance is required for the solution of personal problems.

WHAT IS GUIDANCE?

The term guidance has been used in the above account of the help that psychology can render in the solution of vocational, educational and personal problems. Educational guidance is required in the field of education, vocational guidance in the field of profession and vocation, and personal guidance in the individual's personal life. Before going on to a detailed account of what these three forms entail it would be better to understand what guidance is. Guidance may be defined as the process of helping the individual in selecting, preparing, entering and progressing in the behavioural patterns which comprise human activities in the educational, vocational, recreational field as well as in connection with community service group. This help takes the form of personal help on the psychologist's part. It is, again, in the form of advice. This does not solve problems but only helps the individual in solving his problems. Husband, in his book entitled *Applied Psychology*, has defined the term thus "Guidance may be defined as assisting the individual to prepare for his future life, to fit him for his place in society."[1] In this way, guidance prepares the individual for his life. It informs the individual of the kind of education that the requires, the subjects that he would be advised to choose in his study, the vocation to which he should apply himself when old enough, as well as the means he should employ when faced with problems that he must solve in society every individual has a specific status and certain roles that are concomitant with it. For example, a male member is head of his family, and from this position is derived his responsibility of providing for the needs of the family and keeping in mind the proper development of every member. But an individual does not maintain the same status throughout his life. At one and the same or different times he passes through stages where he occupies the status of son, father, husband, teacher or advocate a citizen of the nation, etc. In each of these different statuses he has distinct and definite roles to play. The person who has ability or sense enough to work as befits his status in society is the one who wins the acclaim of society and its approval as well. It is in the performance of these various roles and duties, which conform to his differing statuses, that he needs guidance. In this way, the psychologist's guidance helps the individual fit into his

1. Husband, *Applied Psychology*, p. 15.

role and status in society. Every individual is not fit to take up any and every position in society. Teaching, doctoring, advocacy and a variety of other professions are not jobs that require the same individual qualities from the person occupied in doing them. Introducing fitness in an individual to occupy some position is a matter that has two aspects. The first is that his ability should be commensurate with the requirements of the job and the second that he should try to become qualified to occupy that position. The second of these aspects has some limitations. Whatever the effort expended every person cannot become an artist or author, because every individual does not have the ability or quality to adopt any and every profession. Even every individual cannot become a successful trader as that requires a definite, shrewd and calculating, mentality that is not possessed by everyone. Hence, in order to prove able for some particular position a person should choose the position that concurs with his capabilities and qualities. Educational psychology helps the individual in his choice. In this way, guidance helps the individual to settle down into positions that are, or are not of his own choosing. As has been said in the preceding definition guidance helps to prepare the individual for this future life. Preparation for the future life implies creating ability in the individual to bear responsibilities that fall to his lot. These future responsibilities can take a variety of forms. Normally, for example, every boy and girl gets married when he and she grows up, creates a family and indulges in prolific procreation. In this manner, every individual is to face in the future responsibilities concerning his children, responsibilities concerning the partner he has chosen for life as well as further responsibilities of the family in general. And in the normal circumstances, again, most young men and some young women have also to adopt some or the other profession, whether to their liking or not. A child grown up to be not only a man but also a citizen of his country and in this position certain rights devolve upon him that bring with them some additional responsibilities. Consequently, when we talk of preparing an individual for the future we mean to prepare him for bearing his responsibilities ably and sufficiently whether he be called upon to do so in the field of family relations, the economic sphere, the political field or any other situation in life. For this every individual boy and girl should turn to a profession that conforms to the education they have had so that they may be in positions for which they have been prepared and act with skill and confidence. They should decide upon the profession that they would like to adopt. They should have the capacity to face and solve the problems as well as the problems that are likely to arise in relation with others. Guidance helps the individual in all these kinds of efforts.

It should be quite apparent from the above detailed discussion on the meaning of the term that guidance helps in determining the objective of life. in establishing a synthesis in life and in solving various kinds of problems In the words of Jones, "Guidance is the personal help that is given by one person to another in developing life goals, in making adjustment and in solving problems that confront him in the attainment of goals".[1] In this manner guidance is personal assistance. Although guidance is sometimes offered at the group level, yet even in these matters every member of the group is also individually given advice. Applied psychology is based on the conception of individual differences. General experience and scientific research have both established that every single individual has certain abilities, problems and difficulties that are distinctly his own, as distinct from those of others. Evidently, if any advice or guidance is to be rendered, it must he rendered individually and personally. This personal help is forthcoming from one individual to another. One of these two individuals is a psychologist, or one who knows psychology and the other a person who is in need of psychological guidance. Guidance, then, is the help rendered to an individual by the psychologist. In its more extensive sense the term may be taken to comprehend the advice rendered by any individual who is in the know concerning psychology to another who is in need of it. For example, if a father guides his son in solving a problem, this, too, amounts to guidance, irrespective of the fact that it may or may not be based on the most correct notion of psychological principles. But this extensive meaning of the term is its general meaning and implication. In a scientific analysis it is not taken in its general meaning but reduced to more definite and precise terms whereby its meaning becomes limited. That is why it is first defined. Guidance in psychology, means a particular thing. It is the personal advice or service rendered by a psychologist, and not by any Tom, Dick and Harry, to another person. This guidance takes the form of advice which helps the guided individual to adjust to various conditions and circumstances. If one would only look at it that way, it would become evident that adjustment is the basic problem of human life. The person who fails to adjust to his circumstances becomes a failure, suffers himself and inflicts it upon others, and is branded an abnormal being. In this way, educational psychology, through its helping the individual in adjusting himself, helps to spread happiness, peace and organisation in society. Problems in human life do not come to an end, because new ones keep on arising, There is no end to trouble. A child, for example, is faced by very new problems, much of his anxiety being centred around the work forced upon him by the teacher, or the means of dealing with the more recalcitrant of his friends and such minor things.

1. Jones, *A.J., Principles of Guidance,* McGraw-Hill Book Co., New York (1951), p. 85.

He has not to worry about keeping the home fires burning. But these are problems that gradually engulf every individual as be grows older. As a general rule most people marry and have children who must go to school and with equal inevitability fall ill and he treated for it, Only to grow up and get married themselves and keep the almost eternal circle moving forward. Thus one trouble grows out of another, and never lets the individual being sit back contented and unhurried. Human psychology is much like this. One desire arises and destroys the being's peace till it is satisfied. Hence, he immediately busies himself. If in searching for the means to satisfy this desire and achieves this after more or less trouble. But the story does not end here, it is followed by the arising of another desire, and the inevitable circle of objective, search for objective, obstacles in search for means of solving the desire, over coming of the obstacles, possession of the satisfying object, satisfaction of the desire, and the arising of another desire. It is evident that every individual is continually faced with new objective the achievement of which entails the facing of many other difficulties. As Jones has stated in his definition, guidance helps the overcoming of these difficulties that beset the achievement of an objective.

KINDS OF GUIDANCE

As has been pointed out, an individual has to run to the psychologist, in the latter's role of a specialist, for personal advice when he fails to solve the problems that confront him. This personal advice is guidance. How this guidance can take effect depends on the fact that it be given in the context of some problem the solution of which is being sought. As a matter of fact it is no easy matter to recount all the possible problems that arise in, various spheres of human life, but some psychologists have attempted a classification of them. For example, Jones has divided the problems of life into eight spheres on the basis of their nature:

(1) Related to health and psychological development, (2) Related to house and family, (3) Related to time for recreation, (4) Concerned with personality, (5) Religious, (6) Educational, (7) Social and (8) Vocational or occupational. Having achieved the classification of problems it becomes possible to classify the kinds or forms of guidance that is to be given correspondingly. For example, vocational guidance is required in connection with profession and educational guidance in the field of education Psychologists have professed many and various kinds of guidance. For example, Myers has mentioned the following eight kinds of guidance:

(1) Vocational Guidance,
(2) Educational Guidance,
(3) Recreational Guidance,
(4) Civic Guidance,
(5) Community Service Guidance,
(6) Social and Moral Guidance,
(7) Health Guidance,
(8) Leadership Guidance.

The present chapter makes a study of three kinds of guidance. The Bureau of Psychology, Uttar Pradesh, has also put guidance in these three categories, and much the same classification of guidance kinds has been followed in the other Indian states as well. These three kinds are: (1) Educational guidance, (2) Vocational guidance and (3) Personal guidance.

If the matter is looked at closely it will be seen that the above three classes in fact include all kinds of classification. If child guidance is considered, for example, and this guidance requires the opening of clinics in various places, it will be found that problems concerning the children are either concerned with education or are of a personal nature. Hence, child guidance is jointly comprehended under educational and personal guidance. Similarly, the various forms of guidance, such as health guidance, recreational guidance, civic guidance, social and moral guidance, community service guidance and leadership guidance are all comprehended in personal guidance.

Dividing of the various spheres of guidance dose not imply that these spheres are completely separated and uncounted. In fact guidance is a dynamic and progressive concept in which advice given on every aspect of human life is comprehended, but nevertheless with a view to convenience in discussion, its aspects and spheres have been differentiated. Educational guidance and vocational guidance are closely related, and both of them are very intimately concerned with personal guidance. The basis of this correlation between the various spheres is that all problems of human beings, are connected with each other. For example, when a person experiences difficulty in selecting a particular curriculum or a definite profession, his indecision may stem from certain personal difficulties. It happens quite often that young men become so engrossed in their love affairs that they are not able to devote any serious thought to their careers and future. Death of a close and loved relative may be another reason why he may be at a loss and grouping in the dark. The fundamental problem here is of a personal nature, with the result that all educational or vocational guidance to such an individual will be modified by the personal guidance given to him. On the other hand, many personal problems may be the consequence of certain deficiencies of education and the lack of educational guidance. If a child runs away from school and becomes vagrant, finds no interest in study but chooses to pursue a life of crime or one of anti social conduct, then it is evident that there is something wrong somewhere and as likely as not it may be that his choice of curriculum may have been undesirable. In much the same manner certain individual and personal problems may be the outcome of an absence of vocational guidance. A young man, for example, in his schooldays may have been a very fine sportsman, and by its virtue he would naturally not appreciate a job that ties him down, offers no opportunity of leadership, and does not allow the development of any of his sportsman like qualities like motivation, patience, adventure and courage. If he is forced to take on such a job for a variety of reason, it would be natural for him to become irritable and lose his mental balance and calm to some extent. This may lead to further complications in the form of personal problems. Here the personal problems have been caused by lack of proper vocational guidance. Similarly, educational, vocational and personal guidance are naturally related.

CLASSIFICATION ACCORDING TO MODE OF GUIDANCE

The above classification that we have been viewing is made on the basis of problems for which such guidance is required. If the mode of guidance is taken into consideration guidance can be classified in the following manner:

(1) Individual Guidance,
(2) Group Guidance.

Before going on to a detailed description of educational, vocational and personal guidance, it would be advisable to comprehend this classification of guidance made on the basis of its modes.

1. **Individual Guidance Method.** In the individual guidance method the person to be guided and his guide, the psychologist, are in direct and personal contact with each other. He invades the ill person's house and makes a study of his family conditions, and for this purpose he interviews the various members of the individual's household. Besides the family background, the individual's social, financial and cultural background is also investigated so that no possible source of information is left untapped. And for this it becomes essential to study his neighbourhood and to collect as many facts of his life as are possible so as to build up fairly complete case history. The schools

and colleges that he has attended are contacted in order to gain information concerning his behaviour and scholastic attainments there. His teachers, too are consulted on the matter.

Study of this type and the collection of all possible information concerning the individual is followed by testing of the individual himself. He is made to take tests of intelligence, specific mental abilities, interests, attitudes and personality. Interview is another weapon that is used to uncover much information and, incidentally, to learn the patient's opinion of himself. Accordingly, then in individual guidance the following information concerning the individual is gathered:

(1) Information concerning his intelligence, mental abilities, interests, attitudes and personality.
(2) Information concerning family conditions.
(3) Information concerning the social, financial and cultural background.
(4) Other relevant information.

Having gathered all this information it is subjected to close and intelligent scrutiny, and then curative measures are introduced to remove the problems which have made this guidance necessary.

Among these efforts are logical arguments, suggestions psychoanalysis.

The individual guidance method has the following qualities:

(1) It renders almost complete information concerning the individual. Hence a proper cure can be effected.
(2) Cures in this method are simpler and more effective.

Despite these advantages, the method suffers from the following drawbacks:

(1) It consumes much time, with the result that a very large number of psychologists are required if there is a big number of patients.
(2) Accordingly, this method is extremely expensive also.
(3) It needs highly trained and specialist psychologists.

(2) **Group Guidance Method.** The shortcomings of the individual guidance method are not found in group method because in this a number of people are guided simultaneously. Group guidance should not be interpreted to imply that it involves guiding the group. Actually, the guidance is aimed at the individual because it consists of the personal assistance rendered by a psychologist. In the group guidance technique a complete group is guided. But this guidance is intended to help the individual members or the group to

solve their own problems, the sole difference being, that the group is comprised of individuals facing more or less the same problems. Evidently, then, there is no need to waste money and time in giving individual guidance to individuals who are facing similar problems and the advice given is likely to be similar. Hence, there can be no questioning of the importance of' the group guidance technique. It economises upon time and money.

Nevertheless, group guidance technique lacks all the advantage that accrues from an application of the individual guidance method. Due to the smaller degree of personal contact between the psychologist and his subjects, the cures are not quite so effective as in the case of individual guidance. When group guidance is administered it is also not possible to gather the same amount of authentic information concerning the subject as is feasible in the individual guidance method. Hence, it may be tentatively concluded that group guidance method can be of value only in circumstances in which the problems faced are similar to a degree without wide individual differences and are also not particularly complex.

EDUCATIONAL GUIDANCE

Defining educational guidance, Jones has written, "Educational guidance, in so far as it can be distinguished from other aspects of guidance, is concerned with the assistance given to pupils in their choices and adjustments with relation to schools, curriculums, courses and school life."[1] This definition of guidance reveals the following facts concerning its nature:

1. **Educational Guidance is administered to Students.** Out of the many problems that the student is often faced with, there are some that he fails to solve of his own accord, and these do not even admit of any fruitful assistance from the teachers or the parents. Solution of these problems calls for the intervention of the specialist, and this specialist is none other than the psychologist.
2. Intended for Educational Selection. One part of the student's education consists in making a variety of selections, the first of them, being the kind of college or school in which he would like to be educated. Then he has to follow this in the selection of the curriculum that he imagines will be suitable for him. Another problem that confronts him is the choice of the subjects that he

1. *Ibid.* p. 357.

wishes to study. It must also be remembered in this connection that normal kind of curriculum is not suitable for either morons, brilliant children or for the backward children. The child himself has normally no way of telling whether he is a moron, a brilliant chap or a backward person. This is something that the psychologist alone can discover through his psychological examination. Hence, the need of guidance in this respect.

3. **Rendered for Adjustment in Education.** A student finds a peculiar atmosphere in the college, the like of which he cannot find outside, and he has to adjust himself to this atmosphere. This atmosphere is at composite of his friends, teachers, daily routine of the institution, method of teaching, curriculum, subjects taught, extracurricular programmes, etc. This environment is the same for every individual student, whatever his personal capability or drawback. Evidently, and, as a result, problems of adjustment arise. One student finds the teaching terribly dull while his more enterprising partner runs away from school. Another child might find himself tired most of the time while another is constantly bored stiff. Some of them indulge in systematically destroying discipline while others turn to crime and delinquency. Educational guidance is rendered for the solution of such problems that arise in the educative process.

Individual Guidance

The following information concerning the individual is required in the individual educational guidance method:

1. **Scholastic Attainments.** As a general rule, if one is to discover these holistic achievements of the students all that is necessary is to secure the results obtained in the various tests or examinations taken by him. But sometimes attainment tests are also given to secure more reliable information on this point.
2. **Personality Characteristics.** Problems of adjustment selection concerning education are influenced in an important way by personality characteristics. Hence the psychologist gathers facts of this through astute testing.
3. **Interest.** Selection in connection with many important elements in education such as curriculum subjects, extra-curricular programmes, etc., depends upon the individual's interests. Hence, in educational guidance, interests of the individual are determined through tests and lists of interests.

4. **Level of Intelligence.** Different subjects require differing levels of intelligence for successful study. Hence, intelligence tests are given to the student to discover his level of intelligence.
5. **Special Mental Abilities.** Selection of curricular subjects requires that attention be paid not only to the level of intelligence but also to special mental abilities. For example, literal subjects require verbal felicity, memory, mathematical ability, logic, flow of thought, etc., while creative subjects require speed in perception, spatial ability, artistic ability etc. Different tests have been devised to discover different mental abilities.
6. **Aptitude.** Educational guidance requires that the student's aptitude also be known.
7. **Health and Physical Development.** Many of the problems of adjustment that arise, in fact, originate in problematic health and physical development. Hence, it is essential that the, selection of curriculum, subjects and extracurricular activities for the student should take into account his health and physical development. For example, students taking up the study of agriculture should be sturdy of body and strong of will.
8. **Family Background and Economic Condition.** Many of the problems of adjustment that appear in the college are in fact born in the family. Hence guidance concerning them requires knowledge of the family background. Similarly, many of the educational problems that arise have an intimate relation with the student's economic condition. It is within the pale of possibility that a student may not have been able to select a desirable and suitable curriculum only because of his economic condition. In such conditions a scholarship should be provided, if the student be deserving.

Having gathered the above mentioned variety an quantity of information concerning the student, the next step in educational guidance is to collect useful information about the curriculum, subjects taught, the college and other allied matters. A psychologist keeps fairly extensive information concerning these things at his disposal. Nowadays colleges specialise in the teaching of specific subjects. Agricultural colleges impart knowledge of agricultural techniques and all that there is to know on the subject while technical institutions or colleges impart technical training. Engineering and medical colleges teach their respective subjects. Besides these, there are some multipurpose colleges that take up the simultaneous teaching of technical subjects along with the sciences as well as humanities. The psychologist keeps extensive information concerning all such colleges, their individual curriculum, their subjects and atmosphere, etc. In educational guidance his function is to help the student to make a choice of curriculum, subjects to be studied and a college, according to his abilities and aptitudes.

Group Educational Guidance Method

Besides individual guidance, educational guidance is also rendered in the form of group guidance. Following are the steps in group guidance:

1. **Orientation Talks.** These talks or lectures, as is apparent from the term, establish a proper orientation for guidance. Before turning to actual group guidance the psychologist first lectures the group on the importance of guidance and encourages them to collect information on the various adjuncts of educational guidance to be rendered.
2. **Psychological Testing.** Following the lecture, the members of the group are then subjected to psychological testing in order to gain some data on their general and individual intelligence mental abilities, interests, aptitudes and personality.
3. **Collection of Data from the School.** A considerable fund of useful information concerning the child is normally available from his school. His scholarly achievement is usually opitomised in the marks that he obtains in the various regular tests held in the class, while interview with the teachers reveals much of the child's general behaviour, interest, personality, etc., and, in most cases, teacher is the only reliable source of such information. The small confined circle that the child has in school is a mine and treasure of information for the psychologist.
4. **Collection of Data from the Family.** The next step is consolidation of information by applying to the child's family. Parents and other members of the family have usually been with the child ever since his birth, and are thereby in a position to reveal many very interesting and unique facts to the psychologist, he being able to make much of them and for them it is a personal matter as they are anxious to solve the child's difficulties. In addition to the report of the child's nature given to him by the parents and relatives, the psychologist also tries to discover the family's economic, cultural and educational status and, in fact, many of the child's problems have their origin in his relations with his parents. Hence, it is very necessary for the psychologist to have adequate knowledge of this relationship.

5. **Interview with the Child.** Finally, the psychologist personally interviews the child occasionally and finds out his views on his past, present and the future that he looks forward to. Self-inventory can be of much help in this respect.
6. **Formation of Profile.** Consolidating and integrating all the above information that the psychologist has compiled a profile of the child is now constructed which supplies a good view of all the aspects of the child. Educational guidance can now be rendered on the basis of this profile.
7. **Follow-up Studies.** Educational guidance does not end with the actual giving of advice but proceeds one step further to the follow up study of the child. Having provided the guidance and advice the psychologist keeps an eye on the child to make sure that the child is in fact benefiting from his labour. If the child fails to show any appreciable progress then he is given more tests and the necessary changes in guidance are affected.

In this manner, what educational guidance amounts to is the personal advice given by the psychologist to the child for solving various problems connected with the process of education. Educational guidance forms the basis of vocational guidance, since, the vocation that the child will ultimately select depends much upon the subjects that he chose in his period of education. Now, a person who has never studied science has the worst possible prospect for an engineer or overseer. But the process being one of reciprocity, educational guidance also depends upon vocational guidance since, once the matriculation level of education has been attained through a more or less general pattern, choice of subjects at the intermediate and university level is determined by the profession to be followed later by the student. Thus, educational and vocational guidance are interdependent.

Functions of Educational Guidance

The objective of guidance in respect of education is the solution of educational problems, helping the student select his curriculum, and to impart to him the ability to adjust to school surroundings arid conditions. Mainly, the following can be said to be the objectives of educational guidance:

(1) Selection of curriculum according to ability and capability,
(2) Improvement in the method of study,
(3) Arrangement of a special method of education for the backward child,

(4) Creation of special education programmes for the gifted children,
(5) Consideration and solution of failures at examinations,
(6) Encouraging the child's inspiration to study,
(7) Removing weakness in particular subjects.

In order to clarify the outlines of educational guidance, it would be useful to go into a detailed description of the above mentioned problems.

1. **Selection of Curriculum according to Ability and Capability.** Researches in psychology have established that success in education depends upon the student's judicious choice of a study curriculum that suits his capability and aptitude. In this, two factors are at work and have to be established. The first is that the student's abilities should be tested and evaluated and the second that the subjects conforming to those abilities determined. To take a simple example, it is essential that the qualities required for the study of mathematics should be known and found to exist in the student before any educational guidance can be rendered. Some definite and reliable knowledge of the various mental abilities required for the study of different distinct subjects has been established through psychological research. Now, the main thing that is to be done is to test the student and find the mental abilities that he happens to possess. This test of the student is designed to reveal his memory, intelligence, power of reasoning imagination, skill in manual work, special interests and his personality. All these various tests have been described at adequate length in the preceding chapters. In this examination while some tests are resorted to, study of the student's living environment is also undertaken. In this manner, the psychologist tests each individual case, and then advises the young student as to the educational course he should profitably pursue. Experiments have shown that advice of this nature, concerning the selection of curriculum, has not only resulted in marked improvement in examination results but has also had the effect of appreciably improving the child's or student's chances of gaining a real ability in his sphere. Educational guidance is normally required at the 8th or 10th class level. The high school or school leaving stage is divided into four courses, one in sciences, the others in the arts, agriculture and commerce. The particular course that a student is to take up has to be determined by the 8th class, by reason of which this class has been called the Delta class. As a general rule the subject that a student chooses in the 10th class is also continued late, but renewed guidance is required at this stage. In India, in particular,

this is all the more necessary since at this stage the student has to decide the profession that he intends to follow and to choose a course to suit that profession. In giving educational guidance at this level, the psychologist has to keep in mind the guidance that he rendered to the same student when the latter was in the 8th class.

In rendering advice besides paying attention to the results of various tests performed upon the student, it is essential to pay attention to his progress in school as well. Much information concerning school progress takes the form of annual, bi-annual and monthly test scores, educational habits regarding general discussion and play and the teacher's evaluation of the student's personality and ability. All this information is collected in, the cumulative record, which is prepared either, by the teacher or by the school psychologist.

Besides the cumulative record, another source of valuable information is the Guardian's Schedule in which the parents of the students record important facts concerning the student. Besides, the student, himself is required to furnish information regarding himself and the subjects that he would prefer to study at a higher level. In this manner, the student prepares a self inventory in which he includes mention of the subjects that he prefers and others that he does not and besides mentions the profession that he finds attractive and suitable. Generally, subjects are chosen from among the following classification of a general nature :

(1) Literary,
(2) Scientific,
(3) Agricultural,
(4) Commercial,
(5) Technical,
(6) Constructive,
(7) Aesthetic.

Making use of the cumulative record, the guardian's schedule and the self-inventory, the psychologist prepares an information, record, following which he interviews the student. In this interview the psychologist may also invite the parent or guardian. Following this interview the guide or psychologist offers his advice to the student. Educational guidance at the delta class level is available to almost all students in the Western countries, but, unfortunately, in India at present only a few students are in a position to benefit by this scheme of things and the paucity of such advice is evident from the fact that a state of the size and population of Uttar Pradesh has only 25 schools that provide facilities for such guidance.

One major difference between the guidance at the 8th class level and the 10th class level is that in the former case the guidance, is limited solely to the concerns of curriculum selection while in the latter stage it must also be concerned with the need for future selection of profession and career. In this manner, the educational guidance after the 10th is more of an educational, vocational nature and hence it naturally requires more information. In this, in addition to the student's educational career records such as the cumulative record, guardian's schedule and self-inventory, the teacher's rating is also solicited, and finally the student is again interviewed. What usually happens is that confronted with all this information in the form of a profile the student is himself able to choose a suitable profession and curriculum, but if for some reasons he is unable to sort out his way, the psychologist has to intervene and offer his assistance.

2. **Improvement in the Method of Study.** The other important aspect is the improvement in the study method of the individual. The study method is comprised of such factors as mode of taking notes, mode of reading, ability to summarize, method of memorising, proper division of time, arrangements for test, etc. It would be useful to go into a slightly detailed account of these factors.

   (i) *Mode of Taking Notes*: Charles Bird has sagaciously observed that study improves if notes are taken, but taking notes on an art that is not given equally to all men. Taking notes does not involve taking down all that the teacher says or in omitting the important points. In fact taking notes implies taking down in brief all that is said. Signs can be used as in the case of shorthand. Notes should not be so brief as to be incomprehensible on a second reading and neither should they be so extensive as to be difficult to memorising. Notes should be so designed that all important facts mentioned should be noted and all extraneous or detailed explanatory matter excluded.

   (ii) *Mode of Reading*: Considerable research has been made psychology concerning the mode of reading. For example, the various conditions under which and the degree to which either the whole or the part method is useful have been discovered. Reading quietly or reading aloud have their own qualities and these too have been discovered. When reading it is essential that sufficient light be available and that least disturbance be present. Speed of reading can be improved by practice and effort.

(iii) *Method of Memorising:* Considerable research on the memorising of facts have been made. The following conclusions concerning the various methods of memorising are recommended:

(a) Recitation. Recitation dose not mean reading a piece of matter over and over again but its repetition. This has advantages over rote learning and over numerous readings. But this does not mean that making more than one reading has no advantage. In fact, recitation and repetition should go on side by side.

(b) Part and Whole Methods. In the part method the matter to be learned is divided into suitable pieces while in the whole method it is learnt as one piece and the method that is to be used in a particular case depends upon the quantity, kind and nature of the matter as well as upon the capability of the learner. A small poem can be learnt whole but if the poem is long it is best to use the part method. Similarly, the whole method is advisable when the matter is difficult as this helps in the understanding of the various individual parts of the matter. But it is perhaps best to use both methods. In practical life, a student has to decide for himself but in choosing between the two methods he must be aware of his own capacity to learn and remember. Individuals who tire of the whole method should use the part method while others who only warm up after a short period of study would probably benefit by using the whole method.

(c) Spaced and Unspaced Methods. In the spaced method, as is evident from the name, memorising is done with intervals introduced between pieces. Contrary to this, in the unspaced method, the entire subject is tackled in a single sitting. As to which method will prove more efficacious depends upon the learner's ability and the extent and nature of the subject being tackled. A small poem with no more than ten or fifteen lines can conveniently be memorised in a single sitting, but if the poem has something like 200 lines it is usually found more practicable to distribute the burden over more than one sitting. And, there is no definite rule as to the space or time period that should be provided between two successive sittings. Roughly speaking, the only thing that can definitely be said is that the second meeting should commence only when the exhaustion of the first is completely removed, and memory impressions of it have had a chance to become permanent. In fact, the spaced method has many advantages. It not only provides opportunity for removing fatigue and creates chance for mental consideration of what has been memorised, it also reduces monotony and helps to concentrate attention upon the work in hand.

(d) **Active and Passive Method.** Memorising by reading out aloud is called the active method while learning quietly without any external aid is known as the passive method. Experiments have indicated that in the active method, as compared with the passive method, attention is disturbed much less, a pattern of the subject is formed in the mind, and the various parts of it establish relations with each other. The learner is aware of all that he has in fact learned and the desire and effort of learning are retained. Yet, it may sometimes be more convenient and profitable to precede the loud reading with a quiet reading of the subject matter.

(e) **Rote and Intelligent Methods.** In the method the learner memorises without understanding what he is learning, whereas in the intelligent method the learner understands its meaning and comprehends it along with memorising it. Experiments and tests have shown almost conclusively that the intelligent method of learning is almost invariably better than the rote method In it thoughts form definite associations, the subject matter sinks into the brain, and the memorising is more permanent an longer lasting. When the above methods of learning and memorising are supplemented with grouping, association and rhythmic learning it becomes possible to be much more expansive when writing on the subject. The importance of learning poetry by rhyming is known to one and all. Association helps the newly memorised subject matter to be related to that which is already in the mind and hence improves its retention. Besides, self-confidence is another important factor in memorising. Memory is further helped by mental set. The objective in learning a piece also, helps its successful retention in the mind. Attention is quite essential as without it memorising is impossible. Mental commentary also helps memory. In this process the subject matter learnt is repeated in the mind. Finally, apperception, or mixing newly learnt with that which is present in the mind, helps the process of memorising.

(f) **Method of Summary.** Another aspect of learning that is very important is the method of summarising. The main thing in this is perception of the heart of the matter, and selection of terms that succinctly sum up all that has been said in the minimum possible number of words.

(g) **Division of Time.** As has been pointed out, much benefit is to be derived by reading over divided periods of time rather than continuously. Division is also two fold division between periods of study and rest, and division of study period according to the subject to be studied. Division of both kinds is essential.

(h) **Provision of Rest.** If one rests after having read for sometime the fatigue caused thereby is relieved boredom is obviated, and all that has been read gets a chance to sink into the mind. Experiments have shown that if one sleeps after reading, all that is read in that period is retained for far greater time than any other material read under differing circumstances. This occurs because sleep provides complete rest to the brain. The extent, of rest required after reading a book depends not only upon the capacity of the student himself, but also upon the material read because if the subject is obstruse and difficult rest will be needed only after a short reading, whereas in the case of a simple or light subject much reading can be done before fatigue set in.

From the above analysis of the results of Psychological investigation in study methods, students can discover the faults and advantages of their own methods and can also effect improvements in them. Students who cannot do this stand in need of a psychologist's guidance and in giving such guidance and advice the psychologist should find out the complete capacity and capability of the student, as this is intimately related to the method of study.

3. **Provision of a Special Method of Education for the Backward Child.** One spiecific aspect of educational guidance is the guidance concerning backward children. This category includes children who usually fail at examinations, or show signs of indiscipline, running away from school, juvenile delinquency, or other defects of such nature. Backwardness in education can be caused by personal causes as well as by the method of teaching or external factors. The advisor must be able to gather all possible relevant information regarding-the backward child whom he is called upon to guide. In this besides getting hold of the cumulative record and guardian's schedule, or the self-inventory it is necessary to gather information from the parents and teachers. It is only on the basis of such information that any advise for the solution of educational problems can be given. In case a child is intellectually of a lower level or suffers from some mental defect, then he requires a special curriculum and a special method of teaching to suit his needs. Psychologists can advise on this matter also. If it is observed that the backward child fails to show any progress despite persistent effort then he would be best advised to go into some technical profession requiring training rather than mental acumen. If the child's backwardness is due to family conditions or the school environment then the psychologist should advise his parents and teachers. Sometimes backwardness can be the result of some mental disease. In such a case the child stands in need of medical treatment rather than guidance. Briefly, the psychologist and the advisor must individually consider the case of each child and give private and separate advice to each patient.

4. **Provision of Special Educational Programmes for the Gifted Children.** While backward children require guidance and care, the unusually gifted children also require a special educational arrangement as otherwise there is fear of their falling into bad

activities. A gifted child does not find the ordinary programme that satisfies and invigorates the average child satisfying and helpful. The psychologist discovers such exceptional children, gathers all available information regarding them and guides their parents and teachers as to the manner in which the child should be treated. Guidance of such cases more usually concerns suggestions for some special extra-curricular programmes that can help the child develop properly and in accordance with his special gifts. Putting in briefly, it can be said that the psychologist arranges a curriculum that suits well with the child's gifts.

5. **Consideration and Failures at Examinations.** In the intermediate and high school examinations held every year by the U.P. Board of High School and Intermediate examination, the results are almost invariably below 50 per cent. More than half the students that appear for the examinations fail to pass them and while one hears a few odd cases of suicide that are the result of this failure there are many more individuals who become discouraged and give up their educational career when it has just begun. Some of the more enterprising turn to antisocial activity, others lose their mental balance, while a major portion of them become morose and frustrated. Almost all educationists are of the view that as a result of this very high rate of failures, the nation's wealth and strength are being greatly undermined. On the face of it, it is a national problem or at best the fault of the state's faulty educational methods and educational organisation that admits of almost no interference on the psychologist's part, but he can nevertheless resolve the factors that lead children to failure in examinations through his guidance.

6. **Encouragement to the child's Inspiration to study.** Another problem that makes itself felt to the psychologists is when a particular child evinces lack of inspiration and enthusiasm to study. Causes of this lack of motivation may both be personal as well as related to the total environment whether social, family or school. Among the personal reasons can be physical factors such as a weak constitution or mental reasons such as anxiety and irritation. Environmental factors are concerned either with the home or the school. As far as the school is concerned it may produce a variety of causes such as uninteresting curriculum and routine, the method of education or teaching being anything but psychological, absence of extra-curricular programmes, etc. The psychologist sifts all these factors and causes, and then advises

the child to create motivation in him. In fact, this can be achieved more by removing causes that destroy motivation than by any guidance. For this the psychologist guides either the teacher or the parents. The parents, teachers and the psychologist can jointly exert themselves to create a condition in which the student will take an interest in his education of his own volition. Then, and only then, can the child be inspired to take an interest in the study of his subjects.

7. **Removal of Weakness in Particular Subjects.** Yet another problem confronts the psychologist when a student shows signs of being weak in some particular subject or subjects. English, for example, is one subject in which most students in Uttar Pradesh are lamentably weak. A major portion of college students failing is of those who fail in the English language papers. Some students evade some subjects as if they were running for the safety of their very lives Mathematics, for example, is another subject that is something of a burden for many people, equalled perhaps only by grammar for the dread it causes. Weakness in a particular subject is not due to lack of the required ability in the student, but more often because the student fails to take a keen interest in that subject. Through tests and observation the psychologist can locate the individual cause that is responsible for the weakness. If it is the study of that subject as soon as possible, or if some ability can possibly be injected into the students, efforts should be made to create it in him. If the cause of weakness is something else, then in that case teachers, parents, the psychologist and the student can cooperate to put an end to the meaningless weakness threatening the student's progress.

   From the above brief outline of the various aspects of educational guidance it becomes evident that it is concerned with the various problems of education. All the problems that have been mentioned in the process are only the major problems, and there can be, besides them, many other problems that may require the intervention of the psychologist.

VOCATIONAL GUIDANCE

Historical Outline

Vocational guidance was defined by the 1954 Committee of the International Labour Organisation in its suggestions concerning vocational guidance, as assistance rendered by an individual to another in the latter's solving of problems related to his progress and vocational selection, keeping in mind the individual's peculiarities or special abilities and their relations with his occupational opportunity. In this manner, the objective of vocational guidance is the proper and complete utilization of a nation's man power through helping the individual to achieve his development and satisfaction in his profession. An individual should choose a profession that suits his abilities in order that both he and the nation may profit. It is not possible for any one individual to be capable of doing every job. Special kinds of job require particular kinds of skill and special know-how. It is possible that it may be asked why guidance thereby becomes necessary since every individual can tell the kind of skill lie has and choose a profession accordingly. But if the situation is objectively viewed it will be found that it is not precisely of this nature as only few people are able to gauge their own abilities and capabilities. A large majority of persons are wrong in their estimate of their own capabilities, many of them over estimating while a fair number denigrating themselves. It is not possible for the proverbial human eye to see the very grit that is in it, it being implied that the human eye rarely lights upon the individual's own defects. If one were to go to any student doing postgraduate work in the university and ask him as to what he proposes to do after obtaining the degree, the most likely reply would be that he would take one of the competitive examinations, preferably the administrative service, and if not fortunate enough to be selected, carry on to do research and finally become a teacher. The audacity and over-weaning self confidence of the student is stupendous. If you were to ask him as to what he will do if neither of these contingencies comes about, then it will only be a regard for your social standing that will prevent him from denouncing you on the spot. The implication is that very, few of the students who fail in these and other competitive examinations realise that they do not possess the requisite qualities. When they fail, they turn their wrath upon the examiner while the more, charitable abuse only their bad luck. There will hardly be one student who will acquiesce in the knowledge that it was he himself who was lacking in the qualities requited in the job. Again, to prevent unnecessary meanings being read into these statements it must be pointed out that the competitive examinations held in the present era can hardly be considered sufficient to gauge an individual's inherent merit. The sole intention of introducing this example is to point out the fact that young men and women do not think rationally and scientifically when faced with the choice of a profession. Vocational guidance helps in the solution of no other than this problem. Scientific testing reveals all that there is to know of the individual to the guide, who then advises the former as to the profession most suitable for him. Experiments have succeeded in pointing out roughly the qualities that a particular kind of profession requires of the individual. For example, efforts were made to establish the intelligence level required for various kinds of jobs. The table at page 420 states the intelligence quotient that a person should possess in order to go in for one or the other profession.

Similarly, other tests and experiments have been conducted to establish some relation between vocation and other mental abilities. For example, engineering and other industrial work requires mechanical skill in the individual, with the result that persons who possess it in a slight degree cannot in the normal course be expected to become successful engineers or skilled technicians. Some kinds of work, for example the repair of chronometers and surgery, require the ability to do minute accurate work skillfully. Lacking this quality no individual can become a good surgeon, watch repairer or experimenter or research worker. In much the same manner other industries and professions require different kinds of expertise and skill.

S.No.	*Professional Class*	*I.Q.*
1.	Administrative work and high level professional work	150 or more
2.	Low level professional and technical work	130 to 153
3.	Clerical or high level skilled labour	115 to 130
4.	Skilled work	100 to 115
5.	Semi skilled work	85 to 100
6.	Work not requiring intelligence	70 to 85
7.	Labour work.	50 to 70

The above description makes evident the importance inherent in vocational guidance. But this hardly means that the guide pays no attention to the person's aptitude. Aptitude is one of the bases of guidance, but one thing that is beyond question is that no individual can attain much success on the sole basis of aptitude. Accordingly, the guide has to collect elaborate and detailed information concerning the individual's aptitudes and capabilities, and give guidance on the basis of such information. Vocational guidance dose not involve categorical declarations that one shall be doctor while such another shall be a clerk or an engineer. It is only a hypothesis and a suggestion that has its own limitations. What the guide says is simply that such and such a person possesses certain qualities in abundance that fit him for such a profession, and there is much greater possibility of success in that profession then in any other for that individual.

Personnel Selection

It was the National Institute of Industrial Psychology that commenced research on matters concerning vocational guidance, and its results have been used much by all the big industries. Every productive unit has a large variety of functions which can best be performed by individuals having different kinds of ability and training. Now, the selection of separate individuals for each of these jobs is what is called personnel selection and this personnel selection is based upon vocational guidance. Here, it is essential that the distinction between personnel selection and vocational guidance be well marked and known. In both it is essential that the qualities fit for different jobs be present in the person being considered for selection or guidance, as the case may be. But, in personnel selection, the qualify required for some particular function is remarked, and one person out of many applicants is selected to perform that function, of course, care being taken that the best of the applicants is thereby selected. In vocational guidance, the qualities of a person are gauged and he is accordingly advised to take up some vocational training or adopt a particular profession that suits him and is likely to bring him satisfaction. Vocational guidance and personnel selection are two branches of vocational psychology. Both these branches are interdependent since the provision of the right man for the right job and right job for the right man requires, on the one hand, analysis of the individual, and an analysis of the job on the other.

PROGRESS OF VOCATIONAL GUIDANCE

The Western nations have done much work concerning vocational guidance, particularly in the United States of America personnel selection is itself a specialised job now. Considerable moderation and improvement work is being carried on there to improve the collection of information regarding the professions and the methods of selection. A Dictionary of Occupational Titles has been prepared to search for and thereby provide information concerning vocations that are open to individuals. Then, an Occupational Code has been prepared by classifying the vocations according to the qualities that they require in the man as well as according to their different levels. Detailed information regarding every profession is collected. Job description, which is an important organ of the information concerning every profession, provides a detailed and exhaustive account of the various factors such as conditions of work, wages, responsibility, etc., that are operative in the industry or vocation. The first dictionary included details of 75 percent vocations and occupations, and it comprehended some 90 percent of working population of that country. This dictionary went through additional and improved editions in 1942, 1944 and 1945 while in its 1959 revised version some 40,40,023 professions were detailed and job analysis in 1942 has been confined to 16 professions.

Vocational Guidance in India

In India, vocational guidance is not easily available, as are few other technical and specialised services. In 1945, the Training and Employment Service Organisation Committee headed by Shri B. Shivarao suggested that occupational information be selected and published. As a result, during the second five year plan period a project was prepared to set up 50 vocational guidance centres to supplement the efforts of the employment exchanges in their personnel selection. There have been certain appointments in this connection but the actual achievement is not very noticeable and the books on occupations that have been published are no scientific research material but merely constitute a description. Besides the efforts of the Government of India, the state governments have also opened some centres, while this in turn has been supplemented by certain non-governmental agencies. Among them the Y.M.C.A. and the Rotary Club have achieved things that deserve mention. As is apparent from the above rather short account, progress in the direction of vocational guidance for a large country like India, is not worthy of praise. It need hardly be pointed out that much of this failure is to be attributed to the lack of organisation.

List of Abilities and Traits

Much important research and modification work has been carried on in connection with finding out the qualities and traits required for different professions. The National Institute of Industrial Psychology of England has prepared a list of approximately 20 psychological abilities and traits. On the basis of this list an industrial survey was undertaken. In this survey, the specialists and senior officers working in the different occupations were requested to supply information as to the qualities and traits required for their respective functions. Specialists of different occupations effected a rating from three standpoints-average, high level, and very high level. Now the specialists of National Institute took the average of the ratings made available from some 80 occupations. This average was categorised in the form of a table and on the basis of this table it is possible to determine whether a particular individual is suitable for a specific profession or not. For example, this table clarifies the qualities that are requisites, for the medical and the legal professions and the qualities that are quite desirable.

Another bit of important research work in connection with various professions and mental abilities was carried on by R.B. Cattell.[1] Cattell tested some 100 adult persons and found out their average intelligence level. This average indicates the approximate level of intelligence required by a person wishing to join some particular profession. This is made apparent in the table shown on page 423.

Tests by Dvorak and Dodge

Dvorak and Dodge also conducted tests upon employees of different professions, of persons successful and unsuccessful within one profession, of people working in the same profession but in differing capacities. This

S.No.	*Professions*	*No of trained people*	*Average I.Q.*
1.	Teachers of universities and inter colleges	30	151
2.	Doctors and surgeons	25	146.5
3.	Teachers of government schools	50	145
4.	Civil engineers	20	142
5.	Mechanical engineers	18	140
6.	Teachers of primary schools	90	137
7.	Managers of industry	20	137
8.	Stenographers	57	129
9.	Clerks	54	127
10.	Travelling representatives	24	123
11.	Nurses	250	122
12.	Telephone department employees	52	115
13.	Workers doing minute work	19	114
14.	Workers doing gross work	—	106 to 78

testing was based upon a wide variety of authentic psychological testing techniques. These tests revealed considerable difference between the

[1] Cattell, R.B., Occupational norms of intelligence and standardization of adult intelligence test, *British Journal of Psychology, Vol XXV,* July 1954.

abilities of motor mechanics, successful or unsuccessful clerks, and other people. But these tests were neither extensive and comprehensive to be applied to a majority of professions nor concentrated enough to have completely distinguished one profession from another. In this manner, it is essential to exercise the greatest care in applying the conclusions in these tests. Dodge himself has acknowledged this fact.

Class level of Intelligence	*Neccessary ability*	*Example*
(a) High level	Highest university education creativee ability and power of argument	Professors, authors, scientists, adovcates etc.
(b) Higher than average	High school and college level of education.	Clerks, photographers foreman, etc.
(c) Average level	High school level of education.	Typists, machanics, etc.
(d) Below average	Junior high school or eighth grade education.	Labourers, porters etc.

Minnesota Occupational Rating Scales

In Minnesota University six mental abilities and their extent were determined for 30 professions and occupations and even in this the ability was individually divided into four categories a, b, c, d. These six mental abilities were Verbal, Mechanical, Sociability, Clerical, Musical and Artistic and these six abilities were divided into four classes each for different professions. For example, the Minnesota occupational rating scale concerning ability of verbal efficacy can be understood from the table given on page 423.

PROCESS OF VOCATIONAL, GUIDANCE

The preceding description of vocational guidance must have made it apparent that it requires two kinds of information or subject matter to be collected, the first concerning indispensable information about the individual, and the second pertaining to knowledge of the industrial or occupational aspect. In this manner, vocational guidance has two aspects:

(1) Study of the individual.
(2) Study of the occupational or professional sphere.

Study of the Individual

Before any vocational guidance can be rendered to an individual, it is essential that adequate information concerning his-education, level of intelligence, mental abilities, aptitudes, interests, physical development, health, nature, personality characteristics and economic status be gathered, because variations in any of them will necessarily require change in guidance.

1. **Education.** Individuals need differing levels of education in order to enter into and succeed in different professions, as for example, the highest education is required for advocates, professors, engineers, doctors, and other such professions, whereas a general and lower level of education can serve the purpose if the profession is clerk, overseer, mechanic, compounder, teacher, etc. Besides these there are certain other occupations in which the medium level of education suffices e.g., business salesmanship. In such professions only the basic necessities of literacy must be fulfilled, as much else depends upon practice. It is only because of this importance of various levels of education being relative and relevant to different professions that most advertisements for applications for job contain specific instructions regarding the educational qualifications. For example, a person teaching students at the high school and Intermediate level need only be a graduate while no mere graduate can teach the college or graduate level. Doctors require medical degrees while in order to qualify as an engineer it is essential that one passes an engineering examination.
2. **Training.** Education does not merely imply the degree obtained at the end of a session by passing a prescribed examination. Now-a-days, most occupational units make it obligatory on all new entrants to be trained in addition to being educated, and this is being carried to the extent that only a trained individual is allowed to fill the post of a high-school teacher. Certain occupations need training inevitably, for example, the occupations of electrician, stenographer, chemist, compounder, etc. As it is the, tendency to employ trained personnel in industry and other occupations is catching on. In certain professions, the individual after having entered it is oriented for a, period of few weeks, and only then is he allowed to handle work on his own responsibility.
3. **Level of Intelligence.** Besides difference in, education, different professions require differing levels of intelligence. For example, the medical, technical, legal, teaching and administrative professions require the highest intelligence level, while on the other hand, the peon and the domestic worker can be selected from people with a much lower level of intelligence. Other professions require only the average level of intelligence, so that evidently, before a person

can be told of the profession that suits his natural endowments, it is essential to know the level of intelligence to which he belongs.

4. **Special Mental Abilities.** Individuals differ not only in respect of their intelligence but also in respect of their special mental abilities. For example, all people do not possess mechanical ability to the same degree and neither is verbal felicity shared by all in equal degree. Different professions require differing mental abilities verbal ability being required by advocates and teachers, etc., mechanical ability by doctors and engineers, etc. Hence, prior to the selection of a profession it is essential for the individual to be aware of his mental abilities.
5. **Aptitudes.** Success in a particular profession seems to depend to some extent upon one's aptitude for it. If a person lacks artistic and creative aptitude, there is not much likelyhood of his succeeding in the role of an artist, and one need not expect it. As a general rule, it is advisable for every person to join the profession for which he has any natural aptitude. Hence, knowledge of a person's aptitudes is also essential before he can be given any vocational guidance.
6. **Interests.** Interest helps to increase the possibility of success in a profession. Interesting work is done enthusiastically and patiently while uninteresting work tends to fall upon most men, and requires very conscious application to be carried through. Success in work requires that serious interest be taken in the work, or that interest in that kind of work be created, and this is possible. Interests are mutable, and it is possible to create interest in work that was once repugnant. But if the individual is originally endowed with interest for a particular occupation and is also possessed of the requisite mental abilities, then he would be best advised to adopt it. It need hardly be repeated, as a slogan is, that a knowledge of the person's interest is essential before any vocational guidance can be rendered.
7. **Health and Physical Development.** As a general rule proper health and physical development are necessarily taken into consideration in every profession, but in certain other occupations success depends almost solely upon these factors. For success in the armed forces or in the police department health and good physical development are quite indispensable. In the absence of these factors the presence of no other qualities of ability will bring success to the individual. Hence, physical development, constitution and health are additional factors that must be taken

into consideration when the question of vocational guidance comes up for consideration.

8. **Nature.** Different people show very pertinent and obvious difference in their nature, some being introverted while others more extroverted and, different kinds of people can successfully settle down only in some specific professions that suit their nature. An extroverted personality, for example, is an essential if one wants to succeed as a salesman, agent, administrator or even as a leader, while on the other hand, gifted introverts male great artists, authors, scholars, scientists, specialists, etc. If choice of profession is contrary to one's natural inclination, it goes against the grain and deprives the individual's life of happiness and contentment, and the profession becomes a burden. While, if the profession conforms to one's nature, then on is happy and enthusiastic in his work, and these conditions are conductive to progress and success. Hence, before vocational guidance can be ventured upon, it is necessary to judge a person's nature also.

9. **Personality Characteristics.** It is a fact generally known that different qualities of the personality are required in such widely separated professions as teaching, artistic creation, selling, labour work, etc. Hence, choice of profession should also be made with a due regard for the qualities of the person's personality.

10. **Financial Status.** As a general rule, it is improper and unnecessary to take into consideration a person's financial status before making a choice of profession but in a country like India where scholarships are hard to come by, the economic status of the students also plays an important part in his choice of the future that he wants to shape for himself. Now a person with middle, class status is in no position to afford a technical or medical education for his child because either of these two special courses involve the expenditure of a considerable amount of money and it is unnecessary and improper to advice a poor and needy person to go in for higher education when he cannot afford it. It is equally useless to advise such a person to choose a profession in which high education and specialised qualifications are desired. Hence, a person should be recommended only to that profession for which he can afford to gain education and any training that may be essential. He must have the means to gain such training. It must also be remembered that economic or financial status can be a bar to earning some profession only under certain circumstances. There are many examples of people

who came from poor families having gained very high education and improved their lot in life. The truth or crux of the matter is that instead of discouraging a student from entertaining thoughts of a profession for which he apparently has not the economic means, the psychologist should expend his effort in arranging scholarships or other facilities whereby he may be able to attain the goal for which the former is striving, as he stands great chances of success. In India, these things are still unexplored, and many individuals fail to gain satisfying and rewarding positions in life that conform to their abilities, interests and aptitudes, for no reason other than that they were born in poor families.

11. **Other Important Factors.** In addition to all these elements pointed out above it is necessary to keep in mind certain other factors concerning the individual before giving vocational guidance. Age of the person, for example, is another factor that must be taken into account since many jobs and occupations set the maximum and minimum age limits on all applicants, so that people not qualifying for them in this respect cannot enter these services. Hence, there is hardly any point in advising them to take up such a profession. Sex of the person is another consideration in vocational guidance upon which much depends because some occupations are more suitable to the male individual while others are within the capacities of the female, and for these she is eminently suitable. Nursing and caring for the diseased in hospitals is one function that can safely and even desirably be allocated to women, while in the armed forces and the police most of the jobs with very few exceptions are suitable only for the male.

Study of Professional World

Having collected all the necessary and desired information regarding the individual under consideration, it is necessary to turn to another aspect of vocational guidance, that of studying the professional world. While the psychologist must necessarily have enough information concerning the person to whom he is imparting vocational guidance, it is equally important that he be well informed on its professional and occupational aspect. Only then can he provide proper and effective assistance. It is enough for the psychologist to be knowing the number and kinds of professions but also the kind of education, training, intelligence, mental abilities, interests, aptitudes, personality, qualities etc., that are desired as well as the conditions of work that prevail therein.

Classification of Occupations

Occupations have been classified in different ways, according to the viewpoint adopted in doing so. Classification is beneficial because the individual comes to know all the professions from one point of view and can select from among them. This has the twofold advantage of narrowing down the range from which the selection is to be made while at the same time it provides a number of alternatives. It will be advantageous now to glance at these various professions.

(a) Classification according to Interest. Professions have been divided into the following classes on the basis of interest:

(1) Occupations concerned with child life,
(2) Mechanical occupations,
(3) Computational occupations,
(4) Scientific occupations,
(5) Occupations concerned with change,
(6) Artistic occupations,
(7) Literary occupations,
(8) Musical occupations,
(9) Occupations concerned with social service,
(10) Clerical occupations.

In each of these classes there are professions belonging to five levels, depicted in the following classification:

(b) Classification on the basis of Educational Level, Mental Ability or Skill, Training, Age and Social Respect. This classification of the professions is the work of Beckman.[1] as follows:

1. **Executive, Managerial and Professional.** This class includes the following three kinds of occupations:
   (i) Verbal — such as advocate, judge, editor, auditor, professor, etc.
   (ii) Scientific — such as doctor, engineer, scientist, accountants, etc.,
   (iii) Executive or managerial—such as the various kinds of managers and executives, etc.
2. **Business and Sub-Professional.** This class includes the following two kinds:
   (i) Business — such as trader, salesman, agent, etc.
   (ii) Sub-professional — such as actor, photographer, designer, etc.
3. **Skilled Occupation.** This class includes the following two kinds of occupations:

---

1. Beckman, R.O., A new scale for gauging occupational rank, *Personnel Journal,* (1954), pp. 223-235.

(i) Physical labour such as electrician, dyer, machine-man, and press mechanic, etc.

(ii) Intellectual such as clerk, supervisor, stenographer cashier, etc.

4. **Semi-skilled Occupation.** Such as policeman, bus conductor, driver, guard, etc.

5. **Unskilled Occupation.** Such as labourer, peon, night-watchman etc.

(c) **Classification according to the Form of Work.** Professions have been divided into the following four classes according to the nature of work done by them:

1. **Social Occupations.** These professions require that the person be possessed of social qualities and a high degree of sociability because he comes into contact with very many individuals. Examples of such professions are advocate, leader, salesman, agent, administrator, manager, teacher, etc.
2. **Occupations of Mental Skill.** In these, professions tools are used for work that requires a high degree of manual skill, examples being carpenter, mechanic, mason, binder, overseer, engineer etc.
3. **Occupations concerned with Offices.** This class includes all people concerned with office organisations such as clerks, cashiers, peons, etc.
4. **Intellectual and Scholarly Occupation.** In this class come the professions that require intellectual acumen and love of academic work of the individual, examples of which are philosopher, author, inventor, poet, scientist, etc.

Job Families

From the above classification of occupations it becomes evident that there are many professions that are similar in respect of their nature of work done, conditions of work, desired skill, interest, mental abilities and personality qualities, etc. When such similar families are put together, a job family is constituted. In one job family the work can be carried on different levels such as high, medium or low. Evidently, then the individual will first have to select a job family, and then level of that family on which he is capable of functioning.

Sources of Information Regarding Occupations

The question that may justifiably intrigue the beginner is the source of all this comprehensive information regarding a profession. The following are the sources from which such information is forthcoming and can be gathered:

(1) Through papers and magazines.
(2) Though information published by government organisations.
(3) Through radio discussions.
(4) From employment exchanges.
(5) From information broadcast by industrial and commercial institutions.
(6) Through lectures delivered by specialists.
(7) Through examination of factories and people working in them.
(8) By working on any particular profession.
(9) From guidance psychologist and vocational adviser.

Significant Facts in Vocational Selection

After gethering information regarding the profession from one or more of the above mentioned sources it is possible to select one's profession, but before committing oneself finally, as has been pointed out before, the following thing must be taken into consideration and made a note of:

(1) Nature of work which includes the kind of work, charge, responsibility, duty, interest, etc.
(2) Working conditions, which include both psychological and physical needs.
(3) Necessary personality traits such as nature, adepts in behaviour, power of leadership, etc.
(4) Level of intelligence.
(5) Mental abilities.
(6) Interest and aptitudes.
(7) Necessary education and training.
(8) Income, chances of promotion and permanency of work.
(9) Procedure of entrance.
(10) Necessary physical development and health.
(11) Social prestige.
(12) Demand of the job.

In this manner, a profession is chosen after analysing the individual on the one hand, and the various occupations upon the other. Analysis of the individual reveals the abilities and qualities present in him while analysis of the job or profession reveals the desired qualities and abilities. Now, all that remains to be done is that the person who possesses abilities and qualities requisite for a particular profession should be prompted to join it.

Steps of the Vocational Guidance Method

Vocational guidance, as in the case of all other forms of guidance, can be given by two methods — the individual method and the collective method. And, in these methods, the steps are the same as were described in the case of educational guidance. In this manner, vocational guidance will involve the following steps:

(1) Orientation talks.
(2) Psychological testing.
(3) Collection of data from the school.
(4) Collection of data from the family.
(5) Interview.
(6) Formation of profile.
(7) Achievement besides the above important steps in vocational guidance, which means that the psychologist, along with providing vocational guidance, also helps the individual to attain to the desired profession. For this he keeps in contact with employment exchange offices and social workers.
(8) Follow up studies.

PERSONAL GUIDANCE

An important part of guidance is personal guidance, and it constitutes the personal and individual advice offered by a guide to an individual for the solution or latter's personal problems. This helps the person to adjust to circumstances in his life. As a general rule problems are a part and parcel of human life, but not everyone is able to solve the problems that arise in his life and ruffle the calm of existence. People who find no way out of the morass of problems need the guidance and opinions of a specialist and expert and, a psychologist is the only one who can provide advice concerning the solving of personal psychological problems.

Need for Personal Guidance

There can not be exact prescription of the number and kind of problems that can be called essentially personal, because while the same person may be faced with a wide variety of problems at different stages of his life, the same problems may assume a different shape when they plague another individual. In this manner, personal problems are so numerous and have so incongruous and varying forms that it is well high impossible to indulge in a description of them, and yet, the main personal problems that beset the human animal can be distinguished. Roughly speaking, human problems of a personal nature can be of two kinds: (1) Personal or individual, (2) Social. Individual problems can also be divided into two classes: (1) Physiological problems such as health, disease, development and concerned problems, (2) Psychological problems such as sex problems, problems concerning the satisfaction of instinctive needs. Among the psychological problems those of emotional adjustment are very important because inability to solve them has very great debilitating influence upon the entire personality of the individual and social more than the personal problems cause anxiety to the person. If the truth be required, it may be declared that human life, from the moment of birth to the time of death, is a continuous and ceaseless process of adjustment with social circumstances. These social conditions keep on changing and being transmuted, with the result that new problems are constantly presented to the person for solution. Now, as to which of these problems is likely to cause disorganisation in his personality, it is not easy to say with any degree of certitude. It is the opinion of psychologists that most men need personal guidance at some or the other occasion in life when the cross that they have to bear becomes a mite too heavy for them. That life continues on its desultory path even without guidance is a mundane truth. Life continues even in strife, poverty, unemployment, disease and trial. But man wants to improve his lot in life with the help of science. The psychologist's guidance helps the individual to solve certain personal problems, the failure to attain which only increases the burden of life, stops all development and progress in the person, even though he may continue to exist and outwardly appear to be hale and hearty. There are many aspects of social adjustment and adaptation because there are more than one dimensions to man's social circumstances. Social problems are generally interpreted to include family problems of school and college if the individual is a student, vocational problems if he is an earning individual, moral and ideal problems. Of these, the family problems are the most prominent and varied, comprehending problems of relations between the child and parents, relations between husband and wife, conjugal problems, relations between brothers and sisters, financial status of the family, mutual adaptations of the individuals and others and, any one of these problems is Herculean enough to destroy the peace and calm of an individual. Problems of conjugal love, for example, compel an infinity of couples to spend their life in utter misery and misunderstanding.

Very often the individual makes some slap dash trial and error efforts to solve his personal problems or turns to good friends for personal advice, or insted turns to the older family members or teachers. Though this advice may have some practical validity, yet scientifically it is difficult to find any justification for it. If we take up for consideration the problem of conjugal love and bliss, then, it will be seen that the advice rendered by the best friends and sages of the family is all based upon their personal experience, and cannot provide any real guidance for a person. The crux of the matter is that the conjugal relations between no two pairs are identical. The conjugal problem of one specific pair is a person particular problem. Examples from other persons and solutions can only provide some general suggestions but it is dangerous to emulate others without paying attention to the particular merits of one specific case, for which the solution is being sought. Evidently then, the individual can tackle his own problem after making a comprehensive study and gathering considerable psychological knowledge, but if this psychological knowledge is present in him then why should that problem arise in the first place? Naturally, it is essential for the person to turn to the psychologist for expert advice. But it must be kept in mind that guidance and advice cannot solve the problem in its entirety. This advice is more of the nature of suggestions, is scientific, and has no qualities of hit and miss about it. If the individual is to profit from such suggestions, he must be possessed of understanding, sympathy and skill.

Process of Personal Guidance

The first condition of personal guidance is that the person to, be guided be fully and completely understood. It is desirable that the individual should himself come forward with all relevant information in the form of life history, present condition, feelings, thoughts, activities and all main facts concerning his life, and pass it on to the psychologists. He should not try to conceal anything irrespective of the inhibitions that may urge him to do so, for it has often been found that the root of the problems to be solved existed in things from which the person wanted to escape, that he not only did not want to reveal to others but of which he did not even want to think himself. Briefly stated, in personal guidance, the psychologist should, with the co-operation of the person himself as well as with the help of various tests, gather all relevant and necessary information concerning the person. Roughly, personal guidance has the following five steps:

(1) Gathering the facts,
(2) Diagnosis of the problem,
(3) Prognosis,
(4) Therapy,
(5) Follow-up studies.

1. **Gathering the Facts.** Gathering of factual information is the first and most important step in personal guidance. These facts, can be of two kinds those connected with the particular problem, and

those concerned with the general life history of the person and, the facts concerned merely with the problem also can be of two kinds. The first concerned with the individual and his characteristic qualities, the second concerned with the external circumstances of the problem and the need for knowing these facts compels the psychologist to turn to observation, interview and various tests that yield it. The person himself is not the only one interviewed, as much valuable information is forthcoming from the interviews of people nearest to him, such as friends and relatives. In an interview it is essential that the psychologist ventures to speak as little as possible, that he asks questions that elicit the correct and desired responses by allowing the interviewed person to carry on the bulk of the talking. As in the case of educational and vocational guidance, in personal guidance, the opportunity for interview arrives only after a profile has been formed from the available information and for this profile, the school, family, and other sources are ransacked for information. This necessitates the use of the cumulative record, the guardian's schedule, the self inventory and the teacher's ratings, besides which a number of tests are also performed. The outline of the profile is something like what is described below:

(a) *Physical Description*: Physical description includes the person's age, sex and physical health.

(b) *Family Description:* In family description are included facts concerning the family background and hereditary relationships, parents (whether real or step, living or dead), brothers and sisters (their mutual relationships, economic status of the family, social standard of the family, mutual relations between all the members of the family, etc.).

(c) *History of Social Development*: This class includes the student's relations with other members of his class, and with other friends outside the class. If the person requiring guidance is not a student, then his relations with his neighbours and relatives outside the family will be studied.

(d) *History of College Life*: This classification includes the student's history in his progress through the primary, secondary and college educational stages which is constituted by results of examinations and record of part taken in extracurricular programmes. If the person being studied and guided is not a student, then his life outside the sphere of his family should be studied to provide equivalent information. If he is engaged in some professional pursuit, it is necessary that the information regarding level of income, conditions of work, relations with other members of the profession or institution, etc. is collected.

(e) *Mental Abilities:* By means of various tests and examinations intended for the purpose, the psychologist gathers information concerning the individual's level of intelligence, mental abilities and aptitudes, etc.

(f) *Qualities of Personality:* Qualities of the personality have an important part in the personal problems. Hence the psychologist finds it incumbent to secure information concerning the person's interests, emotional maturity, motives, ambitions, objectives and ideals, etc.

One very important part of gathering such information is the keeping of proper records so that the information be available in future. Even in interview it is desirable for the psychologist not to depend upon his memory too much but to take adequate notes so that the information revealed is permanently available to him when it is required. But this requires an attitude of co-operation on the subject's part and a reassuring approach on the psychologist's part so that the subject should not become suspicious. If a person finds any objection to his statements being recorded, then modern tape recording machines can be used without the person being informed of them. Facts which do not qualify for this kind can be recorded after the person has been informed of their importance. For example, the psychologist should encourage and praise the subject and lead him into believing that all that he says deserves to be recorded.

2. **Diagnosis of the Problem.** Having gathered all the facts that he wanted to collect the psychologist is now ready to start his own work. He has to search and analyse this information in order to see some system in it as well as any pattern that will help to reveal the cause of the problem under consideration. Such a discovery of patterns is the diagnosis of the problem and this diagnosis is the basis on which the problem is to be solved and the trouble cured. The better and more accurate the diagnosis the better will be the cure ultimately effected and it would be no misnomer to state that with a proper and accurate diagnosis half the psychologist's work is over.

3. **Prognosis.** Prognosis consists in estimating the benefit or result of the guidance. A psychologist tries to visualise the extent to which he will be able to, solve the person's problem or, in other words, to what extent is there hope of the problem being solved. For example, by seeing a person's past performance in mathematics and by measuring his mental abilities, it becomes possible to make some tentative estimate of what he will be able to achieve after the guidance is rendered.
4. **Therapy.** Now the time for therapy or cure has arrived, or in other words it is the time for the psychologist to come forward with a satisfactory solution of the problem. Seeing the profile of the problem from all the information gathered about it as well as from the interviews with the psychologist, the counselee himself gains insight into the problem and sometimes even comes up with some sensible and practicable solution. The truth of the matter is that this in fact should be the aim of the psychologist for he should try to make the counselee see his problem and its patterns, and even to think up a solution for it. If this happens, he will on the one hand gain considerable pleasure from having solved the problem of his own accord, while on the other he will have considerable enthusiasm in solving the problem, and he will exert himself to the maximum limit. Freud, who used to cure mental diseases by the psychoanalytic method, used this method very effectively. When his patients became aware of the unconscious cause of their trouble, much of the problem was solved, whereas if the psychologist insists on giving his own suggestions and advice, then it becomes possible that due to certain tendencies and motives the subject may choose to ignore it. But if the counselee fails to understand the therapeutic measures implied by the psychologists, then the latter has to take positive steps and, in the event of such a condition being precipitated it is always best for the advice not to seem to be authoritative or sermon like, and neither should any of the person's short comings be mentioned. The counselee should be given some hope that his problem will be solved, and it should be so expressed that it may appear to have come from the counselee instead of the Psychologist.
5. **Follow-up Studies.** Personal guidance does not come to an end with therapeutic measures being introduced because the psychologist's job is not only to provide guidance, but also to see the actual success of his advice. Hence, even after the therapy he

has to keep up contact with the subject, and to make inquiries to find out the success that he has and in solving the problem originally entrusted to his care. This not only furthers the help rendered to the counselee but also adds to the experience and knowledge of the psychologist, because much of what is learnt in guidance is through trial and error. Human psychology is so complex that it cannot be tied down by any laws. Success in guidance depends upon the psychologist's own experience and insight, and as has been said before, he is assisted in acquiring these through follow up studies. It need hardly be emphasised at this stage that personal guidance is more or less incomplete without a follow-up study.

Methods of Follow-up Studies

The following methods are utilised in follow-up studies:

1. **Follow-up through Letters.** As is evident from the term applied to this method, in this method the counselee is contacted through the medium of letters. Letters reveal only a small quantity of information, but they do contribute something positively to the study and, if need be, these letters can be used to transit further guidance to the person or even meet him.
2. **Questionnaire Method.** In the questionnaire method, the counselee is sent a questionnaire, and he is asked to answer it, and return it to the psychologist. Most questions selected for the purpose have the quality of requiring short, simple, concise and precise answers, most of them being in terms of positives and negatives. This questionnaire is concerned with various aspects of the progress of a problem concerning which the advice was given. Psychologist tries to find the extent to which he has succeeded in curing the person, and if not, why. The questionnaire method has the advantage of soliciting more varied and comprehensive information than mere letters. But the main disadvantage lies in the small number of questionnaires returned to the psychologists.
3. **Card File Method.** In this method, details of an interview, in terms of the name of counselee, age, address, purpose of interview and details of the problem are inscribed. This is kept in the central office of the guidance centre, so that the counselee can contact his guide at any time that he wishes. The file method also makes use of the tickler file, in which the psychologist keeps an open file of the counselee within easy reach, which keeps details of the further contacts that have to be made. The file is so named because it tickles the guide into contacting the person guided.

The above three methods are prevalent and have beneficial results. There are some other methods also in addition to these main ones, by means of which the contact between the psychologist and the counselee can be kept alive. Telephone, for example, is another instrument that is frequently used in U.S.A. for renewing such contacts and gathering fresh information from the subjects.

It would be very useful to present a realistic example of personal guidance before winding up a description of it. This will improve realisation of the actual causes that are confronted and the extent to which our state provides facilities for dealing with them.

A professor in a local college at Allahabad went to take a look at the central jail there, where he saw a young boy undergoing sentence for breaking in or affecting an entry and thieving, the term being six months. The professor had the boy released on probation and took him into his own household. The boy maltreated the professor and continued on his path of theft and crime. He was also often absent for a couple of days from home. Finally, the professor handed the boy over to the parents who were living within the college campus. The boy was sent to school where he was admitted to the sixth class, but his progress was not satisfactory by any standards. Psychological tests revealed that he was definitely below the average in mental traits and capacities. But his practical skill and ability was somewhat better than the average. His other faculties were definitely weak. He naturally did not pay any attention to his study and took no interest in social activities. At times he was filled with feelings of guilt and remorse, but at other times he showed to be very aggressive and anti-social. This boy was brought to the bureau of psychology for personal guidance, where it was advised that the boy needed a change of environment. It was opined that an understanding and sympathetic person might help to improve his adjustment to life, and that there was no benefit to be derived from further study. He should turn to acquiring training in a mechanical trade. Psychologists also felt that the boy required regular mental treatment but as the bureau was not able to provide this assistance not much could be done in this direction. Even then, the boy did benefit somewhat from the guidance of the psychologists. He learned to understand some of his problems and this helped him in his adjustment.

QUESTIONS FOR EXERCISE

1. Write short note on Educational guidance.
2. Explain personal guidance, give examples.